# Ignite

## Topicwise MCQs

*"Give Fire to **Your Prelims Prep**"*

# Science & Technology

For **Civil Services** & **State PCS**
Preliminary Examination

arihant
SUCCESS AND NOTHING LESS

# Ignite

## Topicwise MCQs

*"Give Fire to **Your Prelims Prep**"*

# Science & Technology

For **Civil Services** & **State PCS**
Preliminary Examination

**ARIHANT PUBLICATION (INDIA) LIMITED**



卐 **Administrative & Production Offices**

**Regd. Office**

'Ramchhaya' 4577/15, Agarwal Road, Darya Ganj, New Delhi -110002
Tele: 011- 47630600, 43518550

卐 **Head Office**

Kalindi, TP Nagar, Meerut (UP) - 250002 Tel: 0121-7156203, 7156204

卐 **Sales & Support Offices**

Agra, Ahmedabad, Bengaluru, Bareilly, Chennai, Delhi, Guwahati, Hyderabad, Jaipur, Jhansi, Kolkata, Lucknow, Nagpur & Pune.

卐 **PRICE:** ₹ 275.00

卐 **PO No :** TXT-XX-XXXXXXX-X-XX

Published by Arihant Publications (India) Ltd.

For further information about the books published by Arihant, log on to www.arihantbooks.com or e-mail at info@arihantbooks.com

Follow us on

# Preface

The *Ignite Series* is more than just a resource - it's your ultimate guide to conquering one of the toughest examinations in India. With nearly **10 lakh aspirants** appearing for the UPSC Civil Services Preliminary Examination each year and **only around 15,000 qualifying for Mains**, the success rate stands at a staggering **1.5%**. Designed by the authors of the bestselling *Pulse Handwritten Notes for Prelims*, this series is meticulously crafted to transform your preparation and significantly enhance your chances of success.

What truly sets the *Ignite Series* apart is its ability to **bridge the gap between rote learning and deep conceptual understanding**. Packed with over **6,000+ carefully designed MCQs**, the series offers comprehensive coverage of the Prelims syllabus, ensuring no topic is left unexplored. Each question is strategically designed to challenge your knowledge and sharpen your problem-solving skills.

In an exam where every mark counts, **standing out isn't optional - it's essential**. To equip you for this challenge, the *Ignite Series* introduces a **three-tiered evaluation system**, testing your knowledge at **Factual, Conceptual and Analytical levels**. This innovative approach mirrors the demands of the UPSC, ensuring you are thoroughly prepared to tackle its dynamic and unpredictable nature. Additionally, **topic-wise Previous Years' Questions (PYQs)** included at the end of each chapter provide valuable insights into trends and patterns, helping you craft a data-driven strategy.

Understanding concepts is important, but **retaining and applying them under pressure** is the key to success. To make this process seamless, every question in this series is accompanied by **detailed explanations**, enriched with **infographics, tables and maps** that simplify complex topics.

Recognizing the importance of self-assessment, the series offers **free access to 3 All India Mock Tests**. These simulated tests replicate real exam conditions, allowing you to benchmark your performance, identify areas of improvement, and refine your preparation strategy. By offering a clear picture of where you stand, these tests ensure that you are not just prepared but **exam-ready**.

With the *Ignite Series*, you're not merely preparing for an exam - you're gearing up to outshine the competition and achieve your dreams. Let this book be the tool that empowers you to break into the top **1.5%** and take a giant step toward becoming a civil servant.

This masterpiece wouldn't have been possible without the **tireless efforts of the entire MentorsHut family**, who dedicated countless hours to creating a resource that truly serves aspirants.

To our daughter, **Prisha Mangtani**, your unwavering patience and love have been our greatest source of strength throughout this journey. Thank you for your sacrifices and for inspiring us to give our best.

We at MentorsHut remain committed to excellence and continuous improvement. Your feedback is invaluable to us. If you have suggestions or ideas to make this series even better, please don't hesitate to reach out to us at **info@mentorshut.com**.

Here's wishing you the very best for your preparation - may this series **ignite the spark of excellence within you** and guide you toward achieving your goals.

**Amit Mangtani**
**CA Shalini Wadhwani**
Founders, MentorsHut

# Contents

## Topical PYQ Trend Last 8 Years'

| Section | 2024 | 2023 | 2022 | 2021 | 2020 | 2019 | 2018 | 2017 |
|---|---|---|---|---|---|---|---|---|
| General Science | 1 | 0 | 2 | 4 | 1 | 2 | 0 | 0 |
| Astronomy and Space | 1 | 2 | 1 | 0 | 1 | 2 | 4 | 2 |
| Defence Technology | 5 | 1 | 1 | 0 | 0 | 0 | 2 | 0 |
| Nuclear Technology | 1 | 0 | 0 | 0 | 1 | 1 | 1 | 1 |
| Health and Diseases | 0 | 2 | 2 | 4 | 1 | 2 | 0 | 1 |
| Biotechnology | 0 | 2 | 2 | 1 | 2 | 3 | 1 | 2 |
| ICT | 0 | 0 | 3 | 0 | 1 | 4 | 3 | 1 |
| Emerging Technologies | 1 | 2 | 4 | 1 | 5 | 1 | 2 | 1 |
| Miscellaneous (including IPRs) | 2 | 1 | 1 | 2 | 1 | 1 | 1 | 2 |
| **Total** | **11** | **10** | **16** | **12** | **13** | **16** | **14** | **10** |

## Overall PYQ Trend Last 8 Years'

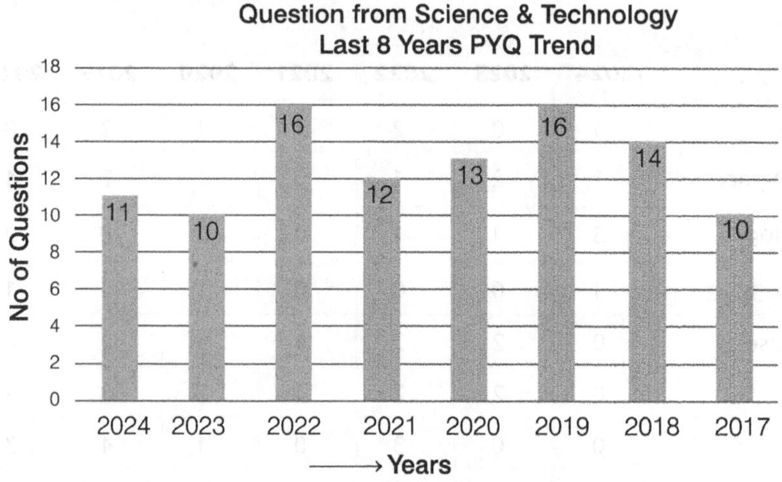


### Key Learnings from the PYQs of 'Science & Technology'

1. A **minimum of 10 questions** can be expected from **Science & Technology** in the UPSC Prelims exam.
2. The questions are broadly categorized into two types: **General Science Applied Science**.
3. **General Science questions** can be easily addressed using **NCERTs**. However, it is unnecessary to read all NCERTs from Class 6 to Class 12. Instead, save time by referring to NCERT summaries or enrolling in an NCERT course focused on General Science.
4. **Applied Science questions** (i.e., technology-based questions) are primarily derived from current affairs. Therefore, consistent newspaper reading and a strong understanding of concepts are essential.
5. It is important to note that technology-based questions are **typically conceptual and informational in nature**.
6. Referring to Pulse Handwritten Notes is highly recommended as a comprehensive resource to achieve the targeted 80% accuracy.

# CHAPTER 01 Astronomy

## Assessment Round

### Topic 1 : Universe

*1.* With reference to the Big Bang Theory, consider the following statements:

1. The Big Bang Theory explains the origin of the universe approximately 13.8 billion years ago.
2. According to the theory, the universe started from a singularity and has been expanding ever since.
3. The Big Bang Theory contradicts the idea that the universe is expanding.

How many of the statements given above is/are correct?

(a) Only one
(b) Only two
(c) All three
(d) None

*2.* With reference to the Big Bang Theory, consider the following statements:

1. Cosmic microwave background radiation is a crucial piece of evidence supporting the Big Bang Theory.
2. The Big Bang was an explosion in space that scattered galaxies across the universe.
3. Edwin Hubble's observations showed that distant galaxies are moving away from us, which supports the idea of an expanding universe.

How many of the statements given above is/are correct?

(a) Only one (b) Only two
(c) All three (d) None

*3.* Consider the following statements:

1. Redshift occurs when an object moves toward the observer.
2. Blueshift occurs when light waves are compressed, indicating that an object is moving away from the observer.
3. Redshift in the light from distant galaxies is evidence for the expansion of the universe.

Which of the given above statement(s) is/are correct?

(a) 1 and 3 only (b) 2 and 3 only
(c) 3 only (d) 1, 2 and 3

*4.* With reference to the Doppler Effect, consider the following statements:

1. The effect applies to both sound waves and light waves.
2. The effect causes a redshift if the source of light is moving away from the observer.
3. A blueshift indicates that the frequency of the light is decreasing.

Which of the given statement(s) is/are correct?

(a) 1 only (b) 1 and 2 only
(c) 1, 2 and 3 (d) 2 and 3 only

**5.** With reference to redshift, consider the following statements:

1. Redshift occurs because of the Doppler Effect when light sources move away from the observer.
2. Cosmological redshift is caused by the expansion of space rather than the motion of galaxies.
3. Redshift can also occur due to gravitational effects in strong gravitational fields.

Which of the statements given above are correct?

(a) 1 and 2 only (b) 2 and 3 only
(c) 1, 2 and 3 (d) 1 and 3 only

**6.** Consider the following.

1. Measuring the speed of stars and galaxies
2. Tracking weather patterns with Doppler radar
3. Measuring the speed of vehicles using radar guns
4. Determining the expansion of the universe

How many of the above is/are applications of the Doppler Effect?

(a) Only one (b) Only two
(c) Only three (d) All four

**7.** Which of the following best describes the concept of 'Singularity' in the context of black holes?

(a) A region in space where time slows down to a complete stop.
(b) A point in space where the curvature of spacetime becomes infinite and the laws of physics break down.
(c) A point of zero gravity at the center of a black hole.
(d) A region of space that emits high levels of radiation due to extreme gravitational forces.

**8.** Arrange the following electromagnetic waves in order of increasing frequency:

1. Microwave 2. Gamma rays
3. Visible light 4. Radio waves

Select the correct order:

(a) 4, 1, 3, 2 (b) 3, 1, 4, 2
(c) 4, 3, 2, 1 (d) 1, 2, 4, 3

**9.** Arrange the following electromagnetic waves in order of decreasing energy:

1. Gamma rays
2. Infrared waves
3. Ultraviolet waves
4. Visible light

Select the correct order:

(a) 1, 3, 4, 2 (b) 2, 4, 1, 3
(c) 4, 3, 1, 2 (d) 3, 2, 1, 4

**10.** Which of the following best describes the Big Bang Theory?

(a) The universe started from a point of infinite density and temperature, and has been expanding ever since.
(b) The Big Bang was a massive explosion in space that scattered galaxies across the cosmos.
(c) The universe was created at a steady state and has always existed in its current form.
(d) The Big Bang Theory suggests that the universe will collapse back into a singularity in the future.

**11.** Consider the following statements:

**Statement I:** Gravitational lensing occurs when light from a distant object, like a galaxy, is bent by the gravitational field of a massive object between the light source and the observer.

**Statement II:** Gravitational lensing supports Einstein's Theory of General Relativity by demonstrating that mass can curve spacetime, affecting the path of light.

Which of the following is correct in respect of the above statement?

(a) Both Statement I and Statement II are correct, and Statement II is the correct explanation for Statement I.
(b) Both Statement I and Statement II are correct, but Statement II is not the correct explanation for Statement I.
(c) Statement I is correct, but Statement II is incorrect.
(d) Statement I is incorrect, but Statement II is correct.

**12.** With reference to Einstein's Theory of General Relativity, consider the following statements.

1. General relativity redefines gravity as the curvature of spacetime caused by mass and energy.
2. The theory predicts the existence of black holes, regions of spacetime where gravity is so intense that nothing, not even light, can escape.
3. General relativity predicts that the speed of light can change depending on the strength of the gravitational field.

How many of the statements given above is/are correct?

(a) Only one (b) Only two
(c) All three (d) None

**13.** Which of the following best describes the 'Saraswati supercluster'?

(a) A large grouping of stars within the Milky Way galaxy.
(b) A massive cluster of galaxies located in the distant universe.
(c) A cluster of black holes orbiting a central quasar.
(d) A collection of exoplanets discovered in the Andromeda galaxy.

**14.** Consider the following:

1. Galactic Bulge 2. Sagittarius A*
3. Spiral arms 4. Andromeda

How many of the given above is/are part of the Milky Way galaxy?

(a) Only one (b) Only two
(c) Only three (d) All four

## Topic 2 : Solar System

**15.** With reference to terrestrial planets, consider the following statements:

1. These planets are primarily composed of rock and metal.
2. These planets have relatively few Moons compared to Jovian planets.
3. Mars is the only terrestrial planet with a thick atmosphere.

Which of the statements given above is/are correct?

(a) 1 and 2 only (b) 2 only
(c) 3 only (d) 1, 2 and 3

**16.** With reference to the 'Jovian Planets', consider the following statements:

1. These planets are mostly composed of gases such as hydrogen and helium.
2. These planets have rings around them.
3. Jupiter and Saturn are considered ice giants due to the presence of icy materials in their composition.

Which of the given above statements is/are correct?

(a) 1 and 2 only (b) 1 and 3 only
(c) 2 only (d) 1, 2 and 3

**17.** With reference to the differences between Terrestrial and Jovian planets, consider the following statements:

1. Terrestrial planets have slower rotational speeds compared to Jovian planets.
2. Jovian planets have stronger magnetic fields than terrestrial planets.
3. Terrestrial planets have a higher density compared to Jovian planets.

Which of the statements given above are correct?

(a) 1 and 2 only (b) 2 and 3 only
(c) 1, 2 and 3 (d) 1 and 3 only

**18.** Where is the headquarters of the International Astronomical Union (IAU) located?

(a) Paris, France (b) Geneva, Switzerland
(c) New York, USA (d) Vienna, Austria

**19.** Which of the following best describes the primary role of the 'International Astronomical Union (IAU)'?

(a) To design and launch international space missions.
(b) To establish universally recognised names and definitions for celestial objects.
(c) To fund global astronomical observatories and research facilities.
(d) To regulate the commercial use of outer space resources.

**20.** Arrange the following planets in the correct order based on the number of confirmed Moons, from the highest to the lowest:

1. Saturn 2. Earth
3. Mars 4. Mercury

Choose the correct order using the codes given below.

(a) 2-1-3-4 (b) 1-2-3-4
(c) 1-3-2-4 (d) 3-1-2-4

**21.** Match the following planets with their largest Moons.

| | Planet | | Largest Moon |
|---|---|---|---|
| A. | Jupiter | 1. | Titan |
| B. | Saturn | 2. | Ganymede |
| C. | Neptune | 3. | Triton |
| D. | Mars | 4. | Phobos |

Select the correctly matched pairs:

(a) A-2, B-1, C-3, D-4
(b) A-1, B-3, C-2, D-4
(c) A-3, B-2, C-1, D-4
(d) A-4, B-2, C-1, D-3

**22.** Which of the following best describes an 'Exoplanet'?

(a) A planet that orbits within our solar system, beyond Neptune.
(b) A planet that orbits a star outside our solar system.
(c) A rogue planet that does not orbit any star.
(d) A hypothetical planet that exists in theoretical astrophysics but has not been observed.

**23.** Which of the following best describes the 'Goldilocks Zone'?

(a) The region in a galaxy where stars are most likely to form.
(b) The region near a black hole where time dilation is at its maximum.
(c) The region around a star where conditions are suitable for liquid water to exist on a planet's surface.
(d) The region in a solar system where gas giants typically form.

**24.** Which of the following best describes the primary purpose of NASA's TESS mission?

(a) To search for exoplanets by monitoring the brightness of nearby stars.
(b) To map the distribution of dark matter in the universe.
(c) To study the atmospheres of gas giants in the outer solar system.
(d) To investigate the origin of gamma-ray bursts in distant galaxies.

**25.** Consider the following statements:

1. A star primarily generates energy through nuclear fusion reactions in its core.
2. Hydrogen is fused into helium in the star's core during the main sequence stage.
3. Stars use nuclear fission to produce energy in later stages of their life cycle.

Which of the statements given above are correct?

(a) 1 and 2 only (b) 2 and 3 only
(c) 1 and 3 only (d) 1, 2 and 3

**26.** Arrange the following stages in the correct order of the life cycle of a low-mass star (like the Sun):

1. Red Giant
2. Main Sequence
3. White Dwarf
4. Planetary Nebula

Select the correct order from the codes given below:

(a) 2, 1, 4, 3 (b) 1, 2, 3, 4
(c) 4, 2, 1, 3 (d) 2, 1, 3, 4

**27.** Arrange the following phases in the correct order for the life cycle of a high-mass star:

1. Supernova
2. Main Sequence
3. Red Supergiant
4. Neutron Star

Select the correct order from the codes given below.

(a) 2, 3, 1, 4 (b) 1, 2, 4, 3
(c) 2, 1, 3, 4 (d) 1, 3, 2, 4

**28.** Identify the phase of a star based on the following characteristics:

1. The star has expanded significantly after exhausting hydrogen in its core.
2. The core starts fusing helium and the outer layers expand.
3. It is much cooler and redder compared to its previous phase.

Select the correct answer from the codes below.

(a) Red Supergiant (b) Red Giant
(c) White Dwarf (d) Neutron Star

**29.** Identify the star type based on the following characteristics:

1. It is the remnant of a low-mass star after it has shed its outer layers.
2. It no longer undergoes fusion reactions.
3. It is incredibly dense, roughly the size of Earth but with the mass of the Sun.

Select the correct answer from the codes given below:

(a) Red Giant (b) White Dwarf
(c) Main Sequence Star (d) Protostar

**30.** With reference to the Chandrasekhar Limit, consider the following statements:

1. The Chandrasekhar Limit defines the maximum mass of a stable white dwarf star.
2. It is approximately 1.4 times the mass of the Sun.
3. A star exceeding this limit is likely to collapse into a neutron star or black hole.

How many of the statements given above is/are correct?

(a) Only one (b) Only two
(c) All three (d) None

**31.** Which of the following best describes the difference between a 'Red Dwarf' and a 'White Dwarf'?

(a) A red dwarf is a hot, dense remnant of a star, while a white dwarf is a cool, small main-sequence star.
(b) A red dwarf is a low-mass main-sequence star that is still burning hydrogen, while a white dwarf is a dense stellar remnant that no longer undergoes nuclear fusion.
(c) A red dwarf is a high-mass star near the end of its life cycle, while a white dwarf is a low-mass star beginning its life cycle.
(d) A red dwarf is a large, bright star, while a white dwarf is a small, dim star that emits no radiation.

**32.** With reference to the planets in our Solar System, consider the following statements:

1. Venus is the hottest planet in the solar system.
2. Jupiter has the shortest day of all planets.
3. Mercury is the smallest planet in the solar system.
4. Saturn is the only planet with rings.

How many of the statements given above is/are correct?

(a) Only one
(b) Only two
(c) Only three
(d) All four

**33.** Consider the following objects.

1. Vesta 2. Ceres
3. Eris 4. Haumea

How many of the given above is/are classified as 'Dwarf Planets'?

(a) Only one
(b) Only two
(c) Only three
(d) All four

**34.** Which of the following best describes the difference between a nebula and a planetary nebula?

(a) A nebula is a region of intense gravitational activity, while a planetary nebula is a dense star cluster.
(b) A nebula is a cloud of gas and dust in space that serves as a stellar nursery, while a planetary nebula is the outer shell of gas ejected by a dying star.
(c) A nebula forms exclusively around black holes, while a planetary nebula forms around young stars.
(d) A nebula emits intense X-rays, while a planetary nebula emits infrared radiation only.

**35.** What is a 'Gamma-Ray Burst (GRB)'?
(a) A high-energy explosion observed in distant galaxies, believed to be associated with the collapse of massive stars or the merger of neutron stars.
(b) A sudden burst of gamma radiation from the Sun, typically associated with solar flares.
(c) A release of gamma rays caused by the collision of asteroids in our solar system.
(d) A type of radiation emitted from the event horizon of a black hole.

**36.** Consider the following:
1. Collapsing massive stars
2. Merging neutron stars
3. Supernova explosions
4. Interactions between black holes and their accretion disks

Which of the above are confirmed causes of gamma-ray bursts?
(a) 1 and 2 only (b) 1, 2 and 3 only
(c) 2, 3 and 4 only (d) 1, 2, 3 and 4

**37.** Consider the following statements about the Cosmic Microwave Background (CMB) Radiation:
1. It is a remnant of the Big Bang and represents the earliest light in the universe.
2. It has a nearly uniform temperature of approximately 2.7 Kelvin.
3. It provides evidence for the expansion of the universe.

Which of the given above statements are correct?
(a) 1 and 2 only
(b) 2 and 3 only
(c) 1 and 3 only
(d) 1, 2 and 3

**38.** Which of the following best describes a singularity in the context of black holes?
(a) A region in space where gravity is strong enough to prevent light from escaping.
(b) A point at the center of a black hole where the curvature of spacetime becomes infinite and the laws of physics break down.
(c) A theoretical boundary surrounding a black hole, also known as the event horizon.
(d) A region in space where matter is stretched infinitely in one direction, forming a singular line.

**39.** Which of the following correctly describes about 'Schwarzschild Black Hole'?
(a) A black hole with no electric charge or angular momentum, characterised only by its mass.
(b) A black hole that emits radiation due to quantum effects near the event horizon.
(c) A rotating black hole with angular momentum but no electric charge.
(d) A black hole that has an electric charge and forms from the collapse of a charged star.

**40.** With reference to the Kuiper Belt, consider the following statements:
1. It lies beyond the orbit of Neptune.
2. Pluto is one of the largest objects in the Kuiper Belt.
3. The Kuiper Belt contains asteroids similar to those in the asteroid belt between Mars and Jupiter.
4. Eris is located in the Kuiper Belt.

How many of the given above statements is/are correct?
(a) Only one
(b) Only two
(c) Only three
(d) All four

**41.** Which of the following planets rotate on their axis in a retrograde (backward) direction?
1. Venus
2. Jupiter
3. Uranus
4. Mars

Select the correct answer from the given codes:
(a) 1 and 2 only
(b) 1 and 3 only
(c) 2 and 4 only
(d) 1, 3 and 4 only

**42.** Arrange the following planets in the correct order of increasing density:
1. Mars
2. Earth
3. Saturn
4. Mercury

Choose the correct order from the codes given below.
(a) 3-1-4-2
(b) 3-4-1-2
(c) 3-1-2-4
(d) 1-3-4-2

**43.** With reference to the Asteroid Belt, consider the following statements.
1. It is located between Mars and Jupiter.
2. The majority of asteroids in the belt are composed of metal and rock.
3. The dwarf planet Ceres is the largest object in the asteroid belt.

How many of the above statements is/are correct?
(a) Only one
(b) Only two
(c) All three
(d) None

**44.** Consider the following pairs:

| | Object | Definition |
|---|---|---|
| 1. | Meteoroid | A small rocky or metallic body traveling through space |
| 2. | Meteor | A meteoroid that enters Earth's atmosphere and burns up, creating a bright streak |
| 3. | Meteorite | A meteor that survives its passage through Earth's atmosphere and lands on the surface |

Which of the pairs given above are correctly matched?
(a) 1 and 2 only
(b) 1 and 3 only
(c) 1, 2 and 3
(d) 2 and 3 only

**45.** What is a meteorite?
(a) A meteoroid that burns up in the Earth's atmosphere
(b) A fragment of a meteor that orbits the Sun
(c) A piece of a meteoroid that survives its passage through the atmosphere and reaches the Earth's surface
(d) A large asteroid that collides with Earth

**46.** Consider the following pairs.

| | Object | Location |
|---|---|---|
| 1. | Asteroid | Mostly located in a belt between Mars and Jupiter |
| 2. | Comet | Found mainly in the Oort Cloud and the Kuiper Belt |
| 3. | Meteorite | Mostly found in the asteroid belt between Mars and Jupiter |

Which of the pair(s) given above is/are correctly matched?
(a) 1 and 2 only
(b) 1 only
(c) 1 and 3 only
(d) 1, 2 and 3

**47.** Consider the following impact sites in India:
1. Lonar Crater
2. Dhala Crater
3. Ramgarh Crater
4. Shiva Crater

How many of the given above is/are confirmed meteorite impact craters?
(a) Only one
(b) Only two
(c) Only three
(d) All four

**48.** Which of the following best describes the 'Oort Cloud'?
(a) A region of the solar system containing the asteroid belt between Mars and Jupiter.
(b) A dense cluster of stars located at the center of the Milky Way galaxy.
(c) A zone of active star formation near the Orion Nebula.
(d) A spherical shell of icy bodies surrounding the solar system, believed to be the source of long-period comets.

## Topic 3 : Gravitational Waves

**49.** With reference to 'Gravitational Waves', consider the following statements:

1. These are ripples in spacetime produced only by events involving black holes.
2. The first direct detection of gravitational waves was made by LIGO in 2015.
3. Gravitational waves travel faster than the speed of light in a vacuum.

Which of the statements given above is/are correct?

(a) 1 and 2 only
(b) 2 only
(c) 1 and 3 only
(d) 1, 2 and 3

**50.** Arrange the following fundamental interactions in the correct order of their relative strength, from weakest to strongest:

1. Weak nuclear force
2. Electromagnetic force
3. Gravitational force
4. Strong nuclear force

Select the correct answer from the codes given below.

(a) 3-1-2-4
(b) 3-2-1-4
(c) 1-3-4-2
(d) 2-1-3-4

**51.** With reference to the LIGO (Laser Interferometer Gravitational-Wave Observatory) project, consider the following statements:

1. LIGO is designed to detect gravitational waves caused by violent cosmic events.
2. LIGO operates in both space and ground-based observatories.
3. India is building its own LIGO facility.

How many of the statements given above is/are correct?

(a) Only one
(b) Only two
(c) All three
(d) None

**52.** With reference to the LIGO-India project, consider the following statements:

1. It will be part of a global network of gravitational wave detectors including Virgo and KAGRA.
2. The LIGO-India project aims to study cosmic phenomena such as merging black holes and neutron stars.
3. It is entirely an independent initiative of the Government of India, without any international collaboration.

Which of the statements given above are correct?

(a) 1, 2 and 3
(b) 2 and 3 only
(c) 1 and 2 only
(d) 1 and 3 only

**53.** With reference to the 'Laser Interferometer Space Antenna (LISA)' project, consider the following statements:

1. LISA is a ground-based gravitational wave detector.
2. It is designed to detect low-frequency gravitational waves emitted by supermassive black holes.
3. The LISA mission is led by the European Space Agency (ESA).

Which of the given above statements are correct?

(a) 1 and 2 only
(b) 2 and 3 only
(c) 1 and 3 only
(d) 1, 2 and 3

**54.** Which of the following best describes the primary goal of the eLISA (Evolved Laser Interferometer Space Antenna) project?

(a) To study the surface of exoplanets for habitability.
(b) To detect and observe gravitational waves from space-based observatories.
(c) To monitor the magnetic field of the Earth from orbit.
(d) To map the distribution of dark matter in the universe.

## Topic 4 : Particle Physics

**55.** Which of the following best describes the primary difference between 'Matter' and 'Anti-matter'?

(a) Matter is composed of protons, neutrons and electrons, while anti-matter is composed of dark matter particles.
(b) Matter consists of particles with a positive charge, while anti-matter consists of particles with a negative charge.
(c) Matter consists of particles, while anti-matter consists of antiparticles with the same mass but opposite charges.
(d) Matter exists in the observable universe, while anti-matter only exists in theoretical models.

**56.** Which of the following statements about matter and antimatter are correct?

1. Matter and anti-matter annihilate each other upon contact, producing energy.
2. Anti-matter particles have the same mass but opposite charges as their matter counterparts.
3. The observable universe is composed mostly of anti-matter due to its stability over matter.

Select the correct answer using the codes given below:

(a) 1 and 2 only (b) 1 and 3 only
(c) 2 and 3 only (d) 1, 2 and 3

**57.** Consider the following pairs of phenomena and their description related to matter and anti-matter:

| | Phenomenon | Description |
|---|---|---|
| 1. | Annihilation | The process where a particle and its antiparticle collide, and convert into energy |
| 2. | Charge Parity (CP) violation | The phenomenon where the laws of physics differ between matter and anti-matter |
| 3. | Baryogenesis | The process theorised to explain the imbalance of matter and anti-matter in the universe |
| 4. | Anti-gravity | The repulsive gravitational force exerted by anti-matter on ordinary matter |

Which of the pairs given above are correctly matched?

(a) 1, 2 and 3 only
(b) 1 and 3 only
(c) 2 and 4 only
(d) 1, 2 and 4 only

**58.** Consider the following properties:

1. Does not interact with electromagnetic forces
2. Affects the expansion rate of the universe
3. Can be detected directly through telescopes
4. Comprises a significant portion of the universe's mass

How many of the given above is/are characteristics of 'Dark Matter'?

(a) Only one
(b) Only two
(c) Only three
(d) All four

**59.** Consider the following statements about 'Dark Energy':

1. Dark energy is thought to be responsible for the accelerated expansion of the universe.
2. Dark energy makes up roughly 68% of the universe's total energy density.
3. Dark energy interacts strongly with visible matter.

How many of the statements given above is/are correct?

(a) Only one
(b) Only two
(c) All three
(d) None

**60.** Which of the following best describes the primary objective of the 'Xenon 1T' experiment?

(a) To study the properties of neutrinos in high-energy particle collisions.
(b) To detect and study Weakly Interacting Massive Particles (WIMPs) as candidates for dark matter.
(c) To investigate the formation of heavy elements through stellar nucleosynthesis.
(d) To measure the cosmic microwave background radiation and its anisotropies.

**61.** Consider the following pairs of bosons and their associated forces:

| | Boson | Associated Force |
|---|---|---|
| 1. | Photon | Electromagnetic Force |
| 2. | Gluon | Strong Nuclear Force |
| 3. | W and Z Bosons | Weak Nuclear Force |
| 4. | Higgs Boson | Gravitational Force |

Which of the pairs given above are correctly matched?

(a) 1, 2 and 3 only (b) 1 and 3 only
(c) 2 and 4 only (d) 1, 2, 3 and 4

**62.** With reference to the Standard Model of particle physics, consider the following statements:

1. Fermions are divided into quarks and leptons.
2. Photons and gluons are examples of fermions.
3. Higgs boson is responsible for giving mass to fundamental particles.

How many of the statements given above is/are correct?

(a) Only one (b) Only two
(c) All three (d) None

**63.** Consider the following particles:

1. Electron 2. Photon
3. Neutron 4. Z Boson

How many of the given above is/are classified as 'Fermions'?

(a) Only one (b) Only two
(c) Only three (d) All four

**64.** Which of the following statements are correct about the 'Neutrinos'?

1. These are electrically neutral particles.
2. These interact with matter very weakly, making them difficult to detect.
3. These are produced in nuclear reactions, such as those occurring in the Sun.
4. Neutrinos travel faster than the speed of light.

Select the correct answer from the codes given below.

(a) 1 and 2 only (b) 1, 2 and 3 only
(c) 1, 3 and 4 only (d) 2 and 4 only

**65.** Which of the following are sources of neutrinos?

1. Nuclear reactors
2. The Sun
3. Cosmic rays interacting with the Earth's atmosphere
4. Black holes

Select the correct answer from the codes given below.

(a) 1 and 2 only (b) 1, 2 and 3 only
(c) 2, 3 and 4 only (d) 1, 2, 3 and 4

**66.** Which of the following statements are correct about CERN's 'Large Hadron Collider (LHC)'?

1. It is the world's largest and most powerful particle accelerator.
2. It is located in a 27-kilometer-long tunnel beneath the border of Switzerland and France.
3. The primary goal of the LHC is to study the Higgs boson and fundamental forces of nature.
4. LHC uses protons as the only particles in its collisions.

Select the correct answer from the codes given below:

(a) 1 and 2 only (b) 1, 2 and 3 only
(c) 2 and 4 only (d) 1, 3 and 4 only

**67.** Where is the proposed site for the India-based Neutrino Observatory (INO) located?

(a) Nilgiri Hills, Tamil Nadu
(b) Bodi West Hills, Tamil Nadu
(c) Aravalli Hills, Rajasthan
(d) Western Ghats, Kerala

**68.** Which of the following best describes the primary objective of the 'IceCube Neutrino Observatory'?

(a) To detect and study cosmic neutrinos originating from distant astrophysical sources.
(b) To monitor changes in polar ice caps due to climate change.
(c) To measure the properties of dark matter particles using underground detectors.
(d) To map the distribution of cosmic microwave background radiation.

# OMR SHEET

**Assessment Round**

| Q | Options | Q | Options | Q | Options | Q | Options |
|---|---|---|---|---|---|---|---|
| 1 | a b c d | 31 | a b c d | 61 | a b c d | 91 | a b c d |
| 2 | a b c d | 32 | a b c d | 62 | a b c d | 92 | a b c d |
| 3 | a b c d | 33 | a b c d | 63 | a b c d | 93 | a b c d |
| 4 | a b c d | 34 | a b c d | 64 | a b c d | 94 | a b c d |
| 5 | a b c d | 35 | a b c d | 65 | a b c d | 95 | a b c d |
| 6 | a b c d | 36 | a b c d | 66 | a b c d | 96 | a b c d |
| 7 | a b c d | 37 | a b c d | 67 | a b c d | 97 | a b c d |
| 8 | a b c d | 38 | a b c d | 68 | a b c d | 98 | a b c d |
| 9 | a b c d | 39 | a b c d | 69 | a b c d | 99 | a b c d |
| 10 | a b c d | 40 | a b c d | 70 | a b c d | 100 | a b c d |
| 11 | a b c d | 41 | a b c d | 71 | a b c d | 101 | a b c d |
| 12 | a b c d | 42 | a b c d | 72 | a b c d | 102 | a b c d |
| 13 | a b c d | 43 | a b c d | 73 | a b c d | 103 | a b c d |
| 14 | a b c d | 44 | a b c d | 74 | a b c d | 104 | a b c d |
| 15 | a b c d | 45 | a b c d | 75 | a b c d | 105 | a b c d |
| 16 | a b c d | 46 | a b c d | 76 | a b c d | 106 | a b c d |
| 17 | a b c d | 47 | a b c d | 77 | a b c d | 107 | a b c d |
| 18 | a b c d | 48 | a b c d | 78 | a b c d | 108 | a b c d |
| 19 | a b c d | 49 | a b c d | 79 | a b c d | 109 | a b c d |
| 20 | a b c d | 50 | a b c d | 80 | a b c d | 110 | a b c d |
| 21 | a b c d | 51 | a b c d | 81 | a b c d | 111 | a b c d |
| 22 | a b c d | 52 | a b c d | 82 | a b c d | 112 | a b c d |
| 23 | a b c d | 53 | a b c d | 83 | a b c d | 113 | a b c d |
| 24 | a b c d | 54 | a b c d | 84 | a b c d | 114 | a b c d |
| 25 | a b c d | 55 | a b c d | 85 | a b c d | 115 | a b c d |
| 26 | a b c d | 56 | a b c d | 86 | a b c d | 116 | a b c d |
| 27 | a b c d | 57 | a b c d | 87 | a b c d | 117 | a b c d |
| 28 | a b c d | 58 | a b c d | 88 | a b c d | 118 | a b c d |
| 29 | a b c d | 59 | a b c d | 89 | a b c d | 119 | a b c d |
| 30 | a b c d | 60 | a b c d | 90 | a b c d | 120 | a b c d |

## Calculate Your Score

**Correct (✓)**

**Incorrect (✓)**

**Unattempted**

**Total Score**

**Accuracy (%)**

## Reasons for Incorrect Answers?

1. Lack of Knowledge/Existing Source Insufficient
2. Lack of Multiple Revision
3. Common Sense Mistakes

**Note :**

1. Calculate total score as correct answers carry 2 marks each 1/3rd marks will deducted for **Incorrect** Answers.
2. Calculate Accuracy (%) by dividing the number of correct answers to the total number of attempted questions.

## Past Learning

**1.** Consider the following statements: **(2024)**

**Statement I** : Giant stars live much longer than dwarf stars.

**Statement II** : Compared to dwarf stars, giant stars have a greater rate of nuclear reactions.

Which one of the following is correct in respect of the above statements?

(a) Both Statement I and Statement II are correct, and Statement II explains Statement I.

(b) Both Statement I and Statement II are correct, but Statement II does not explain Statement I.

(c) Statement I is correct, but Statement II is incorrect.

(d) Statement I is incorrect, but Statement II is correct.

**2.** Consider the following pairs: **(2023)**

| | Objects in space | Description |
|---|---|---|
| 1. | Cepheids | Giant clouds of dust and gas in space |
| 2. | Nebulae | Stars which brighten and dim periodically |
| 3. | Pulsars | Neutron stars that are formed when massive stars run out of fuel and collapse |

How many of the above pairs is/are correctly matched?

(a) Only one (b) Only two

(c) All three (d) None

**3.** 'The experiment will employ a trio of spacecraft flying in formation in the shape of an equilateral triangle that has sides one million kilometres long, with lasers shining between the craft'. The experiment in this question refers to **(2020)**

(a) Voyager-2 (b) New Horizons

(c) LISA Pathfinder (d) Evolved LISA

**4.** Recently, scientists observed the merger of giant 'blackholes' billions of light years away from the Earth. What is the significance of this observation? **(2019)**

(a) 'Higgs boson particles' were detected

(b) 'Gravitational waves' were detected

(c) Possibility of inter-galactic space travel through 'wormhole' was confirmed

(d) It enabled the scientists to understand 'singularity'

**5.** Consider the following phenomena: **(2018)**

1. Light is affected by gravity.
2. The Universe is constantly expanding.
3. Matter warps its surrounding space-time.

Which of the above is/are the predictions of Albert Einstein's General Theory of Relativity, often discussed in media?

(a) 1 and 2 only

(b) 3 only

(c) 1 and 3 only

(d) 1, 2 and 3

**6.** What is the purpose of 'evolved Laser Interferometer Space Antenna (eLISA)' project? **(2017)**

(a) To detect neutrinos

(b) To detect gravitational waves

(c) To detect the effectiveness of missile defence system

(d) To study the effect of solar flares on our communication system

**7.** The terms 'Event Horizon', Singularity', 'String Theory' and 'Standard Model' are sometimes seen in the news in the context of **(2017)**

(a) observations and understanding of the universe

(b) study of the solar and the lunar eclipses

(c) placing satellites in the orbit of the Earth

(d) origin and evolution of living organisms on the Earth

# Detailed Solutions

## Assessment Round

**1.** *(b)* Only two

- **Statement 1 is correct:** The Big Bang Theory posits that the universe originated approximately **13.8 billion years ago** from an extremely hot, dense singularity. This estimate is supported by evidence like the cosmic microwave background radiation and the observed expansion of the universe.
- **Statement 2 is correct:** The theory suggests that the universe began as a singularity and has been expanding continuously since its inception. This expansion is evidenced by Edwin Hubble's discovery of **galactic redshifts** and the cosmic microwave background radiation.
- **Statement 3 is incorrect:** The Big Bang Theory does **not contradict the idea of the universe's expansion**. Instead, the concept of expansion is central to the theory. The redshift of light from distant galaxies and the **cosmic** microwave background radiation both confirms the universe's ongoing expansion.

**Thus, the correct answer is (b) Only two.**

**2.** *(b)* Only two

- **Statement 1 is correct: Cosmic Microwave Background Radiation (CMBR)** is one of the most compelling pieces of evidence for the Big Bang Theory. It represents the afterglow of the universe's early stages, discovered by Arno Penzias and Robert Wilson in 1965.
- **Statement 2 is incorrect:** The Big Bang was **not an explosion in space but rather an expansion of space itself**. Unlike a conventional explosion, which scatters material into existing space, the Big Bang refers to the **stretching of space-time**, carrying galaxies along.
- **Statement 3 is correct:** Edwin Hubble's observations in the 1920s demonstrated that galaxies are moving away from us, as indicated by their redshifted light. This observation is a cornerstone of the Big Bang Theory, supporting the idea of an expanding universe.

**Thus, the correct answer is (b) Only two.**

**3.** *(c)* 3 only

- **Statement 1 is incorrect:** Redshift occurs when an **object moves away** from the observer, not toward them. As light waves stretch, their wavelength increases, shifting them toward the red end of the spectrum.
- **Statement 2 is incorrect:** Blueshift occurs when an **object moves toward the observer**, causing the light waves to compress, which increases their frequency and shifts them toward the blue end of the spectrum.
- **Statement 3 is correct:** Redshift in light from distant galaxies provides strong **evidence for the universe's expansion**. This phenomenon was first observed by Edwin Hubble, leading to the formulation of Hubble's Law, which quantifies **the relationship between a galaxy's distance and its velocity of recession.**

**Thus, the correct answer is (c) 3 only.**

**4.** *(b)* 1 and 2 only

- **Statement 1 is correct:** The Doppler Effect describes the **change in the frequency of waves** as the source and observer move relative to each other. It applies to **sound waves** (e.g., the pitch change of a siren) and **light waves** (e.g., redshift and blueshift in astronomy).
- **Statement 2 is correct:** When a source of light moves away from the observer, its light waves stretch, increasing their wavelength and causing a redshift. This phenomenon is key evidence for the expanding universe.
- **Statement 3 is incorrect:** A blueshift occurs when the source moves toward the observer, compressing the light waves. This increases the frequency and decreases the wavelength. The statement incorrectly describes the effect.

**Thus, the correct answer is (b) 1 and 2 only.**

**5.** *(c)* 1, 2 and 3

- **Statement 1 is correct: Redshift** occurs due to the Doppler Effect when light sources move away from the observer. The stretching of light waves shifts them toward the red end of the spectrum.

- **Statement 2 is correct: Cosmological redshift** arises because space itself is expanding. This stretches the wavelengths of light travelling through space, as opposed to being caused by the motion of galaxies through space.
- **Statement 3 is correct: Gravitational redshift** occurs when light escapes a strong gravitational field. The gravitational force stretches the light waves, shifting them toward the red end of the spectrum.

**Thus, the correct answer is (c) 1, 2 and 3.**

**6.** *(d)* All four

- **Statement 1 is correct:** The **Doppler Effect** is extensively used in astronomy to measure the speed and direction of stars and galaxies relative to Earth.
  - A **redshift** indicates that a celestial object is moving away, while a blueshift suggests it is moving toward us. This application is crucial for understanding galactic motions and the dynamics of celestial objects.
- **Statement 2 is correct: Doppler radar** is widely employed in meteorology to track weather patterns, such as rain, snow and storm systems. It works by analysing the frequency shift in radar waves reflected off precipitation particles, providing data on the velocity and movement of weather systems.
- **Statement 3 is correct: Law enforcement radar** guns use the Doppler Effect to measure vehicle speeds. These devices emit radio waves that reflect off moving vehicles; the change in frequency of the reflected waves determines the vehicle's speed.
- **Statement 4 is correct:** The Doppler Effect is fundamental in understanding the **expansion of the universe.** The observed **redshift** in light from distant galaxies, as discovered by Edwin Hubble, provides evidence for the universe's expansion. This forms a cornerstone of the Big Bang Theory.

**Thus, the correct answer is (d) All four.**

**7.** *(b)* A point in space where the curvature of spacetime becomes infinite and the laws of physics break down.

- In the context of black holes, a **singularity** refers to a theoretical point where the density of matter becomes infinite, resulting in the **infinite curvature of spacetime.** At this point, the known laws of physics, including General Relativity, break down and we currently lack a unified theory to describe the phenomena.

**Thus, option (b) is the correct answer.**

**8.** *(a)* 4, 1, 3, 2

- **Electromagnetic waves** are arranged in the electromagnetic spectrum based on their frequency and wavelength. **Frequency is inversely proportional to wavelength,** meaning waves with longer wavelengths have lower frequencies and *vice-versa.*
- **Radio waves:** These have the **longest wavelength and the lowest frequency** in the electromagnetic spectrum. They are used for communication purposes, such as radio broadcasting and TV signals.
- **Microwaves:** These have a **shorter wavelength and higher frequency** than radio waves. They are commonly used in microwave ovens and satellite communications.
- **Visible light:** This lies in the **middle of the electromagnetic spectrum,** with frequencies higher than microwaves but lower than gamma rays. It is the part of the spectrum that human eyes can detect.
- **Gamma rays:** These have the **shortest wavelength and the highest frequency** in the electromagnetic spectrum. They are highly energetic and are produced in nuclear reactions and certain astronomical phenomena.

**Thus, the correct order is (a) 4, 1, 3, 2.**

**9.** *(a)* 1, 3, 4, 2

- **Gamma rays:** Have the **highest energy** in the electromagnetic spectrum due to their extremely high frequency.
- **Ultraviolet (UV) waves:** Have higher energy than visible light but less than gamma rays.
- **Visible light:** Falls between UV waves and infrared waves in terms of energy.
- **Infrared waves:** Have the lowest energy among the given options.

**Thus, the correct order is (a) 1, 3, 4, 2.**

**10.** *(a)* The universe started from a point of infinite density and temperature and has been expanding ever since.

- **Statement (a) is correct:** The Big Bang Theory explains that the universe began approximately 13.8 billion years ago from a singularity, a point of infinite density and temperature. From this initial state, the universe has been expanding, as evidenced by redshifts in galaxies and the cosmic microwave background radiation (CMBR).
- **Statement (b) is incorrect:** The Big Bang was **not an explosion** in space but rather an expansion of space-time itself.
- **Statement (c) is incorrect:** This describes the **now-discredited Steady State Theory**, which proposed a constant universe with no beginning or end.
- **Statement (d) is incorrect:** The Big Bang Theory **does not predict the future of the universe.** Other models, such as the Big Crunch or Big Freeze, address possible future scenarios.

**Thus, option (a) is the correct answer.**

**11.** *(a)* Both Statement I and Statement II are correct, and Statement II is the correct explanation for Statement I.

- **Statement I is correct:** Gravitational lensing occurs when light from a distant source, such as a galaxy or quasar, passes near a massive object like a galaxy cluster. The gravitational field of the **massive object bends the path of light, similar to how a lens bends light.** This effect can create multiple images, magnify the source, or distort its shape, depending on the alignment of the light source, lens and observer.
- **Statement II is correct:** Gravitational lensing is a direct prediction of **Einstein's General Theory of Relativity,** which states that massive objects cause a curvature in spacetime. Light follows the curved spacetime, resulting in its apparent bending. Observations of gravitational lensing provide strong evidence supporting Einstein's theory.

**Therefore, both statements are correct and Statement II provides the correct explanation for Statement I.**

**12.** *(b)* Only two

- **Statement 1 is correct:** Einstein's General Theory of Relativity redefines gravity as the **curvature of spacetime.** Massive objects, like planets or stars, cause spacetime bend and smaller objects move along these curves, which we perceive as the effect of gravity. This concept **replaced Newton's idea of gravity** as a force acting at a distance.
- **Statement 2 is correct:** General relativity predicts the **existence of black holes,** which are regions of spacetime where gravity is so strong that even light cannot escape.
- Observational evidence, such as gravitational waves from black hole mergers and the first image of a black hole shadow, confirms this prediction.
- **Statement 3 is incorrect:** General relativity **does not suggest that the speed of light in a vacuum change.** The speed of light remains constant at approximately 299,792 kilometers per second, regardless of gravitational field strength. However, the path and frequency of light can be affected by gravity, leading to phenomena like gravitational lensing and redshift.

**Therefore, the correct answer is (b) Only two.**

**13.** *(b)* A massive cluster of galaxies located in the distant universe.

- The **Saraswati supercluster** is a massive structure consisting of thousands of galaxies bound together by gravity. Located approximately **4 billion light-years away,** it spans about **600 million light-years** in diameter. This discovery highlights one of the largest known structures in the universe.
- It is located in the **Pisces constellation** and discovered by Indian astronomers using data from the **Sloan Digital Sky Survey (SDSS).**

**Thus, option (b) is the correct answer.**

**14.** *(c)* Only three

- **Galactic Bulge:** The **Galactic Bulge** is the central region of the Milky Way, composed of a dense concentration of older stars. It plays a critical role in the structure of the galaxy and is part of the Milky Way.
- **Sagittarius A*:** It is a supermassive black hole located at the center of the Milky Way galaxy. It governs the dynamics of the galaxy's core and is a well-established component of the Milky Way.
- **Spiral Arms:** The Milky Way is a **barred spiral galaxy**, with distinct spiral arms that contain young stars, gas and dust. The solar system resides in the Orion Arm, one of the Milky Way's minor spiral arms.
- **Andromeda:** The **Andromeda Galaxy** is not part of the Milky Way. It is a separate galaxy within the local group and the Milky Way's closest large galactic neighbour.

**Thus, the correct answer is (c) Only three.**

**15.** *(a)* 1 and 2 only

- **Statement 1 is correct: Terrestrial planets,** including Mercury, Venus, Earth and Mars, are composed mostly of rock and metal. Their rocky structure is a result of their formation in the inner solar system, where high temperatures prevented lighter gases from condensing.
- **Statement 2 is correct:** Terrestrial planets have fewer Moons compared to Jovian planets. For example, Mercury and Venus have no Moons. Earth has one Moon. Mars has two small Moons, Phobos and Deimos.
  - In contrast, Jovian planets like Jupiter and Saturn have dozens of Moons due to their stronger gravitational pull.
- **Statement 3 is incorrect:** Mars has a thin atmosphere composed primarily of carbon dioxide (~95%) and a very low surface pressure. Venus has the thickest atmosphere among terrestrial planets, composed mainly of carbon dioxide and with a surface pressure 92 times that of Earth.

**Therefore, the correct answer is (a) 1 and 2 only.**

**16.** *(a)* 1 and 2 only

- **Statement 1 is correct: Jovian planets** (Jupiter, Saturn, Uranus and Neptune) are primarily composed of hydrogen and helium, making them gas giants. They lack a solid surface and have thick atmospheres dominated by these light gases.
- **Statement 2 is correct:** All Jovian planets have rings, although Saturn's rings are the most prominent and visible. Rings around other planets, like Jupiter, Uranus and Neptune, are fainter and composed of smaller particles.
- **Statement 3 is incorrect:** Jupiter and Saturn are classified as gas giants, while Uranus and Neptune are ice giants. Ice giants have a higher proportion of icy materials like water, ammonia and methane in their composition.

**Hence, the correct answer is (a) 1 and 2 only.**

**17.** *(c)* 1, 2 and 3

- **Statement 1 is correct:** Terrestrial planets **rotate more slowly compared to Jovian** planets. For example, Earth takes 24 hours for a rotation, whereas Jupiter completes a rotation in about 10 hours.
- **Statement 2 is correct:** Jovian planets have **stronger magnetic fields** due to their larger size, faster rotation and the presence of conducting materials in their interiors. For instance, Jupiter's magnetic field is the strongest in the solar system.
- **Statement 3 is correct: Terrestrial planets are denser than Jovian planets** because they are composed of heavy elements like iron and rock. Jovian planets, being made mostly of gases like hydrogen and helium, have much lower densities.

**Therefore, the correct answer is (c) 1, 2 and 3.**

**18.** *(a)* Paris, France

- The **International Astronomical Union (IAU)** is the preeminent organisation for promoting and safeguarding astronomy globally. It coordinates astronomical research, standardises celestial nomenclature and fosters international collaboration among astronomers.
- Established in **1919**, the IAU is headquartered in **Paris, France.**

- The choice of Paris reflects its historical and scientific significance, as well as its accessibility for the global community of astronomers.
- The IAU's responsibilities include defining planetary criteria (e.g., the reclassification of Pluto as a dwarf planet in 2006) and managing global astronomy education initiatives.

**Therefore, the correct answer is (a) Paris, France.**

**19.** *(b)* To establish universally recognised names and definitions for celestial objects.

The **International Astronomical Union** (IAU) is the globally recognised authority for assigning names and classifications to celestial objects, such as stars, planets, asteroids and surface features like craters. It also defines terms like 'planet' and 'dwarf planet', ensuring universal consistency in astronomical nomenclature and classifications.

**Thus, option (b) is the correct answer.**

**20.** *(c)* 1-3-2-4

- **Saturn:** As of now, Saturn has the highest number of confirmed Moons.
- **Mars:** Mars has two Moons, Phobos and Deimos.
- **Earth** has one natural satellite, the Moon.
- **Mercury:** Mercury has no Moons.

**Thus, the correct order is 1-3-2-4 and the correct answer is (c).**

**21.** *(a)* A-2, B-1, C-3, D-4

- **Ganymede** is the largest Moon of **Jupiter** and the largest Moon in the solar system.
- **Titan** is **Saturn's** largest Moon and the second-largest Moon in the solar system.
- **Triton** is **Neptune's** largest Moon, notable for its retrograde orbit.
- **Phobos** is the largest and closest Moon of **Mars**, with an irregular shape.

**Thus, the correct answer is (a).**

**22.** *(b)* A planet that orbits a star outside our solar system.

An **exoplanet** refers to any planet that orbits a star other than our Sun, meaning it is located outside our solar system. Thousands of exoplanets have been discovered using advanced astronomical methods such as the transit method and radial velocity method. These planets vary in size, composition and orbit, ranging from rocky Earth-like planets to massive gas giants.

**Thus, option (b) is the correct answer.**

**23.** *(c)* The region around a star where conditions are suitable for liquid water to exist on a planet's surface.

The **Goldilocks Zone**, also known as the **habitable zone**, is the region around a star where the temperature range allows for liquid water to exist on a planet's surface. This concept is critical because liquid water is considered essential for the development and sustenance of life as we know it. The location of the Goldilocks Zone depends on the star's size, temperature and luminosity.

**Thus, option (c) is the correct answer.**

**24.** *(a)* To search for exoplanets by monitoring the brightness of nearby stars.

The **TESS (Transiting Exoplanet Survey Satellite)** mission is designed to identify exoplanets by observing the brightness of nearby stars. It looks for periodic dips in brightness caused by planets passing in front of their stars (a method known as the transit method).

**Thus, option (a) is the correct answer.**

**25.** *(a)* 1 and 2 only

- **Statement 1 is correct:** Stars generate energy primarily through **nuclear fusion**, where lighter elements fuse to form heavier elements, releasing enormous energy.
- **Statement 2 is correct:** During the **main sequence stage**, hydrogen nuclei are fused into helium through the proton-proton chain reaction or CNO cycle, depending on the star's size.
- **Statement 3 is incorrect:** Stars do not use **nuclear fission** (the splitting of heavier nuclei into lighter ones) to produce energy. Energy production in stars is dominated by nuclear fusion.

**Thus, the correct answer is (a) 1 and 2 only.**

**26.** *(a)* 2, 1, 4, 3

- **Main Sequence** (2): Low-mass stars spend most of their lives in this phase, where **hydrogen is fused into helium in the core.** This process releases energy, keeping the star stable by balancing gravitational collapse. For the Sun, this phase lasts approximately **10 billion years.**
- **Red Giant** (1): When **hydrogen in the core is depleted**, the core contracts while the outer layers expand. The star becomes a red giant, with a cooler outer shell and a helium-burning core. The Sun in this phase will engulf planets like Mercury and Venus.
- **Planetary Nebula** (4): When **helium fusion ends**, the outer layers are ejected, forming a glowing shell of gas called a planetary nebula. This marks the final shedding of material, enriching the interstellar medium.
- **White Dwarf** (3): The **remaining core becomes a white dwarf**, a dense, hot remnant composed mainly of carbon and oxygen. Over time, it cools and fades into a black dwarf, though this process takes billions of years.

**Thus, the correct order is** (a) **2, 1, 4, 3.**

**27.** *(a)* 2, 3, 1, 4

- **Main Sequence** (2): High-mass stars begin their life **fusing hydrogen into helium**, similar to low-mass stars but at a much faster rate due to their larger size and higher energy output.
- **Red Supergiant** (3): After exhausting hydrogen, the star **expands into a red supergiant** and starts fusing heavier elements in its core, progressing up to iron.
- **Supernova** (1): When fusion reaches iron, energy generation stops. The star collapses under its own gravity, triggering a catastrophic supernova explosion that expels its outer layers.
- **Neutron Star** (4): The core left behind after the supernova becomes a neutron star if the mass is insufficient to form a black hole. A neutron star is incredibly dense, composed mainly of neutrons.

**Hence, the correct order is** (a) **2, 3, 1, 4.**

**28.** *(b)* Red Giant

- The characteristics provided describe a Red Giant phase. Here's a detailed breakdown:
- **Expansion After Hydrogen Exhaustion:** Once hydrogen in the core is depleted, fusion ceases in the core. The core contracts under gravity, heating up, while the outer layers expand. This marks the transition to the red giant phase.
- **Helium Fusion:** The core becomes hot enough to ignite helium fusion, producing heavier elements like carbon and oxygen.
- **Cooler and Redder Appearance:** The expansion of the star lowers its surface temperature, making it appear cooler and redder than during its main sequence phase.

**Therefore, the star described is in the Red Giant phase.**

**29.** *(b)* White Dwarf

- The characteristics described in the question align with the **White Dwarf** phase.
- A **White Dwarf** forms after a low to medium-mass star, like our Sun, completes its Red Giant phase. The star ejects its outer layers as a planetary nebula, leaving behind a dense core.
- White Dwarfs are **no longer capable of nuclear fusion.** They are essentially cooling remnants that emit light due to residual heat from their past.
- White Dwarfs are **extremely dense.** They pack the mass of the Sun into a volume similar to Earth's size due to the gravitational collapse of the core.

**Other options are incorrect:**

(a) **Red Giant:** A Red Giant is a phase before the White Dwarf, characterised by the expansion of the outer layers and ongoing fusion in the core.

(c) **Main Sequence Star:** A Main Sequence Star is in an earlier, stable phase of stellar evolution, undergoing hydrogen fusion in its core.

(d) **Protostar:** A Protostar is an early stage in star formation, where a gas cloud is contracting under gravity before nuclear fusion begins.

**Therefore, the star described is a White Dwarf.**

**30.** *(c)* All three

- **Statement 1 is correct:** The limit represents the point at which electron degeneracy pressure is no longer sufficient to counteract gravity in a white dwarf.
- **Statement 2 is correct:** The Chandrasekhar Limit is calculated to be **around 1.4 solar masses.** A white dwarf exceeding this limit cannot remain stable.
- **Statement 3 is correct:** Stars with masses greater than this limit collapse further, either forming a neutron star or, if massive enough, a black hole.

**Thus, all three statements are correct, making the answer (c) All three.**

**31.** *(b)* A red dwarf is a low-mass main-sequence star that is still burning hydrogen, while a white dwarf is a dense stellar remnant that no longer undergoes nuclear fusion.

- **Red dwarfs** are low-mass stars on the **main sequence,** burning hydrogen in their cores through nuclear fusion. They are cooler, dimmer and have much longer lifespans compared to other stars.
- **White dwarfs** are the **stellar remnants** of stars like the Sun. They are extremely dense, consist mostly of carbon and oxygen and no longer undergo nuclear fusion. Instead, they emit energy slowly as they cool over billions of years.

**Thus, option (b) is the correct answer.**

**32.** *(c)* Only three statements

- **Statement 1 is correct:** Venus is the **hottest planet** due to its thick atmosphere composed of carbon dioxide, which traps heat through a runaway greenhouse effect.
- **Statement 2 is correct:** Jupiter has the **shortest day,** completing one rotation in approximately 10 hours.
- **Statement 3 is correct:** Mercury is the **smallest planet** in the solar system, with a diameter of approximately 4,880 km.
- **Statement 4 is incorrect:** While Saturn is famous for its rings, it is not the only planet with rings. **Jupiter, Uranus** and **Neptune** also have ring systems, although they are less prominent.

**Therefore, three statements are correct so, option (c) is the correct answer.**

**33.** *(c)* Only three

**Criteria for a Dwarf Planet (IAU):**

(i) **Orbits the Sun:** The object must revolve around the Sun.

(ii) **Nearly Round Shape:** It must be massive enough for its gravity to give it a nearly spherical shape (hydrostatic equilibrium).

(iii) **Has Not Cleared Its Orbit:** It shares its orbital path with other objects (e.g., asteroids or Kuiper Belt objects).

(iv) **Not a Satellite:** It cannot be a moon or natural satellite of another body.

- **Option 1 is incorrect:** Vesta is a large **asteroid** located in the asteroid belt between Mars and Jupiter. It is not classified as a dwarf planet because it does not meet the criteria of being in hydrostatic equilibrium (rounded shape due to self-gravity).
- **Option 2 is correct:** Ceres is the **only dwarf planet located in the asteroid belt.** It is in hydrostatic equilibrium and orbits the Sun, meeting all the criteria for a dwarf planet as per the International Astronomical Union (IAU).
- **Option 3 is correct:** Eris is a **dwarf planet** located in the Kuiper Belt. It is larger than Pluto and meets all the criteria for classification as a dwarf planet.
- **Option 4 is correct: Haumea** is an elongated, rapidly rotating dwarf planet in the Kuiper Belt. It has two moons and meets the IAU's criteria for classification as a dwarf planet.

**Thus, three objects (Ceres, Eris and Haumea) are classified as dwarf planets making correct answer (c).**

**34.** *(b)* A nebula is a cloud of gas and dust in space that serves as a stellar nursery, while a planetary nebula is the outer shell of gas ejected by a dying star.

- **Nebula:** A nebula is a vast cloud of gas and dust in space, often acting as a stellar nursery where new stars are born. Examples include the Orion Nebula and the Eagle Nebula.
- **Planetary Nebula:** A planetary nebula is formed when a dying star, typically a red giant, sheds its outer layers, creating a glowing shell of ionised gas surrounding the stellar remnant.

**Thus, option (b) is the correct answer.**

***35.*** *(a)* A high-energy explosion observed in distant galaxies, believed to be associated with the collapse of massive stars or the merger of neutron stars.

GRBs are among the most **energetic and luminous explosions** in the universe, releasing as much energy in a few seconds as the Sun will emit over its entire lifetime. They are detected as brief flashes of gamma radiation, often followed by a slower-fading afterglow in X-ray, ultraviolet, optical and radio wavelengths.

**Cause of GRBs**

- **Long-duration GRBs** are linked to the collapse of massive stars into black holes during supernovae or hypernova.
- **Short-duration GRBs** are associated with the merger of compact objects such as neutron stars or a neutron star and a black hole.

**Thus, option (a) is the correct answer.**

***36.*** *(b)* 1, 2 and 3 only

- **Option 1 is correct: Collapsing massive stars: Long-duration GRBs** are caused by the **collapse of massive stars** at the end of their life cycles, often resulting in black hole formation. This event is usually accompanied by a supernova or hypernova.
- **Option 2 is correct: Merging neutron stars: Short-duration GRBs** are linked to the merger of neutron stars or a neutron star with a black hole. These events produce gravitational waves and are followed by gamma-ray bursts.
- **Option 3 is correct: Supernova explosions:** Some GRBs, particularly long-duration ones, are associated with supernova explosions that occur during the collapse of massive stars.
- **Option 4 is incorrect: Interactions between black holes and their accretion disks:** While black holes and their accretion disks emit X-rays and other forms of radiation, there is **no evidence to suggest that these interactions cause GRBs.**

**Therefore, the correct answer is (b) 1, 2 and 3 only.**

***37.*** *(d)* 1, 2 and 3

- **Statement 1 is correct:** The Cosmic Microwave Background (CMB) radiation is the faint thermal radiation left over from the Big Bang, which occurred approximately 13.8 billion years ago. It is the oldest light observable in the universe.
- **Statement 2 is correct:** The CMB radiation has a nearly uniform temperature of 2.725 Kelvin throughout the universe, with slight fluctuations indicating density variations in the early universe.
- **Statement 3 is correct:** The redshifted nature of the CMB and its uniformity provide strong evidence for the expanding universe model, supporting the Big Bang theory.

**Therefore, all three statements are correct and the correct answer is (d) 1, 2 and 3.**

***38.*** *(b)* A point at the center of a black hole where the curvature of spacetime becomes infinite and the laws of physics break down.

A **singularity** is the central point of a black hole where matter is compressed to infinite density and spacetime curvature becomes infinite. At this point, the known laws of physics, including general relativity, cease to be valid.

- **Option (a):** This describes the event horizon, not the singularity. The event horizon is the boundary beyond which nothing, not even light, can escape.

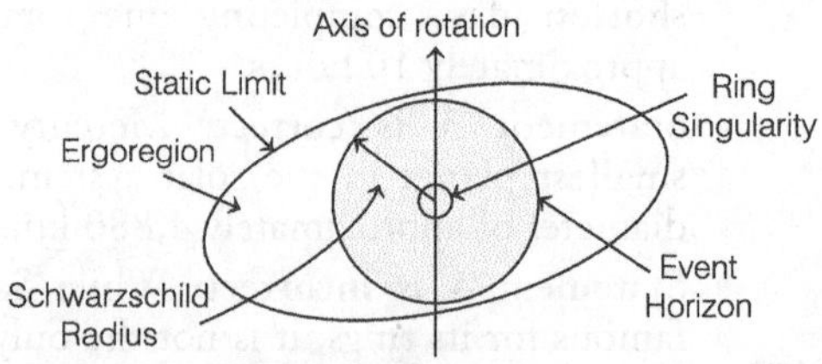


- **Option (c):** Again, this refers to the event horizon, the 'point of no return' for objects near a black hole.

- **Option (d):** A singularity is not a line; it is a point in space with infinite density.

**Thus, the correct answer is (b).**

**39.** *(a)* A black hole with no electric charge or angular momentum, characterised only by its mass.

**Schwarzschild black hole:** This is the simplest type of black hole, described by the Schwarzschild solution to Einstein's field equations. It is **non-rotating,** has **no electric charge** and is entirely characterised by its mass. It is spherically symmetric and static.

**While the other options are incorrect:**

- **Option (b):** This describes Hawking radiation, not a Schwarzschild black hole.
- **Option (c):** A rotating black hole is called a Kerr black hole.
- **Option (d):** A charged black hole is known as a Reissner-Nordström black hole.

**Therefore, the correct answer is (a).**

**40.** *(c)* Only three

- **Statement 1 is correct:** The Kuiper Belt is a region of the solar system located beyond Neptune's orbit, approximately 30-55 AU (astronomical units) from the Sun. **It consists of icy bodies and is the source of short-period comets.**
- **Statement 2 is correct:** Pluto, a dwarf planet, is one of the largest known objects in the Kuiper Belt. Other large Kuiper Belt Objects (KBOs) include Eris, Haumea and Makemake.
- **Statement 3 is incorrect:** As the **Kuiper Belt primarily contains icy bodies and dwarf planets, not the rocky asteroids found in the asteroid belt between Mars and Jupiter.** The objects in the Kuiper Belt are more similar to comets in composition, consisting largely of frozen volatiles like methane, ammonia and water.
- Unlike the asteroid belt, which contains rocky and metallic bodies, the Kuiper Belt is primarily composed of icy bodies, such as frozen methane, ammonia and water.
- **Statement 4 is correct: Dwarf planet Eris** is a member of a group of objects that **orbit in a disc-like zone beyond the orbit of Neptune called the Kuiper Belt.** This distant realm is populated with thousands of miniature icy worlds, which formed early in the history of our solar system about 4.5 billion years ago.

**Therefore, three statements are correct, making the correct answer (c).**

**41.** *(b)* 1 and 3 only

**Retrograde rotation:** A retrograde rotation means the planet rotates in the opposite direction to most other planets in the solar system.

- **Venus: Retrograde rotation.** Venus rotates on its axis in the opposite direction to most planets in the solar system. This means it rotates East to West, which is retrograde.
- **Jupiter: Prograde rotation.** Jupiter rotates on its axis in the normal direction (West to East) and has one of the fastest rotations in the solar system.
- **Uranus: Retrograde rotation.** Uranus is tilted on its side with an axial tilt of about 98 degrees, making its rotation effectively retrograde.
- **Mars: Prograde rotation.** Mars rotates counter-clockwise, similar to Earth.

**Thus, only Venus and Uranus rotate retrograde, making the correct answer (b).**

**42.** *(a)* 3-1-4-2

- **Saturn (Density ~ 0.69 g/cm$^3$):** Saturn has the **lowest density** of all planets. It is less dense than water and would float if placed in a large enough body of water.
- **Mars (Density ~ 3.93 g/cm$^3$):** Mars has a low density compared to Earth and Mercury, as it lacks a large metallic core.
- **Mercury (Density ~ 5.43 g/cm$^3$):** Mercury has a high density due to its large metallic core, contributing to its compact size.
- **Earth (Density ~ 5.52 g/cm$^3$):** Earth has the **highest density** among planets because of its solid inner core and rocky mantle.

**Therefore, the correct order of increasing density is 3-1-4-2, making the answer (a).**

**43.** (c) All three

- **Statement 1 is correct:** The asteroid belt is a region of the solar system located between the orbits of **Mars** and **Jupiter**, containing a large number of rocky and metallic bodies.

- **Statement 2 is correct:** Most asteroids are made up of **silicate rock and metal,** particularly iron and nickel, with some containing carbon-rich materials.
- **Statement 3 is correct:** Ceres, the **largest object** in the asteroid belt, is classified as a **dwarf planet**. It accounts for about 25% of the asteroid belt's total mass.

**Thus, all three statements are correct, making the answer (c).**

**44.** *(c)* 1, 2 and 3

- **Pair 1 is correct:** A **meteoroid** is a small rocky or metallic body travelling through space, typically originating from comets, asteroids, or other celestial debris. These objects orbit the Sun.
- **Pair 2 is correct:** A **meteor** is the visible streak of light created when a meteoroid enters Earth's atmosphere and burns up due to friction with air. This is commonly called a 'shooting star'.
- **Pair 3 is correct:** A **meteorite** is a meteoroid that survives its fiery descent through Earth's atmosphere and lands on the surface, where it can be studied for insights into the solar system's composition.

**Therefore, all three pairs are correctly matched, making the answer (c).**

**45.** *(c)* A piece of a meteoroid that survives its passage through the atmosphere and reaches the Earth's surface.

A meteorite refers to a piece of space debris that survives its passage through Earth's atmosphere and lands on the surface. Meteorites provide critical information about the solar system's formation, as they are remnants of asteroids, comets, or meteoroids.

**Therefore, the correct answer is (c).**

**46.** (a) 1 and 2 only

- **Pair 1 is correct:** Asteroids are primarily rocky or metallic objects found in the **asteroid belt,** a region between Mars and Jupiter.
- **Pair 2 is correct:** Comets, composed of ice, dust and rock, originate from the Kuiper Belt (beyond Neptune) and the **Oort Cloud** (a distant spherical region surrounding the solar system).
- **Pair 3 is incorrect:** Meteorites are fragments of meteoroids that have landed on Earth. They are not objects that remain in the asteroid belt.

**Thus, the correct answer is (a) 1 and 2 only.**

**47.** *(c)* Only three

- **Lonar Crater (Correct):** Located in **Maharashtra,** this is a well-preserved impact crater formed by a meteorite collision approximately 52,000 years ago.
- **Dhala Crater (Correct):** Found in **Madhya Pradesh,** it is one of the oldest known meteorite impact sites, dating back approximately 2.5 billion years.
- **Ramgarh Crater (Correct):** Located in **Rajasthan,** this is another confirmed meteorite impact site.
- **Shiva Crater (Incorrect):** The Shiva Crater is a hypothesized structure in the **Arabian Sea.** Its origin as a meteorite impact site has not been confirmed.

**Thus, three of the four craters are confirmed meteorite impact sites, making the correct answer (c).**

**48.** *(d)* A spherical shell of icy bodies surrounding the solar system, believed to be the source of long-period comets.

The **Oort Cloud** is a theoretical spherical region surrounding the solar system, extending far beyond the orbits of the planets and the Kuiper Belt. It is composed of icy bodies, which are considered the primary source of **long-period comets.** These comets are believed to be occasionally disturbed by gravitational forces, sending them into the inner solar system.

**Thus, option (d) is the correct answer.**

**49.** *(b)* 2 only

- **Statement 1 is incorrect:** Gravitational waves are **ripples in spacetime** caused by the acceleration of massive objects, as predicted by Einstein's General Theory of Relativity. These waves are not produced **only by events involving black holes.**
- They can also be generated by other astrophysical phenomena such as **neutron star mergers, supernovae** and the

interaction of massive bodies in orbit around each other.

- **Statement 2 is correct:** The **first direct detection of gravitational waves** was made in 2015 by the **Laser Interferometer Gravitational-Wave Observatory (LIGO)**. This discovery confirmed the detection of gravitational waves generated by the collision and merger of two black holes approximately 1.3 billion light-years away.
- **Statement 3 is incorrect:** Gravitational waves propagate at the **speed of light in a vacuum**, as predicted by Einstein's Theory of Relativity. They do not travel faster than the speed of light. This characteristic aligns with the laws of physics and our current understanding of the universe.

**Thus, the correct answer is (b) 2 only.**

***50.*** *(a)* 3-1-2-4

- **Gravitational force (Weakest):** The **weakest of the four fundamental forces**, it governs the attraction between masses and operates over long distances. It is responsible for holding planets, stars and galaxies together.
- **Weak nuclear force:** Stronger than gravity but weaker than the electromagnetic and strong nuclear forces, the weak nuclear force governs processes like beta decay in atomic nuclei.
- **Electromagnetic force:** This force is much stronger than gravity and weak nuclear force and is responsible for interactions between charged particles, including light and electricity.
- **Strong nuclear force (Strongest):** The strongest of the fundamental forces, it binds protons and neutrons together in atomic nuclei, overcoming the electromagnetic repulsion between positively charged protons.

**Therefore, the correct order is 3-1-2-4, making the answer (a).**

***51.*** *(b)* Only two

- **Statement 1 is correct: LIGO is a scientific facility designed to detect gravitational waves**, which are ripples in spacetime caused by cosmic events like black hole mergers, neutron star collisions and supernovae. It operates by measuring the tiny disturbances in spacetime using highly sensitive laser interferometers.
- **Statement 2 is incorrect:** LIGO is a **ground-based observatory**, with facilities located in the United States (at Hanford, Washington and Livingston, Louisiana). Space-based gravitational wave detectors, such as **LISA (Laser Interferometer Space Antenna)**, are planned for the future.
- **Statement 3 is correct:** India is developing a LIGO facility called **LIGO-India**, which will be a part of the global LIGO network. It aims to enhance the detection of gravitational waves and improve localisation of wave sources.

**Thus, two statements are correct, making the answer (b).**

***52.*** *(c)* 1 and 2 only

- The LIGO-India observatory is being constructed in **Hingoli, Maharashtra**, strategically chosen for its seismic stability and logistical feasibility. The project is a cutting-edge initiative aimed at advancing gravitational-wave astronomy in India.
- **Statement 1 is correct:** The **LIGO-India project** is part of a **global network of gravitational wave detectors**, which includes **LIGO (USA), Virgo (Italy) and KAGRA (Japan)**. This network is crucial for triangulating the source of gravitational waves and improving the sensitivity and accuracy of detections.
- **Statement 2 is correct:** LIGO-India aims to detect **gravitational waves** and study cosmic phenomena such as the **merger of black holes and neutron stars**, supernovae and other massive cosmic events. This will provide deeper insights into the nature of spacetime and fundamental physics.
- **Statement 3 is incorrect:** While the project is funded and supported by the **Government of India**, it is not an entirely independent initiative. The LIGO-India project involves significant **international collaboration**, particularly with the United States, which is providing technical expertise and transferring components from its existing LIGO facilities.

**Thus, the correct answer is (c) 1 and 2 only.**

**53.** *(b)* 2 and 3 only

- **Statement 1 is incorrect:** LISA is a **space-based gravitational wave detector**, not a ground-based one. It operates in space to detect low-frequency gravitational waves that cannot be observed from Earth due to noise and limitations of ground-based detectors like LIGO.
- **Statement 2 is correct:** LISA is specifically designed to detect **low-frequency gravitational waves** generated by phenomena such as **supermassive black hole** mergers, binary star systems and other massive astrophysical events.
- **Statement 3 is correct:** The **European Space Agency (ESA)** leads the LISA mission in collaboration with NASA and other international partners.

**Thus, the correct answer is (b) 2 and 3 only.**

**54.** *(b)* To detect and observe gravitational waves from space-based observatories.

The **eLISA project**, led by the European Space Agency (ESA), aims to detect and study **gravitational waves** from space. Unlike ground-based detectors like LIGO, eLISA will use a constellation of spacecraft to measure tiny disturbances in spacetime caused by massive cosmic events such as black hole mergers.

**Thus, option (b) is the correct answer.**

**55.** *(c)* Matter consists of particles, while antimatter consists of anti-particles with the same mass but opposite charges.

- Matter consists of particles such as **protons, neutrons** and **electrons.**
- Anti-matter consists of **antiparticles,** which have the **same mass** as their corresponding particles but possess **opposite charges.** For example:
- The antiparticle of an electron is a **positron,** which has the same mass as an electron but a **positive charge.**
- The antiparticle of a proton is an **antiproton,** which has the same mass as a proton but a **negative charge.**

This difference in charge is a defining characteristic of matter and anti-matter.

**56.** *(a)* 1 and 2 only

- **Statement 1 is correct:** When a particle of matter meets its corresponding **anti-particle,** they annihilate each other, releasing energy in the form of **gamma rays.** This property is fundamental to the interaction between matter and anti-matter.
- **Statement 2 is correct:** Anti-matter particles, such as positrons and antiprotons, have the **same mass** as their matter counterparts (e.g., electrons and protons) but carry **opposite charges.**
- **Statement 3 is incorrect:** The observable universe is composed primarily of matter, not anti-matter. The dominance of matter over anti-matter in the universe remains an unsolved problem in physics, referred to as the **matter-anti-matter asymmetry.**

**Thus, the correct answer is (a) 1 and 2 only.**

**57.** *(b)* Only two

- **Dark matter** is a mysterious form of matter that does **not emit, absorb, or reflect light,** making it invisible and detectable **only through its gravitational effects** on visible matter, radiation and the large-scale structure of the universe.
- **Statement 1 is correct:** Dark matter **does not interact with electromagnetic forces, meaning it does not emit, absorb, or reflect light,** making it invisible.
- **Statement 2 is incorrect:** Dark energy is the name that **astronomers gave to the mysterious "something" that is causing the universe to expand at an accelerated rate.** Dark energy has been described by some as having the effect of a negative pressure that is pushing space outward.
- **Statement 3 is incorrect:** Dark matter **cannot be detected directly through telescopes.** Its presence is inferred through its gravitational effects, such as galaxy rotation curves and gravitational lensing.
- **Statement 4 is correct:** Dark matter accounts for approximately **27% of the universe's** total mass-energy content and plays a crucial role in galaxy formation.

**Therefore, only two statements are correct, making the answer (b) Only two.**

**58.** *(a)* 1, 2 and 3 only

- **Pair 1 is correctly matched:** When a particle (e.g., an electron) and its anti-particle (e.g., a positron) collide, they annihilate each other, converting their mass into energy, typically in the form of gamma rays.
- **Pair 2 is correctly matched: CP violation** describes the asymmetry in physical laws governing matter and anti-matter. This violation explains why more matter exists than anti-matter in the universe.
- **Pair 3 is correctly matched: Baryogenesis** is a theoretical process proposed to explain the imbalance of matter and anti-matter in the universe. It is believed to have occurred shortly after the Big Bang.
- **Pair 4 is incorrectly matched:** There is **no experimental evidence** supporting the existence of anti-gravity. Anti-matter is thought to interact gravitationally in the same way as ordinary matter.

**Thus, three pairs are correct, making the answer (a).**

**59.** *(b)* Only two

- **Statement 1 is correct: Dark energy** is a theoretical form of energy that **permeates all of space and is believed to be responsible for the accelerated expansion of the universe.** Observations, such as those of distant supernovae and the cosmic microwave background, suggest that the universe's expansion is speeding up, which is attributed to the repulsive force of dark energy.
- **Statement 2 is correct:** Dark energy is **estimated to make up approximately 68% of the total energy density of the universe.** This estimate comes from data collected by missions like the Planck satellite and studies of the large-scale structure of the universe.
- **Statement 3 is incorrect: Dark energy does not interact strongly-or even at all-with visible matter** or other forces except through its influence on the **universe's expansion rate.** Unlike dark matter, which exerts gravitational influence on visible matter, dark energy operates on a cosmic scale, driving the acceleration of the universe's expansion.

**Thus, the correct answer is (b) Only two.**

**60.** *(b)* To detect and study Weakly Interacting Massive Particles (WIMPs) as candidates for dark matter.

The **Xenon 1T experiment** is a direct detection experiment designed to identify **Weakly Interacting Massive Particles (WIMPs)**, which are one of the most promising candidates for **dark matter.** Using a large tank filled with liquid xenon, the experiment aims to detect rare interactions between WIMPs and xenon nuclei, which would produce measurable light and ionization signals.

**Thus, option (b) is the correct answer.**

**61.** *(a)* 1, 2 and 3 only

- **Pair 1 is correct:** The photon is the force carrier for the **electromagnetic force,** mediating interactions between charged particles.
- **Pair 2 is correct:** Gluons mediate the **strong nuclear force,** which binds quarks together to form protons and neutrons.
- **Pair 3 is correct:** The **W and Z bosons are the mediators of the weak nuclear force,** responsible for processes like radioactive decay.
- **Pair 4 is incorrect:** The Higgs boson is **not associated with the gravitational force.** It is related to the Higgs field, which gives mass to particles.

**Therefore, the correct answer is (a).**

**62.** *(b)* Only two

- **Statement 1 is correct:** In the **Standard Model of particle physics, fermions** are the building blocks of matter. They are divided into two categories:
  (i) **Quarks,** which combine to form protons and neutrons.
  (ii) **Leptons,** which include particles like the electron and neutrinos.
- **Statement 2 is incorrect: Photons** and **gluons** are not fermions; they are **bosons,** specifically gauge bosons. Bosons are force-carrier particles that mediate fundamental forces:

– Photons mediate the electromagnetic force. Gluons mediate the strong nuclear force.

– Fermions, on the other hand, are particles of matter, obeying the Pauli exclusion principle.

- **Statement 3 is correct:** The **Higgs boson,** discovered in 2012 at CERN, is a fundamental particle in the Standard Model. It is responsible for the mechanism that gives mass to other fundamental particles through their interaction with the **Higgs field**. This discovery confirmed the mechanism of electroweak symmetry breaking.

**Thus, the correct answer is (b) Only two.**

**63.** *(c)* Only three

- **Option 1 is correct: Electrons** are **leptons,** which are a type of fermion. They follow the Pauli Exclusion Principle and have a half-integer spin (spin = 1/2).
- **Option 2 is incorrect: Photons** are **bosons,** which are force-carrying particles with an integer spin (spin = 1). They **do not follow the Pauli Exclusion Principle.**
- **Option 3 is correct: Neutrons** are **baryons,** a type of fermion, composed of three quarks. They also have a half-integer spin (spin = 1/2).
- **Option 4 is correct:** The **Z boson** is a force carrier for the weak nuclear force and is classified as a boson, with an integer spin (spin = 1).

**Thus, the electron, neutron and photon are fermions, making the correct answer (c) Only three.**

**64.** *(b)* 1, 2 and 3 only

- **Statement 1 is correct:** Neutrinos are fundamental particles with **no electric charge**. This neutrality allows them to pass through matter without being significantly affected.
- **Statement 2 is correct:** Neutrinos interact with matter only through the **weak nuclear force,** making them challenging to detect. Billions of neutrinos pass through us every second without any interaction.
- **Statement 3 is correct:** Neutrinos are produced in **nuclear reactions**, such as those occurring during nuclear fusion in the Sun, in supernovae and in nuclear reactors.
- **Statement 4 is incorrect:** Neutrinos travel close to the speed of light but do not exceed it. Experiments have consistently confirmed this within the framework of special relativity.

**Thus, the correct answer is (b) 1, 2 and 3 only.**

**65.** *(b)* 1, 2 and 3 only

- **Option 1 is correct:** Nuclear reactors are significant sources of neutrinos, as neutrinos are produced during nuclear fission reactions.
- **Option 2 is correct:** The Sun generates a vast number of neutrinos through **nuclear fusion** in its core. These **solar neutrinos are a primary source of neutrinos** reaching Earth.
- **Option 3 is correct:** Cosmic rays interacting with the Earth's atmosphere produce neutrinos when high-energy particles collide with atmospheric nuclei.
- **Option 4 is incorrect:** Black holes do not directly emit neutrinos. While they affect their surroundings, neutrino production is not directly associated with black holes.

**Thus, the correct answer is (b) 1, 2 and 3 only.**

**66.** *(b)* 1, 2 and 3 only

- The **Large Hadron Collider** (**LHC**) is the world's largest and most powerful particle accelerator, located at the European Organisation for Nuclear Research (CERN) near **Geneva, Switzerland**. It is a monumental facility designed to explore the **fundamental forces** and particles that constitute the universe.
- **Statement 1 is correct:** The LHC is the world's largest and most powerful **particle accelerator**, enabling scientists to study the fundamental particles of nature.
- **Statement 2 is correct:** LHC is located in a **27-kilometer-long circular tunnel** near Geneva, Switzerland, beneath the Swiss-French border.
- **Statement 3 is correct:** One of the LHC's key achievements was the discovery of the **Higgs boson** in 2012. It continues to explore fundamental forces and particles, including dark matter and supersymmetry.

- **Statement 4 is incorrect:** While the LHC primarily collides protons, it also collides heavy ions (e.g., lead ions) for specific experiments.

**Thus, the correct answer is (b) 1, 2 and 3 only.**

**67.** *(b)* Bodi West Hills, Tamil Nadu

The proposed site for the **India-based Neutrino Observatory (INO)** is **in the Bodi West Hills, located in Theni district, Tamil Nadu.** The site was selected for its geological stability and the ability to shield the detector from cosmic ray interference by placing it underground.

**Thus, option (b) is the correct answer.**

**68.** *(a)* To detect and study cosmic neutrinos originating from distant astrophysical sources.

The **IceCube Neutrino Observatory,** located at the South Pole, is designed to detect **high-energy neutrinos** from astrophysical sources such as supernovae, black holes and gamma-ray bursts. It uses an array of sensors embedded deep in the Antarctic ice to capture the faint light signals produced when neutrinos interact with matter.

**Thus, option (a) is the correct answer.**

## Past Learning (Answers)

| | | | | | | |
|---|---|---|---|---|---|---|
| 1 (d) | 2 (a) | 3 (d) | 4 (b) | 5 (d) | 6 (b) | 7 (a) |

CHAPTER 02

# Space Technology

## Assessment Round

### Topic 1 : Organisational Setup and Space Policies

**1.** Consider the following pairs related to ISRO organisations that promote private sector involvement in space activities:

| | Organisation | Description |
|---|---|---|
| 1. | NSIL (New Space India Limited) | Facilitates the transfer of ISRO-developed technologies to private entities. |
| 2. | IN-SPACe (Indian National Space Promotion and Authorisation Center) | Provides a regulatory and promotional framework for private sector participation in the space industry. |
| 3. | Antrix Corporation | Operates as ISRO's commercial arm, focusing on satellite launches and transponder leasing. |

How many of the pairs given above is/are correctly matched?

(a) Only one pair (b) Only two pairs
(c) All three pairs (d) None of the pairs

**2.** Which of the following statements are correct about the role of IN-SPACe in the Indian Space Policy 2023?

1. It is responsible for authorising and promoting private sector participation in India's space activities.
2. It regulates the launch of foreign satellites by private companies in India.
3. It collaborates with the Department of Space (DoS) to create industry standards for space activities.
4. It has the authority to dictate ISRO's research priorities under the new policy.

Select the correct answer using the codes given below:

(a) 1 and 2 only (b) 1, 2 and 3 only
(c) 2 and 4 only (d) 1, 3 and 4 only

**3.** Consider the following pairs of ISRO centers and their respective locations:

| | ISRO Center | Location |
|---|---|---|
| 1. | Vikram Sarabhai Space Centre | Thiruvananthapuram |
| 2. | ISRO Propulsion Complex | Mahendragiri |
| 3. | Master Control Facility | Hassan |
| 4. | Satish Dhawan Space Centre | Sriharikota |

How many of the pairs given above is/are correctly matched?

(a) Only one pair (b) Only two pairs
(c) Only three pairs (d) All four pairs

**4.** Consider the following pairs of space agencies and their headquarters:

| | ISRO Center | Headquarters Location |
|---|---|---|
| 1. | European Space Agency (ESA) | Paris |
| 2. | Japan Aerospace Exploration Agency (JAXA) | Tokyo |
| 3. | Canadian Space Agency (CSA) | Saint-Hubert, Quebec |
| 4. | National Aeronautics and Space Administration (NASA) | Washington D.C. |

Which of the pairs given above are correctly matched?

(a) 1, 3 and 4 only (b) 1 and 4 only
(c) 2 and 3 only (d) 1, 2, 3 and 4

**5.** Which of the following is a key feature of the 'Indian Space Policy, 2023'?
(a) ISRO is limited to research and development while private entities take over operational launches.
(b) The policy restricts foreign collaborations to safeguard national security interests.
(c) IN-SPACe oversees only satellite manufacturing and not launch services by private companies.
(d) All satellite launches must be conducted exclusively through ISRO facilities.

**6.** Which of the following best describes the purpose of the 'Artemis Accords'?
(a) To establish a legally binding international treaty for space exploration.
(b) To create a set of non-binding principles for cooperative exploration of the Moon and beyond.
(c) To mandate the exclusive use of national resources for lunar exploration.
(d) To limit the involvement of private entities in space missions.

**7.** Consider the following countries:
1. United States 2. India
3. Russia 4. Japan
How many of the given above is/are signatories to the Artemis Accords?
(a) Only one (b) Only two
(c) Only three (d) All four

**8.** Consider the following principles:
1. Interoperability between space systems
2. Public release of scientific data
3. Obligation to assist astronauts in distress
4. Prohibition of military use of the Moon
How many of the given above principles is/are part of the Artemis Accords?
(a) Only one (b) Only two
(c) Only three (d) All four

**9.** Which of the following best describes a key principle of the 'Outer Space Treaty'?
(a) Outer space can only be used for scientific purposes and prohibits all forms of military activities.
(b) Outer space and celestial bodies are free for exploration and use by all countries, provided such activities are for the benefit of all mankind.
(c) The Treaty requires nations to establish international space laws governing private sector activities in space.
(d) The Treaty allows nations to claim ownership of celestial bodies for peaceful purposes.

**10.** Which of the following statements about the Outer Space Treaty are correct?
1. The Treaty prohibits placing nuclear weapons or other weapons of mass destruction in outer space.
2. The Treaty allows countries to claim territories on celestial bodies for scientific purposes.
3. The Treaty encourages the exploration and use of outer space for peaceful purposes.
4. The Treaty makes nations responsible for all national space activities, including those by private entities.
Select the correct answer using the codes given below:
(a) 1, 3 and 4 only (b) 1 and 2 only
(c) 2, 3 and 4 only (d) 1, 2 and 3 only

**11.** Consider the following statements:
**Statement I:** National Space Day in India is celebrated on 23rd August each year to mark India's achievements in space science.
**Statement II:** 23rd August commemorates the launch of India's first satellite, Aryabhata, in 1975.
Which one of the following is correct in respect of the above statements?
(a) Both Statement I and Statement II are correct and Statement II is the correct explanation for Statement I.
(b) Both Statement I and Statement II are correct and Statement II is not the correct explanation for Statement I.
(c) Statement I is correct, but Statement II is incorrect.
(d) Statement I is incorrect, but Statement II is correct.

## Topic 2 : Satellite Systems

**12.** Consider the following statements:

1. Perigee is the point of maximum distance from Earth.
2. At apogee, the satellite moves slower than at perigee.
3. At perigee, a satellite experiences the greatest gravitational influence from Earth.
4. Apogee is the point of minimum distance from Earth.

How many of the above statements is/are correct?

(a) Only one (b) Only two
(c) Only three (d) All four

**13.** Which of the following statements are correct about 'Kepler's Laws of Planetary Motion'?

1. First Law states that planets orbit the Sun in elliptical paths, with the Sun at one focus.
2. Second Law implies that a planet moves at a constant speed throughout its orbit around the Sun.
3. Third Law states that the square of a planet's orbital period is proportional to the cube of its average distance from the Sun.
4. Kepler's Second Law implies that a planet moves faster when it is closer to the Sun.

Select the correct answer using the codes given below:

(a) 1, 3 and 4 only (b) 1 and 3 only
(c) 2 and 4 only (d) 1, 2 and 4 only

**14.** Which of the following best describes why objects stay in orbit around Earth?

(a) Objects in orbit are stationary relative to Earth, held in place by gravitational force.
(b) Objects in orbit move at a specific speed where the gravitational pull of Earth provides the centripetal force needed to maintain the orbit.
(c) Objects in orbit are beyond the reach of Earth's gravity, allowing them to float freely in space.
(d) Objects in orbit constantly generate their own energy to counteract Earth's gravitational pull.

**15.** Which of the following best describes the concept of 'Escape Velocity'?

(a) The speed at which an object must travel to enter a stable orbit around Earth.
(b) The minimum speed required for an object to break free from Earth's gravitational pull without additional propulsion.
(c) The speed at which an object experiences zero gravitational force from Earth.
(d) The maximum speed at which an object can move and still remain within Earth's atmosphere.

**16.** Which of the following factors affect the escape velocity of an object on a celestial body?

1. The mass of the celestial body.
2. The radius of the celestial body.
3. The atmospheric composition of the celestial body.
4. The gravitational constant (G).

Select the correct answer using the codes given below:

(a) 1 and 2 only
(b) 1 and 3 only
(c) 1, 2 and 4 only
(d) 2, 3 and 4 only

**17.** With reference to the forces acting on a satellite in orbit, consider the following statements:

1. The gravitational force provides the necessary centripetal force to keep the satellite in orbit.
2. A satellite in a stable orbit experiences no net force acting on it.
3. The centrifugal force experienced by the satellite balances the gravitational pull of the Earth.

How many of the given above statements is/are correct?

(a) Only one
(b) Only two
(c) All three
(d) None

**18.** Consider the following statements:

1. The gravitational force on a satellite decreases as its altitude increases.
2. The orbital velocity is higher for satellites in low Earth orbit compared to geostationary orbit.
3. The centrifugal force experienced by the satellite balances the gravitational pull of the Earth.

How many of the above statements is/are correct?

(a) Only one (b) Only two
(c) All three (d) None

**19.** What is the angle of inclination in orbital mechanics?

(a) The angle between the orbit of a satellite and the equator of the Earth
(b) The angle between the orbit of a satellite and the Earth's surface
(c) The angle between two satellites in the same orbit
(d) The angle between the orbital path and the Sun's position

**20.** With reference to geostationary and geosynchronous orbits, consider the following statements:

1. Geostationary orbits are a specific type of geosynchronous orbit.
2. Satellites in geostationary orbit appear to remain fixed over a single point on Earth's surface.
3. Geosynchronous satellites do not need to orbit the Earth in 24 hours.

How many of the given above statements is/are correct?

(a) Only one (b) Only two
(c) All three (d) None

**21.** Consider the following characteristics of geostationary and geosynchronous orbits:

1. Satellites in geostationary orbit revolve around Earth's equator.
2. Geosynchronous satellites can have inclined orbits, not necessarily equatorial.
3. Both geostationary and geosynchronous satellites complete one orbit in 24 hours.
4. Geostationary orbits are mainly used for GPS applications.

How many of the above characteristics is/are correct?

(a) Only one (b) Only two
(c) Only three (d) All four

**22.** Consider the following purposes:

1. Earth observation and environmental monitoring
2. Continuous communication coverage of specific regions
3. Weather forecasting
4. Military surveillance

How many of the above is/are typical uses of 'Polar Orbits'?

(a) Only one (b) Only two
(c) Only three (d) All four

**23.** Consider the following pairs of orbit types and their unique characteristics:

| | Orbit Type | Characteristic |
|---|---|---|
| 1. | Geostationary Orbit (GSO) | Satellite appears fixed over a single point on the Earth |
| 2. | Low Earth Orbit (LEO) | Satellite completes multiple orbits per day |
| 3. | Medium Earth Orbit (MEO) | Satellite takes exactly 24 hours to orbit the Earth |

Which of the pairs given above are correctly matched?

(a) 1 and 2 only
(b) 2 and 3 only
(c) 1, 2 and 3
(d) 1 and 3 only

**24.** Which of the following correctly describes about 'Dawn-to-Dusk' orbit?

(a) An orbit where the satellite follows the Earth's rotation from dawn until dusk.
(b) An orbit that allows the satellite to always stay in sunlight by following the Earth's terminator line.
(c) An orbit where the satellite passes over the poles every 12 hours.
(d) An orbit that keeps the satellite in the Earth's shadow.

**25.** Which of the following best describes the purpose of a 'Hohmann Transfer Orbit'?
(a) To achieve the fastest possible transition between two points in space regardless of fuel consumption.
(b) To minimise the fuel required for transferring a spacecraft between two circular orbits of different radii.
(c) To enable a spacecraft to escape Earth's gravity and enter deep space exploration.
(d) To maintain a spacecraft's orbit around a celestial body with minimal adjustments.

**26.** With reference to the Van Allen Radiation Belts, consider the following statements:
1. These are layers of charged particles surrounding Earth, trapped by its magnetic field.
2. The inner Van Allen Belt is mainly composed of high-energy protons, while the outer belt primarily consists of electrons.
3. These are situated beyond the orbit of the Moon.

Which of the statements given above are correct?
(a) 1 and 2 only (b) 1 and 3 only
(c) 2 and 3 only (d) 1, 2 and 3

**27.** With reference to the INSAT system, consider the following statements:
1. INSAT is a series of multipurpose geostationary satellites developed by India.
2. The primary functions of INSAT include telecommunications, meteorology and television broadcasting.
3. All INSAT satellites are positioned in low Earth orbit (LEO).

How many of the above statements is/are correct?
(a) Only one
(b) Only two
(c) All three
(d) None

**28.** Consider the following applications:
1. Monitoring agricultural crop health
2. Mapping urban development
3. Monitoring air quality and atmospheric pollutants
4. Predicting earthquakes

How many of the given above is/are possible uses of remote sensing satellites?
(a) Only one (b) Only two
(c) Only three (d) All four

**29.** Which of the following best describes the NISAR satellite collaboration?
(a) A joint mission between ISRO and ESA for studying space weather.
(b) A collaborative effort by ISRO and NASA for Earth observation, focusing on environmental and disaster management.
(c) A partnership between ISRO and Roscosmos for lunar surface mapping.
(d) A collaborative mission between NASA and JAXA for monitoring ocean salinity.

**30.** Which of the following are remote sensing satellites launched by India?
1. Cartosat series
2. RISAT series
3. GSAT series
4. Oceansat series

Select the correct answer using the codes given below:
(a) 1, 2 and 3 only (b) 1, 3 and 4 only
(c) 1, 2 and 4 only (d) 1, 2, 3 and 4

**31.** Which of the following statements are correct about NavIC (Navigation with Indian Constellation)?
1. It is an autonomous global satellite navigation system developed by ISRO.
2. It provides coverage over the Indian subcontinent and an extended area of 1,500 km around it.
3. It is solely designed for civilian use and does not have any military applications.
4. It consists of a constellation of seven satellites in geosynchronous and geostationary orbits.

Select the correct answer using the codes given below:
(a) 1, 2 and 4 only (b) 1, 3 and 4 only
(c) 1, 2, 3 and 4 (d) 2 and 4 only

**32.** Which of the following are true regarding the advantages of NavIC over other global navigation satellite systems (GNSS) in India?
1. NavIC provides higher accuracy within its regional coverage area compared to GPS.
2. NavIC is less dependent on weather conditions and provides reliable signals in all environments.
3. NavIC's Standard Positioning Service (SPS) offers free access to users across India.
4. NavIC allows for direct international data sharing with other countries.

Select the correct answer using the codes given below:
(a) 1, 2 and 3 only
(b) 1, 3 and 4 only
(c) 2, 3 and 4 only
(d) 1 and 4 only

**33.** Consider the following pairs of satellite navigation systems and their respective countries:

| Satellite Navigation System | Country |
|---|---|
| 1. GPS | United States |
| 2. GLONASS | Russia |
| 3. Galileo | European Union |
| 4. BeiDou | China |

How many of the given above pairs is/are correctly matched?
(a) Only one pair
(b) Only two pairs
(c) Only three pairs
(d) All four pairs

**34.** With reference to the GAGAN system, consider the following statements:
1. It is an independent satellite navigation system developed by ISRO and the Airports Authority of India (AAI).
2. It enhances the accuracy of GPS signals within the Indian airspace.
3. It is exclusively used for military applications in India.

Which of the statements given above is/are correct?
(a) 1 and 2 only (b) 2 only
(c) 1, 2 and 3 (d) 1 and 3 only

**35.** With reference to the AstroSat, consider the following statements:
1. It is India's first dedicated multi-wavelength space observatory.
2. It observes the universe only in the visible spectrum.
3. It was launched by ISRO to study stars, galaxies and black holes.

How many of the given above statements is/are correct?
(a) Only one (b) Only two
(c) All three (d) None

## Topic 3 : Launch Vehicles

**36.** Arrange the following launch vehicles based on the year they were first developed or launched, starting from the earliest:
1. GSLV Mk III 2. SLV
3. GSLV 4. ASLV
5. PSLV

Select the correct answer using the codes given below:
(a) 2 - 4 - 5 - 3 - 1
(b) 4 - 2 - 3 - 5 - 1
(c) 2 - 5 - 3 - 4 - 1
(d) 5 - 2 - 4 - 1 - 3

**37.** With reference to GSLV, consider the following statements:
1. It is capable of launching satellites into Geosynchronous Transfer Orbit (GTO).
2. It uses a cryogenic upper stage for its final phase of launch.
3. It was the first Indian launch vehicle to use both solid and liquid propulsion stages.

How many of the above statements is/are correct?
(a) Only one (b) Only two
(c) All three (d) None

**38.** Which of the following best describes the 'Vikas engine'?

(a) A cryogenic engine developed by ISRO for interplanetary missions.

(b) A liquid rocket engine used in the second stage of PSLV and the core stage of GSLV.

(c) A solid rocket booster used for launching small satellites into low Earth orbit.

(d) An electric propulsion engine designed for deep-space missions.

**39.** Consider the following payload capacities:

1. Geosynchronous Transfer Orbit (GTO): Up to 4,000 kg
2. Low Earth Orbit (LEO): Up to 10,000 kg
3. Lunar Orbit: Up to 1,500 kg

How many of the above payload capacities is/are correct for GSLV Mk III?

(a) Only one (b) Only two
(c) All three (d) None

**40.** With reference to the 'Small Satellite Launch Vehicle (SSLV)', consider the following statements:

1. It is designed to carry payloads of up to 500 kg to Low Earth Orbit (LEO).
2. It is a three-stage vehicle using all solid propulsion.
3. It is capable of launching satellites into Geosynchronous Transfer Orbit (GTO).

Which of the statements given above are correct?

(a) 1 and 2 only (b) 2 and 3 only
(c) 1 and 3 only (d) 1, 2 and 3

**41.** Which of the following best describes the purpose of the 'Reusable Launch Vehicle - Technology Demonstrator (RLV-TD)'?

(a) To test India's first fully operational reusable spacecraft for interplanetary missions.

(b) To demonstrate technologies for reducing the cost of satellite launches by enabling partial reusability of launch systems.

(c) To enhance the capability of launching heavier satellites into geosynchronous orbit.

(d) To serve as a prototype for crewed missions under the Gaganyaan programme.

**42.** Consider the following statements:

1. Solid propellants are easier to store and handle compared to liquid propellants.
2. Solid propellants provide better control over burn rates compared to liquid propellants.
3. Solid propellants are more efficient than liquid propellants in terms of specific impulse.

Which of the statements given above is/are correct?

(a) 1 only (b) 2 and 3 only
(c) 1 and 3 only (d) 1, 2 and 3

**43.** Consider the following engines:

1. Ramjet 2. Scramjet
3. Turbojet 4. Rocket engine

How many of the given above is/are 'Air-Breathing Engines'?

(a) Only one (b) Only two
(c) Only three (d) All four

**44.** Which of the following best describes a Pulsejet engine?

(a) An engine that operates by continuously compressing air at high speeds without any moving parts.

(b) An engine that operates using intermittent combustion, producing pulses of thrust.

(c) An engine capable of maintaining supersonic combustion through its entire operation.

(d) An engine that compresses incoming air using a turbine-driven compressor and operates efficiently at subsonic speeds.

**45.** Which of the following statements best defines a Turbojet engine?

(a) An engine that operates efficiently without a compressor, relying on high-speed airflow.

(b) An engine that maintains supersonic airflow in the combustion chamber, suitable for hypersonic speeds.

(c) An engine that creates pulsed thrust using intermittent combustion.

(d) An engine that compresses incoming air with a turbine-driven compressor and is efficient for subsonic and low supersonic speeds.

**46.** With reference to Ramjet and Scramjet engines, consider the following statements:

1. Ramjet engines require high speeds to operate efficiently, as they lack a compressor.
2. Scramjet engines are capable of operating at hypersonic speeds, above Mach 5.
3. Both Ramjet and Scramjet engines can operate at zero airspeed.

How many of the above statements is/are correct?

(a) Only one (b) Only two
(c) All three (d) None

**47.** Consider the following differences between Ramjet and Scramjet engines:

1. Ramjets are used for supersonic speeds while Scramjets are designed for hypersonic speeds.
2. Both engines can operate at low speeds without external assistance.
3. Ramjets use subsonic combustion, whereas Scramjets use supersonic combustion.

How many of the above comparisons is/are correct?

(a) Only one
(b) Only two
(c) All three
(d) None

**48.** What does the term specific impulse indicate in the context of rocket and satellite propulsion?

(a) The fuel efficiency of a rocket engine, indicating how much thrust is produced per unit of fuel consumed per second.
(b) The total amount of fuel a rocket carries for its entire mission.
(c) The time taken for a rocket to reach its orbital velocity.
(d) The weight of the satellite in orbit.

**49.** Which of the following statement(s) is/are correct about the 'Mach Number'?

1. Mach 1 represents the speed of sound in a given medium.
2. Speeds between Mach 1 and Mach 5 are classified as subsonic.
3. Hypersonic speeds are those greater than Mach 5.

Select the correct answer using the codes given below:

(a) 1 and 3 only (b) 1, 2 and 3
(c) 2 only (d) 1 and 2 only

**50.** Consider the following characteristics of cryogenic propulsion:

1. Cryogenic engines require storage and handling at extremely low temperatures.
2. These engines are mainly used in the upper stages of rockets for interplanetary missions.
3. These fuels provide higher energy efficiency than conventional liquid fuels.
4. These engines are simpler in design compared to solid rocket engines.

How many of the given above characteristics is/are correct?

(a) Only one (b) Only two
(c) Only three (d) All four

## Topic 4 : Celestial Bodies and Space Missions

**51.** Regarding the process of nuclear fusion in the Sun's core, consider the following statements:

1. The Sun fuses hydrogen atoms to form helium in a process known as the proton-proton chain reaction.
2. Fusion in the Sun's core produces energy primarily in the form of visible light.
3. The Sun's fusion process releases neutrinos as a byproduct.

How many of the given above statements is/are correct?

(a) Only one (b) Only two
(c) All three (d) None

**52.** Which of the following phenomena are affected by changes in the Solar Cycle?

1. Solar flares
2. Coronal mass ejections (CMEs)
3. Earth's magnetic field strength
4. Aurora intensity on Earth

Select the correct answer using the codes given below:

(a) 1, 2 and 4 only (b) 1 and 3 only
(c) 2 and 4 only (d) 1, 2, 3 and 4

**53.** Arrange the following layers of the Sun in the correct order from the outermost layer to the innermost layer:
1. Convective Zone
2. Photosphere
3. Corona
4. Radiative Zone
5. Chromosphere

Choose the correct order using the codes given below:
(a) 3-5-2-1-4
(b) 3-2-5-1-4
(c) 5-3-2-4-1
(d) 3-5-2-4-1

**54.** Which of the following best describes the 'Solar Cycle'?
(a) A 365-day cycle of the Sun's movement around the Milky Way galaxy.
(b) An approximately 11-year cycle of solar activity, marked by changes in the number of sunspots and solar radiation.
(c) A phenomenon where the Sun's energy output decreases every 22 years, affecting global climates.
(d) A periodic shift in the Sun's position relative to Earth, causing variations in seasons.

**55.** Consider the following impacts:
1. Creation of auroras near the poles
2. Disruption of Global Positioning System (GPS) signals
3. Long-term shifts in Earth's magnetic poles
4. Disruption of satellite communication systems

How many of the given above is/are possible impacts of 'Coronal Mass Ejections (CMEs)'?
(a) Only one
(b) Only two
(c) Only three
(d) All four

**56.** Consider the following statements about 'Sunspots':
1. These are cooler regions on the Sun's surface compared to the surrounding areas.
2. These are the primary cause of solar flares and coronal mass ejections (CMEs).
3. These indicate areas of intense magnetic activity on the Sun.

How many of the above statements is/are correct?
(a) Only one
(b) Only two
(c) All three
(d) None

**57.** Why are auroras primarily observed near the polar regions rather than at the equator?
(a) The magnetic field is strongest at the equator, deflecting solar particles.
(b) Earth's magnetic field lines converge near the poles, guiding solar particles toward these regions.
(c) The polar atmosphere contains special gases that emit light more easily.
(d) Equatorial regions receive less sunlight, reducing auroral visibility.

**58.** With reference to 'Auroras', consider the following statements:
1. Aurora Borealis occurs in the Northern hemisphere.
2. Aurora Australis is observed primarily over Antarctica and surrounding regions.
3. Auroras are caused by solar wind particles interacting with Earth's magnetic field.

How many of the given above statements is/are correct?
(a) Only one
(b) Only two
(c) All three
(d) None

**59.** Which of the following best describes the primary objective of the 'Aditya L-1 mission'?
(a) To explore the Sun's core by sending a probe into its interior.
(b) To study the Sun's atmosphere and its impact on space weather, particularly focusing on the solar corona.
(c) To deploy communication satellites in orbit for solar observations.
(d) To monitor the Sun's magnetic poles for long-term climate predictions on Earth.

**60.** Which of the following statements are correct about various 'Sun-Earth Lagrange Points'?

1. L1 is used by satellites to continuously monitor the Sun for solar flares and space weather.
2. L2 is ideal for astronomical observations of distant galaxies and stars.
3. L3 serves as an ideal point for Earth observation satellites.
4. L4 and L5 provide stable locations where small celestial objects can remain balanced.

Select the correct answer using the codes given below:

(a) 1, 2 and 4 only
(b) 1, 3 and 4 only
(c) 2 and 3 only
(d) 1 and 2 only

**61.** Consider the following pairs of solar missions and their respective space agencies:

| | Solar Mission | Space Agency |
|---|---|---|
| 1. | Parker Solar Probe | NASA |
| 2. | Solar Orbiter | ESA |
| 3. | Aditya L-1 | ISRO |
| 4. | Hinode | JAXA |

How many of the pairs given above is/are correctly matched?

(a) Only one
(b) Only two
(c) Only three
(d) All four

**62.** Which of the following best describes 'Blue Moon' in astronomical terms?

(a) A second full Moon occurring in a calendar month.
(b) A rare occurrence where the Moon appears blue in colour due to atmospheric particles.
(c) A phenomenon where the Moon appears larger than usual due to proximity to Earth.
(d) The first full Moon after the autumn equinox.

**63.** Consider the following pairs of terms and their descriptions:

| | Term | Description |
|---|---|---|
| 1. | Blood Moon | A total lunar eclipse where the Moon appears reddish due to Earth's atmosphere scattering sunlight |
| 2. | Super Moon | A full Moon that occurs when the Moon is at or near its closest point to Earth (perigee) |
| 3. | Harvest Moon | The full Moon that occurs closest to the autumnal equinox, often providing extended evening light |
| 4. | Blue Moon | A lunar event where the Moon appears blue due to atmospheric conditions |

How many of the given above pairs is/are correctly matched?

(a) Only one (b) Only two
(c) Only three (d) All four

**64.** Consider the following Moon missions and the respective countries associated with them:

| | Moon Mission | Country |
|---|---|---|
| 1. | Artemis | United States |
| 2. | Chandrayaan-3 | India |
| 3. | Beresheet | Israel |
| 4. | Hakuto-R | Russia |

How many of the given above pairs is/are correctly matched?

(a) Only one (b) Only two
(c) Only three (d) All four

**65.** Consider the following pairs of Venus missions and the countries that launched them:

| | Mission | Country |
|---|---|---|
| 1. | Venera | Soviet Union |
| 2. | Akatsuki | Japan |
| 3. | Venus Express | European Space Agency |
| 4. | Magellan | China |

How many of the above pairs is/are correctly matched?

(a) Only one (b) Only two
(c) Only three (d) All four

**66.** Which of the following statements are correct about the 'Karman Line'?

1. It is located at an altitude of 100 km above Earth's surface.
2. It marks the threshold where orbital velocity is required to sustain flight.
3. It is universally recognised as the boundary of space by all international organisations.

Select the correct answer using the codes given below:

(a) 1 and 2 only (b) 1 and 3 only
(c) 2 and 3 only (d) 1, 2 and 3

**67.** Which of the following countries are primary partners in the International Space Station (ISS) programme?

1. United States 2. Russia
3. China 4. Japan

Select the correct answer using the codes given below:

(a) 1 and 2 only (b) 1, 2 and 4 only
(c) 2, 3 and 4 only (d) 1, 2, 3 and 4

**68.** Which of the following best describes the 'Kessler Syndrome'?

(a) A phenomenon where satellites are affected by solar wind, leading to disruptions in communication.
(b) A hypothetical scenario in which a cascade of collisions in Earth's orbit causes a chain reaction of space debris.
(c) A condition where Earth's magnetic field intensifies, impacting satellite trajectories.
(d) A theory suggesting the depletion of Earth's orbital resources due to excessive satellite launches.

**69.** Which of the following best describes the primary objective of ISRO's Project NETRA?

(a) To develop advanced satellite communication systems for global connectivity.
(b) To establish a space-based observatory for tracking asteroids and comets.
(c) To enhance India's capability in monitoring, tracking and mitigating space debris.
(d) To launch a network of satellites for environmental monitoring and disaster management.

**70.** Consider the following statements:

1. The Space Debris Mitigation Guidelines of the United Nations are legally binding for all member states.
2. The Outer Space Treaty explicitly defines legal responsibilities for cleaning up space debris.
3. The Artemis Accords promote sustainable use of outer space, including measures to address space debris.

Which of the statements given above is/are correct?

(a) 1 and 2 only (b) 3 only
(c) 2 and 3 only (d) 1, 2 and 3

**71.** Which of the following best describes the concept of 'Microgravity'?

(a) A condition where gravity is completely absent in space.
(b) A state of reduced effective gravity experienced by objects in free-fall or orbit.
(c) A phenomenon caused by the absence of atmospheric pressure in outer space.
(d) A condition where objects become weightless due to the lack of gravitational force from Earth.

**72.** Match the following types of space tourism with their descriptions:

| Type of Space Tourism | Description |
|---|---|
| A. Orbital Space Tourism | 1. A journey to space with suborbital flights offering a few minutes of weightlessness. |
| B. Sub-orbital Space Tourism | 2. Long-duration travel to Earth orbit, typically involving stays aboard space stations. |
| C. Lunar Space Tourism | 3. Travel involving a journey around or to the Moon. |

Select the correctly matched pairs:

(a) A-2, B-1, C-3
(b) A-1, B-3, C-2
(c) A-3, B-2, C-1
(d) A-1, B-2, C-3

**73.** With reference to the Gaganyaan mission, consider the following statements:

1. The Gaganyaan spacecraft will use the GSLV Mk III launch vehicle.
2. The mission will place the spacecraft in a geosynchronous orbit.
3. It is India's first human spaceflight mission, developed by ISRO.

Which of the statements given above is/are correct?

(a) 1 and 2 only (b) 2 and 3 only
(c) 3 only (d) 1 and 3 only

**74.** Consider the following Mars missions with their respective countries:

| | Mars Mission | Country |
|---|---|---|
| 1. | Mars Orbiter Mission (MOM) | India (ISRO) |
| 2. | Mars Atmosphere and Volatile Evolution (MAVEN) | United States (NASA) |
| 3. | Hope Probe | United Arab Emirates (UAE) |
| 4. | Mars Express | Russia |

How many of the above pairs is/are correctly matched?

(a) Only one (b) Only two
(c) Only three (d) All four

**75.** Match the following missions to Jovian planets with their respective descriptions and agencies:

| Mission | Description | Agency |
|---|---|---|
| A. Galileo | Orbiter to study Jupiter and its moons | NASA |
| B. Juno | Polar orbit mission to study Jupiter's atmosphere | NASA |
| C. JUICE | Focus on Ganymede, Callisto, and Europa | ESA |
| D. Pioneer 10 | First spacecraft to perform a flyby of Jupiter | NASA |

Select the correctly matched pairs:

(a) A-2, B-4, C-1, D-3 (b) A-1, B-2, C-3, D-4
(c) A-3, B-2, C-1, D-4 (d) A-4, B-3, C-2, D-1

**76.** Consider the following pairs of missions and their descriptions:

| Mission | Description | Agency |
|---|---|---|
| 1. Voyager 1 | The first spacecraft to leave the heliosphere | NASA |
| 2. Cassini-Huygens | Explored the magnetic field of Saturn and conducted a Titan landing | NASA/ESA |
| 3. New Horizons | The first mission to study Pluto and the Kuiper Belt | NASA |

How many of the above pairs is/are correctly matched?

(a) Only one (b) Only two
(c) All three (d) None

**77.** Consider the following pairs of asteroid probes matched with the asteroids they explored:

| | Asteroid Probe | Asteroid Explored |
|---|---|---|
| 1. | Lucy | Trojans near Jupiter |
| 2. | Hayabusa 2 | Ryugu |
| 3. | OSIRIS-REx | Bennu |
| 4. | Dawn | Eros |

How many of the above pairs is/are correctly matched?

(a) Only one (b) Only two
(c) Only three (d) All four

## Topic 5 : Astronomical Observatories

**78.** With reference to the 'Indian Astronomical Observatory', consider the following statements:

1. It is operated by the Indian Space Research Organisation (ISRO).
2. The IAO houses India's largest optical telescope.
3. The location of the IAO experiences minimal light pollution, making it optimal for night-sky observations.

How many of the above statements is/are correct?

(a) Only one (b) Only two
(c) All three (d) None

**79.** Match the following space-based telescopes with their operational locations:

| Space Telescope | | Operational Orbits |
|---|---|---|
| A. Hubble Space Telescope | 1. | Low Earth Orbit (LEO) |
| B. GLONASS | 2. | Second Lagrange Point (L2) |
| C. Chandra X-Ray Observatory | 3. | High Earth Orbit (HEO) |
| D. Spitzer Space Telescope | 4. | Heliocentric Orbit (trailing Earth) |

Select the correctly matched pairs:
(a) A-1, B-2, C-3, D-4
(b) A-2, B-3, C-4, D-1
(c) A-1, B-3, C-4, D-2
(d) A-4, B-1, C-2, D-3

**80.** Which of the following best describes 'NASA's Great Observatories programme'?
(a) A group of space-based telescopes, each designed to observe the universe in a specific wavelength of light.
(b) A series of ground-based telescopes dedicated to studying planets within the Solar System.
(c) A collection of robotic probes sent to study asteroids and comets.
(d) A programme aimed at establishing a network of radio telescopes on Earth to observe black holes.

**81.** Which of the following statements are correct about 'NASA's Great Observatories programme'?
1. The Hubble Space Telescope focuses on visible, ultraviolet and near-infrared observations.
2. The Spitzer Space Telescope specialises in studying the universe in the gamma-ray spectrum.
3. The Chandra X-ray Observatory is designed to observe high-energy phenomena like black holes and neutron stars.
4. The programme aims to study celestial phenomena across the entire electromagnetic spectrum.

Select the correct answer using the codes given below:
(a) 1 and 2 only (b) 1, 3 and 4 only
(c) 2 and 4 only (d) 1, 2, 3 and 4

**82.** Which of the following are advantages of space-based telescopes over ground-based telescopes?
1. They avoid distortion caused by Earth's atmosphere.
2. They can observe the entire electromagnetic spectrum without atmospheric interference.
3. They are more cost-effective to deploy and operate than ground-based telescopes.

Select the correct answer using the codes given below:
(a) 1 and 2 only (b) 2 and 3 only
(c) 1 and 3 only (d) 1, 2 and 3

**83.** Match the following ground-based telescopes with their respective locations:

| Telescope | | Location |
|---|---|---|
| A. Giant Metrewave Radio Telescope (GMRT) | 1. | Pune, Maharashtra |
| B. Thirty Meter Telescope (TMT) | 2. | Mauna Kea, Hawaii |
| C. Devasthal Optical Telescope (DOT) | 3. | Nainital, Uttarakhand |
| D. Square Kilometre Array Observatory (SKAO) | 4. | South Africa and Australia |

Select the correctly matched pairs:
(a) A-1, B-2, C-3, D-4 (b) A-2, B-3, C-1, D-4
(c) A-3, B-4, C-2, D-1 (d) A-1, B-3, C-4, D-2

**84.** Which of the following are ideal conditions for the location of ground-based telescopes?
1. High altitude to minimise atmospheric interference.
2. Proximity to urban areas for ease of accessibility and maintenance.
3. Dry climate to reduce water vapour in the atmosphere.
4. Remote locations with minimal light pollution.

Select the correct answer using the codes given below:
(a) 1, 3 and 4 only (b) 1 and 2 only
(c) 2, 3 and 4 only (d) 1, 2, 3 and 4

# OMR SHEET

**Assessment Round**

| | | | | | | | |
|---|---|---|---|---|---|---|---|
| 1 | ⓐ ⓑ ⓒ ⓓ | 31 | ⓐ ⓑ ⓒ ⓓ | 61 | ⓐ ⓑ ⓒ ⓓ | 91 | ⓐ ⓑ ⓒ ⓓ |
| 2 | ⓐ ⓑ ⓒ ⓓ | 32 | ⓐ ⓑ ⓒ ⓓ | 62 | ⓐ ⓑ ⓒ ⓓ | 92 | ⓐ ⓑ ⓒ ⓓ |
| 3 | ⓐ ⓑ ⓒ ⓓ | 33 | ⓐ ⓑ ⓒ ⓓ | 63 | ⓐ ⓑ ⓒ ⓓ | 93 | ⓐ ⓑ ⓒ ⓓ |
| 4 | ⓐ ⓑ ⓒ ⓓ | 34 | ⓐ ⓑ ⓒ ⓓ | 64 | ⓐ ⓑ ⓒ ⓓ | 94 | ⓐ ⓑ ⓒ ⓓ |
| 5 | ⓐ ⓑ ⓒ ⓓ | 35 | ⓐ ⓑ ⓒ ⓓ | 65 | ⓐ ⓑ ⓒ ⓓ | 95 | ⓐ ⓑ ⓒ ⓓ |
| 6 | ⓐ ⓑ ⓒ ⓓ | 36 | ⓐ ⓑ ⓒ ⓓ | 66 | ⓐ ⓑ ⓒ ⓓ | 96 | ⓐ ⓑ ⓒ ⓓ |
| 7 | ⓐ ⓑ ⓒ ⓓ | 37 | ⓐ ⓑ ⓒ ⓓ | 67 | ⓐ ⓑ ⓒ ⓓ | 97 | ⓐ ⓑ ⓒ ⓓ |
| 8 | ⓐ ⓑ ⓒ ⓓ | 38 | ⓐ ⓑ ⓒ ⓓ | 68 | ⓐ ⓑ ⓒ ⓓ | 98 | ⓐ ⓑ ⓒ ⓓ |
| 9 | ⓐ ⓑ ⓒ ⓓ | 39 | ⓐ ⓑ ⓒ ⓓ | 69 | ⓐ ⓑ ⓒ ⓓ | 99 | ⓐ ⓑ ⓒ ⓓ |
| 10 | ⓐ ⓑ ⓒ ⓓ | 40 | ⓐ ⓑ ⓒ ⓓ | 70 | ⓐ ⓑ ⓒ ⓓ | 100 | ⓐ ⓑ ⓒ ⓓ |
| 11 | ⓐ ⓑ ⓒ ⓓ | 41 | ⓐ ⓑ ⓒ ⓓ | 71 | ⓐ ⓑ ⓒ ⓓ | 101 | ⓐ ⓑ ⓒ ⓓ |
| 12 | ⓐ ⓑ ⓒ ⓓ | 42 | ⓐ ⓑ ⓒ ⓓ | 72 | ⓐ ⓑ ⓒ ⓓ | 102 | ⓐ ⓑ ⓒ ⓓ |
| 13 | ⓐ ⓑ ⓒ ⓓ | 43 | ⓐ ⓑ ⓒ ⓓ | 73 | ⓐ ⓑ ⓒ ⓓ | 103 | ⓐ ⓑ ⓒ ⓓ |
| 14 | ⓐ ⓑ ⓒ ⓓ | 44 | ⓐ ⓑ ⓒ ⓓ | 74 | ⓐ ⓑ ⓒ ⓓ | 104 | ⓐ ⓑ ⓒ ⓓ |
| 15 | ⓐ ⓑ ⓒ ⓓ | 45 | ⓐ ⓑ ⓒ ⓓ | 75 | ⓐ ⓑ ⓒ ⓓ | 105 | ⓐ ⓑ ⓒ ⓓ |
| 16 | ⓐ ⓑ ⓒ ⓓ | 46 | ⓐ ⓑ ⓒ ⓓ | 76 | ⓐ ⓑ ⓒ ⓓ | 106 | ⓐ ⓑ ⓒ ⓓ |
| 17 | ⓐ ⓑ ⓒ ⓓ | 47 | ⓐ ⓑ ⓒ ⓓ | 77 | ⓐ ⓑ ⓒ ⓓ | 107 | ⓐ ⓑ ⓒ ⓓ |
| 18 | ⓐ ⓑ ⓒ ⓓ | 48 | ⓐ ⓑ ⓒ ⓓ | 78 | ⓐ ⓑ ⓒ ⓓ | 108 | ⓐ ⓑ ⓒ ⓓ |
| 19 | ⓐ ⓑ ⓒ ⓓ | 49 | ⓐ ⓑ ⓒ ⓓ | 79 | ⓐ ⓑ ⓒ ⓓ | 109 | ⓐ ⓑ ⓒ ⓓ |
| 20 | ⓐ ⓑ ⓒ ⓓ | 50 | ⓐ ⓑ ⓒ ⓓ | 80 | ⓐ ⓑ ⓒ ⓓ | 110 | ⓐ ⓑ ⓒ ⓓ |
| 21 | ⓐ ⓑ ⓒ ⓓ | 51 | ⓐ ⓑ ⓒ ⓓ | 81 | ⓐ ⓑ ⓒ ⓓ | 111 | ⓐ ⓑ ⓒ ⓓ |
| 22 | ⓐ ⓑ ⓒ ⓓ | 52 | ⓐ ⓑ ⓒ ⓓ | 82 | ⓐ ⓑ ⓒ ⓓ | 112 | ⓐ ⓑ ⓒ ⓓ |
| 23 | ⓐ ⓑ ⓒ ⓓ | 53 | ⓐ ⓑ ⓒ ⓓ | 83 | ⓐ ⓑ ⓒ ⓓ | 113 | ⓐ ⓑ ⓒ ⓓ |
| 24 | ⓐ ⓑ ⓒ ⓓ | 54 | ⓐ ⓑ ⓒ ⓓ | 84 | ⓐ ⓑ ⓒ ⓓ | 114 | ⓐ ⓑ ⓒ ⓓ |
| 25 | ⓐ ⓑ ⓒ ⓓ | 55 | ⓐ ⓑ ⓒ ⓓ | 85 | ⓐ ⓑ ⓒ ⓓ | 115 | ⓐ ⓑ ⓒ ⓓ |
| 26 | ⓐ ⓑ ⓒ ⓓ | 56 | ⓐ ⓑ ⓒ ⓓ | 86 | ⓐ ⓑ ⓒ ⓓ | 116 | ⓐ ⓑ ⓒ ⓓ |
| 27 | ⓐ ⓑ ⓒ ⓓ | 57 | ⓐ ⓑ ⓒ ⓓ | 87 | ⓐ ⓑ ⓒ ⓓ | 117 | ⓐ ⓑ ⓒ ⓓ |
| 28 | ⓐ ⓑ ⓒ ⓓ | 58 | ⓐ ⓑ ⓒ ⓓ | 88 | ⓐ ⓑ ⓒ ⓓ | 118 | ⓐ ⓑ ⓒ ⓓ |
| 29 | ⓐ ⓑ ⓒ ⓓ | 59 | ⓐ ⓑ ⓒ ⓓ | 89 | ⓐ ⓑ ⓒ ⓓ | 119 | ⓐ ⓑ ⓒ ⓓ |
| 30 | ⓐ ⓑ ⓒ ⓓ | 60 | ⓐ ⓑ ⓒ ⓓ | 90 | ⓐ ⓑ ⓒ ⓓ | 120 | ⓐ ⓑ ⓒ ⓓ |

## Calculate Your Score

| | |
|---|---|
| **Correct (✓)** | |
| **Incorrect (✓)** | |
| **Unattempted** | |
| **Total Score** | |
| **Accuracy (%)** | |

## Reasons for Incorrect Answers?

| | |
|---|---|
| 1. Lack of Knowledge/Existing Source Insufficient | |
| 2. Lack of Multiple Revision | |
| 3. Common Sense Mistakes | |

**Note :**

1. Calculate total score as correct answers carry 2 marks each 1/3rd marks will deducted for **Incorrect** Answers.
2. Calculate Accuracy (%) by dividing the number of correct answers to the total number of attempted questions.

## Past Learning

*1.* Which one of the following countries has its own Satellite Navigation System? **(2023)**

(a) Australia
(b) Canada
(c) Israel
(d) Japan

*2.* If a major solar storm (solar flare) reaches the Earth, which of the following are the possible effects on the Earth? **(2022)**

1. GPS and navigation systems could fail.
2. Tsunamis could occur at equatorial regions.
3. Power grids could be damaged.
4. Intense auroras could occur over much of the Earth.
5. Forest fires could take place over much of the planet.
6. Orbits of the satellites could be disturbed.
7. Shortwave radio communication of the aircraft flying over polar regions could be interrupted.

Select the correct answer using the codes given below:

(a) 1, 2, 4 and 5 only
(b) 2, 3, 5, 6 and 7 only
(c) 1, 3, 4, 6 and 7 only
(d) 1, 2, 3, 4, 5, 6 and 7

*3.* For the measurement/estimation of which of the following are satellite images/remote sensing data used? **(2019)**

1. Chlorophyll content in the vegetation of a specific location.
2. Greenhouse gas emissions from rice paddies of a specific location.
3. Land surface temperatures of a specific location.

Select the correct answer by using the codes given below.

(a) Only 1
(b) 2 and 3
(c) Only 3
(d) 1, 2 and 3

*4.* With reference to the Indian Regional Navigation Satellite System (IRNSS), consider the following statements: **(2018)**

1. IRNSS has three satellites in geostationary and four satellites in geosynchronous orbits.
2. IRNSS covers entire India and about 5500 sq. km beyond its borders.
3. India will have its own satellite navigation system with full global coverage by the middle of 2019.

Which of the statements given above is/are correct?

(a) 1 only (b) 1 and 2 only
(c) 2 and 3 only (d) None of these

*5.* In which of the following areas, can GPS technology be used? **(2018)**

1.Mobile phone operations
2.Banking operations
3.Controlling the power grids

Select the correct answer using the codes given below.

(a) Only 1 (b) 2 and 3 (c) 1 and 3 (d) 1, 2 and 3

*6.* With reference to India's satellite launch vehicles, consider the following statements. **(2018)**

1. PSLVs launch the satellites useful for Earth resources monitoring whereas GSLVs are designed mainly to launch communication satellites.
2. Satellites launched by PSLV appear to remain permanently fixed in the first same position in the sky, as viewed from a particular location on Earth.
3. GSLV Mk III is a four-staged launch vehicle with the first and third stages using solid rocket motors; and the second and fourth stages using liquid rocket engines.

Which of the statements given above is/are correct?

(a) Only 1 (b) 2 and 3
(c) 1 and 2 (d) Only 3

**7.** What is 'Greased Lightning-10 (GL-10)' recently in the news? **(2016)**
(a) Electric plane tested by NASA
(b) Solar-powered, two-seater aircraft designed by Japan
(c) Space observatory launched by China
(d) Reusable rocket designed by ISRO

**8.** Consider the following statements. **(2016)**
The Mangalyaan launched by ISRO
1. is also called the Mars Orbiter Mission.
2. made India the second country to have a spacecraft orbit the Mars after USA.
3. made India the only country to be successful in making its spacecraft orbit the Mars in its very first attempt.

Which of the statements given above is/are correct?
(a) Only 1 (b) 2 and 3
(c) 1 and 3 (d) 1, 2 and 3

**9.** With reference to 'Astrosat', the astronomical observatory launched by India, which of the following statements is/are correct? **(2016)**
1. Other than USA and Russia, India is the only country to have launched a similar observatory into space.
2. Astrosat is a 2000 kg satellite placed in an orbit at 1650 km above the surface of the Earth.

Select the correct answer using the codes given below.
(a) Only 1 (b) Only 2
(c) Both 1 and 2 (d) Neither 1 nor 2

**10.** In which of the following activities are Indian Remote Sensing (IRS) satellites used? **(2015)**
1. Assessment of crop productivity
2. Locating groundwater resources
3. Mineral exploration
4. Telecommunications
5. Traffic studies

Select the correct answer using the codes given below.
(a) 1, 2 and 3 (b) 4 and 5
(c) 1 and 2 (d) 1, 2, 3, 4 and 5

**11.** Which of the following pairs is/are correctly matched? **(2014)**

| Spacecrafts | Purposes |
|---|---|
| 1. Cassini-Huygens | Orbiting the Venus and transmitting data to the Earth |
| 2. Messenger | Mapping and investigating the Mercury |
| 3. Voyager 1 and 2 | Exploring the outer solar system |

Select the correct answer using the codes given below.
(a) Only 1 (b) 2 and 3
(c) 1 and 3 (d) All of these

**12.** An artificial satellite orbiting around the Earth does not fall down. This is so because the attraction of Earth **(2011)**
(a) does not exist at such distance
(b) is neutralised by the attraction of the Moon
(c) provides the necessary speed for its steady motion
(d) provides the necessary acceleration for its motion

**13.** Satellites used for telecommunication relay are kept in a geostationary orbit. A satellite is said to be in such an orbit when **(2011)**
1. the orbit is geosynchronous.
2. the orbit is circular.
3. the orbit lies in the place of the Earth's equator.
4. the orbit is at an altitude of 22236 km.

Select the correct answer using the codes given below.
(a) 1, 2 and 3 (b) 1, 3 and 4
(c) 2 and 4 (d) 1, 2, 3 and 4

# Detailed Solutions

## Assessment Round

**1.** *(c)* All three pairs

- **Pair 1 is correctly matched:** NSIL facilitates the transfer of ISRO-developed technologies to private entities and enables the commercial use of space-related services and products.
- **Pair 2 is correctly matched:** IN-SPACe acts as a regulatory and promotional body for private sector participation in India's space industry, fostering innovation and collaboration.
- **Pair 3 is correctly matched:** Antrix Corporation serves as ISRO's commercial arm, focusing on satellite launch services and transponder leasing for global customers.

**Thus, the correct answer is (c) All three pairs.**

**2.** (b) 1, 2 and 3 only

- **Statement 1 is correct:** IN-SPACe (Indian National Space Promotion and Authorisation Center) is tasked with authorising and promoting private sector participation in space activities, fostering innovation, and creating opportunities for startups and industries in the space domain.
- **Statement 2 is correct:** IN-SPACe regulates the launch of foreign satellites by private companies in India, ensuring compliance with international treaties and national security concerns under the Indian Space Policy 2023.
- **Statement 3 is correct:** IN-SPACe collaborates with the Department of Space (DoS) to establish industry standards and guidelines for private sector involvement, ensuring safety, quality and sustainability in space activities.
- **Statement 4 is incorrect:** IN-SPACe does not dictate ISRO's research priorities. ISRO's research agenda is determined by the Department of Space and national strategic requirements, with IN-SPACe focusing on enabling private participation and regulatory functions.

**Thus, the correct answer is (b) 1, 2 and 3 only.**

**3.** (d) All four pairs

- **Pair 1 is correct:** The Vikram Sarabhai Space Centre (VSSC) in Thiruvananthapuram is a major facility of ISRO dedicated to the development of launch vehicles and space technology.
- **Pair 2 is correct:** The ISRO Propulsion Complex (IPRC) at Mahendragiri handles testing and assembly of propulsion systems for satellites and launch vehicles.
- **Pair 3 is correct:** The Master Control Facility (MCF) in Hassan is responsible for the operation and control of geostationary satellites.
- **Pair 4 is correct:** The Satish Dhawan Space Centre (SDSC) in Sriharikota serves as the primary launch site for India's satellite missions.

**Thus, the correct answer is (d) All four pairs.**

**4.** (d) 1, 2, 3 and 4

- **Pair 1 is correct:** The **European Space Agency (ESA)** is headquartered in **Paris, France**. ESA coordinates space exploration and satellite missions in collaboration with multiple European nations.
- **Pair 2 is correct:** The headquarters of the **Japan Aerospace Exploration Agency (JAXA)** is located in Chofu-city, Tokyo.
- **Pair 3 is correct:** The **Canadian Space Agency (CSA)** is headquartered in **Saint-Hubert, Quebec, Canada**, which is close to Montreal and supports CSA's satellite and space exploration programmes.
- **Pair 4 is correct: The National Aeronautics and Space Administration (NASA)** is headquartered in **Washington, DC, United States.**

**Thus, the correct answer is (d) 1, 2, 3 and 4.**

**5.** *(a)* ISRO is limited to research and development while private entities take over operational launches.

- The Indian Space Policy 2023 introduces a transformative change by **focusing ISRO's role on research and development** (R&D), **advanced space exploration and innovation.** This allows ISRO to channel its resources into cutting-edge missions, such as interplanetary exploration and the development of next-generation technologies.
- At the same time, **operational activities like satellite launches and commercial ventures are being shifted to the private sector, facilitated and regulated by IN-SPACe.** This transition aims to create a thriving space ecosystem, leveraging private industry capabilities for operational efficiencies and innovation.

**Thus, option (a) is the correct answer.**

**6.** *(b)* To create a set of non-binding principles for cooperative exploration of the Moon and beyond.

- **Option (b) is correct:** The Artemis Accords are a set of non-binding principles established by NASA in collaboration with international partners. They aim to provide a framework for peaceful, transparent and cooperative space exploration activities, particularly focusing on the Moon, Mars and other celestial bodies. The Accords encourage sustainable practices, sharing of scientific data, and the preservation of space heritage sites, aligning with the Outer Space Treaty of 1967.
- **Option (a) is incorrect:** The Artemis Accords are not legally binding. Unlike an international treaty, they do not create enforceable obligations. Instead, they are voluntary agreements that nations adopt to adhere to shared principles in space exploration.
- **Option (c) is incorrect:** The Accords do not mandate the exclusive use of national resources. Instead, they promote the responsible use of space resources under internationally recognised principles. Resource utilisation is encouraged in ways that benefit all humanity.
- **Option (d) is incorrect:** The Artemis Accords explicitly welcome the involvement of private entities and recognise their role in advancing space exploration. They promote public-private partnerships while ensuring compliance with the principles of the Accords.

**Thus, option (b) is the correct answer.**

**7.** *(c)* Only three

- **Country 1 is correct:** The United States initiated the Artemis Accords and is a signatory.
- **Country 2 is correct: On 21st June, 2023, the Republic of India became the 27th nation to sign the Artemis Accords,** demonstrating its commitment to sustainable and transparent space activity.
- **Country 3 is incorrect:** Russia has not signed the Artemis Accords, citing concerns over alignment with its national policies and strategies.
- **Country 4 is correct:** Japan is a signatory and a key partner in the Artemis program, contributing to lunar exploration efforts.

**Thus, the correct answer is (c) Only three.**

**8.** *(c)* Only three

- **Statement 1 is correct:** The **Artemis Accords** emphasise **interoperability,** encouraging partner nations to make their space systems compatible with each other for easier collaboration.
- **Statement 2 is correct:** The Accords promote **public release of scientific data** to increase transparency and share knowledge gained from lunar and space exploration.
- **Statement 3 is correct:** The Accords include the **obligation to assist astronauts in distress,** in line with the principle of international cooperation and safety in space.
- **Statement 4 is incorrect:** While the **Outer Space Treaty** prohibits the military use of celestial bodies like the Moon, the Artemis Accords do not specifically mention this prohibition, as it's already covered under international space law.

**Thus, the correct answer is (c) Only three.**

**9.** *(b)* Outer space and celestial bodies are free for exploration and use by all countries, provided such activities are for the benefit of all mankind.

- **Option (b) is correct:** A fundamental principle of the Outer Space Treaty is that **outer space, including the Moon and other celestial bodies, is free for exploration and use by all nations.** Activities conducted in outer space must be carried out for the benefit and in the interest of all countries, irrespective of their level of development, ensuring equal opportunities for humanity as a whole.
- **Option (a) is incorrect:** While **the Treaty prohibits the placement of WMDs and the establishment of military bases, certain non-aggressive military uses like communication and surveillance satellites** are permitted, making this statement overly restrictive.
- **Option (c) is incorrect:** The Outer Space Treaty sets general principles for activities in space but does not mandate the creation of international laws for private sector activities. However, national governments are responsible for ensuring that their private entities comply with the Treaty.
- **Option (d) is incorrect:** The Treaty explicitly forbids nations from claiming sovereignty or ownership over any part of outer space or celestial bodies, even for peaceful purposes.

**Thus, option (b) is the correct answer.**

**10.** *(a)* 1, 3 and 4 only

- **Statement 1 is correct:** The **Outer Space Treaty** prohibits the placement of **nuclear weapons and other weapons of mass destruction** in outer space or on celestial bodies, aiming to prevent the militarisation of space.
- **Statement 2 is incorrect:** The Treaty **explicitly prohibits any country from claiming territory on celestial bodies** for any purpose, including scientific purposes. Outer space is considered the 'province of all humankind.'
- **Statement 3 is correct:** The Treaty promotes **peaceful exploration** of outer space and encourages cooperation among nations for the benefit of all humankind.
- **Statement 4 is correct:** The Treaty requires that **States take responsibility** for national space activities, including those conducted by **private entities.** This means that private companies must be authorised and supervised by their respective governments.

**Thus, the correct answer is (a) 1, 3 and 4 only.**

**11.** *(c)* Statement I is correct, but Statement II is incorrect.

- **Statement I is correct:** National Space Day in India is celebrated on **23rd August** to honour India's significant achievements in space science and technology. The date commemorates India's success in its Chandrayaan-3 mission, which achieved a soft landing on the Moon's South pole in 2023, marking a historic milestone in India's space exploration.
- **Statement II is incorrect:** 23rd August does not commemorate the launch of Aryabhata, India's first satellite. Aryabhata was launched on **19th April, 1975,** from the Soviet Union's Kosmos launch site. The reference to Aryabhata in this context is incorrect and unrelated to National Space Day.

**Thus, the correct answer is (c).**

**12.** *(b)* Only two

- **Statement 1 is incorrect:** Perigee is **not** the point of **maximum distance** from Earth. Instead, it is the point of minimum distance in a satellite's orbit around the Earth. At perigee, the satellite is closest to Earth.
- **Statement 2 is correct:** At apogee, the satellite moves slower than at perigee due to Kepler's laws of planetary motion. Specifically, the satellite's velocity decreases as it moves away from the Earth because the gravitational pull weakens with distance.
- **Statement 3 is correct:** At perigee, the satellite experiences the **greatest gravitational influence** from Earth because gravitational force is strongest when the satellite is closest to the Earth.
- **Statement 4 is incorrect:** Apogee is **not** the point of minimum distance; it is the point of **maximum distance** in a satellite's orbit around Earth. At apogee, the satellite is farthest from the Earth.

**Thus, two statements are correct, making the answer (b) Only two.**

**13.** *(a)* 1, 3 and 4 only

- **Statement 1 is correct: Kepler's First Law** (Law of Ellipses) states that **planets move in**

**elliptical orbits with the Sun at one of the two foci.** This was a fundamental shift from the prior assumption that orbits were circular.

- **Statement 2 is incorrect:** According to **Kepler's Second Law** (Law of Equal Areas), planets **do not move at a constant speed.** Instead, their speed varies, moving faster at **perihelion** (closest to the Sun) and slower at **aphelion** (farthest from the Sun).
- **Statement 3 is correct:** Kepler's **Third Law,** or the Law of Harmonies, states that the square of a planet's orbital period ($T^2$) is directly proportional to the cube of its average distance from the Sun ($R^3$). This law mathematically relates the orbital period to the size of the orbit.
- **Statement 4 is correct:** Kepler's Second Law implies that a **planet's speed changes** depending on its distance from the Sun. It moves faster when it is closer (perihelion) and slower when farther away (aphelion) due to gravitational variations in different parts of its orbit.

**Thus, the correct answer is (a) 1, 3 and 4 only.**

**14.** *(b)* Objects in orbit move at a specific speed where the gravitational pull of Earth provides the centripetal force needed to maintain the orbit.

- **Option (b) is correct:** Objects stay in orbit because their velocity is perfectly balanced with Earth's gravitational pull. The speed of the object creates a centripetal force that counters the pull of gravity, keeping the object in continuous free fall around Earth. This is why satellites and planets remain in stable orbits.
- **Option (a) is incorrect:** Objects in orbit are not stationary but constantly moving at high speeds. Their motion prevents them from falling straight to Earth.
- **Option (c) is incorrect:** Earth's gravity still influences objects in orbit, even at high altitudes, which is why gravitational force is essential for maintaining their trajectory.
- **Option (d) is incorrect:** Objects in orbit do not generate their own energy to counteract gravity; their motion and gravitational forces work together to sustain the orbit.

**Thus, the correct answer is (b).**

**15.** *(b)* The minimum speed required for an object to break free from Earth's gravitational pull without additional propulsion.

- **Option (b) is correct:** Escape velocity is the minimum speed an object needs to overcome Earth's gravitational pull entirely, allowing it to move away from Earth without requiring further propulsion. For Earth, this speed is approximately **11.2 km/s.**
- **Option (a) is incorrect:** This describes orbital velocity, not escape velocity. Orbital velocity is the speed required to maintain a stable orbit around Earth.
- **Option (c) is incorrect:** Gravitational force never becomes zero; escape velocity enables an object to move indefinitely far from Earth, where gravity's influence becomes negligible.
- **Option (d) is incorrect:** This option refers to atmospheric boundaries, which are unrelated to escape velocity.

**Thus, the correct answer is (b).**

**16.** *(c)* 1, 2 and 4 only

- **Factor 1 is correct:** The mass of the celestial body directly affects escape velocity. **A larger mass** increases the gravitational pull, requiring a higher escape velocity.
- **Factor 2 is correct:** The radius of the celestial body also influences escape velocity. A **smaller radius** increases surface gravity, leading to a higher escape velocity.
- **Factor 3 is incorrect: Atmospheric composition does not directly affect escape velocity,** as escape velocity depends solely on gravitational and physical parameters of the celestial body. However, atmospheric drag may affect a spacecraft's trajectory.
- **Factor 4 is correct:** The gravitational constant (G) is a fundamental factor in calculating escape velocity using the formula:

$$v_e = \sqrt{\frac{2GM}{R}}$$

where M is the mass of the celestial body, R is its radius and G is the gravitational constant.

**Thus, the correct answer is (c) 1, 2 and 4 only.**

**17.** *(b)* Only two

- **Statement 1 is correct:** The gravitational force exerted by Earth acts as the centripetal force, keeping the satellite in a circular or elliptical orbit. Without this force, the satellite would not maintain its trajectory.

- **Statement 2 is incorrect:** A satellite in a stable orbit does experience forces (gravitational and centrifugal), but these forces are balanced, resulting in no net acceleration or change in the orbital path.
- **Statement 3 is correct:** The centrifugal force, which arises due to the satellite's motion, counterbalances Earth's gravitational pull, ensuring the satellite remains in orbit instead of falling to Earth.

**Thus, the correct answer is (b) Only two.**

**18.** *(c)* All three

- **Statement 1 is correct:** The gravitational force decreases with altitude because gravitational force is inversely proportional to the square of the distance between the satellite and Earth.
- **Statement 2 is correct:** Satellites in low Earth orbit have a higher orbital velocity compared to those in geostationary orbit because the gravitational force is stronger at lower altitudes, requiring greater speed to maintain orbit.
- **Statement 3 is correct:** The centrifugal force, which arises due to the satellite's motion, counterbalances Earth's gravitational pull, ensuring the satellite remains in orbit instead of falling to Earth.

**Thus, the correct answer is (c) All three.**

**19.** *(a)* The angle between the orbit of a satellite and the equator of the Earth.

- **Angle of inclination** is defined as the angle between the **plane of a satellite's orbit** and the **Earth's equatorial plane.** This angle determines the orbit's tilt relative to Earth's equator, and it plays a critical role in defining the satellite's path and coverage area.
- **Option** (a) accurately describes this angle, while **option** (b) is incorrect as the inclination is measured from the equatorial plane, not the Earth's surface. **Options** (c) **and** (d) are irrelevant to the definition of inclination.

**Thus, the correct answer is (a).**

**20.** *(b)* Only two

- **Statement 1 is correct:** Geostationary orbits are a specific subset of geosynchronous orbits.

A geosynchronous orbit refers to any orbit where the satellite has an orbital period equal to Earth's rotational period (24 hours). A **geostationary orbit is a special case of this, where the satellite orbits in the Earth's equatorial plane** and remains fixed relative to a point on the equator.

- **Statement 2 is correct: Satellites in geostationary orbit appear to remain stationary** over a single point on Earth's surface. This occurs because the satellite's orbital speed matches Earth's rotational speed, and it orbits in the same direction as Earth's rotation (from West to East).
- **Statement 3 is incorrect: Geosynchronous satellites must have an orbital period of exactly 24 hours** to maintain synchronisation with Earth's rotation. While their orbital path may not align with the equatorial plane (unlike geostationary satellites), their orbital period is still 24 hours.

**Thus, two statements are correct, making the answer (b) Only two.**

**21.** *(c)* Only three

- **Characteristic 1 is correct:** Satellites in geostationary orbit revolve around Earth's equatorial plane at an **altitude of approximately 35,786 km.** This specific positioning ensures that they **appear stationary relative to a fixed point** on Earth's surface.
- **Characteristic 2 is correct: Geosynchronous satellites can have inclined orbits,** meaning their orbit is tilted relative to the equator. These satellites still synchronise with Earth's rotation but do not necessarily remain fixed over a single point on the equator like geostationary satellites.
- **Characteristic 3 is correct: Both geostationary and geosynchronous satellites complete one orbit in 24 hours, which matches the rotational period of Earth.** This synchronisation is the defining characteristic of geosynchronous orbits.
- **Characteristic 4 is incorrect: Geostationary orbits are primarily used for communication, weather monitoring and broadcasting, rather than GPS applications.** GPS satellites are placed in medium Earth

orbits (MEO) with different inclinations and altitudes, enabling global coverage.

**Thus, three characteristics are correct, making the answer (c) Only three.**

**22.** *(c)* Only three

- **Statement 1 is correct: Earth observation** satellites in polar orbits provide comprehensive coverage of the planet, essential for mapping and environmental monitoring.
- **Statement 2 is incorrect: Geostationary orbits,** not polar orbits, are better suited for **continuous communication coverage** over specific regions.
- **Statement 3 is correct:** Polar orbiting satellites are used for **weather forecasting,** especially for monitoring global weather patterns, as they can cover the entire Earth.
- **Statement 4 is correct: Military surveillance** often uses polar orbits for extensive, recurring coverage of specific regions, making it easier to monitor areas worldwide.

**Thus, three purposes are typical uses of polar orbits, making the answer (c) Only three.**

**23.** *(a)* 1 and 2 only

- **Pair 1 is correct:** A satellite in a **Geostationary Orbit (GSO)** remains fixed over a single point on Earth's equator, making it ideal for continuous monitoring of one area.
- **Pair 2 is correct:** Satellites in **Low Earth Orbit (LEO)** are close to Earth and move quickly, completing multiple orbits per day (typically 90-120 minutes per orbit).
- **Pair 3 is incorrect:** Satellites in **Medium Earth Orbit (MEO)** do not take exactly 24 hours to orbit; this is specific to geosynchronous orbits. MEO satellites orbit Earth in periods ranging from a few hours to approximately 12 hours, depending on altitude.

**Thus, the correct answer is (a) 1 and 2 only.**

**24.** *(b)* An orbit that allows the satellite to always stay in sunlight by following the Earth's terminator line

- A **dawn-to-dusk orbit** is a type of **sun-synchronous orbit** in which the satellite travels along the **Earth's terminator line** (the line separating day and night). This positioning allows the satellite to remain in **constant sunlight** as it orbits, making it ideal for solar-powered satellites needing continuous exposure to sunlight.
- **Option** (b) correctly describes the dawn-to-dusk orbit.
- **Option** (a) is incorrect as the orbit does not follow Earth's rotation but instead follows the terminator.
- **Option** (c) is unrelated, as dawn-to-dusk orbits do not pass over the poles at a specific interval but maintain alignment with the Sun.
- **Option** (d) is also incorrect because a dawn-to-dusk orbit avoids Earth's shadow.

**Thus, the correct answer is (b).**

**25.** *(b)* To minimise the fuel required for transferring a spacecraft between two circular orbits of different radii.

A Hohmann transfer orbit is an energy-efficient method used to transfer a spacecraft between two circular orbits of different radii around a central body. It involves two burns: one to enter the elliptical transfer orbit and another to circularise the orbit at the destination.

**Thus, option (b) is the correct answer.**

**26.** *(a)* 1 and 2 only

- **Statement 1 is correct:** The **Van Allen Belts** are indeed layers of **charged particles**-mainly electrons and protons - surrounding Earth. These particles are trapped by **Earth's magnetic field,** which creates regions of intense radiation.
- **Statement 2 is correct:** The **inner Van Allen Belt** is primarily composed of **high-energy protons,** while the outer Van Allen Belt contains a larger concentration of **electrons.** This difference in composition is due to the varying sources and behaviours of these particles in Earth's magnetic field.
- **Statement 3 is incorrect:** The **Van Allen Belts** are located much closer to Earth than the orbit of the Moon. The inner belt typically extends from about 1,000 km to 12,000 km above Earth's surface, while the outer belt ranges from roughly 13,000 km to 60,000 km. The **Moon's average distance from Earth is about 384,400 km,** far beyond the extent of the Van Allen Belts.

**Thus, the correct answer is (a) 1 and 2 only.**

**27.** *(b)* Only two

- **Statement 1 is correct:** The **INSAT series** consists of **multi-purpose geostationary satellites** developed by India, providing various essential services to the nation.
- **Statement 2 is correct:** The **primary functions** of INSAT include **telecommunications, meteorology and television broadcasting.** INSAT also supports disaster warning and search and rescue operations.
- **Statement 3 is incorrect:** INSAT satellites are positioned in **geostationary orbit (GEO)**, not low Earth orbit (LEO). Geostationary orbit is ideal for continuous monitoring of specific regions, which is essential for telecommunica -tions and meteorological services.

**Thus, two statements are correct, making the answer (b) Only two.**

**28.** *(c)* Only three

- **Application 1 is correct:** Remote sensing satellites are widely used to monitor agricultural crop health by analysing vegetation indices and detecting stress due to pests or water scarcity.
- **Application 2 is correct:** They are used to map urban development and monitor changes in land use and urban sprawl.
- **Application 3 is correct:** Monitoring air quality and atmospheric pollutants, such as tracking the distribution of greenhouse gases, is a key application of remote sensing satellites.
- **Application 4 is incorrect:** Remote sensing satellites cannot predict earthquakes. Earthquake prediction requires ground-based sensors and geological studies.

**Thus, the correct answer is (c) Only three.**

**29.** *(b)* A collaborative effort by ISRO and NASA for Earth observation, focusing on environmental and disaster management.

- NISAR (NASA-ISRO Synthetic Aperture Radar) is a joint satellite mission between NASA and ISRO aimed at Earth observation.
- It focuses on mapping and monitoring changes in the Earth's surface, including ice sheet dynamics, land deformation and forest biomass, and provides data for disaster management.

**Thus, option (b) is the correct answer.**

**30.** *(c)* 1, 2 and 4 only

- **Cartosat series** are remote sensing satellites used for cartographic applications, urban planning, and disaster management.
- **RISAT series** satellites are equipped with radar imaging capabilities, suitable for monitoring weather and agricultural activities, and are part of India's remote sensing programme.
- **GSAT series** are communication satellites, not remote sensing satellites. They are primarily used for broadcasting and telecommunication services.
- **Oceansat series** are remote sensing satellites designed for oceanographic studies and environmental monitoring.

**Thus, the correct answer is (c) 1, 2 and 4 only.**

**31.** *(d)* 2 and 4 only

- **Statement 1 is incorrect: NavIC** is an **autonomous satellite navigation system** developed by the **Indian Space Research Organisation (ISRO)** to provide accurate positioning information within India and the surrounding region.
- **Statement 2 is correct:** NavIC provides **coverage over the Indian subcontinent** and an extended area up to **1,500 km around India**, making it useful for both regional and domestic navigation needs.
- **Statement 3 is incorrect:** NavIC is designed for **both civilian and military applications.** The system has a Standard Positioning Service (SPS) for civilian use and a Restricted Service (RS) encrypted for authorised users, including the military.
- **Statement 4 is correct:** NavIC's constellation consists of **seven satellites** in **geosynchronous and geostationary orbits,** ensuring continuous coverage of the region.

**Thus, the correct answer is (d) 2 and 4 only.**

**32.** *(a)* 1, 2 and 3 only

- **Statement 1 is correct:** NavIC is designed to provide **high accuracy within its regional coverage**, making it more precise for users in India compared to other global systems like GPS within the same region.

- **Statement 2 is correct:** NavIC signals are designed to work reliably in **all weather conditions**, and its signals have good penetration, offering reliable service across diverse environments in India.
- **Statement 3 is correct:** NavIC's **Standard Positioning Service (SPS)** is available free to users within India, ensuring accessible navigation data for civilians.
- **Statement 4 is incorrect:** NavIC is primarily intended for **regional use** and is not designed for direct international data sharing with other countries, as it is focused on enhancing India's independent navigation capabilities.

**Thus, the correct answer is (a) 1, 2 and 3 only.**

***33.*** *(d)* All four pairs

- **Pair 1 is correct:** GPS (Global Positioning System) is developed and maintained by the United States for global navigation purposes.
- **Pair 2 is correct:** GLONASS (Global Navigation Satellite System) is a navigation system developed by Russia, offering global coverage.
- **Pair 3 is correct:** Galileo is a European Union project aimed at providing accurate global navigation services.
- **Pair 4 is correct:** BeiDou is a satellite navigation system developed by China, providing regional and global services.

**Thus, the correct answer is (d) All four pairs.**

***34.*** *(b)* 2 only

- **Statement 1 is incorrect: GAGAN** is not an independent satellite navigation system; it is an **augmentation system** that works with the existing GPS to improve accuracy and reliability over Indian airspace.
- **Statement 2 is correct:** GAGAN enhances the **accuracy of GPS signals** by providing corrections, making it suitable for precise navigation requirements within India, especially in aviation.
- **Statement 3 is incorrect:** GAGAN is primarily designed for the **aviation sector** and offers **safety-of-life navigation services,** helping to improve flight safety and efficiency in Indian airspace.

**Thus, the correct answer is (b) 2 only.**

***35.*** *(b)* Only two

- **Statement 1 is correct: AstroSat** is indeed India's first dedicated **multi-wavelength space observatory**. It was designed to observe celestial objects across multiple wavelengths.
- **Statement 2 is incorrect:** AstroSat does not observe the universe only in the visible spectrum; it can observe in **X-ray, ultraviolet and visible wavelengths,** making it versatile for studying various cosmic phenomena.
- **Statement 3 is correct:** AstroSat was launched by **ISRO** to study **stars, galaxies, black holes and other celestial objects,** advancing our understanding of the universe.

**Thus, two statements are correct, making the answer (b) Only two.**

***36.*** *(a)* 2 - 4 - 5 - 3 - 1

- **SLV:** Developed and first launched successfully in **1980**, SLV was India's first satellite launch vehicle.
- **ASLV:** Developed as a successor to SLV, **ASLV** had its first successful launch in **1992.**
- **PSLV:** PSLV was developed next and successfully launched in **1994**, with capabilities to place satellites in polar and low Earth orbits.
- **GSLV:** Developed to place satellites into geostationary orbit, GSLV had its first successful launch in **2001**.
- **GSLV Mk III:** This latest and most powerful launch vehicle was first successfully launched in **2017**.

**Thus, the correct order is (a) 2-4-5-3-1.**

***37.*** *(b)* Only two

- **Statement 1 is correct:** The **GSLV** is designed to launch satellites into **Geosynchronous Transfer Orbit (GTO)**, making it suitable for placing communication and weather satellites into orbit.
- **Statement 2 is correct:** GSLV features a **cryogenic upper stage,** which provides greater efficiency in the final stage of launch and enhances payload capacity.
- **Statement 3 is incorrect:** Polar Satellite Launch Vehicle (PSLV) is the **third generation launch vehicle of India.** It is the

**first Indian launch vehicle to be equipped with liquid stages and the first launcher** to gain operational status. It is a 44m tall vehicle, with lift-off mass of 295 ton. It is configured as a **four stage, alternate solid and liquid propellant vehicle.**

**Thus, only two statements are correct, making the answer (b) Only two.**

**38.** *(b)* A liquid rocket engine used in the second stage of PSLV and the core stage of GSLV.

The Vikas engine is a liquid-propellant rocket engine developed by ISRO. It is used in the second stage of the Polar Satellite Launch Vehicle (PSLV) and the core stage of the Geosynchronous Satellite Launch Vehicle (GSLV). It plays a critical role in lifting heavier payloads into space.

**Thus, option (b) is the correct answer.**

**39.** *(c)* All three

- **Capacity 1 is correct:** GSLV Mk III can launch payloads up to **4,000 kg** into Geosynchronous Transfer Orbit (GTO). This capability supports launching communication satellites.
- **Capacity 2 is correct:** The launch vehicle can carry payloads up to **10,000 kg** to Low Earth Orbit (LEO), making it suitable for heavy payload missions.
- **Capacity 3 is correct:** GSLV Mk III is capable of delivering payloads like Chandrayaan-2 and Chandrayaan-3 to lunar orbit, with a capacity of approximately **1,500 kg**.

**Thus, the correct answer is (c) All three.**

**40.** *(a)* 1 and 2 only

- **Statement 1 is correct:** The SSLV is designed to carry payloads of up to 500 kg to Low Earth Orbit (LEO), making it ideal for **launching small satellites.**
  - SSLV is designed for quick turnaround times and minimal launch preparation compared to larger vehicles like PSLV, making it cost-effective and efficient for frequent launches.
- **Statement 2 is correct:** It is a **three-stage launch vehicle that uses solid propulsion** in all its stages, simplifying its design and reducing costs.
- **Statement 3 is incorrect:** SSLV is optimised for Low Earth Orbit (LEO) missions and is not intended for launching satellites into Geosynchronous Transfer Orbit (GTO), which requires higher thrust and more complex systems.

**Thus, the correct answer is (a) 1 and 2 only.**

**41.** *(b)* To demonstrate technologies for reducing the cost of satellite launches by enabling partial reusability of launch systems.

The **Reusable Launch Vehicle - Technology Demonstrator** (RLV-TD) is a scaled-down prototype **developed by ISRO to validate technologies that enable the reuse of launch vehicle components.** This is aimed at significantly reducing the cost of satellite launches. The RLV-TD incorporates advanced technologies such as autonomous navigation, hypersonic flight and thermal protection systems, which are critical for reusability.

**Thus, option (b) is the correct answer.**

**42.** *(a)* 1 only

- **Statement 1 is correct:** Solid propellants are pre-mixed and stored in a stable, solid form, making them easier to store and handle compared to liquid propellants, which require cryogenic or pressurised storage systems.
- **Statement 2 is incorrect:** Liquid propellants allow for precise control, including throttling (adjusting thrust) and shutdown during flight. **Solid propellants, once ignited, burn to completion without the ability to stop or control the burn.**
- **Statement 3 is incorrect: Liquid propellants generally offer a higher specific impulse** (a measure of efficiency) than solid propellants, making them more efficient for certain missions.

**Thus, the correct answer is (a) 1 only.**

**43.** *(c)* Only three

- **Option 1 is correct:** Ramjets are air-breathing engines that compress incoming air through high-speed forward motion and use it for combustion.

- **Option 2 is correct:** Scramjets are air-breathing engines that operate efficiently at hypersonic speeds by compressing air without the use of rotating compressors.
- **Option 3 is correct:** Turbojets are air-breathing engines that use a compressor to pressurise air, mix it with fuel, and ignite it for propulsion.
- **Option 4 is incorrect: Rocket engines are not air-breathing;** they carry both fuel and oxidiser onboard, enabling them to operate in space.

**Thus, the correct answer is (c) Only three.**

**44.** *(b)* An engine that operates using intermittent combustion, producing pulses of thrust

A **Pulsejet engine** uses **intermittent combustion** to produce short bursts, or 'pulses,' of thrust. These engines have a simple design and can function without compressors, making them suitable for low-speed applications.

**Thus, option (b) is the correct answer.**

**45.** *(d)* An engine that compresses incoming air with a turbine-driven compressor and is efficient for subsonic and low supersonic speeds

A **Turbojet engine** compresses air using a **turbine-driven compressor** before it enters the combustion chamber. It is suitable for **subsonic and low supersonic speeds** and was widely used in early jet engines.

**Thus, option (d) is the correct answer.**

**46.** *(b)* Only two

- **Statement 1 is correct:** Ramjet engines **operate efficiently only at supersonic speeds (generally above Mach 2) because they lack a compressor.** Instead, they use the forward motion of the engine to compress incoming air, which is then mixed with fuel for combustion. At lower speeds, the air compression is insufficient for effective operation.
- **Statement 2 is correct:** Scramjet (Supersonic Combustion Ramjet) engines are **designed to operate at hypersonic speeds (above Mach 5).** Unlike ramjets, scramjets allow supersonic airflow through the engine, making them suitable for extremely high-speed propulsion systems, such as in spaceplanes or missiles.
- **Statement 3 is incorrect: Neither ramjet nor scramjet engines can operate at zero airspeed. Both engines rely on the intake of air from high-speed motion for compression and combustion.** At zero airspeed, there is no airflow into the engine, rendering them non-functional.

**Thus, the correct answer is (b) Only two.**

**47.** *(b)* Only two

- **Comparison 1 is correct:** Ramjets are designed to operate efficiently at **supersonic speeds** (typically between Mach 2 and Mach 5). In contrast, scramjets (Supersonic Combustion Ramjets) are specifically designed for **hypersonic speeds** (above Mach 5), where the airflow remains supersonic throughout the engine.
- **Comparison 2 is incorrect: Neither ramjets nor scramjets can operate at low speeds without external assistance. Both engines require high initial speeds for proper air intake compression.** Typically, an external booster or another propulsion system is used to accelerate the vehicle to operational speeds.
- **Comparison 3 is correct:** Ramjets perform **subsonic combustion**, where the air is slowed down to subsonic speeds before mixing with fuel and igniting. In contrast, scramjets allow **supersonic combustion**, where the air remains supersonic while undergoing combustion, enabling efficient propulsion at hypersonic speeds.

**Thus, two comparisons are correct, making the answer (b) Only two.**

**48.** *(a)* The fuel efficiency of a rocket engine, indicating how much thrust is produced per unit of fuel consumed per second

- **Specific impulse** is a measure of the **fuel efficiency** of a rocket engine and is often used to compare the performance of different propulsion systems. It indicates the amount of **thrust produced per unit of fuel** consumed per second and is usually expressed in seconds.
- Higher specific impulse values mean that the engine is more efficient, providing greater thrust for less fuel. This is crucial in satellite missions, as efficient fuel use allows for extended mission lifetimes and greater maneuvering capabilities.

**Thus, the correct answer is (a).**

**49.** *(a)* 1 and 3 only

- **Statement 1 is correct:** The Mach number is a dimensionless quantity representing the ratio of an object's speed to the speed of sound in the surrounding medium. **Mach 1** indicates the speed of sound, which varies with factors such as temperature and the type of medium (air, water, etc.). For example, at sea level, the speed of sound in air is approximately 343 m/s.
- **Statement 2 is incorrect:** Speeds between **Mach 1** and **Mach 5** are classified as **supersonic**, not subsonic. Subsonic speeds are those below Mach 1, where an object is traveling slower than the speed of sound. Supersonic speeds range from Mach 1 (the speed of sound) to Mach 5.
- **Statement 3 is correct: Hypersonic speeds** are defined as speeds greater than Mach 5. Vehicles or objects traveling at hypersonic speeds, such as scramjets or re-entry spacecraft, experience unique aerodynamic and thermal challenges due to the high velocity.

**Thus, the correct answer is (a) 1 and 3 only.**

**50.** *(c)* Only three

- **Statement 1 is correct:** Cryogenic engines require fuels such as **Liquid Oxygen (LOX) and Liquid Hydrogen (LH2), which need to be stored at extremely low temperatures (cryogenic conditions) to remain in a liquid** state. For example, liquid hydrogen is stored at approximately -253°C. Handling these fuels requires specialised technology to ensure safe storage and operation.
- **Statement 2 is correct:** Cryogenic engines are primarily used in the **upper stages of rockets due to their high efficiency and thrust-to-weight ratio,** which is critical for placing payloads into high orbits or conducting interplanetary missions. ISRO's GSLV uses a cryogenic upper stage for launching satellites into geosynchronous orbits.
- **Statement 3 is correct:** Cryogenic fuels provide **higher energy efficiency compared to conventional liquid or solid fuels.** Liquid hydrogen and liquid oxygen have high specific impulse values, making them ideal for missions requiring greater performance and payload capacity.
- **Statement 4 is incorrect:** Cryogenic engines **are complex in design compared to solid rocket engines.** They involve intricate systems such as cryogenic turbopumps, precise insulation, and advanced technology for handling extremely cold temperatures and high-pressure environments.

**Thus, the correct answer is (c) Only three.**

**51.** *(b)* Only two

- **Statement 1 is correct:** The Sun primarily produces energy through **hydrogen fusion** in a sequence called the **proton-proton chain reaction**, where protons (hydrogen nuclei) fuse to form helium nuclei.
- **Statement 2 is incorrect :** While fusion does release energy, it is initially in the form of **gamma rays** and not directly as visible light. These gamma rays gradually lose energy as they move outward, eventually becoming visible light by the time they leave the Sun's surface.
- **Statement 3 is correct: Neutrinos** are indeed a byproduct of the fusion process in the Sun's core. These particles escape the Sun quickly due to their weak interaction with matter, allowing them to reach Earth.

**Thus, two statements are correct, making the answer (b) Only two.**

**52.** *(a)* 1, 2 and 4 only

- **Solar flares** and **coronal mass ejections (CMEs)** are both influenced by the **Solar Cycle.** These phenomena become more frequent during solar maximum when the Sun's magnetic activity is strongest.
- **Earth's magnetic field strength** is not directly affected by the Solar Cycle, although disturbances in space weather caused by solar activity can lead to geomagnetic storms.
- **Auroras** on Earth, such as the Northern and Southern Lights, become more intense during periods of high solar activity, particularly during solar maximum.

**Thus, the correct answer is (a) 1, 2 and 4 only.**

**53.** *(a)* 3-5-2-1-4

The layers of the Sun arranged from the outermost to the innermost are as follows:

- **Corona:** The **corona** is the Sun's outermost layer, extending millions of kilometres into space. It is visible during a total solar eclipse as a faint, white halo. The corona is extremely hot, with temperatures reaching millions of degrees Celsius.
- **Chromosphere:** The **chromosphere** lies beneath the corona and is a thin layer of the Sun's atmosphere. It emits a reddish glow due to the presence of hydrogen and is visible during solar eclipses.

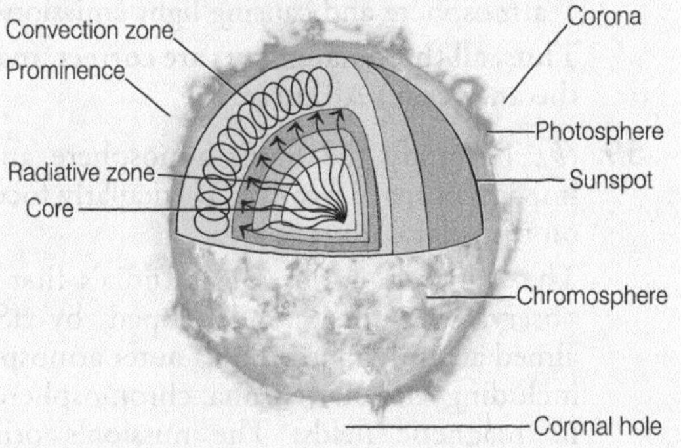


- **Photosphere:** The **photosphere** is the visible surface of the Sun from where most of the Sun's light and heat are emitted. It has a temperature of approximately 5,500°C and appears as a bright, glowing disk.
- **Convective Zone:** The **convective zone** lies below the photosphere and is the region where hot plasma rises and cooler plasma sinks, transferring energy outward through convection currents.
- **Radiative Zone:** The **radiative zone** is the innermost layer responsible for energy transfer through radiation. Energy generated in the Sun's core is transmitted outward through this layer before reaching the convective zone.

**Thus, the correct answer is (a) 3-5-2-1-4.**

**54.** *(b)* An approximately 11-year cycle of solar activity, marked by changes in the number of sunspots and solar radiation.

- The solar cycle is an **approximately 11-year periodic cycle** during which the Sun's activity fluctuates. This cycle is characterised by variations in the number of **sunspots**, which are dark, cooler regions on the Sun's surface caused by intense magnetic activity. During the cycle, the Sun goes through two main phases:
- **Solar Maximum:** A phase with the highest number of sunspots, increased solar flares, and Coronal Mass Ejections (CMEs), which can disrupt space weather and affect satellite communication.
- **Solar Minimum:** A phase with the lowest sunspot activity, indicating reduced solar activity.
- This cycle also impacts solar radiation, influencing space weather and Earth's upper atmosphere.

**Thus, option (b) is the correct answer.**

**55.** *(c)* Only three

- **Option 1 is correct:** Coronal Mass Ejections (CMEs) **create auroras (Northern and Southern lights) near the poles**. When charged particles from CMEs interact with Earth's magnetic field and atmosphere, they excite atmospheric gases, producing the stunning light displays visible near the poles.
- **Option 2 is correct:** CMEs can disrupt the **Global Positioning System (GPS) signals by disturbing the ionosphere**, a layer of Earth's atmosphere crucial for transmitting GPS signals. This interference reduces the accuracy of navigation systems and affects various technologies dependent on GPS.
- **Option 3 is incorrect:** CMEs do not cause **long-term shifts in Earth's magnetic poles.** Such shifts, known as geomagnetic reversals, occur over thousands to millions of years due to changes in Earth's core dynamics and are unrelated to short-term solar activity.
- **Option 4 is correct:** CMEs can disrupt **satellite communication systems** by exposing satellites to intense solar radiation and

electromagnetic disturbances. This interference can degrade or temporarily disable communication, affecting services like television, internet, and telephony.

**Thus, the correct answer is (c) Only three.**

**56.** *(c)* All three

- **Statement 1 is correct:** These are **cooler regions** on the Sun's surface compared to the surrounding areas. While the Sun's surface (photosphere) has a temperature of about 5,500°C, sunspots are cooler at approximately 3,500°C to 4,000°C, making them appear darker.
- **Statement 2 is correct:** Sunspots are dark, planet-sized regions that appear on the surface of the Sun. They are caused by twisting, chaotic magnetic fields from within the Sun's convective zone. These powerful magnetic disturbances produce active regions on the Sun, which can often create solar flares and Coronal Mass Ejections (CMEs).
- **Statement 3 is correct:** These are areas of **intense magnetic activity** on the Sun. The Sun's magnetic field lines become twisted and concentrated in these regions, inhibiting convection and causing the cooler, darker appearance of sunspots. This magnetic activity is also linked to the solar cycle.

**Thus, the correct answer is (c) All three.**

**57.** *(b)* Earth's magnetic field lines converge near the poles, guiding solar particles toward these regions.

- Auroras are most commonly observed near the **polar regions** because Earth's **magnetic field lines converge** near the North and South Poles.
- These field lines act as pathways that direct charged particles from the **solar wind** toward the poles, where they interact with the atmosphere, leading to the formation of auroras.
- This convergence makes the **polar regions** more susceptible to auroral displays than the equator, where magnetic field lines are more dispersed and less likely to funnel solar particles toward the atmosphere.

**Thus, the correct answer is (b).**

**58.** *(c)* All three

- **Statement 1 is correct: Aurora Borealis** is known as the Northern Lights because it occurs in the **Northern hemisphere**, typically near the Arctic regions.
- **Statement 2 is correct: Aurora Australis,** also known as the Southern Lights, is observed in the **Southern hemisphere**, particularly over **Antarctica** and the Southern polar region.
- **Statement 3 is correct:** Auroras are caused by **solar wind particles** (charged particles from the Sun) that interact with Earth's **magnetic field**, exciting particles in the atmosphere and causing light emissions.

**Thus, all three statements are correct, making the answer (c) All three.**

**59.** *(b)* To study the Sun's atmosphere and its impact on space weather, particularly focusing on the solar corona.

The **Aditya L-1 mission** is India's first solar observatory mission, developed by ISRO, aimed at studying the Sun's outer atmosphere, including the **solar corona**, chromosphere and its magnetic fields. The mission's primary objective is to understand the dynamics of the solar atmosphere and its impact on **space weather**, which can affect satellites, power grids, and communication systems on Earth. It will also study solar wind properties and their interaction with the interplanetary medium.

**Thus, option (b) is the correct answer.**

**60.** *(a)* 1, 2 and 4 only

- **Statement 1 is correct:** The **L1 point** is a favored position for satellites like SOHO that **monitor the Sun** for solar flares, solar wind, and space weather phenomena.
- **Statement 2 is correct:** The **L2 point** offers a stable, shadowed environment ideal for **deep-space astronomical observations**, like those made by the James Webb Space Telescope.
- **Statement 3 is incorrect:** L3 is not used for Earth observation, as it is located on the opposite side of the Sun, hidden from Earth's view.

- **Statement 4 is correct: L4 and L5** are stable points where **small celestial objects** or Trojan asteroids can remain balanced, as gravitational forces and orbital motions keep them in place.

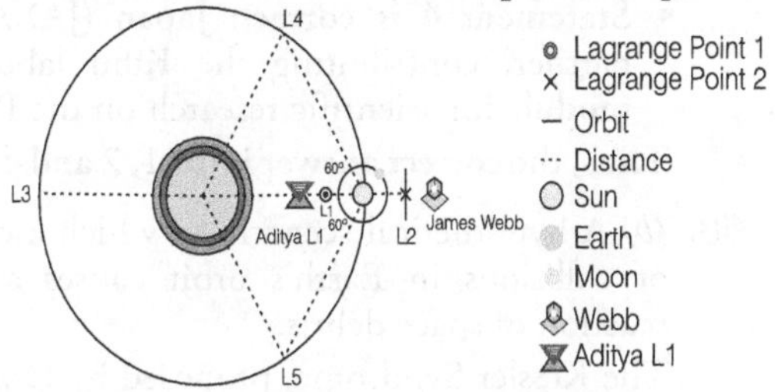


**Thus, the correct answer is (a) 1, 2 and 4 only.**

***61.*** *(d)* All four

- **Pair 1 is correct:** Parker Solar Probe is a mission by NASA, designed to study the Sun's outer corona and gather data on solar wind.
- **Pair 2 is correct:** Solar Orbiter is a collaboration between the European Space Agency (ESA) and NASA, focusing on studying the Sun's poles and heliosphere.
- **Pair 3 is correct:** Aditya L-1 is India's first solar mission, developed by ISRO to study the solar corona and its effects on space weather.
- **Pair 4 is correct:** Hinode is a Japanese solar mission launched by JAXA (Japan Aerospace Exploration Agency) to observe the Sun's magnetic field and its interactions with the solar corona.

**Thus, the correct answer is (d) All four.**

***62.*** *(a)* A second full Moon occurring in a calendar month.

A **Blue Moon** traditionally refers to a **second full moon** within a single calendar month, which is a rare occurrence since each lunar cycle is approximately 29.5 days. Typically, there is only one full Moon per month, so a Blue Moon only happens every two to three years. While atmospheric particles like volcanic ash or smoke can give the Moon a bluish hue, this is not the astronomical definition of a Blue Moon.

**Thus, the correct answer is (a).**

***63.*** *(c)* Only three

- **Pair 1 is correct:** A **Blood Moon** occurs during a total lunar eclipse, where sunlight filtering through Earth's atmosphere casts a reddish hue onto the Moon's surface.
- **Pair 2 is correct:** A **Super Moon** happens when the full Moon is closest to Earth (perigee), making it appear larger and brighter than usual.
- **Pair 3 is correct:** The **Harvest Moon** is the full Moon closest to the autumnal equinox, traditionally providing extra light for farmers during the harvest season.
- **Pair 4 is incorrect:** A **Blue Moon** is not associated with the Moon appearing blue due to atmospheric conditions. Instead, it generally refers to the second full Moon in a calendar month or an extra full Moon in a season.

**Thus, three pairs are correctly matched, making the answer (c) Only three.**

***64.*** *(c)* Only three

- **Pair 1 is correct:** The **Artemis** programme is NASA's latest lunar exploration initiative, led by United States' aiming to return humans to the Moon and establish a sustainable presence.
- **Pair 2 is correct: Chandrayaan-3** is India's second lunar mission under ISRO, aiming to explore the lunar surface and search for water ice.
- **Pair 3 is correct: Beresheet** was a privately funded lunar lander developed by Israel's **SpaceIL**; though the mission ended in a crash landing, it marked Israel's entry into lunar exploration.
- **Pair 4 is incorrect: Hakuto-R** is a Japanese commercial lunar mission developed by ispace. Russia's lunar missions have been part of the Soviet **Luna** programme and recent **Luna-25**.

**Thus, three pairs are correctly matched, making the answer (c) Only three.**

***65.*** *(c)* Only three

- **Pair 1 is correct:** The **Venera series** was a program by the **Soviet Union** that sent numerous missions to Venus, including both flybys and landers, making it one of the most extensive exploration programmes for Venus.
- **Pair 2 is correct: Akatsuki**, also known as the Venus Climate Orbiter, was launched by

Japan (JAXA) in 2010 to study the atmosphere of Venus and its weather patterns.

- **Pair 3 is correct: Venus Express** was a mission by the **European Space Agency** (ESA), launched in 2005 to study Venus's atmosphere and surface characteristics.
- **Pair 4 is incorrect: Magellan** was a mission launched by **NASA** (United States) in 1989, which mapped the surface of Venus using radar. China has not launched a Venus mission named Magellan.

**Thus, three pairs are correctly matched, making the answer (c) Only three.**

**66.** *(a)* 1 and 2 only

- **Statement 1 is correct:** The **Karman Line** is defined at an altitude of **100 km (62 miles)** above Earth's surface. This is based on the calculation of where the atmosphere becomes too thin to support aerodynamic flight, marking the beginning of outer space.
- **Statement 2 is correct:** At the Karman Line, a vehicle must achieve **orbital velocity** (approximately 7.9 km/s) to sustain flight. Below this altitude, lift generated by the atmosphere can support flight, but beyond this point, vehicles rely entirely on orbital mechanics to stay aloft.
- **Statement 3 is incorrect:** While the **Federation Aeronautique Internationale (FAI)** recognises the Karman Line as the boundary of space, it is not universally accepted by all organisations. For instance, NASA and the US military define the boundary of space as **80 km (50 miles)** above Earth's surface.

**Thus, the correct answer is (a) 1 and 2 only.**

**67.** *(b)* 1, 2 and 4 only

- **Statement 1 is correct: The United States** (NASA) is a primary partner in the ISS, contributing significant modules, scientific research, and funding.
- **Statement 2 is correct: Russia** (Roscosmos) is also a major partner in the ISS program, providing key modules such as **Zvezda** and **Zarya,** which are critical for life support and orbital adjustments.
- **Statement 3 is incorrect: China** is not a participant in the ISS program. Instead, China has built its own space station, **Tiangong.**
- **Statement 4 is correct: Japan** (JAXA) is a partner, contributing the **Kibo laboratory module** for scientific research on the ISS.

**Thus, the correct answer is (b) 1, 2 and 4 only.**

**68.** *(b)* A hypothetical scenario in which a cascade of collisions in Earth's orbit causes a chain reaction of space debris.

The Kessler Syndrome, proposed by Donald J. Kessler in 1978, describes a scenario where collisions between objects in Earth's orbit create a cascade of debris. This debris could lead to further collisions, making certain orbits unusable due to the high density of debris.

**Thus, option (b) is the correct answer.**

**69.** *(c)* To enhance India's capability in monitoring, tracking and mitigating space debris.

Project NETRA (Network for Space Object Tracking and Analysis) is ISRO's initiative to monitor and track space debris, ensuring the safety of Indian satellites and other assets in orbit.

**Thus, option (c) is the correct answer.**

**70.** *(b)* 3 only

- **Statement 1 is incorrect:** The **Space Debris Mitigation Guidelines** of the United Nations are **not legally binding.** These guidelines provide recommendations to member states and organisations for mitigating the generation of space debris. They are advisory in nature and rely on voluntary compliance rather than enforcement through legal obligations.
- **Statement 2 is incorrect:** The **Outer Space Treaty (1967)** establishes general principles for the peaceful use of outer space, but it does not **explicitly define legal responsibilities** for cleaning up space debris.
- **Statement 3 is correct:** The **Artemis Accords,** signed by multiple nations, include provisions for the **sustainable use of outer space.** They emphasise cooperative measures to mitigate space debris, ensuring long-term sustainability of outer space activities.

**Thus, the correct answer is (b) 3 only.**

**71.** *(b)* A state of reduced effective gravity experienced by objects in free-fall or orbit.

Microgravity refers to the condition where objects experience very low effective gravity. This occurs because they are in a state of free-fall, such as in orbit around Earth, where gravitational force is present but does not produce a noticeable effect due to the constant free-fall motion.

**Thus, option (b) is the correct answer.**

**72.** *(a)* A-2, B-1, C-3

- **A-2 (Orbital Space Tourism)**: Orbital space tourism involves traveling to Earth's orbit and may include long-duration stays aboard space stations like the ISS.
- **B-1 (Suborbital Space Tourism)**: Suborbital flights reach the edge of space, allowing passengers to experience weightlessness for a few minutes before returning to Earth.
- **C-3 (Lunar Space Tourism)**: Lunar tourism involves travelling around or landing on the Moon, a more advanced and costly form of space tourism.

**Thus, the correct answer is (a).**

**73.** *(d)* 1 and 3 only

- **Statement 1 is correct**: The Gaganyaan mission will use the **GSLV Mk III (LVM-3)** launch vehicle, which is India's most powerful rocket. It is capable of carrying the crew module and other systems required for the mission into orbit. This vehicle is specifically chosen for its reliability and capacity to place the spacecraft in the required orbit.
- **Statement 2 is incorrect**: The Gaganyaan spacecraft will be placed in a **Low Earth Orbit** (LEO), at an altitude of approximately **300-400 km**. It will not be placed in a **geosynchronous orbit**, which is much higher (around 35,786 km above Earth) and typically used for communication satellites.
- **Statement 3 is correct**: Gaganyaan is India's first **human spaceflight mission**, developed by ISRO as part of its initiative to establish a sustainable human space exploration programme. The mission represents a significant milestone in India's space capabilities.

**Thus, the correct answer is (d) 1 and 3 only.**

**74.** *(c)* Only three

- **Pair 1 is correct:** The **Mars Orbiter Mission (MOM)**, also known as **Mangalyaan**, was launched by **India's ISRO** in 2013, marking India's first interplanetary mission and achieving Mars orbit on the first attempt.
- **Pair 2 is correct:** The **MAVEN** mission was launched by **NASA** (United States) in 2013 to study Mars's atmosphere and understand how its climate evolved over time.
- **Pair 3 is correct:** The **Hope Probe** is a Mars mission launched by the **United Arab Emirates** (UAE) in 2020, becoming the UAE's first interplanetary mission and aiming to study Mars's atmosphere and weather.
- **Pair 4 is incorrect: Mars Express** is a mission launched by the **European Space Agency** (ESA), not Russia. Launched in 2003, it studies the Martian atmosphere, surface and subsurface.

**Thus, three pairs are correctly matched, making the answer (c) Only three.**

**75.** *(b)* A-1, B-2, C-3, D-4

- **A-1 (Galileo - NASA)**: The **Galileo mission was an orbiter sent by NASA** to study Jupiter and its moons in detail.
- **B-2 (Juno - NASA): Juno is a NASA** mission currently studying Jupiter's polar regions, atmosphere and magnetic field.
- **C-3 (JUICE - ESA)**: The **Jupiter Icy Moons Explorer (JUICE), developed by ESA**, focuses on exploring Jupiter's icy moons - Ganymede (largest moon of our solar system), Callisto and Europa.
- **D-4 (Pioneer 10 - NASA)**: **Pioneer 10** was the **first spacecraft to perform a flyby of Jupiter** and provided the first close-up images of the planet.

**Thus, the correct answer is (b).**

**76.** *(c)* All three

- **Pair 1 is correct:** Voyager 1 became the first spacecraft to leave the heliosphere, entering interstellar space in 2012, after conducting flybys of Jupiter and Saturn.

- **Pair 2 is correct:** Cassini-Huygens explored Saturn's magnetic field and carried out groundbreaking studies of its rings and moons, including the successful landing of the Huygens probe on Titan.
- **Pair 3 is correct:** New Horizons was the first mission to study Pluto and its moons, and it continued its journey to explore the Kuiper Belt, expanding our understanding of the outer Solar System.

**Thus, the correct answer is (c) All three.**

***77.*** *(c)* Only three

- **Pair 1 is correct:** Lucy, a NASA mission, is en route to study Trojan asteroids near Jupiter, which are remnants from the early Solar System.
- **Pair 2 is correct:** Hayabusa2, another JAXA mission, studied asteroid Ryugu and returned samples in 2020.
- **Pair 3 is correct:** OSIRIS-REx, a NASA mission, explored asteroid Bennu and returned samples to Earth in 2023.
- **Pair 4 is incorrect:** The Dawn mission explored Vesta and Ceres, not Eros. NEAR Shoemaker was the mission that explored Eros.

**Thus, the correct answer is (c) Only three.**

***78.*** *(a)* Only one

- **Statement 1 is incorrect:** The **Indian Astronomical Observatory** is operated by the **Indian Institute of Astrophysics (IIA)**, not ISRO. The IIA is responsible for developing and managing astronomical facilities in India.
- **Statement 2 is incorrect:** The IAO houses **the Himalayan Chandra Telescope (HCT)**, which is one of India's largest optical telescopes and is used for various astronomical studies.
  - **The Devasthal Optical Telescope (DOT) is India's largest optical telescope,** located at Aryabhatt Research Institute of Experimental Sciences in Nainital.
- **Statement 3 is correct:** The location in **Hanle, Ladakh**, experiences minimal light pollution due to its remote setting and elevation, making it highly suitable for **night-sky observations.**

**Thus, only one statement is correct, making the answer (a) Only one.**

***79.*** *(a)* A-1, B-2, C-3, D-4

- **A-1 (Hubble Space Telescope - Low Earth Orbit):** The Hubble Space Telescope operates in **Low Earth Orbit (LEO)** at an altitude of about 540 km.
- **B-2 (James Webb Telescope - Second Lagrange Point):** The James Webb Space Telescope (JWST) is located at the **Second Lagrange Point (L2)**, about 1.5 million km from Earth.
- **C-3 (Chandra X-Ray Observatory - High Earth Orbit):** The Chandra Observatory operates in a highly elliptical **High Earth Orbit (HEO)** to avoid interference from Earth's atmosphere.
- **D-4 (Spitzer Space Telescope - Heliocentric Orbit):** Spitzer is in a **heliocentric orbit,** trailing Earth as it observes infrared emissions.

**Thus, the correct answer is (a) A-1, B-2, C-3, D-4.**

***80.*** *(a)* A group of space-based telescopes, each designed to observe the universe in a specific wavelength of light.

NASA's Great Observatories programme includes space-based telescopes such as the Hubble Space Telescope, Chandra X-ray Observatory, Spitzer Space Telescope and Compton Gamma Ray Observatory. Each telescope observes the universe in different wavelengths (visible light, X-rays, infrared, and gamma rays), providing a comprehensive view of astronomical phenomena.

**Thus, option (a) is the correct answer.**

***81.*** *(b)* 1, 3 and 4 only

- **Statement 1 is correct:** The Hubble Space Telescope observes the universe in **visible light,** ultraviolet and near-infrared wavelengths, making it one of the most versatile observatories.
- **Statement 2 is incorrect:** The Spitzer Space Telescope focuses on the **infrared spectrum,** not gamma rays. The gamma-ray spectrum was observed by the Compton Gamma Ray Observatory.

- **Statement 3 is correct:** The Chandra X-ray Observatory is designed to detect high-energy X-rays emitted by phenomena like **black holes**, neutron stars and supernova remnants.
- **Statement 4 is correct:** The Great Observatories programme collectively aims to study celestial phenomena across the **entire electromagnetic spectrum**, using specialised telescopes for different wavelengths.

**Thus, the correct answer is (b) 1, 3 and 4 only.**

***82.*** *(a)* 1 and 2 only

- **Statement 1 is correct:** Space-based telescopes avoid atmospheric distortion, enabling clearer and sharper observations compared to ground-based telescopes.
  - They operate above Earth's atmosphere, remaining unaffected by weather conditions like clouds or rain that hinder ground-based telescopes.
- **Statement 2 is correct:** They can observe wavelengths like ultraviolet, X-rays and gamma rays, which are absorbed by Earth's atmosphere.
- **Statement 3 is incorrect:** Space-based telescopes are generally more expensive to deploy and operate due to launch and maintenance costs.

**Thus, the correct answer is (a) 1 and 2 only.**

***83.*** *(a)* A-1, B-2, C-3, D-4

- A-1 : The **Giant Metrewave Radio Telescope (GMRT)** is located near Pune, Maharashtra. It is one of the world's largest arrays of radio telescopes, designed to study low-frequency radio waves emitted by cosmic sources.
- B-2 : The **Thirty Meter Telescope (TMT)** is a advanced optical and infrared observatory planned for construction at Mauna Kea, Hawaii. It will provide unparalleled resolution for studying the universe.
- C-3 : The **Devasthal Optical Telescope** (DOT), located in Nainital, Uttarakhand, is India's largest fully steerable optical telescope. It supports studies in optical and near-infrared astronomy.
- D-4 : The **Square Kilometre Array Observatory** (SKAO) is an international collaboration to build the world's largest radio telescope network. It spans sites in **South Africa** and **Australia**, enabling large-scale studies of the cosmos.

**Thus, the correct answer is (a) A-1, B-2, C-3, D-4.**

***84.*** *(a)* 1, 3 and 4 only

- **Statement 1 is correct:** High-altitude locations are ideal for ground-based telescopes because they **minimise the thickness of the atmosphere that light from celestial objects must pass through.**
- **Statement 2 is incorrect:** Proximity to urban areas is not an ideal condition. **Urban environments typically have significant light pollution and atmospheric disturbances** caused by heat and pollution, which adversely affect observations.
- **Statement 3 is correct:** A dry climate is crucial as it reduces **water vapour** in the atmosphere. **Water vapour absorbs certain wavelengths of light**, such as infrared, which is critical for some astronomical observations.
- **Statement 4 is correct:** Remote locations with minimal **light pollution** are ideal for ground-based telescopes as they provide darker skies, allowing for the observation of faint celestial objects without interference from artificial lights.

**Thus, the correct answer is (a) 1, 3 and 4 only.**

## Past Learning (Answers)

| | | | | | | | | | |
|---|---|---|---|---|---|---|---|---|---|
| 1 (d) | 2 (c) | 3 (d) | 4 (a) | 5 (d) | 6 (a) | 7 (a) | 8 (c) | 9 (d) | 10 (a) |
| 11 (b) | 12 (d) | 13 (a) | | | | | | | |

# CHAPTER 03 Defence Technology

## Assessment Round

### Topic 1 : Organisational Setup

**1.** Who holds the position of Supreme Commander of the Indian Armed Forces?
(a) Chief of Defence Staff
(b) Prime Minister of India
(c) President of India
(d) Defence Minister of India

**2.** Arrange the branches of the Indian Armed Forces in descending order of their personnel strength:
1. Indian Army
2. Indian Navy
3. Indian Air Force

Choose the correct order:
(a) 1-2-3
(b) 1-3-2
(c) 2-1-3
(d) 3-1-2

**3.** With reference to the 'Chief of Defence Staff (CDS)' in India, consider the following statements:
1. It is the principal military advisor to the government on all tri-service matters.
2. The CDS heads the Department of Military Affairs (DMA) under the Ministry of Defence.
3. The position of the CDS was established under the Defence Reorganisation Act, 2019.

Which of the above statements is/are correct?
(a) 1 only
(b) 1 and 2 only
(c) 2 and 3 only
(d) 1, 2 and 3

**4.** Consider the following committees:
1. Naresh Chandra Committee
2. D.B. Shekatkar Committee
3. Kargil Review Committee

How many of the above committees was/were specifically focused on structural and operational reforms in the Indian defence sector?
(a) Only one
(b) Only two
(c) All three
(d) None

**5.** Which of the following are members of the Cabinet Committee on Security (CCS)?
1. Prime Minister
2. Union Minister of Defence
3. Union Minister of Home Affairs
4. Union Minister of Finance
5. Union Minister of External Affairs

Select the correct answer using the codes given below:
(a) 1, 2 and 3 only
(b) 1, 3 and 4 only
(c) 1, 2, 3, 4 and 5
(d) 2, 3, 4 and 5 only

**6.** Which of the following statements are correct about 'India's Nuclear Command Authority (NCA)'?

1. The NCA is chaired by the Prime Minister of India.
2. The NCA is responsible for the deployment and operational command of nuclear weapons.
3. The Executive Council of the NCA is headed by the National Security Advisor (NSA).

Select the correct answer using the codes given below:

(a) 1 and 2 only (b) 2 and 3 only
(c) 1 and 3 only (d) 1, 2 and 3

## Topic 2 : Missile Programmes of India

**7.** With reference to the 'Ballistic Missiles', consider the following statements:

1. Ballistic missiles follow a parabolic trajectory.
2. They are only capable of carrying conventional warheads.
3. Ballistic missiles can be classified based on their range.

How many of the above statements is/are correct?

(a) Only one (b) Only two
(c) All three (d) None

**8.** With reference to cruise missiles, consider the following statements:

1. Cruise missiles fly at low altitudes to avoid radar detection.
2. They are designed to follow a pre-determined path and cannot adjust their course mid-flight.
3. Cruise missiles can carry both conventional and nuclear warheads.

How many of the above statements is/are correct?

(a) Only one
(b) Only two
(c) All three
(d) None

**9.** Consider the following missiles with their respective types:

| | Missile | Type |
|---|---|---|
| 1. | Prithvi | Surface-to-surface tactical missile |
| 2. | Agni | Ballistic missile |
| 3. | BrahMos | European Union |
| 4. | Nirbhay | Anti-ship missile |

How many of the pairs given above is/are correctly matched?

(a) Only one (b) Only two
(c) Only three (d) All four

**10.** Consider the following pairs of Indian missiles and their launch platforms:

| | Missile | Launch Platform |
|---|---|---|
| 1. | Agni | United States |
| 2. | Prithvi | Land-based and mobile launchers |
| 3. | Trishul | Sea-based platform |
| 4. | Akash | Land-based launcher with radar guidance |

How many of the pairs given above is/are correctly matched?

(a) Only one (b) Only two
(c) Only three (d) All four

**11.** Who is known as the 'Missile Man of India'?

(a) Dr. Vikram Sarabhai
(b) Dr. Homi J. Bhabha
(c) Dr. APJ Abdul Kalam
(d) Rakesh Sharma

**12.** Consider the following missiles developed as part of the Integrated Guided Missile Development Programme (IGMDP):

1. Prithvi 2. Agni
3. Trishul 4. Nag

How many of the above is/are surface-to-surface missiles?

(a) Only one (b) Only two
(c) Only three (d) All four

**13.** With reference to the differences between ballistic and cruise missiles, consider the following statements:

1. Ballistic missiles follow a parabolic trajectory, while cruise missiles travel close to the ground.
2. Ballistic missiles are powered only during the initial phase of flight, whereas cruise missiles are powered throughout their flight.
3. Cruise missiles are generally slower than ballistic missiles.

Which of the statements given above are correct?

(a) 1 and 2 only (b) 1 and 3 only
(c) 2 and 3 only (d) 1, 2 and 3

**14.** Which of the following are ballistic missiles developed by India?

1. Agni
2. Prithvi
3. BrahMos
4. Nirbhay

Select the correct answer using the codes given below:

(a) 1 and 2 only (b) 3 and 4 only
(c) 1, 2 and 3 only (d) 1, 2, 3 and 4

**15.** Which of the following missiles are cruise missiles?

1. BrahMos
2. Nirbhay
3. Shaurya
4. Dhanush

Select the correct answer using the codes given below:

(a) 1 and 2 only (b) 2 and 4 only
(c) 3 and 4 only (d) 1, 2 and 4 only

**16.** Which of the following statements are correct about the 'BrahMos Missile'?

1. It is a supersonic cruise missile jointly developed by India and Russia.
2. The BrahMos missile can be launched from land, sea, air, and submarine platforms.
3. It is designed exclusively for anti-ship roles.
4. The missile has a speed of around Mach 3.

Select the correct answer from the codes given below:

(a) 1 and 2 only (b) 1, 2 and 4 only
(c) 2 and 3 only (d) 1, 2, 3 and 4

**17.** Which of the following anti-tank missiles are developed by India?

1. Nag 2. Spike
3. Helina 4. Javelin

Select the correct answer using the codes given below:

(a) 1 and 3 only (b) 2 and 4 only
(c) 1, 2 and 3 only (d) 1, 2, 3 and 4

**18.** Consider the following missiles with their correct descriptions:

| | Satellite Navigation System | Description |
|---|---|---|
| 1. | Trishul | Surface-to-air missile used for short-range defense |
| 2. | Prahaar | Short-range ballistic missile designed for tactical strikes |
| 3. | Pranash | Short-range tactical missile with a range of 200 km |
| 4. | Shaurya | Hypersonic surface-to-surface missile with nuclear capability |

How many of the pairs given above is/are correctly matched?

(a) Only one (b) Only two
(c) Only three (d) All four

**19.** Which of the following are air-to-air missiles used by the Indian Air Force?

1. Astra
2. MICA
3. BrahMos
4. Python-5

Select the correct answer using the codes given below:

(a) 1 and 3 only (b) 1, 2 and 4 only
(c) 2, 3 and 4 only (d) 1, 2, 3 and 4

**20.** With reference to the Iron Dome air defense system, consider the following statements:

1. Iron Dome is capable of intercepting short-range rockets and artillery shells.
2. It was jointly developed by Israel and the United States.
3. The system is designed to operate only in urban areas.

How many of the above statements is/are correct?

(a) Only one (b) Only two
(c) All three (d) None

**21.** Which of the following best describes 'Multiple Independently Targetable Re-entry Vehicle (MIRV)' technology?

(a) A missile technology that allows a single missile to carry multiple warheads, each capable of striking different targets independently.
(b) A space exploration technology used to send multiple payloads into orbit simultaneously.
(c) A missile defense system designed to intercept and destroy incoming ballistic missiles.
(d) A satellite communication system designed for secure military communication.

**22.** Consider the following countries:

1. United States
2. Russia
3. India
4. Germany

How many of the above countries currently possess 'Intercontinental Ballistic Missiles (ICBMs)'?

(a) Only two (b) Only three
(c) Only four (d) All four

**23.** Which of the following missiles contribute to India's sea-based nuclear deterrence?

1. K-15 (Sagarika) 2. Agni-III
3. K-4 4. Dhanush

Select the correct answer using the codes given below:

(a) 1 and 3 only (b) 1, 3 and 4 only
(c) 2 and 4 only (d) 1, 2, 3 and 4

**24.** With reference to India's Ballistic Missile Defense (BMD) shield, consider the following statements:

1. The BMD shield is designed to intercept and neutralise incoming ballistic missiles at multiple altitudes.
2. India's BMD system has both exo-atmospheric and endo-atmospheric interception capabilities.
3. The BMD shield was developed in collaboration with Russia.

How many of the statements given above is/are correct?

(a) Only one (b) Only two
(c) All three (d) None

**25.** Consider the following statements:

1. Pinaka is a multiple rocket launcher system developed by India.
2. Rudra is an armed variant of the Dhruv helicopter used by the Indian Army.
3. ASAT is an air-to-air missile developed by DRDO.

How many of the given above statements is/are correct?

(a) Only one (b) Only two
(c) All three (d) None

**26.** With regard to India's ASAT (Anti-Satellite Weapon) capabilities, consider the following statements:

1. ASAT can intercept and destroy satellites in low Earth orbit (LEO).
2. ASAT was first tested by India in 2019 under Mission Shakti.
3. ASAT is specifically designed to target ballistic missiles.

How many of the given statements is/are correct?

(a) Only one (b) Only two
(c) All three (d) None

**27.** Which of the following best describes the Pinaka Mk-II variant's capability?

(a) Short-range anti-ship missile
(b) Long-range artillery rocket system with precision targeting
(c) Low-altitude air defense system
(d) Underwater mine detection

## Topic 3 : Naval Programme

**28.** Which of the following best describes Archimedes' Principle?

(a) An object immersed in fluid experiences a force equal to the weight of the fluid displaced by it
(b) Objects fall at the same rate in a vacuum regardless of mass
(c) Energy cannot be created or destroyed, only transformed
(d) The pressure in a fluid decrease as the speed of the fluid increases

**29.** Which of the following statements best describes the primary differences between frigates and destroyers?

1. Frigates are primarily used for escorting and patrolling, while destroyers focus on multi-threat combat capabilities.
2. Destroyers are smaller and faster, designed for rapid-response missions, while frigates handle long-range power projection.
3. Frigates are often employed in anti-submarine roles, while destroyers provide layered air defense.
4. Both frigates and destroyers are designed exclusively for defensive roles.

Select the correct answer from the codes given below:

(a) 1 and 3 only
(b) 1, 2 and 4 only
(c) 2 and 4 only
(d) 1, 2, 3 and 4

**30.** Which of the following statements are correct regarding India's aircraft carriers?

1. INS Vikrant is India's first indigenously built aircraft carrier.
2. INS Viraat was retired in 2017 after serving in the Indian Navy for nearly 30 years.
3. INS Vikramaditya was purchased from the United States and commissioned into the Indian Navy.

Select the correct answer from the codes given below:

(a) 1 and 2 only
(b) 1, 2 and 3
(c) 2 and 3 only
(d) 1 and 3 only

**31.** Which of the following best describes the key difference between diesel-electric and nuclear-powered submarines?

(a) Diesel-electric submarines can remain submerged indefinitely, while nuclear-powered submarines must surface regularly.
(b) Nuclear-powered submarines use nuclear reactors for propulsion, allowing longer endurance, while diesel-electric submarines rely on battery-powered electric propulsion.
(c) Diesel-electric submarines are faster and more powerful than nuclear-powered submarines.
(d) Nuclear-powered submarines are exclusively used for reconnaissance missions, while diesel-electric submarines are used for combat.

**32.** Which of the following features are unique to nuclear-powered submarines compared to diesel-electric submarines?

1. Very high underwater endurance.
2. Requires regular surfacing for air and battery recharge.
3. Larger size and capability to carry more weapons.
4. Quieter operation in shallow waters.

Select the correct answer using the codes given below:

(a) 1 and 3 only
(b) 2 and 4 only
(c) 1, 2 and 3 only
(d) 1, 3 and 4 only

**33.** Match the following Indian submarines with their respective types:

| | Submarine | | Type |
|---|---|---|---|
| A. | INS Arihant | 1. | Nuclear-powered ballistic missile submarine (SSBN) |
| B. | INS Kalvari | 2. | Diesel-electric attack submarine (SSK) |
| C. | INS Chakra | 3. | Nuclear-powered attack submarine (SSN) |
| D. | INS Sindhughosh | 4. | Diesel-electric submarine (Kilo-class) |

Select the correctly matched pairs from below:
(a) A-1, B-2, C-3, D-4
(b) A-2, B-3, C-4, D-1
(c) A-3, B-4, C-1, D-2
(d) A-1, B-4, C-2, D-3

**34.** With reference to Project 75, consider the following statements:
1. It involves the construction of Scorpène-class submarines for the Indian Navy.
2. The submarines under Project 75 are being built in collaboration with France.
3. INS Kalvari is the first submarine commissioned under Project 75.

Which of the above statements are correct?
(a) 1 and 2 only
(b) 2 and 3 only
(c) 1 and 3 only
(d) All of the above

**35.** With reference to Project 15, consider the following statements:
1. Project 15 focuses on building guided-missile destroyers for the Indian Navy.
2. INS Kolkata is the lead ship of Project 15.
3. The destroyers under Project 15 are named after Indian cities.

Which of the above statements are correct?
(a) 1 and 2 only (b) 1 and 3 only
(c) 2 and 3 only (d) All of these

**36.** With reference to torpedoes used in naval warfare, consider the following statements:
1. Torpedoes are self-propelled underwater weapons designed to strike targets at sea.
2. The speed and range of a torpedo are unaffected by the density of seawater.
3. Torpedoes can be launched from submarines, ships and aircraft.

How many of the given statements is/are correct?
(a) Only one
(b) Only two
(c) All three
(d) None

**37.** Consider the following statements about India's Varunastra torpedo:
1. It is an indigenously developed heavyweight torpedo.
2. It is designed specifically for use by submarines.
3. Varunastra can engage surface vessels and submarines.

How many of the above statements is/are correct?
(a) Only one
(b) Only two
(c) All three
(d) None

## Topic 4 : Aircrafts and Tanks

**38.** With reference to Indian combat aircraft, consider the following statements:
1. Tejas is an indigenously developed multi-role fighter jet.
2. The Su-30MKI was developed by India in collaboration with the United States.
3. The Rafale is a twin-engine aircraft acquired by India from France.

How many of the statements given above is/are correct?
(a) Only one
(b) Only two
(c) All three
(d) None

**39.** Which of the following statements are correct about the HAL Tejas fighter aircraft?
1. Tejas is an indigenously developed light combat aircraft.
2. It is powered by an engine developed by India.
3. Tejas can carry both air-to-air and air-to-ground weapons.
4. It is a twin-engine aircraft designed for high-speed interception missions.

Select the correct answer using the codes given below:
(a) 1 and 3 only (b) 1, 2 and 4 only
(c) 2, 3 and 4 only (d) 1, 2, 3 and 4

**40.** Which of the following best describes the purpose of stealth technology in defense systems?
(a) To reduce the noise generated by military vehicles.
(b) To enhance the manoeuvrability of fighter jets in combat scenarios.
(c) To protect military equipment from extreme weather conditions.
(d) To make an aircraft or vessel invisible to radar, infrared and other detection systems.

**41.** Which of the following are features of stealth technology used in defense systems?
1. Use of radar-absorbent materials (RAM).
2. Angled surfaces to deflect radar waves.
3. Reduction of infrared emissions.
4. Increased speed to outrun radar detection.

Select the correct answer using the codes given below:
(a) 1 and 2 only
(b) 1, 2 and 3 only
(c) 2, 3 and 4 only
(d) 1, 2, 3 and 4

**42.** Consider the following aircrafts:
1. F-22 Raptor
2. Tejas
3. Dassault Rafale
4. F-35 Lightning II

How many of the above is/are classified as fifth-generation fighter aircrafts?
(a) Only one (b) Only two
(c) Only three (d) All four

**43.** Which of the following are key roles of the 'Airborne Warning and Control System (AWACS)'?
1. Airspace surveillance and threat detection.
2. Coordinating fighter jets and ground operations.
3. Delivering aerial refuelling to military aircraft.
4. Acting as a mobile command centre during combat operations.

Select the correct answer using the codes given below:
(a) 1 and 2 only (b) 1, 2 and 4 only
(c) 2, 3 and 4 only (d) 1, 3 and 4 only

**44.** With reference to MUNTRA (Mission Unmanned Tracked) developed by India, consider the following statements:
1. It is India's first indigenously developed unmanned ground vehicle (UGV).
2. It is primarily designed for mine detection and reconnaissance.
3. It can operate underwater for detecting naval mines.

How many of the above statements is/are correct?
(a) Only one (b) Only two
(c) All three (d) None

**45.** With reference to tanks used by the Indian Army, consider the following statements:
1. The Arjun tank is an indigenously developed main battle tank (MBT) of India.
2. T-90 Bhishma is a Russian-made tank customised for the Indian Army.
3. The T-72 Ajeya tank is primarily used for reconnaissance missions in the Indian Army.

How many of the given statements is/are correct?
(a) Only one (b) Only two
(c) All three (d) None

## Topic 5 : Drone Technology

**46.** With reference to India's indigenous drone technology, consider the following statements:

1. The Rustom drone is developed by DRDO for reconnaissance and surveillance missions.
2. Nishant is an armed drone developed for strike operations.
3. The Panchi UAV is a wheeled variant of Nishant designed for runway takeoff and landing.

How many of the statements given above is/are correct?

(a) Only one (b) Only two
(c) All three (d) None

**47.** Which of the following UAVs are developed indigenously in India?

1. Rustom
2. Heron
3. Nishant
4. Harop

Select the correct answer from the codes given below:

(a) 1 and 3 only
(b) 1, 2 and 3 only
(c) 2, 3 and 4 only
(d) 1, 2, 3 and 4

**48.** Consider the following categories of drones in India with their respective weight classifications:

| Space Telescope | Operational Orbits |
|---|---|
| 1. Nano | Up to 250 grams |
| 2. Micro | 250 grams to 2 kilograms |
| 3. Small | 2 kilograms to 25 kilograms |
| 4. Medium | 25 kilograms to 150 kilograms |

How many of the above pairs is/are correctly matched?

(a) Only one (b) Only two
(c) Only three (d) All four

**49.** With reference to military drones in India, consider the following statements:

1. Rustom is an indigenously developed medium-altitude long-endurance (MALE) drone.
2. Nishant is designed for high-altitude intelligence gathering.
3. Heron is an armed drone acquired from Israel.

How many of the given statements is/are correct?

(a) Only one (b) Only two
(c) All three (d) None

**50.** Consider the following drones and their features used by the Indian military:

1. Nishant is designed for low-altitude tactical reconnaissance.
2. Rustom-2 has a combat capability and can carry precision-guided munitions.
3. Harop can loiter over target areas and perform kamikaze missions.
4. Heron is a high-altitude surveillance drone with around 48 hours of endurance.

How many of the above statements is/are correct?

(a) Only one (b) Only two
(c) Only three (d) All four

**51.** Consider the following Indian military drones with their primary roles:

| Drone | Primary Role |
|---|---|
| 1. Rustom-2 | Tactical reconnaissance in low-altitude regions |
| 2. Nishant | High-altitude, long-endurance surveillance |
| 3. Harop | Loitering munition for kamikaze missions |
| 4. Heron | Intelligence, surveillance, and reconnaissance in medium-altitude regions |

How many of the above pairs is/are correctly matched?

(a) Only one (b) Only two
(c) Only three (d) All four

**52.** Consider the following Indian military drones with their country of origin:

| Drone | Country of Origin |
|---|---|
| 1. Heron | United States |
| 2. Rustom | India |
| 3. Predator | Russia |
| 4. Harop | Israel |

How many of the above pairs is/are correctly matched?

(a) Only one (b) Only two
(c) Only three (d) All four

**53.** Which of the following roles do drones perform in the field of disaster management?

1. Providing real-time imagery of disaster-hit areas
2. Delivering essential supplies to remote or isolated locations
3. Conducting rapid search and rescue operations
4. Enforcing crowd control during large gatherings

Select the correct answer from the codes given below:

(a) 1 and 2 only
(b) 1, 2 and 3 only
(c) 2, 3 and 4 only
(d) 1, 2, 3 and 4

**54.** Which of the following are applications of drones in environmental conservation?

1. Monitoring deforestation and illegal logging
2. Surveying wildlife and tracking endangered species
3. Measuring air quality in urban areas
4. Identifying illegal fishing activities in coastal waters

Select the correct answer using the codes given below:

(a) 1 and 2 only
(b) 1, 2 and 4 only
(c) 2, 3 and 4 only
(d) 1, 2, 3 and 4

**55.** With reference to Drone Rules 2021 in India, consider the following statements:

1. All drone operators are required to register their drones and obtain a unique identification number (UIN).
2. Drones weighing less than 250 grams and used for recreational purposes are exempt from UIN requirements.
3. Drone corridors are planned to facilitate cargo deliveries.

How many of the above statements is/are correct?

(a) Only one (b) Only two
(c) All three (d) None

## Topic 6 : Other Defence Developments

**56.** Consider the following radar types with their unique characteristics:

| Radar Type | Unique Characteristic |
|---|---|
| 1. Doppler Radar | Measures velocity using frequency shift |
| 2. Pulse Radar | Emits short bursts of energy to detect range |
| 3. Continuous Wave Radar | Measures relative speed without range detection |
| 4. Synthetic Aperture Radar (SAR) | Creates detailed images of terrain using movement |

How many of the above pairs is/are correctly matched?

(a) Only one (b) Only two
(c) Only three (d) All four

**57.** Which of the following best describes the purpose of the Rajendra Radar system?

(a) To provide weather forecasting data to Indian Meteorological Department (IMD).
(b) To track and guide surface-to-air missiles in real-time during combat operations.
(c) To enhance the navigation capabilities of Indian naval ships.
(d) To monitor and secure India's space assets from potential threats.

**58.** Which of the following best describes the 'Doppler Effect'?
(a) A phenomenon where the wavelength of light changes due to the movement of a source.
(b) A change in the frequency or wavelength of a wave in relation to an observer moving relative to the source of the wave.
(c) A phenomenon where the speed of light changes based on the observer's position.
(d) A shift in energy levels due to gravitational force.

**59.** With reference to the Sonar technology, consider the following statements:
1. It stands for Sound Navigation and Ranging.
2. This technology is used only in military applications.
3. Sonar can be used for both detection and communication underwater.

How many of the above statements is/are correct?
(a) Only one
(b) Only two
(c) All three
(d) None

**60.** Consider the following statements about active and passive Sonar systems:
1. Active Sonar emits sound waves and listens for echoes to detect objects.
2. Passive Sonar detects sounds made by objects without emitting any sound waves.
3. Both active and passive Sonar are used to measure ocean depth.

How many of the given above statements is/are correct?
(a) Only one
(b) Only two
(c) All three
(d) None

**61.** Which of the following statements are correct about electronic warfare systems in India?
1. Sangraha is primarily used by the Indian Army to enhance land-based operations.
2. Shakti is developed for the Indian Navy to protect against maritime threats.
3. Netra provides airborne surveillance and electronic support measures.
4. Kavach is used to protect naval ships by creating radar decoys.

Select the correct answer using the codes given below:
(a) 1 and 2 only
(b) 2, 3 and 4 only
(c) 1, 3 and 4 only
(d) 1, 2, 3 and 4

**62.** Which of the following statements correctly describe the characteristics of thermobaric bombs?
1. They use oxygen from the atmosphere to generate an explosion.
2. They are primarily used for deep underground penetration.
3. They produce a prolonged blast wave and intense heat.
4. They are also known as fuel-air explosives.

Select the correct answer using the codes given below:
(a) 1 and 2 only
(b) 1, 3 and 4 only
(c) 2, 3 and 4 only
(d) 1, 2, 3 and 4

**63.** Which of the following characteristics of hydrogen bomb differentiate it from an atomic bomb?
1. It uses fusion instead of fission as the primary source of energy.
2. It requires an initial fission reaction to initiate the fusion process.
3. It produces far more destructive power than a fission bomb.
4. It contains a chain reaction that is difficult to control once initiated.

Select the correct answer using the codes given below:
(a) 1 and 2 only
(b) 1, 2 and 3 only
(c) 2, 3 and 4 only
(d) 1, 2, 3 and 4

**64.** With reference to nuclear bombs, consider the following statements:

1. Nuclear bombs release energy primarily through nuclear fission or fusion.
2. The first nuclear bomb used in warfare was a fusion bomb.
3. Nuclear bombs have long-lasting environmental impacts, including radiation fallout.

How many of the above statements is/are correct?

(a) Only one (b) Only two
(c) All three (d) None

**65.** With reference to the hydrogen bomb, consider the following statements:

1. A hydrogen bomb uses nuclear fusion to release energy.
2. It is significantly more powerful than an atomic bomb.
3. The initial stage of a hydrogen bomb uses nuclear fission to trigger fusion.

How many of the above statements is/are correct?

(a) Only one (b) Only two
(c) All three (d) None

**66.** Which of the following countries are currently not signatories to the Chemical Weapons Convention (CWC) of 1993?

1. Egypt
2. North Korea
3. South Sudan
4. Israel

Select the correct answer using the codes given below:

(a) 1 and 2 only (b) 1, 2 and 3 only
(c) 2, 3 and 4 only (d) 1, 2, 3 and 4

**67.** Consider the following objectives:

1. To verify the destruction of chemical weapons stockpiles.
2. To monitor the use of dual-use chemicals in member states.
3. To promote international cooperation for peaceful use of chemicals.
4. To provide military assistance to member states against chemical attacks.

How many of the given objectives is/are correct of the Organisation for the Prohibition of Chemical Weapons (OPCW)?

(a) Only one (b) Only two
(c) Only three (d) All four

**68.** Which of the following countries are currently not signatory or state parties to the Biological Weapons Convention (BWC) of 1972?

1. Israel 2. North Korea
3. South Sudan 4. Myanmar

Select the correct answer using the codes given below:

(a) 1 and 2 only (b) 1 and 3 only
(c) 2, 3 and 4 only (d) 1, 2, 3 and 4

**69.** With reference to the Biological Weapons Convention (BWC), consider the following statements:

1. The BWC permits research on biological agents strictly for peaceful purposes.
2. The BWC includes penalties for violations of its provisions.
3. The BWC mandates periodic reviews to address advances in biological sciences.

How many of the above statements is/are correct?

(a) Only one (b) Only two
(c) All three (d) None

**70.** Which of the following types of warfare were banned by the Geneva Protocol of 1925?

1. Chemical warfare
2. Biological warfare
3. Nuclear warfare
4. Conventional warfare

Select the correct answer using the codes given below:

(a) 1 and 2 only (b) 1, 2 and 3 only
(c) 2, 3 and 4 only (d) 1, 2, 3 and 4

**71.** Consider the following:

1. Nerve agents 2. Blister agents
3. Choking agents 4. Incendiary agents

How many of the given categories is/are classified as chemical warfare agents?

(a) Only one (b) Only two
(c) Only three (d) All four

**72.** Consider the following:
1. Bacteria
2. Viruses
3. Fungi
4. Nerve agents

How many of the given is/are correctly classified as biological warfare agents?
(a) Only one (b) Only two
(c) Only three (d) All four

**73.** With reference to biological warfare agents, consider the following statements:
1. Biological warfare agents are living organisms or toxins that can cause diseases.
2. Biological warfare has been banned internationally under the Geneva Protocol.
3. Anthrax is a common example of a biological warfare agent.

How many of the above statements is/are correct?
(a) Only one (b) Only two
(c) All three (d) None

**74.** Which of the following export control regimes is India a member of ?
1. Missile Technology Control Regime (MTCR)
2. Nuclear Suppliers Group (NSG)
3. Wassenaar Arrangement
4. Australia Group

Select the correct answer using the codes given below:
(a) 1 and 2 only (b) 1, 3 and 4 only
(c) 2, 3 and 4 only (d) 1, 2, 3 and 4

**75.** Consider the following:
1. Limiting the transfer of missile technology
2. Preventing the export of conventional arms
3. Controlling the export of dual-use technologies
4. Promoting transparency in global arms trade

How many of the above goals is/are correctly associated with the Wassenaar Arrangement?
(a) Only one (b) Only two
(c) Only three (d) All four

**76.** Consider the following statements:
1. India joined the Australia Group in 2018.
2. The Wassenaar Arrangement primarily focuses on nuclear non-proliferation.
3. India is currently the only non-NPT country to be a member of the Missile Technology Control Regime (MTCR).

How many of the given statements is/are correct?
(a) Only one
(b) Only two
(c) All three
(d) None

**77.** With reference to carbon bombs, consider the following statements:
1. Carbon bombs release fine carbon filaments that disrupt electrical circuits.
2. They are lethal weapons designed to maximise human casualties.
3. Carbon bombs are primarily intended to incapacitate enemy infrastructure.

How many of the given statements is/are correct?
(a) Only one
(b) Only two
(c) All three
(d) None

**78.** Which of the following statements accurately describe the characteristics of white phosphorus bombs?
1. They produce intense heat and light upon detonation.
2. They are used to create smoke screens on the battlefield.
3. White phosphorus can cause severe chemical burns.
4. These bombs are prohibited under all international laws.

Select the correct answer using the codes given below:
(a) 1 and 2 only
(b) 1, 2 and 3 only
(c) 2, 3 and 4 only
(d) 1, 2, 3 and 4

**79.** Match the following international groups with their primary focus areas:

| Group | Focus Area |
|---|---|
| 1. Nuclear Suppliers Group (NSG) | A. Regulates trade in conventional arms and dual-use goods |
| 2. Australia Group | B. Prevents the proliferation of nuclear materials and technology |
| 3. Missile Technology Control Regime (MTCR) | C. Controls exports related to chemical and biological weapons |
| 4. Wassenaar Arrangement | D. Prevents the spread of missile and unmanned aerial vehicle technology |

Select the correct answer using the codes given below:

(a) 1-B, 2-C, 3-D, 4-A
(b) 1-A, 2-B, 3-C, 4-D
(c) 1-C, 2-B, 3-A, 4-D
(d) 1-D, 2-A, 3-B, 4-C

**80.** Consider the following features statements about CAATSA (Countering America's Adversaries Through Sanctions Act, 2017):

1. It mandates sanctions on nations purchasing major defence equipment from Russia.
2. CAATSA sanctions are mandatory for all countries that engage in transactions with Russia's defense sector.
3. India has been granted a permanent waiver from CAATSA sanctions for its defense purchases from Russia.

Which of the given above statements are correct?

(a) 1 and 2 only
(b) 1 and 3 only
(c) 2 and 3 only
(d) 1, 2 and 3

# OMR SHEET

**Assessment Round**

| Q. | Options | Q. | Options | Q. | Options | Q. | Options |
|---|---|---|---|---|---|---|---|
| 1 | ⓐ ⓑ ⓒ ⓓ | 31 | ⓐ ⓑ ⓒ ⓓ | 61 | ⓐ ⓑ ⓒ ⓓ | 91 | ⓐ ⓑ ⓒ ⓓ |
| 2 | ⓐ ⓑ ⓒ ⓓ | 32 | ⓐ ⓑ ⓒ ⓓ | 62 | ⓐ ⓑ ⓒ ⓓ | 92 | ⓐ ⓑ ⓒ ⓓ |
| 3 | ⓐ ⓑ ⓒ ⓓ | 33 | ⓐ ⓑ ⓒ ⓓ | 63 | ⓐ ⓑ ⓒ ⓓ | 93 | ⓐ ⓑ ⓒ ⓓ |
| 4 | ⓐ ⓑ ⓒ ⓓ | 34 | ⓐ ⓑ ⓒ ⓓ | 64 | ⓐ ⓑ ⓒ ⓓ | 94 | ⓐ ⓑ ⓒ ⓓ |
| 5 | ⓐ ⓑ ⓒ ⓓ | 35 | ⓐ ⓑ ⓒ ⓓ | 65 | ⓐ ⓑ ⓒ ⓓ | 95 | ⓐ ⓑ ⓒ ⓓ |
| 6 | ⓐ ⓑ ⓒ ⓓ | 36 | ⓐ ⓑ ⓒ ⓓ | 66 | ⓐ ⓑ ⓒ ⓓ | 96 | ⓐ ⓑ ⓒ ⓓ |
| 7 | ⓐ ⓑ ⓒ ⓓ | 37 | ⓐ ⓑ ⓒ ⓓ | 67 | ⓐ ⓑ ⓒ ⓓ | 97 | ⓐ ⓑ ⓒ ⓓ |
| 8 | ⓐ ⓑ ⓒ ⓓ | 38 | ⓐ ⓑ ⓒ ⓓ | 68 | ⓐ ⓑ ⓒ ⓓ | 98 | ⓐ ⓑ ⓒ ⓓ |
| 9 | ⓐ ⓑ ⓒ ⓓ | 39 | ⓐ ⓑ ⓒ ⓓ | 69 | ⓐ ⓑ ⓒ ⓓ | 99 | ⓐ ⓑ ⓒ ⓓ |
| 10 | ⓐ ⓑ ⓒ ⓓ | 40 | ⓐ ⓑ ⓒ ⓓ | 70 | ⓐ ⓑ ⓒ ⓓ | 100 | ⓐ ⓑ ⓒ ⓓ |
| 11 | ⓐ ⓑ ⓒ ⓓ | 41 | ⓐ ⓑ ⓒ ⓓ | 71 | ⓐ ⓑ ⓒ ⓓ | 101 | ⓐ ⓑ ⓒ ⓓ |
| 12 | ⓐ ⓑ ⓒ ⓓ | 42 | ⓐ ⓑ ⓒ ⓓ | 72 | ⓐ ⓑ ⓒ ⓓ | 102 | ⓐ ⓑ ⓒ ⓓ |
| 13 | ⓐ ⓑ ⓒ ⓓ | 43 | ⓐ ⓑ ⓒ ⓓ | 73 | ⓐ ⓑ ⓒ ⓓ | 103 | ⓐ ⓑ ⓒ ⓓ |
| 14 | ⓐ ⓑ ⓒ ⓓ | 44 | ⓐ ⓑ ⓒ ⓓ | 74 | ⓐ ⓑ ⓒ ⓓ | 104 | ⓐ ⓑ ⓒ ⓓ |
| 15 | ⓐ ⓑ ⓒ ⓓ | 45 | ⓐ ⓑ ⓒ ⓓ | 75 | ⓐ ⓑ ⓒ ⓓ | 105 | ⓐ ⓑ ⓒ ⓓ |
| 16 | ⓐ ⓑ ⓒ ⓓ | 46 | ⓐ ⓑ ⓒ ⓓ | 76 | ⓐ ⓑ ⓒ ⓓ | 106 | ⓐ ⓑ ⓒ ⓓ |
| 17 | ⓐ ⓑ ⓒ ⓓ | 47 | ⓐ ⓑ ⓒ ⓓ | 77 | ⓐ ⓑ ⓒ ⓓ | 107 | ⓐ ⓑ ⓒ ⓓ |
| 18 | ⓐ ⓑ ⓒ ⓓ | 48 | ⓐ ⓑ ⓒ ⓓ | 78 | ⓐ ⓑ ⓒ ⓓ | 108 | ⓐ ⓑ ⓒ ⓓ |
| 19 | ⓐ ⓑ ⓒ ⓓ | 49 | ⓐ ⓑ ⓒ ⓓ | 79 | ⓐ ⓑ ⓒ ⓓ | 109 | ⓐ ⓑ ⓒ ⓓ |
| 20 | ⓐ ⓑ ⓒ ⓓ | 50 | ⓐ ⓑ ⓒ ⓓ | 80 | ⓐ ⓑ ⓒ ⓓ | 110 | ⓐ ⓑ ⓒ ⓓ |
| 21 | ⓐ ⓑ ⓒ ⓓ | 51 | ⓐ ⓑ ⓒ ⓓ | 81 | ⓐ ⓑ ⓒ ⓓ | 111 | ⓐ ⓑ ⓒ ⓓ |
| 22 | ⓐ ⓑ ⓒ ⓓ | 52 | ⓐ ⓑ ⓒ ⓓ | 82 | ⓐ ⓑ ⓒ ⓓ | 112 | ⓐ ⓑ ⓒ ⓓ |
| 23 | ⓐ ⓑ ⓒ ⓓ | 53 | ⓐ ⓑ ⓒ ⓓ | 83 | ⓐ ⓑ ⓒ ⓓ | 113 | ⓐ ⓑ ⓒ ⓓ |
| 24 | ⓐ ⓑ ⓒ ⓓ | 54 | ⓐ ⓑ ⓒ ⓓ | 84 | ⓐ ⓑ ⓒ ⓓ | 114 | ⓐ ⓑ ⓒ ⓓ |
| 25 | ⓐ ⓑ ⓒ ⓓ | 55 | ⓐ ⓑ ⓒ ⓓ | 85 | ⓐ ⓑ ⓒ ⓓ | 115 | ⓐ ⓑ ⓒ ⓓ |
| 26 | ⓐ ⓑ ⓒ ⓓ | 56 | ⓐ ⓑ ⓒ ⓓ | 86 | ⓐ ⓑ ⓒ ⓓ | 116 | ⓐ ⓑ ⓒ ⓓ |
| 27 | ⓐ ⓑ ⓒ ⓓ | 57 | ⓐ ⓑ ⓒ ⓓ | 87 | ⓐ ⓑ ⓒ ⓓ | 117 | ⓐ ⓑ ⓒ ⓓ |
| 28 | ⓐ ⓑ ⓒ ⓓ | 58 | ⓐ ⓑ ⓒ ⓓ | 88 | ⓐ ⓑ ⓒ ⓓ | 118 | ⓐ ⓑ ⓒ ⓓ |
| 29 | ⓐ ⓑ ⓒ ⓓ | 59 | ⓐ ⓑ ⓒ ⓓ | 89 | ⓐ ⓑ ⓒ ⓓ | 119 | ⓐ ⓑ ⓒ ⓓ |
| 30 | ⓐ ⓑ ⓒ ⓓ | 60 | ⓐ ⓑ ⓒ ⓓ | 90 | ⓐ ⓑ ⓒ ⓓ | 120 | ⓐ ⓑ ⓒ ⓓ |

## Calculate Your Score

| | |
|---|---|
| **Correct (✓)** | |
| **Incorrect (✓)** | |
| **Unattempted** | |
| **Total Score** | |
| **Accuracy (%)** | |

## Reasons for Incorrect Answers?

| | |
|---|---|
| 1. Lack of Knowledge/Existing Source Insufficient | |
| 2. Lack of Multiple Revision | |
| 3. Common Sense Mistakes | |

**Note :**

1. Calculate total score as correct answers carry 2 marks each 1/3rd marks will deducted for **Incorrect** Answers.
2. Calculate Accuracy (%) by dividing the number of correct answers to the total number of attempted questions.

## Past Learning

**1.** Consider the following activities. **(2024)**

1. Identification of narcotics on passengers at airports or in aircraft
2. Monitoring of precipitation
3. Tracking the migration of animals

In how many of the above activities can the radars be used?

(a) Only one (b) Only two
(c) All three (d) None of these

**2.** Consider the following aircraft: **(2024)**

1. Rafael 2. MiG-29
3. Tejas MK-I

How many of the above is/are considered fifth generation fighter aircraft?

(a) Only one (b) Only two
(c) All three (d) None of these

**3.** Which of the following statements about 'Exercise Mitra Shakti-2023' are correct?

1. This was a joint military exercise between India and Bangladesh. **(2024)**
2. It commenced in Aundh (Pune).
3. Joint response during counter-terrorism operation was a goal of this operation.
4. Indian Air Force was a part of this exercise.

Select the answer using the codes given below:

(a) 1, 2 and 3 (b) 1, 2 and 4
(c) 1, 3 and 4 (d) 2, 3 and 4

**4.** Consider the following statements. **(2023)**

1. Ballistic missiles are jet-propelled at subsonic speeds throughout their flights, while cruise missiles are rocket-powered only in the initial phase of flight.
2. Agni-V is a medium-range supersonic cruise missile, while BrahMos is solid-fuelled intercontinental ballistic missile.

Which of the statements given above is/are correct?

(a) Only 1 (b) Only 2
(c) Both 1 and 2 (d) Neither 1 nor 2

**5.** Which one of the following statements best reflects the idea behind the 'Fractional Orbital Bombardment System' often talked about in media? **(2022)**

(a) A hypersonic missile is launched into space to counter the asteroid approaching the Earth and explode it in space.
(b) A spacecraft lands on another planet after making several orbital motions.
(c) A missile is put into a stable orbit around the Earth and deorbits over a target on the Earth.
(d) A spacecraft moves along a comet with the same speed and places a probe on its surface.

**6.** What is Terminal High Altitude Area Defense (THAAD), sometimes seen in the news? **(2018)**

(a) An Israeli Radar System
(b) India's indigenous anti-missile programme
(c) An American anti-missile system
(d) A defence collaboration between Japan and South Korea

**7.** Which one of the following is the best description of 'INS Astradharini', that was in the news recently? **(2016)**

(a) Amphibious warfare ship
(b) Nuclear-powered submarine
(c) Torpedo launch and recovery vessel
(d) Nuclear-powered aircraft carrier

**8.** With reference to Agni-IV Missile, which of the following statements is/are correct?

1. It is a surface-to-surface missile. **(2014)**
2. It is fuelled by liquid propellant only.
3. It can deliver one-tonne nuclear warheads about 7500 km away.

Select the correct answer using the codes given below.

(a) Only 1 (b) 2 and 3 only
(c) 1 and 3 only (d) 1, 2 and 3

# Detailed **Solutions**

## Assessment Round

**1.** *(c)* President of India

The **President of India** is designated as the **Supreme Commander of the Indian Armed Forces** under the Constitution of India. This role includes the authority to oversee and exercise supreme command over the Army, Navy, and Air Force of India. However, the operational command and decision-making are primarily handled by the Ministry of Defence, and the Chief of Defence Staff, with the President's role being largely ceremonial, and constitutional.

**Therefore, the correct answer is (c) President of India.**

**2.** *(b)* 1-3-2

- **Indian Army** has the largest personnel strength among the three branches of the Indian Armed Forces, as it is responsible for ground-based defense and has a large force due to the country's territorial, and border security needs.
- **Indian Air Force** has the second-largest personnel strength, focusing on aerial defense, airspace protection and air support for other branches.
- **Indian Navy** has the smallest personnel strength of the three branches, as it focuses on maritime security and requires a smaller, but highly specialised force.

**Thus, the correct order is (b) 1-3-2.**

**3.** *(b)* 1 and 2 only

- **Statement 1 is correct:** The **Chief of Defence Staff (CDS)** acts as the **principal military advisor** to the government, especially for matters involving coordination among the three services-Army, Navy and Air Force. The CDS is tasked with ensuring synergy and unified planning in operations, procurement, and policy formulation across the services.
- **Statement 2 is correct:** The CDS heads the **Department of Military Affairs (DMA)**, a specialised department under the **Ministry of Defence.** The DMA oversees policy-making for the armed forces, including matters related to procurement, restructuring and the implementation of joint operations. This role ensures greater integration and efficiency within the defence setup.
- **Statement 3 is incorrect:** The position of the CDS was announced by the Indian Government in 2019, but it was not established under any specific legislation like a **Defence Reorganisation Act, 2019.** Instead, it was implemented as a part of military reforms to modernise the armed forces and enhance inter-service coordination.

**Thus, the correct answer is (b) 1 and 2 only.**

**4.** *(c)* All three

- **Naresh Chandra Committee:** This committee, constituted in 2011, was focused on **defence and national security reforms,** including modernisation, intelligence-sharing mechanisms, and enhancing operational capabilities of the armed forces. It recommended strengthening the role of the Chief of Defence Staff (CDS).
- **D.B. Shekatkar Committee:** Established in 2016, this committee focused on **enhancing combat capabilities** and rebalancing defence expenditure. It provided recommendations to improve efficiency and reduce wasteful expenditure in the Indian armed forces.
- **Kargil Review Committee:** Formed in 1999 post the Kargil conflict, this committee aimed at **reviewing the state of national security,** with a focus on intelligence-sharing, border security and modernising the armed forces.
- **Justice Reddy Committee:** This committee was primarily related to **defence land disputes and cantonment-related issues,** rather than operational, and structural reforms.

**Thus, the correct answer is (c) All three.**

**5.** *(c)* 1, 2, 3, 4 and 5

- The **Cabinet Committee on Security (CCS)** is one of the most important committees in the Indian Government, tasked with decision-making on national security and defense matters.
- **Prime Minister:** Heads the CCS and plays a central role in decision-making.
- **Union Minister of Defence:** Responsible for military policies and national defense strategy.
- **Union Minister of Home Affairs:** Manages internal security, and counter-terrorism strategies.
- **Union Minister of Finance:** Ensures financial oversight and resource allocation for security and defense needs.
- **Union Minister of External Affairs:** Handles foreign policy decisions related to national security.

**Thus, the correct answer is (c) 1, 2, 3, 4 and 5.**

**6.** *(c)* 1 and 3 only

- **Statement 1 is correct:** The **Political Council** of the **Nuclear Command Authority** (NCA), which is the apex decision-making body, is chaired by the **Prime Minister of India.**
- **Statement 2 is incorrect:** The NCA is responsible for **policy-making** and overseeing India's nuclear strategy, but the actual deployment, and operational command of nuclear weapons are delegated to the armed forces through the Strategic Forces Command (SFC).
- **Statement 3 is correct:** The **Executive Council**, which advises the Political Council, is headed by the **National Security Advisor** (NSA). It ensures the implementation of decisions related to nuclear operations.

**Thus, the correct answer is (c) 1 and 3 only.**

**7.** *(b)* Only two

- **Statement 1 is correct: Ballistic missiles** follow a **parabolic trajectory** after an initial powered boost phase. They ascend into the upper atmosphere or space and then descend towards their target in a ballistic path.
- **Statement 2 is incorrect:** Ballistic missiles can carry both **conventional and nuclear warheads**, depending on the intended use.
- **Statement 3 is correct:** Ballistic missiles are classified by range, including **short-range, medium-range**, intermediate-range, and **intercontinental** ballistic missiles.

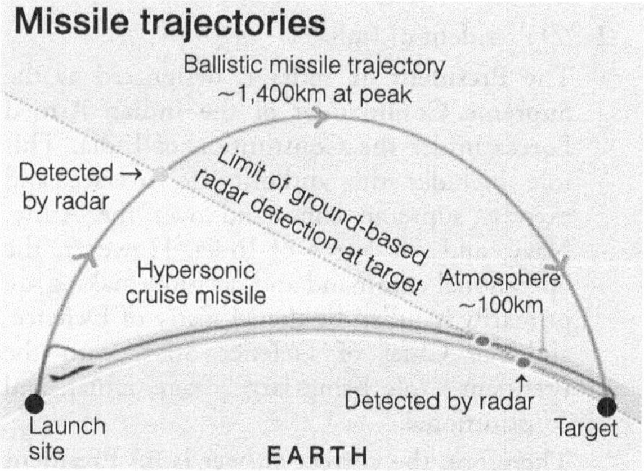


**Therefore, two statements are correct, making the answer (b) Only two.**

**8.** *(b)* Only two

- **Statement 1 is correct: Cruise missiles** often fly at **low altitudes**, following the terrain (terrain-hugging capability) to avoid radar detection, making them harder to track.
- **Statement 2 is incorrect:** Cruise missiles can adjust their **course mid-flight** based on guidance systems, allowing them to make precise adjustments toward their target.
- **Statement 3 is correct:** Cruise missiles can carry both **conventional and nuclear warheads,** making them versatile for a range of mission objectives.

**Therefore, two statements are correct, making the answer (b) Only two.**

**9.** *(c)* Only three

- **Pair 1 is correct: Prithvi** is a **surface-to-surface tactical missile** developed for short-range strikes, mainly for battlefield support.
- **Pair 2 is correct: Agni** is a **ballistic missile** series, developed for medium to long-range strategic targeting, including nuclear deterrence.
- **Pair 3 is correct: BrahMos** is a **supersonic cruise missile** known for its high speed and precision, capable of targeting **sea**, and land assets.

- **Pair 4 is incorrect: Nirbhay** is not specifically an anti-ship missile; it is a **subsonic cruise missile** developed for long-range, precision strikes, capable of carrying both nuclear and conventional warheads.

**Thus, three pairs are correctly matched, making the answer (c) Only three.**

***10.*** *(c)* Only three

- **Pair 1 is correct: Agni** missiles are primarily **land-based** ballistic missiles, developed for strategic deterrence.
- **Pair 2 is correct: Prithvi** can be launched from both **land-based and mobile platforms,** making it flexible for battlefield deployment.
- **Pair 3 is incorrect: Trishul** was developed as a **short-range surface-to-air missile,** not for sea-based platforms, it was intended for quick-reaction defense against low-flying threats.
- **Pair 4 is correct: Akash** is a land-based, surface-to-air missile system, designed with **radar guidance** for tracking and intercepting aerial threats.

**Therefore, three pairs are correctly matched, making the answer (c) Only three.**

***11.*** *(c)* Dr. APJ Abdul Kalam

**Dr. APJ Abdul Kalam** is widely recognised as the 'Missile Man of India' due to his pivotal role in India's missile development and defense technology. His work as the chief of the **Integrated Guided Missile Development Program (IGMDP)** led to the successful development of missiles like **Agni** and **Prithvi,** strengthening India's defense capabilities. Dr. Kalam's contributions in the field of aerospace and defense earned him this title, and he later served as the **11th President of India.**

**Thus, the correct answer is (c) Dr. APJ Abdul Kalam.**

***12.*** *(b)* Only two

The **Integrated Guided Missile Development Programme (IGMDP)** was initiated by the Government of India in 1983 under the leadership of Dr. A.P.J. Abdul Kalam. The programme aimed to make India **self-reliant in the development and production of guided missiles.** It was spearheaded by the Defence Research and Development Organisation (DRDO).

- **Option 1 is correct: Prithvi** is a **surface-to-surface tactical missile,** primarily designed for short-range strikes on land targets.
- **Option 2 is correct: Agni** is a **surface-to-surface ballistic missile** series, capable of medium to long-range attacks and often used for strategic deterrence.
- **Option 3 is incorrect: Trishul** is a **surface-to-air missile,** not a surface-to-surface missile, designed to engage aerial targets.
- **Option 4 is incorrect: Nag** is an **anti-tank guided missile** designed to destroy armoured vehicles, not for surface-to-surface engagements.

**Therefore, two missiles (Prithvi and Agni) are surface-to-surface missiles, making the answer (b) Only two.**

***13.*** *(d)* 1, 2 and 3

- **Statement 1 is correct: Ballistic missiles** follow a **parabolic trajectory** after the initial powered phase, reaching high altitudes before descending towards the target. **Cruise missiles,** on the other hand, travel at low altitudes, often following the terrain to avoid radar detection.
- **Statement 2 is correct: Ballistic missiles** are powered only during the **boost (initial) phase** and then rely on momentum, and gravity in their unpowered descent phase. In contrast, **cruise missiles are powered throughout their flight,** maintaining a constant speed and trajectory.
- **Statement 3 is correct: Cruise missiles** typically fly at **subsonic or supersonic speeds,** generally slower than ballistic missiles, which can reach hypersonic speeds in their descent phase.

**Therefore, the correct answer is (d) 1, 2 and 3.**

***14.*** *(a)* 1 and 2 only

- **Option 1 is correct:** The **Agni series** is a family of **ballistic missiles** developed for long-range strategic capabilities, including nuclear deterrence.

- **Option 2 is correct: Prithvi:** The **Prithvi series** is a **short-range ballistic missile** designed for tactical battlefield use, providing ground support in conventional and nuclear roles.
- **Option 3 is incorrect: BrahMos: BrahMos** is a **supersonic cruise missile** developed jointly by India and Russia, intended for precision strikes, and anti-ship roles, not a ballistic missile.
- **Option 4 is incorrect: Nirbhay: Nirbhay** is a **long-range subsonic cruise missile** designed for precision targeting, capable of carrying conventional and nuclear warheads.

**Therefore, the correct answer is (a) 1 and 2 only, as Agni and Prithvi are ballistic missiles.**

**15.** *(a)* 1 and 2 only

- **Option 1 is correct: BrahMos: BrahMos** is a **supersonic cruise missile** with high speed and precision, capable of targeting land, and sea assets, developed through a collaboration between India, and Russia.
- **Option 2 is correct: Nirbhay: Nirbhay** is a **subsonic cruise missile** with long-range capabilities, designed for precise strikes, including potential nuclear deployment.
- **Option 3 is incorrect: Shaurya: Shaurya** is a **ballistic missile** with tactical use, developed for short to medium ranges and capable of carrying nuclear warheads.
- **Option 4 is incorrect: Dhanush: Dhanush** is a **short-range ballistic missile** that can be launched from ships, modified from the Prithvi missile series.

**Thus, the correct answer is (a) 1 and 2 only, as BrahMos and Nirbhay are cruise missiles.**

**16.** *(b)* 1, 2 and 4 only

- **Statement 1 is correct: BrahMos** is a **supersonic cruise missile** developed through a collaboration between India's DRDO and Russia's NPO Mashinostroyenia.
- **Statement 2 is correct:** The BrahMos can be launched from **multiple platforms:** land-based launchers, naval ships, submarines and aircraft.
- **Statement 3 is incorrect:** While BrahMos is often used for **anti-ship roles,** it is also designed for **land-attack** missions, making it versatile.
- **Statement 4 is correct:** The missile has a speed of approximately **Mach 3** (three times the speed of sound), making it one of the fastest cruise missiles in the world.

**Therefore, the correct answer is (b) 1, 2 and 4 only.**

**17.** *(a)* 1 and 3 only

- **Option 1 is correct: Nag** is an indigenous **anti-tank guided missile (ATGM)** developed by India's Defense Research and Development Organisation (DRDO) under the Integrated Guided Missile Development Programme (IGMDP). It is designed to target and destroy enemy tanks.
- **Option 2 is incorrect: Spike** is an anti-tank missile developed by **Israel** and has been procured by India for use, but it was not developed by India.
- **Option 3 is correct: Helina** is the **air-launched version of the Nag missile,** specifically designed to be launched from helicopters to target armoured vehicles.
- **Option 4 is incorrect: Javelin** is a **shoulder-fired anti-tank missile** developed by the United States, known for its 'fire-and-forget' capability and top-attack mode against armoured targets.

**Therefore, the correct answer is (a) 1 and 3 only, as Nag and Helina are indigenous anti-tank missiles developed by India.**

**18.** *(d)* All four

- **Pair 1 is correct: Trishul** is a **surface-to-air missile (SAM)** developed for short-range defense against low-flying aerial threats.
- **Pair 2 is correct: Prahaar** is a **short-range ballistic missile** designed for tactical battlefield use, providing precision strikes with a range of approximately 150 km.
- **Pair 3 is correct: Pranash** is an **upcoming short-range tactical missile** with an estimated range of around **200 km,** being developed to meet tactical strike requirements.

- **Pair 4 is correct: Shaurya is a hypersonic surface-to-surface missile** capable of carrying nuclear warheads, offering high speed and accuracy over long distances.

**Therefore, all four pairs are correctly matched, making the answer (d) All four.**

**19.** *(b)* 1, 2 and 4 only

- **Option 1 is correct: Astra is an indigenously developed beyond-visual-range (BVR) air-to-air missile** by India, designed for engaging enemy aircraft at long distances.
- **Option 2 is correct: MICA is a French-made air-to-air missile** used by the Indian Air Force for both visual and beyond-visual range engagements.
- **Option 3 is incorrect: BrahMos** is a **supersonic cruise missile** primarily used for surface-to-surface and anti-ship roles, not as an air-to-air missile.
- **Option 4 is correct: Python-5** is an advanced **air-to-air missile developed by Israel** and used by the Indian Air Force for close-combat, short-range engagements.

**Thus, the correct answer is (b) 1, 2 and 4 only, as Astra, MICA, and Python-5 are air-to-air missiles used by the Indian Air Force.**

**20.** *(b)* Only two

- **Statement 1 is correct: Iron Dome** is designed to intercept **short-range rockets, artillery shells and mortars**, providing a shield against incoming threats with a high success rate.
- **Statement 2 is correct:** Iron Dome was developed by **Israel's Rafael Advanced Defense Systems** with funding support from the United States, but not co-development. This has led to extensive support and operational alignment with the US
- **Statement 3 is incorrect:** Although Iron Dome is highly effective in urban areas, it is not limited to them. The system can be deployed in various locations to protect infrastructure and population centers as needed.

**Therefore, two statements are correct, making the answer (b) Only two.**

**21.** *(a)* A missile technology that allows a single missile to carry multiple warheads, each capable of striking different targets independently.

- **MIRV technology** refers to a ballistic missile's ability to carry and deliver multiple warheads, each of which can be independently targeted. This enhances strike efficiency and complicates missile defense systems.
- **Agni-V:** India's most advanced intercontinental ballistic missile (ICBM) with a range exceeding 5,000 km is reported to have MIRV capabilities. This allows it to target multiple locations across continents with a single missile.

**Thus, option (a) is the correct answer.**

**22.** *(b)* Only three

- **Option 1 is correct: United States:** The USA has advanced ICBMs like the **Minuteman III**, capable of striking targets across continents.
- **Option 2 is correct: Russia:** Russia possesses one of the world's largest ICBM arsenals, including missiles like the **RS-28 Sarmat** and **Topol-M**.
- **Option 3 is incorrect: India:** India has developed and successfully tested ICBMs like the **Agni-V**, with a range exceeding 5,000 km. While not officially declared as an ICBM country, **Agni-V** places India in the ICBM-capable category.
- **Option 4 is incorrect: Germany:** Germany does not possess ICBMs, as it is a non-nuclear weapons state under the **Non-Proliferation Treaty (NPT)**.

**Thus, the correct answer is (b) Only three.**

**23.** *(b)* 1, 3 and 4 only

- **Option 1 is correct: K-15 (Sagarika)**: A short-range submarine-launched ballistic missile (SLBM), K-15 is pivotal for India's **sea-based deterrence** as part of the Arihant-class submarine arsenal.

- **Option 2 is correct: Agni-III:** While Agni-III is a medium-range ballistic missile (MRBM), it is part of India's **land-based deterrence** and does not contribute directly to sea-based capabilities.
- **Option 3 is correct: K-4:** This medium-range SLBM strengthens India's second-strike capability from nuclear-powered submarines, a core aspect of the nuclear triad.
- **Option 4 is correct: Dhanush:** A ship-launched ballistic missile, Dhanush complements the K-series SLBMs and contributes to India's **sea-based nuclear deterrence.**

**Thus, the correct answer is (b) 1, 3 and 4 only.**

**24.** *(b)* Only two

India's **Ballistic Missile Defence (BMD)** program is an indigenous initiative developed by the **Defence Research and Development Organisation (DRDO)** to protect the country from incoming ballistic missile threats. It aims to provide a robust defence against nuclear-capable and conventional missiles. The BMD programme is integrated with India's broader air defense network, which includes **Akash, Barak-8** and other surface-to-air missiles.

- **Statement 1 is correct:** The Indian BMD shield is designed to intercept ballistic missiles at **multiple altitudes**, providing layered defense with different interception ranges.
- **Statement 2 is correct:** India's BMD system includes both **exo-atmospheric (outside the atmosphere) and endo-atmospheric (within the atmosphere) interception capabilities,** allowing it to engage incoming missiles at high and low altitudes.
- **Statement 3 is incorrect:** The BMD shield is an **indigenous programme** developed by DRDO (Defense Research and Development Organisation), with no major collaboration with Russia.

**Thus, two statements are correct, making the answer (b) Only two.**

**25.** *(b)* Only two

- **Statement 1 is correct: Pinaka** is an **indigenous multiple rocket launcher system** developed by DRDO, capable of delivering rapid firepower over a large area.
- **Statement 2 is correct:** Rudra is an **armed variant of the Dhruv Advanced Light Helicopter** (ALH), fitted with weapon systems for close combat support.
- **Statement 3 is incorrect: ASAT (Anti-Satellite Weapon)** is not an air-to-air missile; it is designed to neutralise satellites in space and was developed by DRDO for space defense.

**Thus, two statements are correct,** making the answer **(b) Only two.**

**26.** *(b)* Only two

- **Statement 1 is correct:** India's ASAT capability demonstrated under **Mission Shakti** allows it to target and destroy satellites in **Low Earth orbit (LEO).** The successful test showcased India's ability to neutralise potential threats in space.
- **Statement 2 is correct:** India conducted its first-ever ASAT test in **2019** under the code-name **Mission Shakti,** making it the fourth country (after the USA, Russia and China) to develop such capabilities.
- **Statement 3 is incorrect:** ASAT is specifically designed to **target satellites,** not ballistic missiles. While there are systems for ballistic missile defense (BMD), they are separate from ASAT technologies.

**Thus, the correct answer is (b) Only two.**

**27.** *(b)* Long-range artillery rocket system with precision targeting

The **Pinaka Mk-II variant** is an advanced version of the Pinaka multiple rocket launcher, capable of **longer-range targeting** (up to around 75 kilometers) with **enhanced precision guidance.** This system was developed to increase the range and accuracy of area saturation capabilities, supporting artillery roles on the battlefield. Unlike anti-ship, air defense, or underwater systems, Pinaka Mk-II is strictly focused on **land-based long-range artillery support.**

**Thus, option (b) is the correct answer.**

**28.** *(a)* An object immersed in fluid experiences a force equal to the weight of the fluid displaced by it

**Archimedes' Principle** states that any object, partially or fully submerged in a fluid, experiences an **upward buoyant force** equal to the **weight of the fluid displaced by the object.** This principle is fundamental in understanding buoyancy, as it explains why some objects float while others sink, depending on the weight of the displaced fluid relative to the object's weight.

**Thus, option (a) is the correct answer.**

**29.** *(a)* 1 and 3 only

- **Statement 1 is correct: Frigates** are often used for **escort and patrol missions**, while destroyers have more comprehensive combat capabilities, focusing on handling multiple threats simultaneously.
- **Statement 2 is incorrect: Destroyers are larger and more heavily armed** than frigates, with greater capacity for advanced radar and weapons systems.
- **Statement 3 is correct: Frigates are typically employed in anti-submarine warfare**, while destroyers are equipped with air defense systems for layered protection.
- **Statement 4 is incorrect:** Both frigates and destroyers can have **offensive and defensive roles**, with destroyers often taking on more offensive operations.

**Thus, the correct answer is (a) 1 and 3 only.**

**30.** *(a)* 1 and 2 only

- **Statement 1 is correct: INS Vikrant** is India's first **indigenously built aircraft carrier**, commissioned in 2022, representing a significant milestone in India's naval capabilities.
- **Statement 2 is correct: INS Viraat** was decommissioned in 2017 after nearly **30 years** of service in the Indian Navy. It was originally a British carrier before being acquired by India.
- **Statement 3 is incorrect: INS Vikramaditya** was purchased from Russia (originally the Soviet carrier Admiral Gorshkov) and commissioned into the Indian Navy in 2013, not from the United States.

**Therefore, the correct answer is (a) 1 and 2 only.**

**31.** *(b)* Nuclear-powered submarines use nuclear reactors for propulsion, allowing longer endurance, while diesel-electric submarines rely on battery-powered electric propulsion.

- **Option (b) is correct: Nuclear-powered submarines** use nuclear reactors to generate power for propulsion and onboard systems, allowing them to remain submerged for extended periods without surfacing. In contrast, **diesel-electric submarines** rely on diesel engines to charge batteries, which power electric motors for propulsion. These submarines must surface periodically to recharge.
- **Option (a) is incorrect:** It is diesel-electric submarines, not nuclear-powered ones, that must surface regularly for recharging batteries. Nuclear-powered submarines can stay submerged indefinitely, limited only by food supplies and crew endurance.
- **Option (c) is incorrect:** Nuclear-powered submarines are typically faster and have greater endurance compared to diesel-electric submarines.
- **Option (d) is incorrect:** Both types of submarines can be used for reconnaissance and combat missions; their roles depend on specific mission objectives.

**Thus, option (b) the correct answer.**

**32.** *(a)* 1 and 3 only

- **Statement 1 is correct:** Nuclear-powered submarines can operate underwater for unlimited periods, constrained only by food supplies and crew endurance.
- **Statement 2 is incorrect:** Diesel-electric submarines, not nuclear-powered submarines, require regular surfacing for battery recharging.

- **Statement 3 is correct:** Due to their larger size, nuclear-powered submarines can carry more weapons, including nuclear-tipped missiles, making them suitable for strategic deterrence missions.
- **Statement 4 is incorrect:** When running on **battery power**, diesel-electric submarines are quieter than nuclear-powered submarines, making them ideal for stealth operations in shallow waters.

**Thus, the correct answer is (a) 1 and 3 only.**

**33.** *(a)* A-1, B-2, C-3, D-4

- **INS Arihant** : It is India's first **nuclear-powered ballistic missile submarine** (SSBN), forming a crucial part of India's nuclear triad.
- **INS Kalvari** : A **diesel-electric attack submarine** (SSK) and part of the Kalvari-class (Scorpène-class), it is designed for stealth, and efficiency.
- **INS Chakra** : A **nuclear-powered attack submarine** (SSN) leased from Russia, capable of long underwater operations.
- **INS Sindhughosh** : A **diesel-electric submarine** of the Kilo-class, it has been in service with the Indian Navy for decades.

**Thus, the correct answer is (a) A-1, B-2, C-3, D-4.**

**34.** *(d)* All of the above

- **Statement 1 is correct: Project 75** focuses on the construction of **Scorpène-class submarines,** designed for stealth, anti-surface warfare and anti-submarine warfare capabilities.
- **Statement 2 is correct:** The submarines are being developed in collaboration with the Naval Group (formerly DCNS) of **France** and are constructed at Mazagon Dock Shipbuilders Limited (MDL) in Mumbai under a technology transfer agreement.
- **Statement 3 is correct: INS Kalvari** was the first Scorpène-class submarine commissioned under Project 75 in December 2017, marking a major milestone in India's indigenous submarine-building program.

**Thus, all three statements are correct so, the correct answer is (d) All of the above.**

**35.** *(b)* 1 and 3 only

- **Statement 1 is correct: Project 15** involves the construction of Delhi-class guided-missile destroyers, which are heavily armed with advanced weapons and systems.
- **Statement 2 is incorrect:** INS Delhi is the lead ship of **Project 15.** INS Kolkata is the lead ship of Project 15A, an upgraded version of Project 15.
- **Statement 3 is correct:** Destroyers under Project 15 are named after Indian cities, including INS Delhi, INS Mysore and INS Mumbai.

**Therefore, the correct answer is (b) 1 and 3 only.**

**36.** *(b)* Only two

- **Statement 1 is correct:** Torpedoes are **self-propelled underwater weapons** primarily designed for targeting and striking other naval vessels or submarines.
- **Statement 2 is incorrect:** The **speed and range of a torpedo** can be affected by the **density of seawater,** as denser water can increase resistance, potentially slowing it down or affecting its range.
- **Statement 3 is correct:** Torpedoes are versatile and can be launched from various platforms, including **submarines, ships and aircraft.**

**Thus, two statements are correct, making the answer (b) Only two.**

**37.** *(b)* Only two

- **Statement 1 is correct: Varunastra** is an indigenously developed **heavyweight torpedo** produced by the Defence Research and Development Organisation (DRDO) of India.
- **Statement 2 is incorrect:** Varunastra is designed for use by **surface ships,** not submarines. It is launched from naval vessels to target underwater threats.
- **Statement 3 is correct:** Varunastra is capable of engaging both **surface vessels and submarines,** making it versatile in anti-submarine warfare.

- The Varunastra was developed by the Naval Science and Technological Laboratory (NSTL) of DRDO. It was officially inducted into the Indian Navy in 2016, marking a significant milestone in India's defense capabilities. The torpedo has undergone extensive trials to validate its performance in various combat scenarios.

**Thus, two statements are correct, making the answer (b) Only two.**

**38.** *(b)* Only two

- **Statement 1 is correct:** Tejas is an indigenously developed **multi-role light fighter aircraft** designed by HAL (Hindustan Aeronautics Limited) for the Indian Air Force.
- **Statement 2 is incorrect:** The **Su-30MKI** was developed in collaboration with **Russia**, not the United States. It is a variant of the Sukhoi Su-30 customised for India.
- **Statement 3 is correct:** The **Rafale** is a **twin-engine fighter jet** that India acquired from **France** for multi-role combat operations.

**Thus, two statements are correct, making the answer (b) Only two.**

**39.** *(a)* 1 and 3 only

- **Statement 1 is correct: Tejas** is an **indigenously developed Light Combat Aircraft (LCA)** by Hindustan Aeronautics Limited (HAL), developed under India's LCA program.
- **Statement 2 is incorrect:** Currently, Tejas is powered by an **American-made General Electric (GE)** engine. India's indigenous Kaveri engine, initially intended for Tejas, is still under development.
- **Statement 3 is correct:** Tejas has the capability to carry a range of **air-to-air and air-to-ground** weapons, enhancing its multi-role capabilities.

**Statement 4 is incorrect:** Tejas is a **single-engine aircraft**, not a twin-engine design. It is intended for multi-role missions rather than specialised high-speed interception.

**Therefore, the correct answer is (a) 1 and 3 only.**

**40.** *(d)* To make an aircraft or vessel invisible to radar, infrared and other detection systems.

**Stealth technology** is designed to reduce the detectability of military assets, such as aircraft, ships and missiles, by making them invisible or less visible to radar, infrared, and other detection methods. It ensures tactical advantages by evading enemy surveillance systems.

**Thus, option (d) is the correct answer.**

**41.** *(b)* 1, 2 and 3 only

- **Statement 1 is correct: Radar-absorbent materials (RAM)** are used to reduce the reflection of radar signals, making the object less visible to radar detection.
- **Statement 2 is correct:** Angled surfaces in stealth aircraft and vessels deflect radar waves away from the radar source, reducing their radar cross-section (RCS).
- **Statement 3 is correct:** Stealth technology reduces **infrared emissions** to minimise the chances of detection by heat-seeking devices.
- **Statement 4 is incorrect:** Increased speed is not a feature of stealth technology. Instead, stealth focuses on minimising detection, not evading radar through speed.

**Thus, the correct answer is (b) 1, 2 and 3 only.**

**42.** *(b)* Only two

- **Option 1 is correct: F-22 Raptor:** It is a **fifth-generation fighter aircraft developed by Lockheed Martin for the United States Air Force.** It is characterised by its **stealth technology,** advanced avionics, and supermaneuverability. It was the world's first operational fifth-generation fighter and remains one of the most advanced in its class.
- **Option 2 is incorrect: Tejas:** The **Tejas, developed by Hindustan Aeronautics Limited (HAL),** is a **fourth-generation light combat aircraft** (LCA). While highly capable, it lacks the full stealth capabilities, sensor fusion and advanced avionics required to classify it as a fifth-generation aircraft.
- **Option 3 is incorrect: Dassault Rafale:** The **Rafale,** developed by Dassault Aviation, is classified as a **4.5-generation fighter aircraft.**

While it features advanced avionics, agility and radar capabilities, it does not possess the full stealth technology or other characteristics required for fifth-generation classification.

- **Option 4 is correct: F-35 Lightning II:** The **F-35 Lightning II**, developed by Lockheed Martin, is a **fifth-generation fighter** aircraft with **stealth capabilities, advanced integrated sensors** and networked warfare systems. It is designed for multi-role capabilities, including air superiority, ground attack, and reconnaissance.

**Thus, the correct answer is (b) Only two.**

**43.** *(b)* 1, 2 and 4 only

- **Statement 1 is correct:** AWACS systems are designed to perform **airspace surveillance**, detect incoming threats and monitor enemy aircraft, and missile movements over long distances.
- **Statement 2 is correct:** AWACS plays a critical role in **coordinating fighter jets, ground operations and naval assets** during military engagements, ensuring a synchronised defense, and attack strategy.
- **Statement 3 is incorrect:** AWACS does not have aerial refueling capabilities, this is the role of **tanker aircraft**.
- **Statement 4 is correct:** AWACS serves as a **mobile command and control center**, providing real-time intelligence, and decision-making support in combat scenarios.

**Thus, the correct answer is (b) 1, 2 and 4 only.**

**44.** *(b)* Only two

- **Statement 1 is correct: MUNTRA** is indeed India's **first indigenously developed unmanned ground vehicle** (UGV).
- **Statement 2 is correct:** MUNTRA is designed for **mine detection and reconnaissance**, among other functions, to support military operations in hazardous areas.
- **Statement 3 is incorrect:** MUNTRA is a **ground-based vehicle** and is not designed for underwater operations. It is used for land-based mine detection and reconnaissance, not for detecting naval mines.

**Thus, two statements are correct, making the answer (b) Only two.**

**45.** *(b)* Only two

- **Statement 1 is correct: Arjun** is an **indigenously developed main battle tank** (MBT) designed and built in India by DRDO to meet the needs of the Indian Army.
- **Statement 2 is correct:** The **T-90 Bhishma** is a Russian-made tank that has been customised with advanced systems for Indian Army requirements.
- **Statement 3 is incorrect:** The **T-72 Ajeya** is primarily used as a **main battle tank (MBT)** for frontline combat, not specifically for reconnaissance missions.

**Therefore, two statements are correct, making the answer (b) Only two.**

**46.** *(b)* Only two

- **Statement 1 is correct: Rustom** is a **medium-altitude long-endurance** (MALE) **drone** developed by DRDO for surveillance, reconnaissance and intelligence missions for the Indian Army, Navy and Air Force.
- **Statement 2 is incorrect: Nishant** is an **unarmed surveillance drone** developed by DRDO for reconnaissance and target tracking. It is not designed for strike operations.
- **Statement 3 is correct: Panchi** is a wheeled variant of the Nishant UAV, designed for **takeoff and landing on runways.** Unlike Nishant, which is launched using a catapult system, Panchi offers runway-based operation flexibility.

**Thus, two statements are correct, making the answer (b) Only two.**

**47.** *(a)* 1 and 3 only

- **Option 1 is correct: Rustom** is an **indigenous medium-altitude long-endurance** (MALE) UAV developed by DRDO, intended for surveillance and intelligence missions.
- **Option 2 is incorrect: Heron** is an **Israeli-made** UAV developed by Israel Aerospace Industries (IAI), used by the Indian military for intelligence gathering.
- **Option 3 is correct: Nishant** is also **indigenously developed** by DRDO for

surveillance and reconnaissance, making it an Indian UAV.

- **Option 4 is incorrect: Harop** is an **Israeli-made loitering munition** used by the Indian armed forces, designed for kamikaze-style strikes on enemy targets.

**Thus, the correct answer is (a) 1 and 3 only.**

***48.*** *(d)* All four

India follows the **Drone Rules, 2021**, which categorise drones based on their weight. These classifications govern the registration, operation and usage of drones in various sectors, ensuring compliance with safety, and security norms.

- **Statement 1 is correct: Nano drones** are classified as drones weighing **up to 250 grams** in India.
- **Statement 2 is correct: Micro drones** are classified as those weighing **between 250 grams and 2 kilograms.**
- **Statement 3 is correct:** Small drones are classified within the 2 **kilograms** to **25 kilograms** range, often used for commercial and industrial applications.
- **Statement 4 is correct: Medium drones** weigh between 25 **kilograms** and **150 kilograms,** and are generally used in specialised operations like logistics, and agriculture.

**Hence, all four statements are correctly matched, making the answer (d) All four.**

***49.*** *(a)* Only one

- **Statement 1 is correct: Rustom** is an indigenously developed **medium-altitude long-endurance** (MALE) drone created by DRDO for intelligence, surveillance and reconnaissance (ISR) missions.
- **Statement 2 is incorrect: Nishant** is designed for **short-range, low-altitude reconnaissance** and is not suited for high-altitude intelligence gathering.
- **Statement 3 is incorrect:** The **Heron** drone, acquired from **Israel,** is used by the Indian military for surveillance and reconnaissance. It is **not armed,** but is equipped with advanced sensors for ISR.

**Therefore, only one statement is correct, making the answer (a) Only one.**

***50.*** *(b)* Only two

- **Statement 1 is correct: Nishant** is used for **low-altitude tactical reconnaissance** by the Indian Army, providing real-time intelligence in battlefield environments.
- **Statement 2 is incorrect:** While **Rustom-2** is designed for ISR missions, it is not yet armed with **precision-guided munitions.** It has the potential to be weaponised, but currently serves primarily for surveillance.
- **Statement 3 is correct: Harop** is a **loitering munition** capable of hovering over target areas and performing kamikaze strikes, used by the Indian Air Force.
- **Statement 4 is incorrect: Heron, acquired from Israel,** is capable of high-altitude, long-endurance surveillance missions and has operational endurance of **nearly 45 hours** at an altitude of up to 35,000 feet.

**Hence, two statements are correct, making the answer (b) Only two.**

***51.*** *(b)* Only two

- **Pair 1 is incorrect: Rustom-2** is designed for **medium-altitude long-endurance** (MALE) used for **intelligence, surveillance and reconnaissance** (ISR) missions, enhancing India's border patrol, and security capabilities.
- **Pair 2 is incorrect: Nishant** is a **short-range, low-altitude tactical reconnaissance drone,** primarily used for battlefield intelligence and not high-altitude surveillance.
- **Pair 3 is correct: Harop** serves as a **loitering munition,** capable of hovering over potential targets and performing kamikaze strikes if required.
- **Pair 4 is correct: Heron** is used by India for **medium-altitude, long-endurance surveillance** and can conduct extensive reconnaissance over border areas.

**Therefore, two pairs are correctly matched, making the answer (b) Only two.**

***52.*** *(b)* Only two

- **Pair 1 is incorrect:** The **Heron drone** is an unmanned aerial vehicle (UAV) developed by **Israel** Aerospace Industries (IAI) and is widely used by the Indian military for surveillance.

- **Pair 2 is correct:** The **Rustom** is an **indigenous drone** developed by the Defence Research and Development Organisation (DRDO) in India for reconnaissance, and surveillance.
- **Pair 3 is incorrect:** The **MQ-9 Predator** is a high-end UAV developed by General Atomics in the **United States** and used for combat, and surveillance purposes.
- **Pair 4 is correct:** The **Harop** is a loitering munition developed by **Israel** Aerospace Industries (IAI), designed for kamikaze-style attacks on enemy assets.

**Therefore, only two pairs are correct, the correct answer is (b) Only two.**

**53.** *(b)* 1, 2 and 3 only

- **Statement 1 is correct:** Drones are valuable in **disaster management** for providing **real-time aerial imagery**, helping rescue teams assess damage and locate affected areas quickly.
- **Statement 2 is correct:** Drones can be used to **deliver essential supplies** such as food, water and medical kits to remote or inaccessible locations, supporting relief operations.
- **Statement 3 is correct:** Drones play a role in **search and rescue** by scanning large areas quickly, and locating people who may be trapped.
- **Statement 4 is incorrect:** While drones provide surveillance, **crowd control** typically involves law enforcement and ground-based strategies, rather than drone intervention.

**Therefore, the correct answer is (b) 1, 2 and 3 only.**

**54.** *(d)* 1, 2, 3 and 4

- **Statement 1 is correct:** Drones can monitor **deforestation and illegal logging** activities by capturing aerial imagery, providing authorities with data on forest health, and illegal activities.
- **Statement 2 is correct:** Drones are used in **wildlife conservation** to survey habitats, track animal movement and monitor endangered species without disturbing their environment.
- **Statement 3 is correct:** Drones equipped with sensors can measure **air quality** and collect data on pollutants, which is particularly useful in urban areas for environmental monitoring.
- **Statement 4 is correct:** Drones are used to monitor **illegal fishing** in coastal waters by providing real-time surveillance and alerting authorities to unauthorised activities.

**Hence, the correct answer is (d) 1, 2, 3 and 4.**

**55.** *(c)* All three

- **Statement 1 is correct:** According to **Drone Rules 2021**, all drones must be registered and assigned a **unique identification number** (UIN) unless exempted, such as nano drones used for recreational purposes.
- **Statement 2 is correct: Drones weighing less than 250 grams (nano drones)** used for recreational purposes are **exempt from UIN requirements** under these rules.
- **Statement 3 is correct: Drone corridors** have been proposed to **facilitate cargo deliveries** and are intended to separate commercial drone operations from traditional air traffic.

**Thus, all three statements are correct, making the answer (c) All three.**

**56.** *(d)* All four

- **Pair 1 is correct: Doppler Radar** uses the **Doppler shift** to measure the **velocity of objects** based on frequency changes, widely applied in weather forecasting and speed detection.
- **Pair 2 is correct: Pulse Radar** sends out **short bursts or pulses of energy** to determine the range of an object, used in navigation and basic tracking systems.
- **Pair 3 is correct: Continuous Wave Radar** continuously transmits waves and measures **relative speed without providing range information,** making it useful for applications like speed detection in law enforcement.
- **Pair 4 is correct: Synthetic Aperture Radar** (SAR) uses **movement to simulate a larger antenna**, creating **high-resolution images** of the terrain, which is valuable for remote sensing and Earth observation.

**Therefore, all four pairs are correctly matched, making the answer (d) All four.**

**57.** *(b)* To track and guide surface-to-air missiles in real-time during combat operations.

The **Rajendra Radar** is a multi-functional radar system used in India's **Akash missile defense system**. It performs tracking, engagement and guidance functions, enabling real-time operation of surface-to-air missiles against aerial threats.

**Thus, option (b) is the correct answer.**

**58.** *(b)* A change in the frequency or wavelength of a wave in relation to an observer moving relative to the source of the wave.

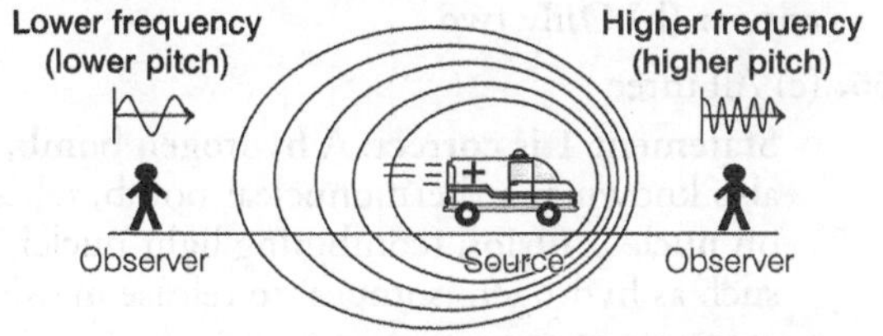


The **Doppler Effect** refers to the **change in frequency or wavelength** of a wave (such as sound or light) when the source of the wave is moving relative to the observer. This effect is observed, for example, when an ambulance passes by and the siren sound frequency appears to change as it approaches, and then moves away.

**Thus, option (b) is the correct answer.**

**59.** *(b)* Only two

- **Statement 1 is correct: Sonar** stands for **Sound Navigation and Ranging,** and is a technology used to detect objects underwater by emitting sound waves, and analysing their reflections.
- **Statement 2 is incorrect:** Sonar is not limited to military applications; it is also used in **civilian applications** like fishing, underwater mapping and environmental monitoring.
- **Statement 3 is correct:** Sonar technology can indeed be used for both **detection and communication** underwater, making it versatile for various purposes.

**Therefore, two statements are correct, making the answer (b) Only two.**

**60.** *(b)* Only two

**Sonar (Sound Navigation and Ranging)** is a technology that uses sound waves to detect, and locate objects underwater. It is primarily used in naval operations, underwater research and fisheries.

- **Statement 1 is correct: Active Sonar** works by emitting sound waves and detecting their echoes, helping determine the location of underwater objects.
- **Statement 2 is correct: Passive Sonar** only listens for sounds made by objects (such as submarine engines) without emitting any sound waves.
- **Statement 3 is incorrect:** Only **active Sonar** is used to measure **ocean depth,** as passive Sonar cannot emit signals needed for depth measurement.

**Thus, two statements are correct, making the answer (b) Only two.**

**61.** *(b)* 2, 3 and 4 only

- **Statement 1 is incorrect: Sangraha** is an electronic warfare suite primarily used by the **Indian Navy,** not the Army, to provide radar and communication jamming capabilities in maritime environments.
- **Statement 2 is correct: Shakti** is designed for the **Indian Navy,** providing electronic warfare capabilities to protect ships from radar-guided threats and enhance maritime defense.
- **Statement 3 is correct: Netra** is an **airborne surveillance** system that includes electronic support measures, assisting in detecting and tracking threats from the air.
- **Statement 4 is correct: Kavach** is a chaff-dispensing system that creates **radar decoys,** protecting naval ships by confusing enemy radar and missile guidance systems.

**Therefore, the correct answer is (b) 2, 3 and 4 only.**

**62.** (b) 1, 3 and 4 only

- **Statement 1 is correct: Thermobaric bombs** utilize **oxygen from the surrounding atmosphere** to fuel the explosion, making them highly effective in open or semi-enclosed spaces.
- **Statement 2 is incorrect:** Thermobaric bombs are not designed specifically for deep underground penetration; rather, they are most effective in creating powerful surface blasts.
- **Statement 3 is correct:** These bombs produce an intense **blast wave and heat,** leading to significant overpressure, capable of collapsing buildings and causing severe injuries.
- **Statement 4 is correct:** Thermobaric bombs are also known as **fuel-air explosives** because they release a fuel-air mixture before ignition.

**Therefore, the correct answer is (b) 1, 3, and 4 only.**

**63.** (b) 1, 2 and 3 only

- **Statement 1 is correct: A hydrogen bomb** primarily uses **nuclear fusion** to generate energy, while an atomic bomb relies on nuclear fission.
- **Statement 2 is correct:** A hydrogen bomb uses an initial **fission reaction to achieve the high temperatures needed to initiate fusion.**
- **Statement 3 is correct:** A hydrogen bomb is far more powerful than a **fission (atomic) bomb,** as fusion releases significantly more energy.
- **Statement 4 is incorrect:** While both types of bombs involve a chain reaction, **the fission chain reaction in atomic bombs** is typically more difficult to control, whereas the hydrogen bomb's fusion reaction is triggered in a controlled manner after the initial fission stage.

**Thus, the correct answer is (b) 1, 2 and 3 only.**

**64.** (b) Only two

- **Statement 1 is correct:** Nuclear bombs release massive energy through **nuclear fission or fusion** reactions, with atomic bombs relying on fission and hydrogen bombs relying on fusion.
- **Statement 2 is incorrect:** The first nuclear bombs used in warfare (Hiroshima and Nagasaki) were fission bombs, not fusion bombs. Fusion-based hydrogen bombs were developed later.
- **Statement 3 is correct:** Nuclear bombs have **long-lasting** environmental impacts, including radiation fallout, which can lead to health risks and environmental contamination over decades.

**Thus, two statements are correct, making the answer (b) Only two.**

**65.** (c) All three

- **Statement 1 is correct:** A **hydrogen bomb,** also known as a thermonuclear bomb, relies on **nuclear fusion** (combining light nuclei, such as hydrogen isotopes) to release massive amounts of energy.
- **Statement 2 is correct:** Hydrogen bombs are **significantly more powerful** than atomic bombs, which rely solely on nuclear fission.
- **Statement 3 is correct:** The hydrogen bomb uses a **two-stage process,** where an initial **fission reaction** triggers the fusion reaction, resulting in an explosive force many times greater than that of a conventional atomic bomb.

**Thus, all three statements are correct, making the answer (c) All three.**

**66.** (b) 1, 2, and 3 only

The **Chemical Weapons Convention** (CWC) is an international treaty that aims to eliminate the development, production, acquisition, stockpiling, transfer, and use of chemical weapons. It represents a global effort to prevent the use of chemical weapons and ensure chemical safety.

- **Statement 1 is correct: Egypt** has not signed or ratified the Chemical Weapons Convention, often citing regional security concerns, particularly with neighboring countries in the Middle East.
- **Statement 2 is correct: North Korea** is also not a signatory to the CWC, and its stance on chemical weapons is a matter of significant international concern due to its history with weapons of mass destruction.

- **Statement 3 is correct: South Sudan**, as a newer nation established in 2011, has not signed the CWC, although it has expressed interest in future compliance with various international treaties.
- **Statement 4 is incorrect: Israel** has signed the CWC but has not ratified it. This means it has not fully committed to the treaty's obligations, though it has agreed to the terms in principle by signing.

**Therefore, the correct answer is (b) 1, 2 and 3 only.**

**67.** *(c)* Only three

The **Organisation for the Prohibition of Chemical Weapons (OPCW)** is an international organisation responsible for implementing and overseeing the **Chemical Weapons Convention (CWC)** of 1993. It works to eliminate chemical weapons globally and prevent their re-emergence.

- **Statement 1 is correct:** The OPCW is responsible for **verifying the destruction** of chemical weapons stockpiles and ensuring compliance with the CWC.
- **Statement 2 is correct:** The OPCW **monitors dual-use chemicals** (chemicals that can be used for both civilian and potential weapon-making purposes) to prevent their misuse.
- **Statement 3 is correct:** The OPCW promotes **international cooperation** and the **peaceful use of chemicals** through training, research, and technological assistance.
- **Statement 4 is incorrect:** The OPCW does not **provide military** assistance, but offers protective equipment, training and technical assistance in response to chemical threats.

**Therefore, three objectives are part of the OPCW's role, making the answer (c) Only three.**

**68.** *(b)* 1 and 3 only

- The **Biological Weapons Convention (BWC)** is an international treaty that prohibits the development, production, acquisition, stockpiling and use of biological, and toxin weapons. It was the first multilateral disarmament treaty to ban an entire category of weapons.
- **Option 1 is correct: Israel** has not signed or ratified the BWC, maintaining a policy of ambiguity regarding its capabilities.
- **Option 2 is incorrect: North Korea** accede to the Biological Weapons Convention (BWC) in 1987. However, there is evidence that North Korea may have a biological weapons program that violates the BWC.
- **Option 3 is correct: South Sudan** is one of the few countries that has not signed the BWC, as it is a relatively new nation formed in 2011.
- **Option 4 is incorrect: Myanmar** initially was not a signatory but has acceded to the BWC in 2014.

**Therefore, the correct answer is (b) 1 and 3 only.**

**69.** *(b)* Only two

- **Statement 1 is correct:** The BWC permits **research on biological agents** if it is conducted for **peaceful purposes**, such as medical, pharmaceutical, or public health research.
- **Statement 2 is incorrect:** The BWC does not include specific **penalties or enforcement mechanisms** for violations, relying instead on cooperation and political pressure among member states to ensure compliance.
- **Statement 3 is correct:** The BWC mandates **periodic review conferences** to assess the treaty's relevance and address emerging threats from advances in **biological sciences and biotechnology**.

**Therefore, two statements are correct, making the answer (b) Only two.**

**70.** *(a)* 1 and 2 only

The **Geneva Protocol of 1925** is a landmark international treaty that prohibits the use of **chemical and biological weapons in war**. It was adopted in response to the widespread use of poison gas during **World War I**, which caused immense suffering and devastation.

- **Option 1 is correct:** The **Geneva Protocol of 1925** specifically banned the use of **chemical warfare** agents due to their indiscriminate and highly destructive effects.

- **Option 2 is correct:** The protocol also banned **biological warfare** agents, marking an early international effort to restrict weapons of mass destruction.
- **Option 3 is incorrect: Nuclear warfare** was not addressed in the Geneva Protocol, as nuclear weapons had not yet been developed in 1925.
- **Option 4 is incorrect:** The protocol does not over **conventional warfare**, which includes traditional weaponry used within the rules of war.

**Therefore, the correct answer is (a) 1 and 2 only.**

**71.** *(c)* Only three

- **Option 1 is correct: Nerve agents** (e.g., sarin, VX) disrupt the nervous system and are classified as chemical warfare agents.
- **Option 2 is correct: Blister agents** (e.g., mustard gas) cause severe skin and tissue damage, and are considered chemical warfare agents.
- **Option 3 is correct: Choking agents** (e.g., chlorine gas) attack the respiratory system, causing suffocation and are used in chemical warfare.
- **Option 4 is incorrect: Incendiary agents** are designed to ignite or burn, but they are generally not classified under chemical warfare; they are more commonly considered part of conventional or incendiary weaponry.

**Therefore, three categories are classified as chemical warfare agents, making the answer (c) Only three.**

**72.** *(c)* Only three

- **Option 1 is correct: Bacteria,** like anthrax (Bacillus anthracis), are biological agents that can cause severe diseases when weaponized.
- **Option 2 is correct: Viruses,** such as smallpox and Ebola, are also biological agents, and can be used to infect, and spread disease among populations.
- **Option 3 is correct: Fungi,** such as those causing **wheat rust or rice blast,** can be used in biological warfare, especially against crops, leading to economic damage and food scarcity.
- **Option 4 is incorrect: Nerve agents** are chemical agents, not biological agents. Examples include sarin and VX, which disrupt the nervous system.

**Thus, three types are correctly classified as biological warfare agents, making the answer (c) Only three.**

**73.** *(c)* All three

- **Statement 1 is correct: Biological warfare agents** are living organisms (like bacteria, viruses, or fungi) or toxins that can cause diseases in humans, animals, or plants.
- **Statement 2 is correct:** Biological warfare was banned under the **Geneva Protocol of 1925** and later reinforced by the **Biological Weapons Convention (BWC)** of 1972.
- **Statement 3 is correct: Anthrax,** caused by the bacterium Bacillus anthracis, is a well-known biological warfare agent due to its lethality and ability to be spread via spores.

**Therefore, all three statements are correct, making the answer (c) All three.**

**74.** *(b)* 1, 3 and 4 only

- **Option 1 is correct:** India joined the **Missile Technology Control Regime (MTCR)** in **2016,** which aims to prevent the proliferation of missile and unmanned aerial vehicle (UAV) technology capable of delivering weapons of mass destruction.
- **Option 2 is incorrect:** India is not a member of the **Nuclear Suppliers Group (NSG).** Its membership has been stalled due to objections from some member countries over India's non-signatory status to the Nuclear Non-Proliferation Treaty (NPT).
- **Option 3 is correct:** India became a member of the **Wassenaar Arrangement** in **2017,** which controls exports of conventional arms and dual-use goods and technologies.
- **Option 4 is correct:** India joined the **Australia Group** in **2018,** which seeks to prevent the spread of chemical and biological weapons by controlling related exports.

**Hence, the correct answer is (b) 1, 3 and 4 only.**

**75.** *(c)* Only three

The **Wassenaar Arrangement** is a multi-lateral export control regime established to promote transparency and responsible transfers of conventional arms, and dual-use goods, and technologies. It aims to prevent destabilising accumulations of these items while ensuring they are used for legitimate purposes.

- **Statement 1 is incorrect:** The **Wassenaar Arrangement** does not focus on missile technology control, this is primarily covered by the MTCR.
- **Statement 2 is correct:** The Wassenaar Arrangement includes **preventing the export of conventional** arms as one of its primary goals.
- **Statement 3 is correct: Controlling dual-use technologies** to prevent them from being used for military purposes is a key focus of the Wassenaar Arrangement.
- **Statement 4 is correct: Promoting transparency** in the global arms trade is also an objective, encouraging member states to share information on exports and transfers.

**Therefore, three goals are correctly associated, making the answer (c) Only three.**

**76.** *(b)* Only two

- **Statement 1 is correct:** India joined the **Australia Group** in **2018**, which controls the export of chemical and biological weapons-related materials.
- **Statement 2 is incorrect:** The **Wassenaar Arrangement** primarily focuses on the **export of conventional arms and dual-use goods, and technologies**, not specifically on nuclear non-proliferation.
- **Statement 3 is correct:** India is the only **non-NPT country** that is a member of the **MTCR**, which controls the export of missile and UAV technology.

**Thus, two statements are correct, making the answer (b) Only two.**

**77.** *(b)* Only two

- **Statement 1 is correct: Carbon bombs release fine carbon or graphite filaments,** which can cause short circuits in electrical systems, disrupting power and communications.
- **Statement 2 is incorrect:** Carbon bombs are **not designed to be lethal to humans**; instead, they target electronic infrastructure to disable operations.
- **Statement 3 is correct:** The primary purpose of carbon bombs is to **incapacitate enemy infrastructure** by disrupting power grids and other electrical systems.

**Therefore, two statements are correct, making the answer (b) Only two.**

**78.** *(b)* 1, 2 and 3 only

- **Statement 1 is correct: White phosphorus** ignites upon exposure to oxygen, producing **intense heat and light**, which makes it both visually, and physically impactful.
- **Statement 2 is correct:** White phosphorus is often used to create **smoke screens** that obscure vision and hinder enemy forces.
- **Statement 3 is correct:** When in contact with human skin, **white phosphorus causes severe chemical burns** that can penetrate tissue and cause significant injury.
- **Statement 4 is incorrect:** White phosphorus bombs are **not entirely prohibited under international law.** While its use is restricted, particularly against civilian populations, it is not universally banned and may be legally used in certain military operations.

**Hence, the correct answer is (b) 1, 2 and 3 only.**

**79.** *(a)* 1-B, 2-C, 3-D, 4-A

- **Nuclear Suppliers Group** (NSG) : The NSG was established to prevent the spread of nuclear weapons by controlling the export of materials, equipment and technology that can be used to develop nuclear weapons. It focuses specifically on nuclear materials and technology.
- **Australia Group** : The Australia Group is an informal forum of countries that aims to prevent the spread of chemical and biological weapons. It achieves this by regulating the export of related technologies and materials that could be used to develop these weapons.

- **Missile Technology Control Regime (MTCR)** : The MTCR seeks to **limit the proliferation of missile and unmanned aerial vehicle technology** capable of delivering weapons of mass destruction (WMDs). Its focus is on restricting exports of missile systems and technology that could be used in nuclear delivery systems.
- **Wassenaar Arrangement** : The Wassenaar Arrangement promotes transparency and responsibility in **the export of conventional arms, and dual-use goods, and technologies.** It aims to prevent destabilising accumulations of weapons by regulating trade in these areas.

**Therefore, the correct answer is (a) 1-B, 2-C, 3-D, 4-A.**

***80.*** *(a)* 1 and 2 only

- **Statement 1 is correct:** CAATSA requires the imposition of sanctions on countries engaging in significant defence or intelligence transactions with **Russia.**
- **Statement 2 is correct:** While sanctions are **mandatory,** the law includes provisions for **presidential waivers,** which allows flexibility in certain cases, such as India's S-400 purchase.
- **Statement 3 is incorrect:** India does not have a **permanent waiver.** Waivers are granted on a **case-by-case basis** by the U.S. President, based on strategic considerations.

**Hence, the correct answer is (a) 1 and 2 only.**

## Past Learning (Answers)

| | | | | | | | |
|---|---|---|---|---|---|---|---|
| 1 (b) | 2 (d) | 3 (d) | 4 (d) | 5 (c) | 6 (c) | 7 (c) | 8 (a) |

# CHAPTER 04 Nuclear Technology

## Assessment Round

### Topic 1 : Nuclear Science

*1.* Which of the following statements best describes isotopes?
(a) Isotopes are atoms of the same element with the same number of neutrons but different numbers of electrons.
(b) Isotopes are atoms of different elements that have the same number of protons but different numbers of neutrons.
(c) Isotopes are atoms of the same element with the same number of protons but different numbers of neutrons.
(d) Isotopes are atoms with the same atomic number but entirely different chemical properties.

*2.* Consider the following statements regarding hydrogen isotopes and their roles in nuclear reactions:
1. Deuterium and Tritium isotopes of hydrogen are commonly used in nuclear fusion reactions.
2. Protium, the most abundant hydrogen isotope, is primarily used in fusion reactions.
3. Tritium is radioactive and is often produced artificially for use in nuclear reactors and weapons.

How many of the given above statements is/are correct?
(a) Only one
(b) Only two
(c) All three
(d) None

*3.* Which of the following best explains the difference between 'Nuclear Fusion' and 'Nuclear Fission'?
(a) Nuclear fusion splits heavy atomic nuclei, while nuclear fission combines light nuclei to form a heavier nucleus.
(b) Nuclear fusion combines light nuclei to form a heavier nucleus, releasing large amounts of energy, while nuclear fission splits a heavy nucleus into lighter nuclei, also releasing energy.
(c) Nuclear fusion and fission are both processes that involve only chemical reactions.
(d) Nuclear fission powers the Sun, while nuclear fusion is used in nuclear reactors on Earth.

*4.* Which of the following statements accurately distinguishes between fissile and fertile materials in nuclear science?
(a) Fissile materials can sustain a nuclear chain reaction, while fertile materials can directly undergo fission without needing any conversion.
(b) Fertile materials are those that can sustain a nuclear chain reaction, while fissile materials require neutron absorption to become fissile.
(c) Fissile materials can sustain a nuclear chain reaction on their own, while fertile materials need to absorb neutrons to convert into fissile materials.
(d) Fertile materials are capable of chain reactions at room temperature, while fissile materials only react at high temperatures.

**5.** Consider the following materials and identify how many of them are fertile materials:

1. Uranium-238 2. Thorium-232
3. Plutonium-239 4. Uranium-235

Select the correct answer from the codes given below:

(a) Only one
(b) Only two
(c) Only three
(d) All four

**6.** Consider the following statements:

1. Uranium-235 is a fissile isotope commonly used as fuel in nuclear reactors.
2. Uranium-238 is the most abundant isotope of uranium and can undergo fission directly to release energy.
3. Enriched uranium contains a higher proportion of Uranium-235 than natural uranium.

How many of the given above statements is/are correct?

(a) Only one (b) Only two
(c) All three (d) None

**7.** In the context of India's nuclear resource deposits, which of the following statements are correct?

1. India has one of the largest reserves of thorium in the world.
2. Thorium-rich monazite sands are abundantly found along the coastal regions of Kerala and Tamil Nadu.
3. Uranium deposits in India are primarily concentrated in the states of Kerala and Tamil Nadu.

Select the correct answer from the codes given below:

(a) 1 and 2 only
(b) 2 and 3 only
(c) 1 and 3 only
(d) 1, 2 and 3

**8.** What type of nuclear reaction primarily takes place in the Sun's core to produce energy?

(a) Nuclear fission of heavy elements
(b) Fusion of hydrogen nuclei into helium
(c) Radioactive decay of uranium
(d) Chemical reactions involving oxygen and hydrogen

**9.** Consider the following statements.

**Statement I :** Nuclear fission reactions produce a large amount of radioactive waste, which poses significant challenges for long-term disposal and environmental safety.

**Statement II :** In nuclear fission, heavy nuclei like Uranium-235 are split into lighter elements, resulting in the formation of radioactive by-products that contribute to nuclear waste.

Which one of the following is correct in respect of the above statements?

(a) Both Statement I and Statement II are correct, and Statement II is the correct explanation for Statement I.
(b) Both Statement I and Statement II are correct, but Statement II is not the correct explanation for Statement I.
(c) Statement I is correct, but Statement II is incorrect.
(d) Statement I is incorrect, but Statement II is correct.

**10.** Which of the following statements best describes Uranium Enrichment?

(a) Uranium enrichment is the process of increasing the percentage of Uranium-238 in uranium fuel to make it suitable for nuclear reactors.
(b) Uranium enrichment is the process of reducing the radioactivity of uranium by removing radioactive isotopes.
(c) Uranium enrichment increases the concentration of Uranium-235 in uranium fuel, making it capable of sustaining a chain reaction for energy production.
(d) Uranium enrichment involves combining uranium with other elements to stabilise its atomic structure.

**11.** Which of the following methods is commonly used for nuclear enrichment?

(a) Electrolysis
(b) Gas centrifugation
(c) Fractional distillation
(d) Magnetic separation

**12.** Which of the following statements about percentages of Uranium enrichment and their typical uses are correct?

1. Low-enriched uranium (LEU), enriched to 3-5% Uranium-235, is commonly used as fuel in nuclear power reactors.
2. Highly enriched uranium (HEU), enriched to over 20% Uranium-235, is primarily used for research reactors and certain types of nuclear weapons.
3. Natural uranium, with about 0.7% Uranium-235, is sufficient for use in standard nuclear reactors without further enrichment.

Select the correct answer using the codes given below:

(a) 1 and 2 only (b) 1 and 3 only
(c) 2 and 3 only (d) 1, 2 and 3

**13.** Which of the following best describes the purpose of the 'AUKUS Agreement'?

(a) A trilateral security pact between Australia, the UK and the US to develop nuclear-powered submarines for Australia.
(b) An economic treaty aimed at eliminating trade barriers between Australia, the UK and the US.
(c) A global climate pact focused on renewable energy collaboration among the member nations.
(d) A military agreement for joint missile defence systems across the Pacific.

**14.** Consider the following statements with respect to the Uranium Enrichment in 'INS Arihant':

1. It is powered by a nuclear reactor that uses highly enriched uranium (HEU) fuel.
2. The uranium enrichment level for INS Arihant's reactor is above 90%, similar to enrichment levels used in U.S. and U.K. naval reactors.
3. The submarine operates with uranium fuel enriched to weapons-grade levels, similar to enrichment in nuclear weapons.

How many of the above statements is/are correct?

(a) Only one (b) Only two
(c) All three (d) None

## Topic 2 : Nuclear Reactor

**15.** What does 'Criticality' signify in a nuclear reactor?

(a) The reactor has been permanently shut down.
(b) The reactor has achieved a stable, self-sustaining chain reaction, marking a key operational step.
(c) The reactor is fully loaded with fuel, ready for construction.
(d) The reactor is under maintenance and not producing power.

**16.** Which of the following components in a nuclear reactor is primarily responsible for absorbing excess neutrons to prevent the reactor from overheating?

1. Control rods
2. Coolant
3. Moderator
4. Turbine

Select the correct answer using the codes given below:

(a) 1 only (b) 2 and 3 only
(c) 3 and 4 only (d) 1, 2 and 4

**17.** Match the following components of a nuclear reactor with their primary functions.

| | Component | | Function |
|---|---|---|---|
| 1. | Control Rods | A. | Slows down neutrons to sustain a controlled chain reaction |
| 2. | Moderator | B. | Transfers heat from the reactor core |
| 3. | Coolant | C. | Absorbs excess neutrons to control the fission rate |
| 4. | Reactor Core | D. | Area where nuclear fission occurs, containing fuel assemblies |

Select the correct answer using the codes given below:

(a) 1-C, 2-A, 3-B, 4-D
(b) 1-B, 2-C, 3-A, 4-D
(c) 1-D, 2-A, 3-C, 4-B
(d) 1-A, 2-B, 3-D, 4-C

**18.** Consider the following statements about 'Thermal Neutron Reactors'.
1. Thermal neutron reactors use a moderator to slow down neutrons.
2. These reactors generally use natural uranium as fuel without any need for enrichment.
3. Heavy water and graphite are commonly used as moderators in thermal neutron reactors.

How many of the above statements is/are correct?
(a) Only one (b) Only two
(c) All three (d) None

**19.** Which of the following statements are correct with respect to various nuclear reactors?
1. Pressurised Water Reactors (PWR) use water as both a coolant and a moderator.
2. Fast Breeder Reactors (FBR) do not use a moderator and are designed to produce more fissile material than they consume.
3. Boiling Water Reactors (BWR) use heavy water as a moderator to sustain the nuclear reaction.

Select the correct answer using the codes given below:
(a) 1 and 2 only (b) 1 and 3 only
(c) 2 and 3 only (d) 1, 2 and 3

**20.** Which of the following characteristics are associated with Breeder reactors?
1. They convert fertile isotopes like Uranium-238 into fissile isotopes such as Plutonium-239.
2. They use a neutron moderator to slow down neutrons for efficient breeding.
3. Liquid sodium is commonly used as a coolant in fast breeder reactors.
4. They are designed to consume more fissile material than they produce.

Select the correct answer using the codes given below:
(a) 1 and 3 only
(b) 1, 2 and 4 only
(c) 2 and 4 only
(d) 1, 2, 3 and 4

**21.** The world's first floating nuclear power plant, nicknamed 'Chernobyl on Ice', was developed by which country?
(a) United States (b) China
(c) Japan (d) Russia

**22.** Match the following operational nuclear reactors in India with their respective locations.

| | Nuclear Reactor | | Location |
|---|---|---|---|
| 1. | Tarapur Atomic Power Station | A. | Tamil Nadu |
| 2. | Kakrapar Atomic Power Station | B. | Maharashtra |
| 3. | Kudankulam Nuclear Power Plant | C. | Karnataka |
| 4. | Kaiga Atomic Power Station | D. | Gujarat |

Select the correct answer using the codes given below:
(a) 1-B, 2-D, 3-A, 4-C
(b) 1-C, 2-A, 3-D, 4-B
(c) 1-A, 2-C, 3-B, 4-D
(d) 1-D, 2-B, 3-A, 4-C

**23.** Match the following nuclear power plants in India with their respective reactor types.

| | Nuclear Power Plant | | Reactor Type |
|---|---|---|---|
| 1. | Narora Nuclear Power Plant | A. | Pressurised Heavy Water Reactor (PHWR) |
| 2. | Kudankulam Nuclear Power Plant | B. | Pressurised Water Reactor (PWR) |
| 3. | Kalpakkam Nuclear Power Plant | C. | Fast Breeder Reactor (FBR) |
| 4. | Tarapur Atomic Power Station | D. | Boiling Water Reactor (BWR) |

Select the correct answer using the codes given below:
(a) 1-A, 2-B, 3-C, 4-D
(b) 1-B, 2-A, 3-D, 4-C
(c) 1-C, 2-D, 3-B, 4-A
(d) 1-D, 2-C, 3-A, 4-B

## Topic 3 : India's Nuclear Power Programme

**24.** Which of the following statements accurately describe the APSARA Nuclear Reactor Programme in India?

1. APSARA was the first research reactor in India and also the first in Asia.
2. The original APSARA reactor operated on low-enriched uranium (LEU) fuel from the beginning.
3. APSARA-U, the upgraded version, was commissioned in 2018 and has a higher neutron flux for enhanced research capabilities.

Select the correct answer using the codes given below:

(a) 1 and 2 only (b) 1 and 3 only
(c) 2 and 3 only (d) 1, 2 and 3

**25.** Which of the following reactors were part of India's Initial Nuclear Research Programme?

1. APSARA 2. CIRUS
3. DHRUV 4. KAMINI

Select the correct answer using the codes given below:

(a) 1 and 2 only (b) 1, 2 and 3 only
(c) 2, 3 and 4 only (d) 1, 2, 3 and 4

**26.** Consider the following statements regarding the first stage of India's Nuclear Power Programme:

1. The first stage primarily uses natural uranium as fuel in Pressurised Heavy Water Reactors (PHWRs).
2. The primary goal of the first stage is to produce Plutonium-239, which will be used in the second stage.
3. The reactors in the first stage are designed to operate without a neutron moderator.

How many of the above statements is/are correct?

(a) Only one (b) Only two
(c) All three (d) None

**27.** Consider the following statements with respect to the third stage of India's Nuclear Power Programme (NPP).

1. The third stage aims to use Thorium-232 to breed Uranium-233, which is a fissile material.
2. Advanced Heavy Water Reactors (AHWRs) are part of the third stage, designed to utilise India's abundant thorium resources.
3. The third stage is currently fully operational, with several thorium-based reactors contributing to India's power grid.

How many of the above statements is/are correct?

(a) Only one (b) Only two
(c) All three (d) None

**28.** Consider the following pairs of elements and their usage in India's Three-Stage Nuclear Programme.

| | Element | Usage |
|---|---|---|
| 1. | Uranium-235 | Fuel for Pressurised Heavy Water Reactors (PHWRs) in the first stage |
| 2. | Plutonium-239 | Fuel for Fast Breeder Reactors (FBRs) in the second stage |
| 3. | Thorium-232 | Source material for producing Uranium-233 in the third stage |

How many of the given above pairs is/are correctly matched?

(a) Only one pair (b) Only two pairs
(c) All three pairs (d) None

**29.** Which of the following statements correctly describe features of India's Nuclear Power Programme?

1. India's Nuclear Power Programme is structured in three stages, focusing on utilising uranium, plutonium and thorium resources.
2. The first stage involves using Pressurised Heavy Water Reactors (PHWRs) fuelled by natural uranium.
3. The third stage aims to use thorium-based reactors, leveraging India's vast thorium reserves for long-term energy security.

Select the correct answer from the codes given below:

(a) 1 and 2 only (b) 1 and 3 only
(c) 2 and 3 only (d) 1, 2 and 3

**30.** What is the primary purpose of a 'Tokamak'?

(a) To produce chemical reactions for industrial applications.

(b) To confine plasma using magnetic fields to sustain nuclear fusion reactions.

(c) To enrich uranium for nuclear power plants.

(d) To split atomic nuclei and release energy through nuclear fission.

**31.** Which of the following statements correctly describe the 'International Thermonuclear Experimental Reactor (ITER)' project?

1. ITER is designed to demonstrate the feasibility of nuclear fusion as a large-scale, clean energy source.
2. The ITER project is located in the United States and is solely funded by European Union countries.
3. The reactor aims to produce a tenfold energy gain, generating 500 MW of fusion power from 50 MW of input power.

Select the correct answer from the codes given below:

(a) 1 and 2 only (b) 1 and 3 only
(c) 2 and 3 only (d) 1, 2 and 3

**32.** Match the following Tokamak experiments with their respective countries.

| Tokamak Experiment | | Country |
|---|---|---|
| 1. Aditya | A. | United States |
| 2. KSTAR | B. | China |
| 3. EAST | C. | South Korea |
| 4. LIFE | D. | India |

Select the correct answer using the codes given below:

(a) 1-D, 2-C, 3-B, 4-A (b) 1-B, 2-D, 3-A, 4-C
(c) 1-D, 2-B, 3-C, 4-A (d) 1-A, 2-C, 3-B, 4-D

## Topic 4 : Nuclear Governance

**33.** Consider the following statements about the role of various institutions in India's Nuclear Programme governance :

1. Atomic Energy Commission (AEC) oversees policy formulation for India's nuclear programme.
2. Department of Atomic Energy (DAE) is responsible for both research and the construction of nuclear power plants.
3. Nuclear Power Corporation of India Ltd (NPCIL) operates India's nuclear power plants.

How many of the above statements is/are correct?

(a) Only one (b) Only two
(c) All three (d) None

**34.** Which of the following statements correctly describes the functions of the Bhabha Atomic Research Centre (BARC)?

1. BARC is responsible for nuclear research and technology development for both civilian and defence applications in India.
2. It operates under the Ministry of Science and Technology.
3. It is involved in developing nuclear technology for medical, agricultural and industrial applications.

Select the correct answer using the codes given below:

(a) 1 and 2 only (b) 1 and 3 only
(c) 2 and 3 only (d) 1, 2 and 3

**35.** Which of the following statements accurately describe the 'Nuclear Power Corporation of India Ltd (NPCIL)'?

1. NPCIL was established as a Public Sector Undertaking (PSU) under the Companies Act.
2. It operates under the administrative control of the Department of Atomic Energy (DAE).
3. It is responsible for both civilian nuclear energy production and nuclear weapons development.

Select the correct answer using the codes given below:

(a) 1 and 2 only

(b) 1 and 3 only

(c) 2 and 3 only

(d) 1, 2 and 3

**36.** Consider the following statements about 'Bharatiya Nabhikiya Vidyut Nigam Ltd (BHAVINI)'.

1. BHAVINI focuses on developing nuclear reactors that use thorium as fuel.
2. It operates under the Department of Atomic Energy (DAE).
3. It manages uranium mining and processing operations in India.

How many of the above statements is/are correct?

(a) Only one (b) Only two
(c) All three (d) None

**37.** Which of the following operators is responsible for operating Fast Breeder Reactors in India?

(a) Nuclear Power Corporation of India Ltd (NPCIL)
(b) Bharatiya Nabhikiya Vidyut Nigam Ltd (BHAVINI)
(c) Bhabha Atomic Research Centre (BARC)
(d) Uranium Corporation of India Ltd (UCIL)

**38.** Match the following operators in India's nuclear programme with their primary roles.

| Operator | Role |
|---|---|
| 1. Nuclear Power Corporation of India Ltd (NPCIL) | A. Mining and processing of uranium ore |
| 2. Bharatiya Nabhikiya Vidyut Nigam Ltd (BHAVINI) | B. Research and development in nuclear technology for civilian and strategic applications |
| 3. Bhabha Atomic Research Centre (BARC) | C. Development and operation of Fast Breeder Reactors |
| 4. Uranium Corporation of India Ltd (UCIL) | D. Construction and operation of nuclear power plants |

Select the correct answer from the codes given below:

(a) 1-A, 2-B, 3-D, 4-C
(b) 1-D, 2-C, 3-B, 4-A
(c) 1-C, 2-A, 3-D, 4-B
(d) 1-B, 2-D, 3-C, 4-A

**39.** With reference to the Atomic Energy Regulatory Board (AERB) in India, which of the following statements are correct?

1. AERB sets safety regulations for nuclear and radiation facilities to protect the public and the environment.
2. AERB is involved in the promotion of nuclear power development across India.
3. AERB oversees the safe handling, transport and disposal of radioactive materials.

Select the correct answer from the codes given below:

(a) 1 and 2 only (b) 1 and 3 only
(c) 2 and 3 only (d) 1, 2 and 3

## Topic 5 : Nuclear Treaties and Cooperation

**40.** Which of the following statements correctly describe the role and functions of the International Atomic Energy Agency (IAEA)?

1. The IAEA promotes the peaceful use of nuclear energy and prevents its diversion to military purposes.
2. It has the authority to enforce nuclear disarmament treaties among member states.
3. It can conduct inspections of civilian nuclear facilities to ensure compliance with non-proliferation agreements.

Select the correct answer using the codes given below:

(a) 1 and 2 only (b) 1 and 3 only
(c) 2 and 3 only (d) 1, 2 and 3

**41.** Which of the following statement(s) about the International Atomic Energy Agency (IAEA) is/are correct?

1. The IAEA was established in 1957 to promote the peaceful use of nuclear energy.
2. The headquarters of the IAEA is located in New York, USA.
3. India is not a member of the IAEA.

Select the correct answer using the codes given below:

(a) 1 only (b) 1 and 3 only
(c) 2 and 3 only (d) 1, 2 and 3

**42.** Which of the following statements correctly describe the India-U.S. Nuclear Deal?

1. The deal made India the only non-NPT signatory allowed to engage in civilian nuclear trade.
2. India committed to separating its civilian and military nuclear facilities as part of the agreement.
3. The deal requires all of India's nuclear reactors to be under International Atomic Energy Agency (IAEA) safeguards.

Select the correct answer using the codes given below:

(a) 1 and 2 only
(b) 1 and 3 only
(c) 2 and 3 only
(d) 1, 2 and 3

**43.** Which of the following countries have signed civil nuclear cooperation agreements with India, allowing India to access nuclear technology or fuel for civilian purposes?

(a) United States, Russia, Japan and Canada
(b) France, South Korea, Australia and Pakistan
(c) United Kingdom, China, Canada and Kazakhstan
(d) Germany, Japan, Pakistan and Australia

**44.** Arrange the following events of India's nuclear history in the correct chronological order.

1. India conducts its first nuclear test, known as Operation Buddha.
2. The Nuclear Non-Proliferation Treaty (NPT) is opened for signatures.
3. India is granted a waiver by the Nuclear Suppliers Group (NSG), allowing it to engage in civilian nuclear trade.
4. India conducts a series of nuclear tests under Operation Shakti.

Select the correct answer using the codes given below:

(a) 2-1-4-3
(b) 1-2-3-4
(c) 2-4-1-3
(d) 1-3-2-4

**45.** Which of the following statement(s) is/are correct about the Nuclear Non-Proliferation Treaty (NPT)?

1. To join the NPT as a nuclear-weapon state, a country must have conducted a nuclear test before 1967.
2. Nuclear-weapon states are required to dismantle their nuclear weapons by a specific deadline.
3. All United Nations member states are required to sign the NPT.

Select the correct answer using the codes given below:

(a) 1 only
(b) 2 and 3 only
(c) 1 and 3 only
(d) 1, 2 and 3

**46.** Consider the following statements regarding the Nuclear Liability Act, 2010 in India.

1. The Act holds the operator of a nuclear facility liable in the event of a nuclear accident.
2. The Act defines a maximum liability amount for nuclear operators in the case of an accident.
3. The Act provides a right of recourse, allowing operators to seek compensation from suppliers under certain circumstances.

How many of the above statements is/are correct?

(a) Only one
(b) Only two
(c) All three
(d) None

**47.** The concept of Nuclear Liability in the Nuclear Liability Act, 2010, is based on which principle?

(a) Shared Responsibility between the government and operator
(b) Absolute Liability, where the operator is liable regardless of fault
(c) Limited Liability, where negligence must be proven
(d) Supplier-Operator Shared Liability

**48.** Which of the following statements correctly describe the 'Comprehensive Nuclear-Test-Ban Treaty (CTBT)'?

1. The CTBT bans all nuclear explosions for both civilian and military purposes.
2. The treaty has been signed by all nuclear-armed states but has not yet entered into force.
3. India has signed but not ratified the CTBT.

Select the correct answer using the codes given below:

(a) 1 and 2 only (b) 1 and 3 only
(c) 2 and 3 only (d) 1, 2 and 3

**49.** Which of the following best describes the concept of a 'Nuclear Triad'?

(a) A defense strategy involving three types of nuclear delivery systems: land-based missiles, submarine-launched missiles and air-delivered weapons.
(b) A framework for international agreements limiting nuclear proliferation.
(c) A three-stage process for developing nuclear weapons involving research, testing and deployment.
(d) A treaty among three nations for joint nuclear defense.

**50.** Which phenomenon is primarily associated with a Nuclear Winter scenario?

(a) Accelerated ozone layer depletion due to ultraviolet radiation
(b) Prolonged darkness and cooling caused by atmospheric soot from nuclear explosions
(c) Intensified greenhouse gas accumulation causing rapid warming
(d) Short-term climatic changes with minimal ecological impact

# OMR SHEET

**Assessment Round**

| | | | | | | | | | | | | | | | | | | | |
|---|---|---|---|---|---|---|---|---|---|---|---|---|---|---|---|---|---|---|---|
| 1 | a | b | c | d | 31 | a | b | c | d | 61 | a | b | c | d | 91 | a | b | c | d |
| 2 | a | b | c | d | 32 | a | b | c | d | 62 | a | b | c | d | 92 | a | b | c | d |
| 3 | a | b | c | d | 33 | a | b | c | d | 63 | a | b | c | d | 93 | a | b | c | d |
| 4 | a | b | c | d | 34 | a | b | c | d | 64 | a | b | c | d | 94 | a | b | c | d |
| 5 | a | b | c | d | 35 | a | b | c | d | 65 | a | b | c | d | 95 | a | b | c | d |
| 6 | a | b | c | d | 36 | a | b | c | d | 66 | a | b | c | d | 96 | a | b | c | d |
| 7 | a | b | c | d | 37 | a | b | c | d | 67 | a | b | c | d | 97 | a | b | c | d |
| 8 | a | b | c | d | 38 | a | b | c | d | 68 | a | b | c | d | 98 | a | b | c | d |
| 9 | a | b | c | d | 39 | a | b | c | d | 69 | a | b | c | d | 99 | a | b | c | d |
| 10 | a | b | c | d | 40 | a | b | c | d | 70 | a | b | c | d | 100 | a | b | c | d |
| 11 | a | b | c | d | 41 | a | b | c | d | 71 | a | b | c | d | 101 | a | b | c | d |
| 12 | a | b | c | d | 42 | a | b | c | d | 72 | a | b | c | d | 102 | a | b | c | d |
| 13 | a | b | c | d | 43 | a | b | c | d | 73 | a | b | c | d | 103 | a | b | c | d |
| 14 | a | b | c | d | 44 | a | b | c | d | 74 | a | b | c | d | 104 | a | b | c | d |
| 15 | a | b | c | d | 45 | a | b | c | d | 75 | a | b | c | d | 105 | a | b | c | d |
| 16 | a | b | c | d | 46 | a | b | c | d | 76 | a | b | c | d | 106 | a | b | c | d |
| 17 | a | b | c | d | 47 | a | b | c | d | 77 | a | b | c | d | 107 | a | b | c | d |
| 18 | a | b | c | d | 48 | a | b | c | d | 78 | a | b | c | d | 108 | a | b | c | d |
| 19 | a | b | c | d | 49 | a | b | c | d | 79 | a | b | c | d | 109 | a | b | c | d |
| 20 | a | b | c | d | 50 | a | b | c | d | 80 | a | b | c | d | 110 | a | b | c | d |
| 21 | a | b | c | d | 51 | a | b | c | d | 81 | a | b | c | d | 111 | a | b | c | d |
| 22 | a | b | c | d | 52 | a | b | c | d | 82 | a | b | c | d | 112 | a | b | c | d |
| 23 | a | b | c | d | 53 | a | b | c | d | 83 | a | b | c | d | 113 | a | b | c | d |
| 24 | a | b | c | d | 54 | a | b | c | d | 84 | a | b | c | d | 114 | a | b | c | d |
| 25 | a | b | c | d | 55 | a | b | c | d | 85 | a | b | c | d | 115 | a | b | c | d |
| 26 | a | b | c | d | 56 | a | b | c | d | 86 | a | b | c | d | 116 | a | b | c | d |
| 27 | a | b | c | d | 57 | a | b | c | d | 87 | a | b | c | d | 117 | a | b | c | d |
| 28 | a | b | c | d | 58 | a | b | c | d | 88 | a | b | c | d | 118 | a | b | c | d |
| 29 | a | b | c | d | 59 | a | b | c | d | 89 | a | b | c | d | 119 | a | b | c | d |
| 30 | a | b | c | d | 60 | a | b | c | d | 90 | a | b | c | d | 120 | a | b | c | d |

## Calculate Your Score

| | |
|---|---|
| **Correct (✓)** | |
| **Incorrect (✓)** | |
| **Unattempted** | |
| **Total Score** | |
| **Accuracy (%)** | |

## Reasons for Incorrect Answers?

| | |
|---|---|
| 1. Lack of Knowledge/Existing Source Insufficient | |
| 2. Lack of Multiple Revision | |
| 3. Common Sense Mistakes | |

**Note :**

1. Calculate total score as correct answers carry 2 marks each 1/3rd marks will deducted for **Incorrect** Answers.
2. Calculate Accuracy (%) by dividing the number of correct answers to the total number of attempted questions.

## Past Learning

**1.** With reference to radioisotope thermoelectric generators (RTGs), consider the following statements. **(2024)**

1. RTGs are miniature fission reactors.
2. RTGs are used for powering the onboard systems of spacecrafts.
3. RTGs can use Plutonium-238, which is a by-product of weapons development.

Which of the statements given above are correct?

(a) 1 and 2 only (b) 2 and 3 only
(c) 1 and 3 only (d) 1, 2 and 3

**2.** In India, why are some nuclear reactors kept under 'IAEA Safeguards' while others are riot? **(2020)**

(a) Some use uranium and others use thorium.
(b) Some use imported uranium and others use domestic supplies.
(c) Some are operated by foreign enterprises and others are operated by domestic enterprises.
(d) Some are state-owned and others are privately-owned.

**3.** Recently, India signed a deal known as 'Action Plan for Prioritisation and Implementation of Cooperation Areas in the Nuclear Field' with which of the following countries? **(2019)**

(a) Japan
(b) Russia
(c) The United Kingdom
(d) The United States of America

**4.** Consider the following statements. **(2017)**

1. The nuclear security summits are periodically held under the aegis of the United Nations.
2. The international panel on fissile materials is an organ of International Atomic Energy Agency.

Which of the statements given above is/are correct?

(a) 1 only
(b) 2 only
(c) Both 1 and 2
(d) Neither 1 nor 2

**5.** India is an important member of the 'International Thermonuclear Experimental Reactor'. If this experiment succeeds, what is the immediate advantage for India? **(2016)**

(a) It can use thorium in place of uranium for power generation.
(b) It can attain a global role in satellite navigation.
(c) It can drastically improve the efficiency of its fusion reactors in power generation.
(d) It can build fusion reactors for power generation.

**6.** To meet its rapidly growing energy demand, some opine that India should pursue research and development on thorium as the future fuel of nuclear energy. In this context, what advantage does thorium hold over uranium? **(2012)**

1. Thorium is far more abundant in nature than uranium.
2. On the basis of per unit mass of mined mineral, thorium can generate more energy compared to natural uranium.
3. Thorium produces less harmful waste compared to uranium.

Which of the statements given above is/are correct?

(a) Only 1
(b) 2 and 3
(c) 1 and 3
(d) 1, 2 and 3

# Detailed Solutions

## Assessment Round

**1.** *(c)* Isotopes are atoms of the same element with the same number of protons but different numbers of neutrons.

- **Isotopes** are variants of the same chemical element that have the **same atomic number** (number of protons) but **different atomic masses** due to a different number of neutrons. This leads to similar chemical properties but slightly different physical properties.

For example, **Hydrogen** has three isotopes.

- **Protium (Hydrogen-1):** Contains 1 proton and no neutrons.
- **Deuterium (Hydrogen-2):** Contains 1 proton and 1 neutron.
- **Tritium (Hydrogen-3):** Contains 1 proton and 2 neutrons.

All three are hydrogen isotopes but differ in mass due to the varying number of neutrons.

**Thus, option (c) is the correct answer.**

**2.** *(b)* Only two

- **Statement 1 is correct: Deuterium (Hydrogen-2) and Tritium (Hydrogen-3)** are indeed used in nuclear fusion reactions. When these isotopes are fused under high temperatures and pressure, they release a large amount of energy, which is why they are important in research for potential fusion power sources.
- **Statement 2 is incorrect: Protium (Hydrogen-1)**, the most abundant isotope with no neutrons, is not typically used in fusion reactions because it lacks the required mass and energy release potential. Deuterium and Tritium are more suitable for fusion due to their additional neutrons, which facilitate the reaction.
- **Statement 3 is correct: Tritium** is radioactive and is not commonly found in nature. It is produced artificially in nuclear reactors by bombarding lithium with neutrons. Tritium is used in nuclear weapons and as a fuel in experimental nuclear fusion reactors.

**Thus, the correct answer is (b) Only two.**

**3.** *(b)* Nuclear fusion combines light nuclei to form a heavier nucleus, releasing large amounts of energy, while nuclear fission splits a heavy nucleus into lighter nuclei, also releasing energy.

- **Option (a) is incorrect: Nuclear fusion does not split heavy nuclei; instead, it combines light atomic nuclei** like hydrogen isotopes (deuterium and tritium) into heavier nuclei (e.g., helium). **Nuclear fission, on the other hand, involves the splitting of a heavy nucleus** (like uranium-235 or plutonium-239) into smaller nuclei.
- **Option (b) is correct:** Nuclear fusion involves the combination of light atomic nuclei to form a heavier nucleus, releasing immense energy due to mass-to-energy conversion as described by Einstein's equation $E=mc^2$. Nuclear fission splits a heavy nucleus into lighter nuclei, also releasing energy. **Both processes are capable of generating significant energy but operate on different principles.**
- **Option (c) is incorrect: Nuclear fusion and fission are nuclear reactions, not chemical reactions.** They involve changes in the nucleus of an atom, unlike chemical reactions, which involve electron interactions and bonding.
- **Option (d) is incorrect:** Nuclear fusion powers the Sun and other stars by fusing hydrogen into helium. Nuclear fission, however, is used in nuclear reactors on Earth to produce energy by splitting heavy elements.

**Thus, the correct answer is (b).**

**4.** *(c)* Fissile materials can sustain a nuclear chain reaction on their own, while fertile materials need to absorb neutrons to convert into fissile materials.

- **Fissile materials, such as Uranium-235 and Plutonium-239,** can directly sustain a nuclear chain reaction because they can undergo fission when struck by thermal neutrons.

- **Fertile materials, like Uranium-238,** require neutron absorption to convert into fissile materials capable of sustaining a chain reaction. They cannot directly undergo fission without conversion.

**Thus, the correct answer is** (c).

**5.** *(b)* Only two

- **Uranium-238** is a **fertile** material that, upon absorbing a neutron, can convert into Plutonium-239, which is fissile.
- **Thorium-232** is also a fertile material and can convert into Uranium-233, a fissile material, after neutron absorption.
- **Plutonium-239** is a fissile material and does not need conversion to sustain a chain reaction.
- **Uranium-235** is also fissile and can directly sustain a chain reaction.

**Thus, the correct answer is (b) Only two.**

**6.** *(b)* Only two

- **Statement 1 is correct: Uranium-235** is indeed a fissile isotope, meaning it can sustain a chain reaction, making it suitable as fuel in nuclear reactors.
- **Statement 2 is incorrect: Uranium-238** is the most abundant isotope of uranium, but it does not undergo fission directly. Instead, it can be converted into Plutonium-239, another fissile material, through neutron absorption.
- **Statement 3 is correct: Enriched uranium** has an increased proportion of Uranium-235 compared to natural uranium, which enhances its ability to sustain a chain reaction, making it more effective for use in nuclear reactors.

**Therefore, the correct answer is (b) Only two.**

**7.** *(a)* 1 and 2 only

- **Statement 1 is correct:** India has significant reserves of thorium, primarily in monazite sands along the eastern (Odisha) and western (Kerala and Tamil Nadu) coasts. **India has 21% of world reserves followed by Australia, Kazakhstan and Canada.**
- **Statement 2 is correct:** Thorium-rich monazite sands are commonly found along the coastal regions of Kerala, Tamil Nadu and Odisha, making India one of the largest holders of thorium reserves.
- **Statement 3 is incorrect:** Major uranium deposits are not found in Kerala and Tamil Nadu; they are primarily located in Jharkhand, and Andhra Pradesh.

**Therefore, the correct answer is (a) 1 and 2 only.**

**8.** *(b)* Fusion of hydrogen nuclei into helium

The primary nuclear reaction in the Sun's core is **nuclear fusion**, where **hydrogen nuclei (protons) combine to form helium.** This process occurs under extreme temperatures and pressures, reaching millions of degrees Celsius in the Sun's core. Fusion releases a tremendous amount of energy in the form of light and heat, which is radiated outwards and ultimately reaches Earth as sunlight.

**Thus, option (b) is the correct answer.**

**9.** *(a)* Both Statement I and Statement II are correct and Statement II is the correct for Statement I.

- **Statement I is correct:** Nuclear fission reactions indeed produce radioactive waste, which poses challenges for disposal and environmental safety due to its long-lived radioactivity.
- **Statement II is also correct:** In nuclear fission, when heavy nuclei like Uranium-235 split, they produce lighter radioactive elements as by-products, which are a significant component of nuclear waste. This explains why fission reactions generate hazardous waste that requires careful handling and disposal.

**Therefore, the correct answer is (a).**

**10.** *(c)* Uranium enrichment increases the concentration of Uranium-235 in uranium fuel, making it capable of sustaining a chain reaction for energy production.

Uranium enrichment is the process of **increasing the percentage of Uranium-235 in uranium fuel, as Uranium-235 is a fissile isotope capable of sustaining a nuclear chain**

**reaction.** Natural uranium contains only about 0.7% Uranium-235 and enrichment raises this concentration to levels required for use in nuclear reactors or, at higher levels, for nuclear weapons.

**Thus, option (c) is the correct answer.**

***11.*** *(b)* Gas centrifugation

- **Gas centrifugation** is a widely used method for uranium enrichment, where uranium hexafluoride gas is spun at high speeds to **separate isotopes based on mass.** This process enriches Uranium-235, making it suitable for use in nuclear reactors or weapons.
- **Electrolysis** is a process that uses an electric current to split compounds, typically used for separating ions in aqueous solutions, such as splitting water into hydrogen and oxygen. This technique is not applicable to uranium enrichment, as uranium isotopes are not separated based on their ionic properties but rather by their slight differences in mass.
- **Fractional distillation** is primarily used to separate liquid mixtures based on differences in boiling points, commonly applied in refining petroleum products or separating gases like nitrogen and oxygen.
- **Magnetic separation** is a method used to separate magnetic materials from non-magnetic ones, such as in mineral processing. Since both Uranium-235 and Uranium-238 isotopes exhibit similar magnetic properties, this method cannot be used to separate them.

**Thus, option (b) is the correct answer.**

***12.*** *(a)* 1 and 2 only

- **Statement 1 is correct: Low-enriched uranium** (LEU), typically enriched to 3-5% Uranium-235, **is widely used as fuel in nuclear power reactors.** This level of enrichment provides enough fissionable material to sustain a controlled nuclear chain reaction without being overly hazardous or weaponisable.
- **Statement 2 is correct:** Uranium enriched to more than 20% Uranium-235 is defined as highly enriched uranium (HEU). **All HEU is weapons-usable,** but the lower the enrichment level the greater the amount of material required to achieve a critical mass—the amount of material required to build a bomb.
  - **States with nuclear weapons typically use so-called weapons-grade HEU, which is typically defined as 90% HEU or above,** to minimise weapons' size. Smaller and lighter nuclear weapons are much easier to deliver; ballistic missiles in particular can only deliver highly miniaturised nuclear weapons.
- **Statement 3 is incorrect:** Natural uranium contains about 0.7% Uranium-235, which is insufficient for most standard nuclear reactors. Most reactors require uranium enrichment to increase the proportion of Uranium-235 to make the fuel viable for sustained energy production.

**Thus, the correct answer is (a) 1 and 2 only.**

***13.*** *(a)* A trilateral security pact between Australia, the UK and the US to develop nuclear-powered submarines for Australia.

AUKUS, launched in 2021, is a trilateral security partnership between Australia, the UK and the US, primarily aimed at developing nuclear-powered submarines for Australia to enhance its defense capabilities in the Indo-Pacific region.

**Thus, option (a) is the correct answer.**

***14.*** *(a)* Only one

- **Statement 1 is correct:** INS Arihant's nuclear reactor is fuelled by highly enriched uranium (HEU). The enrichment of uranium for this reactor provides the submarine with a reliable, long-term power source, enabling it to operate submerged for extended periods without surfacing.
- **Statement 2 is incorrect:** The uranium enrichment level for INS Arihant's reactor is believed to be between 20-40%, lower than the >90% enrichment level used in US and UK naval reactors.
- **Statement 3 is incorrect:** INS Arihant's reactor is not weapons-grade. Weapons-grade uranium is typically enriched to over 90% Uranium-235, whereas INS Arihant uses a lower enrichment level for propulsion.

**Therefore, the correct answer is (a) Only one.**

**15.** *(b)* The reactor has achieved a stable, self-sustaining chain reaction, marking a key operational step.

**Reaching criticality indicates that the reactor has begun a self-sustaining nuclear chain reaction, a critical step before it starts regular power production.** This is the key step in the life of the reactor, as it signals the shift from building the reactor to running it. Once criticality is achieved, the reactor starts producing heat, which is later turned into electricity. Managing this process with care is crucial, as it ensures the reactor runs safely within its designed limits.

**Thus, option (b) is the correct answer.**

**16.** *(a)* 1 only

- **Control rods** are used in a nuclear reactor to **absorb excess neutrons,** which helps regulate the chain reaction and prevents overheating. **Ex – Cadmium, Hafnium, Boron, etc.**
- **Coolant** removes heat from the reactor core, but it doesn't absorb neutrons.
- **Moderator** slows down neutrons but doesn't absorb them. Ex – Graphite, Heavy Water (D2O), Beryllium oxide and some organic liquids.
- **Turbine** is not related to neutron absorption; it is used to generate electricity from the steam produced by the reactor.

**Thus, the correct answer is (a) 1 only.**

**17.** *(a)* 1-C, 2-A, 3-B, 4-D

- **Control Rods (1-C) :** Control rods absorb excess neutrons to regulate the fission rate and prevent the reactor from overheating.
- **Moderator (2-A) :** The moderator slows down fast-moving neutrons, making it easier to sustain a controlled chain reaction.
- **Coolant (3-B) :** The coolant transfers heat from the reactor core to a steam generator or directly to turbines for power generation.
- **Reactor Core (4-D) :** The reactor core is the area where nuclear fission takes place and contains the fuel assemblies.

**Thus, the correct answer is (a) 1-C, 2-A, 3-B, 4-D.**

**18.** *(b)* Only two

- **Statement 1 is correct:** Thermal neutron reactors use a moderator to slow down fast-moving neutrons, making them more likely to induce fission in fissile material. Moderators, such as water or graphite, reduce the kinetic energy of neutrons to thermal levels.
- **Statement 2 is incorrect:** Most thermal neutron reactors use enriched uranium as fuel, as natural uranium does not contain enough fissile material (Uranium-235) to sustain a chain reaction efficiently. Although some reactors such as Pressurised Heavy Water Reactor (PHWR) can use natural uranium in a nuclear fission reaction.
- **Statement 3 is correct:** Heavy water (D2O) and graphite are common moderators in thermal neutron reactors because of their efficiency in slowing down neutrons without excessive absorption.

**Thus, the correct answer is (b) Only two.**

**19.** *(a)* 1 and 2 only

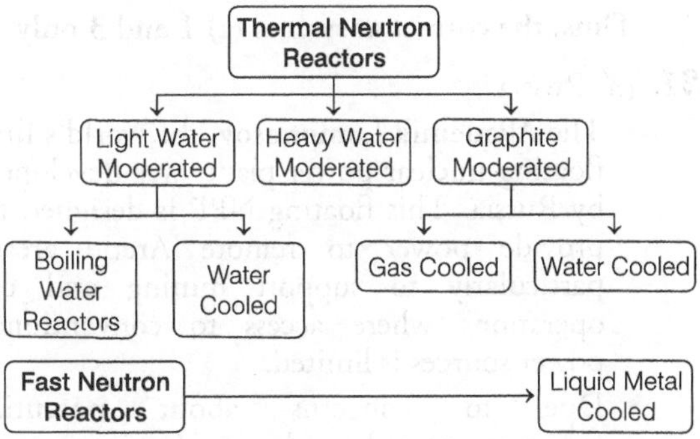


- **Statement 1 is correct:** Pressurised Water Reactors (PWR) use **ordinary (light) water** as both coolant and moderator, and the water is kept at high pressure to prevent it from boiling.
- **Statement 2 is correct:** Fast Breeder Reactors (FBR) **do not use a moderator** and are designed to 'breed' more fissile material (like Plutonium-239) than they consume.

- **Statement 3 is incorrect:** Boiling Water Reactors (BWR) use ordinary (light) water as both coolant and moderator, **not heavy water (deuterium oxide).**

**Therefore, the correct answer is (a) 1 and 2 only.**

***20.*** *(a)* 1 and 3 only

- **Statement 1 is correct:** Breeder reactors are **designed to convert fertile isotopes** like Uranium-238 into fissile isotopes like Plutonium-239, effectively 'breeding' new fuel.
- **Statement 2 is incorrect:** Breeder reactors, especially fast breeder reactors, **do not use a neutron moderator**. They operate with fast neutrons to achieve the breeding process.
- **Statement 3 is correct:** Fast breeder reactors commonly use **liquid sodium** as a coolant due to its high heat transfer capabilities and ability to operate at low pressures.
- **Statement 4 is incorrect:** Breeder reactors are designed to produce **more fissile material than they consume**, not the other way around.

**Thus, the correct answer is (a) 1 and 3 only.**

***21.*** *(d)* Russia

- The **Akademik Lomonosov**, the world's first floating nuclear power plant, was developed by Russia. This floating NPP is designed to provide power to remote Arctic areas, particularly to support mining and oil operations where access to conventional power sources is limited.
- Due to concerns about potential environmental hazards in Arctic waters, especially if an accident were to occur, the plant has been nicknamed 'Chernobyl on Ice'.

**Thus, option (d) is the correct answer.**

***22.*** *(a)* 1-B, 2-D, 3-A, 4-C

- Tarapur Atomic Power Station is located in Maharashtra.
- Kakrapar Atomic Power Station is located in Gujarat.
- Kudankulam Nuclear Power Plant is located in Tamil Nadu.
- Kaiga Atomic Power Station is located in Karnataka.

**Thus, the correct answer is (a) 1-B, 2-D, 3-A, 4-C.**

***23.*** *(a)* 1-A, 2-B, 3-C, 4-D

**Operational Nuclear Power Plants in India**

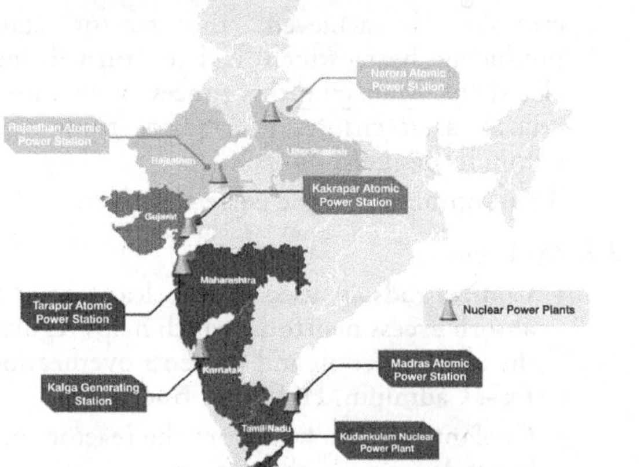


- Narora Nuclear Power Plant in Uttar Pradesh uses a Pressurised Heavy Water Reactor (PHWR).
- Kudankulam Nuclear Power Plant in Tamil Nadu uses a Pressurised Water Reactor (PWR).
- Kalpakkam Nuclear Power Plant also in Tamil Nadu includes a Fast Breeder Reactor (FBR).
- Tarapur Atomic Power Station in Maharashtra uses a Boiling Water Reactor (BWR).

**Thus, the correct answer is (a) 1-A, 2-B, 3-C, 4-D.**

***24.*** *(b)* 1 and 3 only

- **Statement 1 is correct:** APSARA was indeed **India's first research reactor** and the first of its kind in Asia.
- **Statement 2 is incorrect:** The original APSARA reactor initially used **highly enriched uranium** (HEU) fuel, not low-enriched uranium (LEU).
- **Statement 3 is correct: APSARA-U** was commissioned in 2018 and has a higher neutron flux, which enhances its capability for research and radioisotope production.

**Therefore, the correct answer is (b) 1 and 3 only.**

**25.** *(a)* 1 and 2 only

- **APSARA** was India's first nuclear research reactor, commissioned in 1956, marking the beginning of India's nuclear programme.
- **CIRUS (Canada-India Reactor, US)** was a significant part of India's early nuclear programme and was commissioned in 1960 for research and isotope production.
- **DHRUV** is a more advanced reactor commissioned in 1985, so it was not part of the initial programme.
- **KAMINI** is a later reactor commissioned in 1996 and is not part of India's initial nuclear research programme.

**Thus, the correct answer is (a) 1 and 2 only.**

**26.** *(b)* Only two

- **Statement 1 is correct:** The first stage of India's Nuclear Programme primarily uses natural uranium as fuel in Pressurised Heavy Water Reactors (PHWRs).
- **Statement 2 is correct:** The first stage aims to produce Plutonium-239 as a by-product, which will be used as fuel in the second stage.
- **Statement 3 is incorrect:** PHWRs use heavy water as a neutron moderator to sustain the fission reaction, so a moderator is indeed used in the first stage.

**Therefore, the correct answer is (b) Only two.**

**27.** *(b)* Only two

- **Statement 1 is correct:** The third stage of India's Nuclear Programme aims to use Thorium-232 to breed Uranium-233, a fissile material for sustainable nuclear power.
- **Statement 2 is correct:** Advanced Heavy Water Reactors (AHWRs) are part of the third stage and are designed to harness India's abundant thorium reserves.
- **Statement 3 is incorrect:** The third stage is still in the research and development phase, and thorium-based reactors are not yet fully operational in India.

**Thus, the correct answer is (b) Only two.**

**28.** *(b)* Only two pairs

- **Pair 1 is incorrectly matched:** The first stage primarily uses **natural uranium** (Uranium-238) as fuel in Pressurised Heavy Water Reactors (PHWRs). This because natural uranium, not enriched Uranium-235, is used.
- **Pair 2 is correctly matched:** Plutonium-239 is the element produced in the first stage and used as fuel in Fast Breeder Reactors (FBRs) during the second stage.
- **Pair 3 is correctly matched:** In the third stage, Thorium-232 is used as a source material to produce Uranium-233, a fissile material, through neutron absorption.

**Thus, the correct answer is (b) Only two pairs.**

**29.** *(d)* 1, 2 and 3

- **Statement 1 is correct:** India's nuclear power program is indeed designed in three stages to progressively utilise indigenous uranium, plutonium and thorium resources.
- **Statement 2 is correct:** The first stage of India's nuclear programme uses Pressurised Heavy Water Reactors (PHWRs) fuelled by natural uranium, which produces plutonium as a by-product.
- **Statement 3 is correct:** The third stage aims to develop thorium-based reactors using Thorium-232, which India has in abundance, to produce Uranium-233 for sustainable, long-term energy security.

**Therefore, the correct answer is (d) 1, 2 and 3.**

**30.** *(b)* To confine plasma using magnetic fields to sustain nuclear fusion reactions.

A **Tokamak** is a device designed to **confine hot plasma using powerful magnetic fields** to sustain nuclear **fusion reactions.** This approach aims to replicate the energy- producing process of the Sun, with the goal of achieving controlled fusion as a source of nearly limitless, clean energy.

**Thus, option (b) is the correct answer.**

**31.** *(b)* 1 and 3 only

- **Statement 1 is correct:** The **ITER project** is indeed focused on proving that **nuclear fusion** can be a feasible, large-scale and clean energy source for the future.
- **Statement 2 is incorrect:** ITER is located in **Cadarache, France** and involves contributions from 35 countries, including the **European Union, United States, Russia, China, Japan, India and South Korea.**

- **Statement 3 is correct:** ITER aims to achieve a **tenfold energy gain** by producing **500 MW** of fusion power from an input of **50 MW**.

**Thus, the correct answer is (b) 1 and 3 only.**

**32.** *(a)* 1-D, 2-C, 3-B, 4-A

- **Aditya** : The Aditya Tokamak is an Indian experiment focused on studying plasma confinement and fusion.
- **KSTAR** : KSTAR (Korean Superconducting Tokamak Advanced Research) is a South Korean experiment dedicated to stable nuclear fusion research.
- **EAST** : EAST (Experimental Advanced Superconducting Tokamak) is a Chinese project aimed at long-duration nuclear fusion experiments.
- **LIFE** : The LIFE (Laser Inertial Fusion Energy) project is a United States-based initiative, though focused on inertial fusion rather than magnetic confinement like tokamaks.

**Thus, the correct answer is (a) 1-D, 2-C, 3-B, 4-A.**

**33.** *(b)* Only two

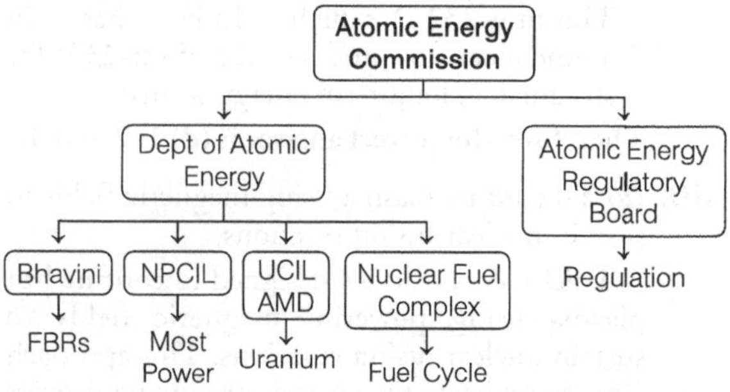


- **Statement 1 is correct:** The Atomic Energy Commission (AEC) is the apex body which is responsible for policy formulation and overseeing India's nuclear programme.
- **Statement 2 is incorrect:** While the Department of Atomic Energy (DAE) oversees nuclear activities, research is primarily handled by institutions like BARC, while NPCIL manages plant construction and operations.
- **Statement 3 is correct:** NPCIL is responsible for the operation and construction of nuclear power plants in India.

**Thus, the correct answer is (b) Only two.**

**34.** *(b)* 1 and 3 only

- The **Bhabha Atomic Research Centre (BARC)** is India's premier nuclear research facility, located in **Trombay, Maharashtra.** It was established in **1954** by Dr. Homi J. Bhabha, regarded as the father of India's nuclear programme, to advance nuclear research and technology development in India.
- **Statement 1 is correct:** BARC is responsible for nuclear research and technology development in various fields, including **civilian and strategic defence** applications.
- **Statement 2 is incorrect:** BARC operates under the **Department of Atomic Energy** (DAE), not the Ministry of Science and Technology.
- **Statement 3 is correct:** BARC plays a key role in developing nuclear technology with applications in medicine, agriculture and industry. For example, **Bhabhatron** is an indigenous teletherapy machine developed by BARC for cost-effective cancer treatment and it also uses **radiation-induced mutation breeding** to develop improved crop varieties for agriculture.

**Thus, the correct answer is (b) 1 and 3 only.**

**35.** *(a)* 1 and 2 only

- **Statement 1 is correct: NPCIL** was established in **1987** as a **public sector enterprise** under the **Companies Act, 1956.** It operates as a **Government of India Enterprise** and is fully owned by the **Government of India.**
- **Statement 2 is correct:** NPCIL operates under the **Department of Atomic Energy** (DAE).
- **Statement 3 is incorrect:** NPCIL is focused solely on **civilian nuclear energy production** and does not engage in nuclear weapons development.

**Thus, the correct answer is (a) 1 and 2 only.**

**36.** *(a)* Only one

- **Statement 1 is incorrect:** Although India's long-term goal includes using thorium as fuel, BHAVINI focuses on Fast Breeder Reactors, which primarily use plutonium.

- **Statement 2 is correct:** BHAVINI operates under the Department of Atomic Energy (DAE).
- **Statement 3 is incorrect:** Uranium mining and processing are handled by the Uranium Corporation of India Ltd (UCIL), not BHAVINI.

**Thus, the correct answer is (a) Only one.**

**37.** *(b)* Bharatiya Nabhikiya Vidyut Nigam Ltd (BHAVINI)

BHAVINI is specifically responsible for the development and operation of Fast Breeder Reactors (FBRs) in India, as part of the three-stage nuclear programme focused on utilising plutonium and thorium resources. The other operators—NPCIL, BARC, and UCIL—have distinct roles but are not directly involved in the operation of Fast Breeder Reactors.

**Thus, option (b) is the correct answer.**

**38.** *(b)* 1-D, 2-C, 3-B, 4-A

- **NPCIL** is responsible for the **construction and operation of nuclear power plants.**
- **BHAVINI** focuses on the **development and operation of Fast Breeder Reactors.**
- **BARC** is involved in **research and development** for both civilian and strategic nuclear applications.
- **UCIL** handles the **mining and processing of uranium.**

**Thus, the correct answer is (b) 1-D, 2-C, 3-B, 4-A.**

**39.** *(b)* 1 and 3 only

**The Atomic Energy Regulatory Board** (AERB) was established under the provisions of the **Atomic Energy Act, 1962.** This act provides the legal framework for regulating nuclear and radiation activities in India, including safety standards and the operation of nuclear facilities.

- **Statement 1 is correct:** The **AERB** is responsible for setting **safety regulations** for nuclear and radiation facilities to protect public health and the environment.
- **Statement 2 is incorrect:** AERB does not promote nuclear power development; it serves as a regulatory body focusing on safety, not promotion. **Nuclear Power Corporation of India Ltd (NPCIL) is responsible for the promotion of nuclear power development across India.**
- **Statement 3 is correct:** AERB oversees the **safe handling, transport and disposal** of radioactive materials to ensure safety standards are met.

**Therefore, the correct answer is (b) 1 and 3 only.**

**40.** *(b)* 1 and 3 only

- **Statement 1 is correct:** The IAEA promotes the peaceful use of nuclear energy and works to prevent the diversion of nuclear materials for military purposes.
- **Statement 2 is incorrect:** The IAEA does not have the authority to enforce nuclear disarmament; its mandate focuses on promoting peaceful nuclear use and non-proliferation rather than disarmament enforcement.
- **Statement 3 is correct:** The IAEA conducts inspections of civilian nuclear facilities to verify that nuclear materials are used only for peaceful purposes, in line with non-proliferation agreements.

**Thus, the correct answer is (b) 1 and 3 only.**

**41.** *(a)* 1 only

- **Statement 1 is correct:** The IAEA was established in 1957 with a mandate to promote the peaceful use of nuclear energy and prevent its misuse for military purposes.
- **Statement 2 is incorrect:** The headquarters of the IAEA is located in **Vienna, Austria.**
- **Statement 3 is incorrect:** India is a member of the IAEA and participates actively in its programmes, particularly those related to peaceful nuclear applications.

**Thus, the correct answer is (a) 1 only.**

**42.** *(a)* 1 and 2 only

- The **123 Agreement** between India and the United States is a civil nuclear cooperation agreement that enables India to access US nuclear technology and fuel for civilian purposes, despite being a non-signatory of the Nuclear Non-Proliferation Treaty (NPT). This agreement has allowed India to participate in international nuclear trade for its civilian nuclear energy programmes.

- **Statement 1 is correct:** The India-US Nuclear deal made India the **only non-NPT signatory** allowed to engage in civilian nuclear trade, enabling India to access nuclear technology and fuel from other countries.
- **Statement 2 is correct:** As part of the agreement, India committed to separating its civilian and military nuclear facilities to ensure that only civilian facilities would benefit from international cooperation and safeguards.
- **Statement 3 is incorrect:** The deal does **not require all of India's nuclear reactors** to be under IAEA safeguards, **only the civilian reactors** that are part of the agreement.

**Thus, the correct answer is (a) 1 and 2 only.**

***43.*** *(a)* United States, Russia, Japan and Canada.

India has signed civil nuclear cooperation agreements with several countries to access nuclear technology, fuel and reactors for civilian use. Key partners include the United States, Russia, Japan, Canada, France, Australia and Kazakhstan. These agreements provide India with the resources necessary for its civilian nuclear energy expansion while ensuring compliance with non-proliferation commitments.

**Thus, option (a) is the correct answer.**

***44.*** *(a)* 2-1-4-3

- **The Nuclear Non-Proliferation Treaty (NPT)** was opened for signatures in 1968, aiming to prevent the spread of nuclear weapons. India chose not to sign the treaty.
- **Operation Buddha,** India's first nuclear test, was conducted in 1974 in Pokhran, marking India's entry as a nuclear-capable state.
- **Operation Shakti**, a series of nuclear tests, was conducted by India in 1998 at Pokhran, further solidifying India's nuclear capability.
- In 2008, India was granted a waiver by the **Nuclear Suppliers Group (NSG)**, allowing it to engage in civilian nuclear trade without being a signatory to the NPT.

**Hence, the correct chronological order is** (a) 2-1-4-3.

***45.*** *(a)* 1 only

- **Statement 1 is correct:** The NPT defines nuclear-weapon states as countries that conducted nuclear tests before 1967 (the U.S., Russia, China, France and the UK).
- **Statement 2 is incorrect:** While the NPT promotes disarmament, it does not set a specific deadline for nuclear-weapon states to dismantle their arsenals.
- **Statement 3 is incorrect:** NPT membership is not compulsory for all UN members; several countries, including India, Pakistan and Israel, have not signed the treaty.

**Thus, the correct answer is (a) 1 only.**

***46.*** *(c)* All three

- **Statement 1 is correct:** The Nuclear Liability Act, 2010 holds the operator liable for damages in the event of a nuclear accident.
- **Statement 2 is correct:** The Nuclear Liability Act, 2010 sets a maximum liability cap for nuclear operators in case of a nuclear accident, helping to define the financial responsibilities in the event of damages.
- **Statement 3 is correct:** The Act includes a right of recourse, allowing operators to claim compensation from suppliers under specific conditions.

**Therefore, the correct answer is (c) All three.**

***47.*** *(b)* Absolute Liability, where the operator is liable regardless of fault.

- The Nuclear Liability Act, 2010, is based on the **Principle of Absolute Liability,** meaning the operator of a nuclear facility is fully responsible for compensating damages arising from a nuclear incident, regardless of fault or negligence. This ensures victims are compensated without the need to prove negligence, providing an assured mechanism for financial responsibility.
- **For example,** suppose there is a minor accident at a nuclear power plant in India, resulting in a release of radiation that affects

the health of nearby residents. Under the **Absolute Liability** principle, the **nuclear** operator (such as NPCIL) is required to compensate affected individuals for their medical expenses, health impacts and other damages, regardless of whether the operator was at fault or negligent in causing the accident.

**Thus, option (b) is the correct answer.**

***48.*** *(a)* 1 and 2 only

- **Statement 1 is correct:** The **CTBT** bans **all nuclear explosions** for both civilian and military purposes, including tests and detonations.
- **Statement 2 is correct:** Although the treaty has been signed by many countries, it has not yet **entered into force** because certain nuclear-armed states, including the US and China, have not ratified it.
- **Statement 3 is incorrect:** India has neither **signed nor ratified** the CTBT due to concerns about the treaty's perceived discriminatory nature and its impact on India's security needs.

**Thus, the correct answer is (a) 1 and 2 only.**

***49.*** *(a)* A defense strategy involving three types of nuclear delivery systems: land-based missiles, submarine-launched missiles and air-delivered weapons.

The Nuclear Triad refers to a military strategy that ensures the delivery of nuclear weapons through three distinct platforms: land-based intercontinental ballistic missiles (ICBMs), submarine-launched ballistic missiles (SLBMs) and strategic bombers. This approach ensures survivability and strategic deterrence.

**Thus, option (a) is the correct answer.**

***50.*** *(b)* Prolonged darkness and cooling caused by atmospheric soot from nuclear explosions.

Nuclear Winter occurs due to the injection of large amounts of soot and aerosols into the stratosphere from nuclear explosions and subsequent fires. These particles block sunlight, leading to prolonged darkness, cooling and significant ecological, and agricultural disruptions.

**Thus, option (b) is the correct answer**

## Past Learning (Answers)

**1** (b) **2** (b) **3** (b) **4** (d) **5** (d) **6** (d)

# CHAPTER 05 Intellectual Property Rights (IPRs)

## Assessment Round

**1.** Consider the following treaties:
1. Paris Convention
2. Berne Convention
3. TRIPS Agreement
4. Madrid Protocol

How many of the above treaties have influenced India's Intellectual Property Rights (IPR) framework significantly?
(a) Only one (b) Only two
(c) Only three (d) All four

**2.** With reference to the 'World Intellectual Property Organisation (WIPO)', consider the following statements:
1. It is a specialised agency of the United Nations established to promote the protection of intellectual property worldwide.
2. WIPO administers international treaties such as the Patent Cooperation Treaty and the Madrid system for trademarks.
3. All countries that are members of the United Nations are automatically members of WIPO.

Which of the above statements are correct?
(a) 1 and 2 only (b) 2 and 3 only
(c) 1 and 3 only (d) 1, 2 and 3

**3.** Consider the following statements about WIPO.
1. It oversees the Global Innovation Index, which ranks countries based on their innovation performance.
2. It can enforce IP laws in the member countries.
3. It solely focuses on trademark protection and excludes patents from its scope.

Which of the given above statements is/are correct?
(a) 1 and 2 only
(b) 1 only
(c) 2 and 3 only
(d) 1, 2 and 3

**4.** Which of the following statement(s) is/are correct about the TRIPs Agreement?
1. It was one of the original agreements negotiated under the GATT in 1947.
2. It was fully implemented by all WTO members in 1995.
3. The Doha Declaration (2001) acknowledged the right to protect public health.

Select the correct answer using the codes given below:
(a) 1 and 3 only
(b) 3 only
(c) 1, 2 and 3
(d) 1 and 2 only

**5.** Which of the following best describes a 'TRIPS-Plus measure'?
(a) Provisions that mandate the patenting of plants and animals.
(b) Requirements under the TRIPS Agreement for all WTO member states.
(c) Additional intellectual property protections that go beyond the requirements of the TRIPS Agreement.
(d) Provisions that limit the duration of copyright protection to 20 years.

**6.** Consider the following types of intellectual property.

1. Copyright
2. Patents
3. Trade Secrets
4. Traditional Knowledge

How many of the above is/are explicitly protected under the WTO TRIPs Agreement?

(a) Only one (b) Only two
(c) Only three (d) All four

**7.** Consider the following statements:

1. The TRIPs Agreement allows compulsory licensing under certain conditions but India has never issued compulsory licenses in the pharmaceutical sector.
2. Under TRIPs, patents must be granted for at least 30 years from the date of application.
3. India amended its Patent Act in 2005 to comply with the TRIPs requirements, allowing product patents in pharmaceuticals and agricultural chemicals.

How many of the statements given above is/are correct?

(a) Only one (b) Only two
(c) All three (d) None

**8.** Consider the following statements with reference to the various features of TRIPs Agreement:

1. The TRIPs Agreement obligates WTO members to provide protection for industrial designs for at least 10 years.
2. The Agreement includes provisions for safeguarding confidential information, known as trade secrets.
3. It requires all WTO members to establish a uniform system for IP enforcement without any flexibility.

Which of the statements given above is/are correct?

(a) 1 and 2 only (b) 2 only
(c) 1 and 3 only (d) 1, 2 and 3

**9.** Which of the following best describes the purpose of 'Special 301 Report'?

(a) To monitor global economic growth rates.
(b) To evaluate and rank countries based on their compliance with Intellectual Property Rights (IPR) Standards.
(c) To set trade tariffs for countries engaged in intellectual property violations.
(d) To recommend global IPR enforcement strategies to the World Trade Organisation (WTO).

**10.** Arrange the following milestones in the evolution of Intellectual Property Rights (IPR) regulation in India in chronological order.

1. Enactment of the Patents Act
2. India's accession to the TRIPS Agreement under the WTO
3. Establishment of the Geographical Indications (GI) of Goods (Registration and Protection) Act
4. Amendments to the Patents Act to comply with TRIPS Agreement

Select the correct answer using the codes given below.

(a) 1-2-3-4 (b) 1-3-2-4
(c) 1-2-4-3 (d) 2-1-3-4

**11.** Arrange the following treaties and agreements influencing India's IPR framework in the order of their adoption by India.

1. Accession to the Berne Convention
2. The signing of the Paris Convention for Industrial Property
3. Membership in the TRIPS Agreement
4. Ratification of the Madrid Protocol

Select the correct answer using the codes given below.

(a) 2-1-3-4 (b) 1-2-4-3
(c) 2-3-1-4 (d) 1-4-3-2

**12.** With reference to the regulatory bodies of Intellectual Property Rights (IPR) in India, consider the following statements.

1. Controller General of Patents, Designs and Trademarks (CGPDTM) is responsible for administering patents, trademarks and designs in India.
2. National Biodiversity Authority (NBA) regulates patents related to biological resources in India.
3. Cell for IPR Promotion and Management (CIPAM) operates under the Ministry of Commerce and Industry and is responsible for implementing the National IPR Policy.

Which of the statements given above are correct?

(a) 1 and 2 only (b) 1 and 3 only
(c) 2 and 3 only (d) 1, 2 and 3

**13.** Consider the following types of intellectual property with their respective legislations.

| | Intellectual Property Type | Legislation |
|---|---|---|
| 1. | Industrial Design | Copyright Act, 1957 |
| 2. | Plant Variety | Indian Patents Act, 2005 |
| 3. | Trade Secret | Trade Marks Act, 1999 |
| 4. | Geographical Indication | The Geographical Indications of Goods (Registration and Protection) Act, 1999 |

How many pairs is/are correctly matched?

(a) Only one pair
(b) Only two pairs
(c) Only three pairs
(d) All four pairs

**14.** Which of the following statements correctly describe the features of the Indian Patent Act (Amendment), 2005?

1. The Act allows for product patents in the fields of pharmaceuticals and agricultural chemicals.
2. The Act provides a patent protection period of 20 years from the date of filing.
3. The Indian Patent Act, 2005 introduced the concept of compulsory licensing.
4. The Act prohibits evergreening of patents by rejecting claims for minor modifications of existing products.

Select the correct answer using the codes given below.

(a) 1 and 2 only
(b) 1, 2 and 4 only
(c) 3 and 4 only
(d) 1, 3 and 4 only

**15.** Which of the following statements correctly distinguishes between a product patent and a process patent?

(a) A product patent provides protection for the specific method or technique of manufacturing a product, while a process patent protects the end product itself.
(b) A product patent grants the inventor exclusive rights over the creation of the end product, while a process patent grants exclusive rights over the method or process of making a product.
(c) A product patent allows anyone to use the patented item but restricts the process of manufacturing it, while a process patent prevents anyone from using the product itself.
(d) Both product and process patents protect only the marketing aspects of a product, not the manufacturing details.

**16.** With reference to the concept of 'Compulsory Licensing', consider the following statements:

1. Compulsory licensing allows a government to permit someone else to produce a patented product without the consent of the patent owner.
2. Under the TRIPs Agreement, compulsory licenses can be issued only for life-saving drugs.
3. In India, the first compulsory license was issued for a cancer drug in 2012.

How many of the statements given above is/are correct?

(a) Only one (b) Only two
(c) All three (d) None

**17.** What does the term 'evergreening of patents' refer to in the context of intellectual property rights?
(a) Extending the life of a patent by making minor changes to the original product or process.
(b) Granting patent protection to an invention for an indefinite period.
(c) Allowing multiple companies to share the same patent for a product.
(d) Preventing any modifications to a patented product during its protection period.

**18.** What does the term 'parallel importation' refer to in the context of intellectual property rights?
(a) The importation of counterfeit goods into a country without authorisation.
(b) The importation of genuine goods into a country without the permission of the intellectual property rights holder.
(c) The exclusive right of the patent holder to import goods into a country.
(d) The prohibition of all imports to protect domestic industries.

**19.** With reference to the protection of Geographical Indications (GIs) in India, consider the following statements:
1. A registered GI is valid for an initial period of 10 years and can be renewed indefinitely.
2. Only agricultural products can be registered as GI under the Indian law.
3. Products with a GI tag is given special protection under the Paris Convention for the Protection of Industrial Property.

How many of the statements given above is/are correct?
(a) Only one (b) Only two
(c) All three (d) None

**20.** With reference to the Geographical Indications (GIs) in India, consider the following statements:
1. The Controller General of Patents, Designs and Trade Marks also serves as the Registrar of Geographical Indications in India.
2. Geographical Indications Registry, which administers GI registrations, is located in Mumbai.
3. The registration of a GI can be challenged by any aggrieved person before the Intellectual Property Appellate Board.

Which of the statements given above is/are correct?
(a) 1 and 2 only (b) 2 and 3 only
(c) 1 and 3 only (d) 1, 2 and 3

**21.** Consider the following statements about the 'Protection of Plant Varieties and Farmers' Rights (PPV&FR) Act, 2001'.
1. The PPV&FR Act, 2001 provides for the registration of both new plant varieties and extant varieties.
2. Farmers are not allowed to register any plant varieties under this Act.
3. The Act establishes the Protection of Plant Varieties and Farmers' Rights Authority as the regulatory body.

How many of the statements given above is/are correct?
(a) Only one (b) Only two
(c) All three (d) None

**22.** Which of the following statements correctly describe the rights granted under the Protection of Plant Varieties and Farmers' Rights Act, 2001?
1. Farmers can register new plant varieties developed by them under this Act.
2. Breeders have exclusive rights to produce and market their registered varieties.
3. The Act allows researchers to use registered varieties for conducting experiments.
4. Farmers cannot save seeds of registered varieties for future use under any circumstances.

Select the correct answer using the codes given below.
(a) 1 and 2 only
(b) 1, 2 and 3 only
(c) 2 and 4 only
(d) 1, 3 and 4 only

**23.** Which of the following rights are granted to farmers under the Protection of Plant Varieties and Farmers' Rights (PPV&FR) Act, 2001?

1. Right to save, use, sow, re-sow, exchange and share seeds of protected varieties
2. Right to sell branded seeds of registered varieties
3. Right to claim compensation for any variety that fails to perform as claimed
4. Right to produce seeds of protected varieties for commercial purposes without any limitations

Select the correct answer from the codes given below.

(a) 1 and 2 only
(b) 1 and 3 only
(c) 2, 3 and 4 only
(d) 1, 3 and 4 only

**24.** With reference to the UPOV Convention, consider the following statements:

1. The UPOV Convention grants intellectual property rights to plant breeders for developing distinct plant varieties.
2. India has not joined the UPOV Convention as its legal framework prioritises farmers' rights.

Which of the given above statement(s) is/are correct?

(a) 1 only
(b) 2 only
(c) Both 1 and 2
(d) Neither 1 nor 2

**25.** With reference to the 'National IPR Policy (2016)', consider the following statements.

1. The policy aims to create an awareness of intellectual property rights among all sections of society.
2. It establishes the DPIIT as the nodal agency for IPR policy implementation in India.
3. The policy promotes commercialisation of intellectual property assets to boost economic growth.

How many of the statements given above is/are correct?

(a) Only one (b) Only two
(c) All three (d) None

**26.** With reference to the National IPR Policy 2016, consider the following statements:

1. The policy proposes setting up specialised IP courts for faster adjudication of IPR disputes.
2. The policy is intended to encourage the development of Traditional Knowledge Digital Libraries.
3. The policy mandates all public-funded research organisations to register their IP assets with the government.

Which of the statements given above is/are correct?

(a) 1 and 2 only (b) 2 only
(c) 1 and 3 only (d) 1, 2 and 3

**27.** Consider the following types of Intellectual Property Rights (IPR) with their descriptions.

| Type of IPR | Description |
|---|---|
| 1. Trademark | Protects the exclusive use of a word, symbol, or logo to identify goods or services. |
| 2. Copyright | Grants legal protection for original literary, artistic and musical works. |
| 3. Patent | Provides exclusive rights to inventors for their novel inventions. |
| 4. Geographical Indication | Identifies goods originating from a specific location with unique qualities or reputation. |

How many of the given above pairs is/are correctly matched?

(a) Only one pair
(b) Only two pairs
(c) Only three pairs
(d) All four pairs

**28.** With reference to the 'Traditional Knowledge Digital Library (TKDL)', consider the following statements.

1. It is managed jointly by the Council of Scientific and Industrial Research (CSIR) and the Ministry of Ayush.
2. It includes codified information about medicinal formulations derived from texts like Ayurveda, Unani and Siddha.
3. It is a database established to prevent the misappropriation of India's traditional knowledge, especially through biopiracy.

Which of the above statements is/are correct?

(a) 1 and 2 only
(b) 2 and 3 only
(c) 1, 2 and 3
(d) None

## Past Learning

**1.** Consider the following statements. **(2019)**

1. According to the Indian Patents Act, a biological process to create seed can be patented in India.
2. In India, there is no Intellectual Property Appellate Board.
3. Plant varieties are not eligible to be patented in India.

Which of the statements given above is/are correct?

(a) 1 and 3 only
(b) 2 and 3 only
(c) 3 only
(d) 1, 2 and 3

**2.** With reference to the 'National Intellectual Property Rights Policy', consider the following statements: **(2017)**

1. It reiterates India's commitment to the Doha Development Agenda and the TRIPS Agreement.
2. Department of Industrial Policy and Promotion is the nodal agency for regulating intellectual property rights in India.

Which of the above statements is/are correct?

(a) 1 only
(b) 2 only
(c) Both 1 and 2
(d) Neither 1 nor 2

# OMR SHEET

**Assessment Round**

| | | | | | | | | | | | | | | | | | | | |
|---|---|---|---|---|---|---|---|---|---|---|---|---|---|---|---|---|---|---|---|
| 1 | a | b | c | d | 31 | a | b | c | d | 61 | a | b | c | d | 91 | a | b | c | d |
| 2 | a | b | c | d | 32 | a | b | c | d | 62 | a | b | c | d | 92 | a | b | c | d |
| 3 | a | b | c | d | 33 | a | b | c | d | 63 | a | b | c | d | 93 | a | b | c | d |
| 4 | a | b | c | d | 34 | a | b | c | d | 64 | a | b | c | d | 94 | a | b | c | d |
| 5 | a | b | c | d | 35 | a | b | c | d | 65 | a | b | c | d | 95 | a | b | c | d |
| 6 | a | b | c | d | 36 | a | b | c | d | 66 | a | b | c | d | 96 | a | b | c | d |
| 7 | a | b | c | d | 37 | a | b | c | d | 67 | a | b | c | d | 97 | a | b | c | d |
| 8 | a | b | c | d | 38 | a | b | c | d | 68 | a | b | c | d | 98 | a | b | c | d |
| 9 | a | b | c | d | 39 | a | b | c | d | 69 | a | b | c | d | 99 | a | b | c | d |
| 10 | a | b | c | d | 40 | a | b | c | d | 70 | a | b | c | d | 100 | a | b | c | d |
| 11 | a | b | c | d | 41 | a | b | c | d | 71 | a | b | c | d | 101 | a | b | c | d |
| 12 | a | b | c | d | 42 | a | b | c | d | 72 | a | b | c | d | 102 | a | b | c | d |
| 13 | a | b | c | d | 43 | a | b | c | d | 73 | a | b | c | d | 103 | a | b | c | d |
| 14 | a | b | c | d | 44 | a | b | c | d | 74 | a | b | c | d | 104 | a | b | c | d |
| 15 | a | b | c | d | 45 | a | b | c | d | 75 | a | b | c | d | 105 | a | b | c | d |
| 16 | a | b | c | d | 46 | a | b | c | d | 76 | a | b | c | d | 106 | a | b | c | d |
| 17 | a | b | c | d | 47 | a | b | c | d | 77 | a | b | c | d | 107 | a | b | c | d |
| 18 | a | b | c | d | 48 | a | b | c | d | 78 | a | b | c | d | 108 | a | b | c | d |
| 19 | a | b | c | d | 49 | a | b | c | d | 79 | a | b | c | d | 109 | a | b | c | d |
| 20 | a | b | c | d | 50 | a | b | c | d | 80 | a | b | c | d | 110 | a | b | c | d |
| 21 | a | b | c | d | 51 | a | b | c | d | 81 | a | b | c | d | 111 | a | b | c | d |
| 22 | a | b | c | d | 52 | a | b | c | d | 82 | a | b | c | d | 112 | a | b | c | d |
| 23 | a | b | c | d | 53 | a | b | c | d | 83 | a | b | c | d | 113 | a | b | c | d |
| 24 | a | b | c | d | 54 | a | b | c | d | 84 | a | b | c | d | 114 | a | b | c | d |
| 25 | a | b | c | d | 55 | a | b | c | d | 85 | a | b | c | d | 115 | a | b | c | d |
| 26 | a | b | c | d | 56 | a | b | c | d | 86 | a | b | c | d | 116 | a | b | c | d |
| 27 | a | b | c | d | 57 | a | b | c | d | 87 | a | b | c | d | 117 | a | b | c | d |
| 28 | a | b | c | d | 58 | a | b | c | d | 88 | a | b | c | d | 118 | a | b | c | d |
| 29 | a | b | c | d | 59 | a | b | c | d | 89 | a | b | c | d | 119 | a | b | c | d |
| 30 | a | b | c | d | 60 | a | b | c | d | 90 | a | b | c | d | 120 | a | b | c | d |

## Calculate Your Score

| | |
|---|---|
| **Correct (✓)** | |
| **Incorrect (✓)** | |
| **Unattempted** | |
| **Total Score** | |
| **Accuracy (%)** | |

## Reasons for Incorrect Answers?

| | |
|---|---|
| 1. Lack of Knowledge/Existing Source Insufficient | |
| 2. Lack of Multiple Revision | |
| 3. Common Sense Mistakes | |

**Note :**

1. Calculate total score as correct answers carry 2 marks each 1/3rd marks will deducted for **Incorrect** Answers.
2. Calculate Accuracy (%) by dividing the number of correct answers to the total number of attempted questions.

# Detailed Solutions

## Assessment Round

**1.** *(c)* Only three

- **Paris Convention:** Established in 1883, it laid the groundwork for protection of patents and trademarks across member countries. India, as a member, ensures national treatment for foreign applicants in patents and trademarks.
- **Berne Convention:** Focused on the protection of literary and artistic works, this convention influenced India's copyright laws, aligning them with global standards, especially for moral rights.
- **TRIPS Agreement:** Introduced by the WTO, TRIPS required India to adopt comprehensive protections for all forms of intellectual property, including patents, trademarks and copyrights, significantly transforming its IPR regime.
- **Madrid Protocol:** While India joined the Madrid Protocol in 2013 to streamline trademark applications internationally, its role is more recent and specific to trademarks rather than the broader IPR framework.

**Thus, the correct answer is (c) Only three.**

**2.** *(a)* 1 and 2 only

- **Statement 1 is correct:** The World Intellectual Property Organisation (WIPO) is indeed a **specialised agency of the United Nations, established in 1967** to promote the protection and use of intellectual property (IP) globally. Its objective is to foster innovation and creativity by creating a balanced and accessible international IP system.
- **Statement 2 is correct:** WIPO administers several key international treaties, including the **Patent Cooperation Treaty (PCT)**, which simplifies the patent application process in multiple countries and the **Madrid system,** which allows for the international registration of trademarks through a single application.
- **Statement 3 is incorrect:** Membership in WIPO is not automatic for United Nations member states. Countries must explicitly join WIPO to become members. As of now, WIPO has 193 member states, slightly fewer than the total number of UN member states.

**Thus, the correct answer is (a) 1 and 2 only.**

**3.** *(b)* 1 only

- **Statement 1 is correct: WIPO oversees the Global Innovation Index (GII),** which evaluates and ranks countries based on their innovation performance. This index provides insights into the strengths and weaknesses of national innovation ecosystems.
- **Statement 2 is incorrect: WIPO does not have enforcement powers over intellectual property (IP) laws** in its member countries. It facilitates cooperation and provides frameworks and treaties for IP protection but relies on member nations to enforce IP laws within their jurisdictions.
- **Statement 3 is incorrect:** WIPO's scope is comprehensive, covering **patents, trademarks, copyrights** and other forms of IP. It administers treaties like the **Patent Cooperation Treaty (PCT)** and the **Madrid system for trademarks.**

**Thus, the correct answer is (b) 1 only.**

**4.** *(b)* 3 only

- **Statement 1 is incorrect:** The TRIPs Agreement was not part of the original GATT in 1947; it was negotiated during the **Uruguay Round (1986–1994).**
- **Statement 2 is incorrect:** There was a **transition period** for developing and least-developed countries to implement the TRIPs Agreement.
  - **Developing countries were given transition periods of 10 years** to implement patent protection, especially for pharmaceutical products.
  - A 2005 amendment allowed least-developed countries to delay implementing pharmaceutical patent protection until 2033.

- **Statement 3 is correct:** The **Doha Declaration** on TRIPs and Public Health in 2001 recognised members' rights to protect public health, allowing for measures like **compulsory licensing.**

**Therefore, the correct answer is (b) 3 only.**

**5.** *(c)* Additional intellectual property protections that go beyond the requirements of the TRIPS Agreement.

- **Statement (c) is correct:** TRIPS-Plus refers to **additional Intellectual Property Rights (IPR) standards** that exceed those in the TRIPS Agreement. These are often included in bilateral or regional trade agreements, requiring stricter IPR enforcement.
- **Statement (a) is incorrect:** While TRIPS-Plus measures may include patenting certain living organisms, they are not limited to plants and animals alone.
- **Statement (b) is incorrect:** TRIPS-Plus is not part of the core TRIPS Agreement; it represents provisions adopted beyond TRIPS obligations.
- **Statement (d) is incorrect:** TRIPS-Plus often extends copyright protection rather than reducing it.

**Thus, the correct answer is (c).**

**6.** *(c)* Only three

The TRIPs Agreement explicitly covers **Copyright, Patents** and **Trade Secrets** as types of intellectual property. However, **Traditional Knowledge** is not specifically covered under TRIPs, though discussions about its protection exist at the WTO.

**Following are the types of intellectual property cover under TRIPs :**

- **Copyright and Related Rights:** Protects original literary and artistic works (e.g., books, music, films, computer software) and rights of performers, producers of sound recordings and broadcasting organisations.
- **Trademarks:** Protects signs, symbols, logos, or any combination that distinguish goods or services of one entity from others.
- **Geographical Indications (GIs):** Protects names or signs used on products that correspond to a specific geographical location or origin (e.g., Champagne from France, Darjeeling tea from India).
- **Industrial Designs:** Protects the aesthetic or ornamental aspects of an article, including shape, pattern or colour combination.
- **Patents:** Grants exclusive rights to inventors for a new and useful invention (product or process) for a specified period, typically 20 years.
- **Layout Designs of Integrated Circuits:** Protects the three-dimensional configuration of electronic circuits in integrated circuit products.
- **Trade Secrets:** Protects confidential business information, such as formulas, practices, designs, or processes, which provide a competitive edge to the business.

These categories encompass a broad range of intellectual property rights, ensuring comprehensive protection and enforcement under the TRIPS Agreement.

**Therefore, the correct answer is (c) Only three.**

**7.** *(a)* Only one

- **Statement 1 is incorrect: Compulsory licensing** is a special type of grant given by the government to allows someone else to produce a patented product or process **without the consent of the patent owner.** This special provision is rare i.e. it granted in cases like emergencies or against life-threatening diseases. It has legal backing under the TRIPS, which allows a country to grant such a provision.
  - **India issued its first compulsory license in March 2012** to the Indian pharmaceutical company Natco Pharma. This license allowed Natco to **produce a generic version of Bayer's cancer drug, Nexavar,** due to its high cost, which made it inaccessible to many patients.
  - The compulsory license was issued under Section 84 of the Indian Patents Act, which permits such licensing when patented drugs are not available at an affordable price or are inadequately supplied in the Indian market.
- **Statement 2 is incorrect:** The TRIPs Agreement mandates a minimum patent protection period of **20 years** not 30 years.

- **Statement 3 is correct:** India amended its Patent Act in 2005 to allow product patents in pharmaceuticals and agricultural chemicals in compliance with TRIPs.

**Therefore, the correct answer is (a) Only one.**

**8.** *(a)* 1 and 2 only

- **Statement 1 is correct:** The TRIPs Agreement requires WTO members to provide protection for **industrial designs** for a minimum term of **10 years.** This helps to safeguard the unique designs of industrial products and maintain fair competition.
- **Statement 2 is correct:** The Agreement includes **provisions for the protection of trade secrets,** or **confidential information,** which are considered part of intellectual property rights under TRIPs.
- **Statement 3 is incorrect:** The TRIPs Agreement allows **flexibility** for member countries in how they implement IP enforcement. Countries can adapt enforcement mechanisms to suit their legal and economic circumstances, so it does not mandate a **uniform system.**

**Therefore, the correct answer is (a) 1 and 2 only.**

**9.** *(b)* To evaluate and rank countries based on their compliance with Intellectual Property Rights (IPR) standards.

**The Special 301 Report is published annually by the United States Trade Representative (USTR).** It identifies trading partners that do not adequately or effectively protect and enforce IPR or that deny market access to U.S. entities relying on IPR.

**Thus, option (b) is the correct answer.**

**10.** *(a)* 1-2-3-4

- **The Patents Act, 1970:** This landmark legislation replaced the colonial-era Patents and Designs Act, 1911, focusing on self-reliant innovation.
- **TRIPS Agreement Accession:** India joined the World Trade Organisation (WTO) in 1995 and became a signatory to the TRIPS Agreement, requiring alignment of domestic IP laws with global standards.
- **GI Act, 1999:** To protect geographical indications like Darjeeling Tea and Pashmina, India enacted this specialised legislation.
- **Patents Act Amendment (2005):** To meet TRIPS obligations, product patents were introduced in pharmaceuticals and agriculture.

**Thus, the correct chronological sequence is 1-2-3-4.**

**11.** *(a)* 2-1-3-4

- **Paris Convention for Industrial Property:** India adopted this in 1998 to foster international cooperation in protecting industrial property like patents and trademarks.
- **Berne Convention:** India joined this treaty in 1928 to protect the rights of authors and creators.
- **TRIPS Agreement:** India signed this agreement in 1995 upon joining the WTO, harmonising its IPR framework with global standards.
- **Madrid Protocol:** India became a member in 2013, simplifying trademark registration across multiple jurisdictions.

**Thus, the correct chronological sequence is 2-1-3-4.**

**12.** *(d)* 1, 2 and 3

- **Statement 1 is correct:** The **Controller General of Patents, Designs and Trademarks (CGPDTM) is the key regulatory authority managing the administration of patents, trademarks and industrial designs in India.** It plays a vital role in granting and overseeing intellectual property rights.
- **Statement 2 is correct:** The **National Biodiversity Authority (NBA) is a statutory body** established under the Biological Diversity Act, 2002. It **regulates the access and use of biological resources and oversees patents** involving such resources to ensure compliance with biodiversity laws.
- **Statement 3 is correct: The Cell for IPR Promotion and Management (CIPAM) functions under the Department for Promotion of Industry and Internal Trade**

(DPIIT) within the Ministry of Commerce and Industry. It is tasked with implementing the National IPR Policy and promoting awareness, capacity building and combating counterfeiting and piracy.

**Thus, the correct answer is (d) 1, 2 and 3.**

***13.*** *(a)* Only one pair

- **Pair 1 is incorrect: Industrial Design** is protected under **The Designs Act, 2000** not with Copyright Act, 1957.
- **Pair 2 is incorrect: Plant Variety** is protected under **Protection of Plant Varieties and Farmers' Rights Act, 2001.**
- **Pair 3 is incorrect:** There is **no specific legislation for trade secrets in India.** Trade secrets are protected by various laws like the Indian Contract Act, 1872 and the Information Technology Act, 2000.
- **Pair 4 is correct: Geographical Indication is** correctly matched with **The Geographical Indications of Goods (Registration and Protection) Act, 1999.**

**Therefore, the correct answer is (a) Only one pair.**

***14.*** *(b)* 1, 2 and 4 only

- **Statement 1 is correct:** The 2005 amendment allowed product patents in pharmaceuticals and agricultural chemicals, aligning with the TRIPs Agreement.
- **Statement 2 is correct:** The Act provides a 20-year patent protection period from the filing date or 20 years from the date of publication, whichever is earlier.
- **Statement 3 is incorrect:** Compulsory licensing was **introduced earlier, in the 1970** version of the Patent Act, not in the 2005 amendment.
- **Statement 4 is correct:** Evergreening refers to the practice of extending the life of a patent by making minor modifications to the invention. The Indian Patent Act, 2005, prevent evergreening by rejecting patent claims on the ground that are merely incremental improvements over existing inventions.

**Thus, the correct answer is (b) 1, 2 and 4 only.**

***15.*** *(b)* A product patent grants the inventor exclusive rights over the creation of the end product, while a process patent grants exclusive rights over the method or process of making a product.

- **Product Patent:** Protects the final product itself, giving exclusive rights to the inventor to make, use, sell, or distribute the product.
- **Process Patent:** Protects the specific method or process of manufacturing a product, allowing others to manufacture the product if they use a different process.

**Process patents protect the unique method or procedure used to create a specific outcome, while product patents safeguard the physical object, device, or composition itself.**

**Thus, option (b) is the correct answer.**

***16.*** *(b)* Only two

- **Statement 1 is correct:** Compulsory licensing allows the government to authorise the production of a patented product without the patent holder's consent.
- **Statement 2 is incorrect:** Under the TRIPs Agreement, compulsory licenses can be issued for various reasons, not just for life-saving drugs, such as to address public health crises or national emergencies.
- **Statement 3 is correct:** India issued its first compulsory license in 2012 for the cancer drug Nexavar (Sorafenib Tosylate) which is used to treat liver and kidney cancer.

**Thus, the correct answer is (b) Only two.**

***17.*** *(a)* Extending the life of a patent by making minor changes to the original product or process.

Evergreening refers to the practice of extending the life of a patent by making minor modifications to the invention. The Indian Patent Act, 2005, prevent evergreening by rejecting patent claims on the ground that are merely incremental improvements over existing inventions.

**Thus, option (a) is the correct answer.**

***18.*** *(b)* The importation of genuine goods into a country without the permission of the intellectual property rights holder.

Parallel importation refers to the practice of importing genuine products into a country without the authorisation of the intellectual property rights holder. This occurs when products are purchased in one country, where they may be sold at a lower price and imported into another country without the consent of the rights holder, often to take advantage of price differences.

**Thus, option (b) is the correct answer.**

**19.** *(b)* Only two

- **Statement 1 is correct:** A **registered Geographical Indication (GI)** is valid for an **initial period of 10 years** and can be **renewed indefinitely** under the **Geographical Indications of Goods (Registration and Protection) Act, 1999.**
- **Statement 2 is incorrect:** In India, GIs can be registered for **agricultural, natural, manufactured products, handicrafts and industrial goods.** It is not limited to agricultural products only.
- **Statement 3 is correct:** Products with a GI tag is indeed covered under the provisions of the Paris Convention.

**Therefore, the correct answer is (b) Only two.**

**20.** *(c)* 1 and 3 only

- **Statement 1 is correct:** The Controller General of Patents, Designs and Trade Marks is responsible for the administration of GI registration and acts as the Registrar of GIs.
- **Statement 2 is incorrect:** The Geographical Indications Registry is located in Chennai, not Mumbai.
- **Statement 3 is correct:** An aggrieved person can challenge the GI registration before the Intellectual Property Appellate Board. However, it's important to note that after the Tribunal Reforms Act, 2021, the IPAB was abolished and such appeals would now be handled by the appropriate high court.

**Therefore, the correct answer is (c) 1 and 3 only.**

**21.** *(b)* Only two

- **Statement 1 is correct: The Protection of Plant Varieties and Farmers' Rights (PPV&FR) Act, 2001 provides for the registration of both new plant varieties and extant varieties** (varieties already in existence).
- **Statement 2 is incorrect:** Farmers are allowed to register plant varieties under the Act. They can also save, use, sow, re-sow, exchange, share, or sell farm produce including seeds of a variety protected under this Act.
- **Statement 3 is correct:** The Act establishes the **Protection of Plant Varieties and Farmers' Rights Authority** as the regulatory body responsible for implementing the provisions of the Act.

**Therefore, the correct answer is (b) Only two.**

**22.** *(b)* 1, 2 and 3 only

- **Statement 1 is correct:** Under the Protection of Plant Varieties and Farmers' Rights Act, 2001, farmers have the right to register new plant varieties that they develop.
- **Statement 2 is correct:** Breeders who register their plant varieties under this Act have **exclusive rights** to produce, sell, market, distribute, import and export their registered varieties.
- **Statement 3 is correct:** Researchers can use registered varieties for experiments or research purposes.
- **Statement 4 is incorrect:** The Act allows **farmers to save, use, sow, re-sow, exchange, share, or sell farm produce including seeds** of a registered variety. However, farmers cannot sell branded seeds of the registered variety.

**Thus, the correct answer is (b) 1, 2 and 3 only.**

**23.** *(b)* 1 and 3 only

- **Statement 1 is correct:** Under the **Protection of Plant Varieties and Farmers' Rights (PPV&FR) Act, 2001,** farmers have the **right to save, use, sow, re-sow, exchange and share seeds** of protected varieties, similar to what they have been doing traditionally.
- **Statement 2 is incorrect:** Farmers **cannot sell branded seeds** of registered varieties. They are allowed to sell farm produce, including seeds, but not as branded seeds of a registered variety.
- **Statement 3 is correct:** Farmers have the **right to claim compensation** if the registered variety fails to perform as promised by the breeder.
- **Statement 4 is incorrect:** The Act does not grant farmers the **right to produce seeds of protected varieties for commercial purposes** without limitations. There are restrictions

when it comes to the commercial production and sale of seeds of protected varieties.

**Thus, the correct answer is (b) 1 and 3 only.**

**24.** *(c)* Both 1 and 2

- **Statement 1 is correct:** The UPOV Convention (International Union for the Protection of New Varieties of Plants) establishes intellectual property rights for plant breeders who develop new, distinct and stable plant varieties.
- **Statement 2 is correct:** India has not joined the UPOV Convention. Instead, it adopted the Protection of Plant Varieties and Farmers' Rights Act (PPV&FRA), 2001, which balances breeders' rights with farmers' rights.

**Thus, the correct answer is (c) Both 1 and 2.**

**25.** *(c)* All three

- **Statement 1 is correct:** The National IPR Policy (2016) aims to create awareness about intellectual property rights among all sections of society, enhancing respect for IP in the interests of economic growth.
- **Statement 2 is correct:** The policy designates the Department for Promotion of Industry and Internal Trade (DPIIT) as the nodal agency responsible for the implementation, coordination and promotion of Intellectual Property Rights in India.
- **Statement 3 is correct:** The policy encourages the commercialisation of intellectual property assets to promote economic growth and transform IP assets into marketable products, thereby driving innovation and entrepreneurship.

**Thus, the correct answer is (c) All three.**

**26.** *(d)* 1, 2 and 3

- **Statement 1 is correct:** The **National IPR Policy (2016)** proposes the establishment of **specialised IP courts** or **IPR cells** within existing courts to ensure **faster adjudication** of IPR disputes, thereby reducing the pendency of cases.
- **Statement 2 is correct:** The policy aims to **promote the development and use of Traditional Knowledge Digital Libraries (TKDL)** to protect India's traditional knowledge and prevent its misappropriation by unauthorised parties.
- **Statement 3 is correct:** The **National IPR Policy** mandates that all publicly funded research organisations register their IP assets with the government and aims to promote the commercialisation and protection of research outputs generated with public funds.

**Thus, the correct answer is (d) 1, 2 and 3.**

**27.** *(d)* All four pairs

- **Pair 1 is correct :** Trademarks are used to protect symbols, names, or slogans that differentiate goods or services.
- **Pair 2 is correct :** Copyright provides protection for creative works like books, movies and music.
- **Pair 3 is correct :** Patents protect inventions that are novel, non-obvious and industrially applicable.
- **Pair 4 is correct :** GIs protect products linked to a specific region, such as Darjeeling Tea or Kolhapuri Chappals.

**Thus, the correct answer is (d) All four pairs.**

**28.** *(c)* 1, 2 and 3

- **Statement 1 is correct :** The Traditional Knowledge Digital Library (TKDL) is a **collaborative effort between the Council of Scientific and Industrial Research (CSIR) and the Ministry of Ayush.**
- **Statement 2 is correct:** TKDL includes codified information on **medicinal formulations from ancient systems like Ayurveda, Unani, Siddha and Sowa Rigpa.**
- **Statement 3 is correct:** The library serves as a critical tool to prevent the **misappropriation of India's traditional knowledge**, particularly in the context of biopiracy, by ensuring that prior knowledge is documented and available as evidence against wrongful patent claims.

**Thus, the correct answer is (c) 1, 2 and 3.**

## Past Learning (Answers)

| | | | |
|---|---|---|---|
| 1 | (c) | 2 | (c) |

# CHAPTER 06 Health and Diseases

## Assessment Round

### Topic 1 : Nutrients

1. Consider the following examples of nutrients:
   1. Vitamin C
   2. Calcium
   3. Carbohydrates
   4. Iron

   How many of the given above is/are considered 'Micronutrients'?
   (a) Only one (b) Only two
   (c) Only three (d) All four

2. Consider the following statements:
   1. Macronutrients are primarily needed for energy production and growth.
   2. Micronutrients play a key role in metabolic processes and immunity.
   3. Macronutrients include vitamins and minerals.

   How many of the above statements is/are correct?
   (a) Only one (b) Only two
   (c) All three (d) None

3. Which of the following are macronutrients?
   1. Protein
   2. Vitamin A
   3. Fiber
   4. Carbohydrates

   Select the correct answer using the codes given below:
   (a) 1 and 4 only (b) 1, 3 and 4 only
   (c) 2, 3 and 4 only (d) 1, 2, 3 and 4

4. Which of the following are fat-soluble vitamins?
   1. Vitamin A 2. Vitamin C
   3. Vitamin D 4. Vitamin B12

   Select the correct answer using the codes given below:
   (a) 1 and 2 only (b) 1 and 3 only
   (c) 2 and 4 only (d) 3 and 4 only

5. Which of the following vitamins are classified as water-soluble?
   1. Vitamin B1
   2. Vitamin A
   3. Vitamin D
   4. Vitamin B12

   Select the correct answer using the codes given below:
   (a) 1 and 4 only (b) 1, 2 and 3 only
   (c) 2, 3 and 4 only (d) 1, 2, 3 and 4

6. Consider the following vitamins with the diseases caused by their deficiency:

| | Vitamin | Disease |
|---|---|---|
| 1. | Vitamin B1 | Scurvy |
| 2. | Vitamin C | Beriberi |
| 3. | Vitamin D | Rickets |
| 4. | Vitamin A | Night blindness |

   How many of the pairs above is/are correctly matched?
   (a) Only one (b) Only two
   (c) Only three (d) All four

**7.** Which of the following vitamin(s) is/are directly responsible for proper blood clotting and can lead to hemorrhagic disease if deficient?

1. Vitamin K
2. Vitamin D
3. Vitamin C
4. Vitamin A

Select the correct answer using the codes given below:

(a) 1 only
(b) 1 and 3 only
(c) 2 and 4 only
(d) 1, 2, 3 and 4

**8.** Consider the following vitamins with their primary food sources:

| Vitamin | Source |
|---|---|
| 1. Vitamin A | Carrots |
| 2. Vitamin C | Citrus fruits |
| 3. Vitamin D | Fish oil |
| 4. Vitamin K | Leafy green vegetables |

How many of the above pairs is/are correctly matched?

(a) Only one
(b) Only two
(c) Only three
(d) All four

**9.** With reference to proteins, consider the following statements:

1. Proteins are made up of amino acids.
2. Proteins are essential for muscle growth and repair.
3. Proteins are stored in the body for long-term energy needs.

How many of the above statements is/are correct?

(a) Only one
(b) Only two
(c) All three
(d) None

**10.** Consider the following types of proteins with their primary functions:

| Type of Protein | Primary Function |
|---|---|
| 1. Enzymes | A. Act as biological catalysts |
| 2. Antibodies | B. Transport oxygen in the blood |
| 3. Hemoglobin | C. Support immune function |
| 4. Structural proteins | D. Provide structure and support to cells |

How many of the above pairs is/are correctly matched?

(a) Only one (b) Only two
(c) Only three (d) All four

**11.** Consider the following statements about the types of dietary fats:

1. Monounsaturated fats are generally considered healthy and are found in foods like olive oil and avocados.
2. Trans fats are artificially created fats that have been linked to increased risk of heart disease.
3. Omega-3 and Omega-6 fatty acids are types of trans fats essential for the body.

How many of the above statements is/are correct?

(a) Only one (b) Only two
(c) All three (d) None

**12.** Which of the following statements correctly describe the characteristics of saturated and unsaturated fats?

1. Saturated fats are typically solid at room temperature.
2. Unsaturated fats are generally considered healthier than saturated fats.
3. Saturated fats are mostly found in plant-based oils.
4. Unsaturated fats can help reduce bad cholesterol levels.

Select the correct answer using the codes given below:

(a) 1 and 2 only (b) 1, 2 and 4 only
(c) 3 and 4 only (d) 1, 2, 3 and 4

**13.** Which of the following best describes the effect of hydrogenation on fats?
(a) It converts unsaturated fats into saturated fats, making them liquid at room temperature.
(b) It converts unsaturated fats into trans fats, which can increase the risk of heart disease.
(c) It enhances the nutritional value of fats by increasing their essential fatty acid content.
(d) It reduces the calorific content of fats by breaking down fatty acid chains.

**14.** Consider the following food sources and the type of fatty acids they are rich in:

| | |
|---|---|
| 1. Avocado | Monounsaturated fatty acids |
| 2. Walnuts | Polyunsaturated fatty acids |
| 3. Salmon | Polyunsaturated fatty acids |
| 4. Coconut oil | Monounsaturated fatty acids |

How many of the above pairs is/are correctly matched?
(a) Only one
(b) Only two
(c) Only three
(d) All four

**15.** With reference to cholesterol, consider the following statements:
1. Cholesterol is only obtained from dietary sources.
2. High-density lipoprotein (HDL) is considered 'good' cholesterol.
3. Low-density lipoprotein (LDL) can contribute to plaque buildup in arteries.

How many of the above statements is/are correct?
(a) Only one (b) Only two
(c) All three (d) None

**16.** What is a blubber?
(a) A type of muscle tissue in marine mammals.
(b) A thick layer of fat found in marine mammals.
(c) A type of bone structure that helps marine animals float.
(d) A substance that marine animals secrete to regulate body temperature.

**17.** Consider the following terms with their definitions:

| Term | Definition |
|---|---|
| 1. Ischemia | Death of tissue due to lack of blood supply |
| 2. Infarction | Narrowing of arteries due to plaque buildup |
| 3. Atherosclerosis | Reduced blood flow to tissues |

How many of the above pairs is/are correctly matched?
(a) Only one
(b) Only two
(c) All three
(d) None

**18.** With reference to the Food Safety and Standards Authority of India (FSSAI), consider the following statements:
1. It is responsible for setting standards for food safety in India.
2. It operates under the Ministry of Health and Family Welfare, Government of India.
3. It has the authority to conduct food safety inspections and issue licenses to food businesses.

How many of the above statements is/are correct?
(a) Only one (b) Only two
(c) All three (d) None

**19.** Consider the following:
1. Ensuring food safety and promoting public health
2. Regulating the import and export of food products
3. Conducting food safety research and spreading awareness
4. Providing licenses to food businesses

How many of the given above functions is/are performed by FSSAI?
(a) Only one
(b) Only two
(c) Only three
(d) All four

**20.** Consider the following:

1. Reducing industrially produced trans fats in food products to less than 2%.
2. Promoting public awareness about the health risks associated with trans fats.
3. Encouraging the food industry to adopt healthier fat alternatives.
4. Increasing the export of trans fat-free food products.

How many of the given above objectives is/are part of the 'Freedom from Trans Fat@75' initiative?

(a) Only one (b) Only two
(c) Only three (d) All four

**21.** Consider the following nutrients:

1. Iron 2. Vitamin A
3. Calcium 4. Iodine

How many of the above nutrients is/are typically added in food fortification programmes in India?

(a) Only one (b) Only two
(c) Only three (d) All four

**22.** Which of the following statements about FSSAI's food fortification standards in India are correct?

1. FSSAI has established standards for fortified wheat flour.
2. FSSAI mandates labeling of fortified products with a specific logo.
3. FSSAI only permits fortification for dairy products.

Select the correct answer using the codes given below:

(a) 1 and 2 only (b) 2 and 3 only
(c) 1 and 3 only (d) 1, 2 and 3

**23.** Which of the following nutrients are typically added to fortified rice in India to address malnutrition?

1. Iron 2. Folic acid
3. Vitamin B12 4. Calcium

Select the correct answer using the codes given below:

(a) 1 and 3 only (b) 1, 2 and 3 only
(c) 2, 3 and 4 only (d) 1, 2, 3 and 4

## Topic 2 : Immunity

**24.** Which of the following are characteristics of antigens?

1. Antigens are substances that trigger an immune response.
2. Antigens are always harmful to the body.
3. Each antigen is specific to a particular pathogen.
4. Antigens can include proteins, polysaccharides, or toxins.

Select the correct answer using the codes given below:

(a) 1 and 3 only (b) 1, 3 and 4 only
(c) 2 and 4 only (d) 1, 2, 3 and 4

**25.** Which of the following statements correctly describes the function of antibodies?

1. They neutralise pathogens by binding to antigens.
2. They directly destroy pathogens through phagocytosis.
3. Antibodies mark pathogens for destruction by immune cells.
4. They provide long-term immunity after an infection.

Select the correct answer using the codes given below:

(a) 1 and 3 only (b) 2 and 4 only
(c) 1, 3 and 4 only (d) 1, 2, 3 and 4

**26.** Which of the following statements are correct about antibody and antigen interaction?

1. Antibodies bind to specific sites on antigens called epitopes.
2. The antibody-antigen complex helps neutralise pathogens.
3. Antibody-antigen interactions are non-specific.
4. Antigens and antibodies form a 'lock-and-key' mechanism for immune recognition.

Select the correct answer using the codes given below:

(a) 1 and 2 only
(b) 1, 2 and 4 only
(c) 2, 3 and 4 only
(d) 1, 2, 3 and 4

**27.** Which of the following correctly describes 'Herd Immunity'?

(a) Immunity that an individual acquires after recovering from an infection

(b) Protection from infectious diseases that occurs when a large percentage of a population is immune

(c) Immunity achieved through natural infection only

(d) A form of immunity specific to animals in herds

**28.** Which of the following are components of acquired (adaptive) immunity?

1. T-cells
2. B-cells
3. Antibodies
4. Natural killer cells

Select the correct answer using the codes given below:

(a) 1 and 2 only

(b) 1, 2 and 3 only

(c) 2, 3 and 4 only

(d) 1, 2, 3 and 4

**29.** Which of the following are characteristics of innate immunity?

1. It provides a rapid response to pathogens.
2. It has memory and adapts to specific pathogens over time.
3. It includes physical barriers like skin and mucous membranes.
4. It is highly specific to particular pathogens.

Select the correct answer using the codes given below:

(a) 1 and 3 only

(b) 2 and 4 only

(c) 1, 2 and 3 only

(d) 1, 2, 3 and 4

**30.** Consider the following types of immune barriers with their descriptions:

| Barrier Type | Description |
|---|---|
| 1. Physical Barrier | Involves specialised immune cells that destroy pathogens |
| 2. Physiological Barrier | Involves chemicals like stomach acid to prevent infection |
| 3. Cellular Barrier | Includes skin and mucous membranes as the first line of defense |
| 4. Cytokine Barrier | Involves proteins that mediate immune responses and inflammation |

How many of the above pairs is/are correctly matched?

(a) Only one (b) Only two

(c) Only three (d) All four

**31.** Consider the following immune components with the barrier type they belong to:

| Immune Component | Barrier Type |
|---|---|
| 1. Skin | Physical Barrier |
| 2. Tears and Saliva | Physiological Barrier |
| 3. Neutrophils | Cellular Barrier |
| 4. Interferons | Cytokine Barrier |

How many of the above pairs is/are correctly matched?

(a) Only one (b) Only two

(c) Only three (d) All four

**32.** What are cytokine barriers?

(a) Physical barriers that prevent pathogens from entering the body

(b) Chemical signals produced by cells to modulate immune responses

(c) Specialised immune cells that directly destroy pathogens

(d) Enzymes that break down pathogens within cells

**33.** Which of the following correctly describes the relationship between T cells and B cells in the immune system?

1. T cells help activate B cells to produce antibodies.
2. B cells present antigens to T cells to initiate their activation.
3. T cells produce cytokines to help regulate the activity of B cells.
4. B cells can destroy infected cells directly without T cell assistance.

Select the correct answer using the codes given below:

(a) 1 and 4 only (b) 1, 2 and 3 only
(c) 2, 3 and 4 only (d) 1, 2, 3 and 4

## Topic 3 : Vaccination

**34.** Consider the following types of vaccines with their descriptions:

| Vaccine Type | Description |
|---|---|
| 1. Inactivated Vaccine | Contains weakened forms of the virus or bacteria |
| 2. Live Attenuated Vaccine | Contains parts of the virus, such as proteins |
| 3. Subunit Vaccine | Contains killed pathogens that cannot replicate |
| 4. mRNA Vaccine | Uses genetic material to instruct cells to produce viral proteins |

How many of the given above pairs is/are correctly matched?

(a) Only one (b) Only two
(c) Only three (d) All four

**35.** Consider the following types of vaccines with examples:

| Vaccine Type | Example |
|---|---|
| 1. Live Attenuated Vaccine | Hepatitis B vaccine |
| 2. Inactivated Vaccine | Polio vaccine (IPV) |
| 3. Subunit Vaccine | Influenza vaccine (Flu shot) |
| 4. mRNA Vaccine | COVID-19 vaccines (Pfizer-BioNTech, Moderna) |

How many of the above pairs is/are correctly matched?

(a) Only one
(b) Only two
(c) Only three
(d) All four

**36.** What type of vaccine is iNCOVACC, India's first nasal COVID-19 vaccine?

(a) mRNA vaccine
(b) Viral vector vaccine
(c) Protein subunit vaccine
(d) Inactivated virus vaccine

**37.** With reference to toxoid vaccines, consider the following statements:

1. Toxoid vaccines contain inactivated toxins produced by bacteria.
2. Toxoid vaccines provide immunity against the toxins rather than the bacteria itself.
3. Toxoid vaccines are primarily used to prevent viral infections.

How many of the above statements is/are correct?

(a) Only one
(b) Only two
(c) All three
(d) None

**38.** With reference to conjugate vaccines, consider the following statements:

1. Conjugate vaccines are designed to protect against bacteria with polysaccharide outer coats.
2. Conjugate vaccines are created by attaching a weak antigen to a strong carrier protein.

Which of the given above statement(s) is/are correct?

(a) 1 only (b) 2 only
(c) Both 1 and 2 (d) Neither 1 nor 2

**39.** Consider the following diseases:
1. Tetanus
2. Pertussis
3. Diphtheria
4. Influenza

How many of the above diseases can be commonly prevented by toxoid vaccines?
(a) Only one
(b) Only two
(c) Only three
(d) All four

**40.** With reference to mRNA vaccines, consider the following statements:
1. mRNA vaccines contain a live, weakened virus.
2. mRNA vaccines instruct cells to produce a viral protein, which triggers an immune response.
3. mRNA vaccines are known for their rapid development and easy modification.

How many of the above statements is/are correct?
(a) Only one
(b) Only two
(c) All three
(d) None

**41.** Which of the following COVID-19 vaccines are examples of RNA vaccines?
1. Pfizer-BioNTech
2. Moderna
3. ZyCoV-D
4. Johnson & Johnson

Select the correct answer using the codes given below:
(a) 1 and 2 only
(b) 1, 2 and 3 only
(c) 2, 3 and 4 only
(d) 1, 2, 3 and 4

**42.** Which of the following statements correctly describe DNA vaccines?
1. They deliver genetic material directly into cells to produce viral proteins.
2. They require specialised cold storage for stability.
3. ZyCoV-D, a COVID-19 vaccine by Zydus Cadila, is an example of a DNA vaccine.
4. They use mRNA to stimulate an immune response.

Select the correct answer using the codes given below:
(a) 1 and 3 only (b) 1, 2 and 3 only
(c) 2, 3 and 4 only (d) 1, 2, 3 and 4

**43.** Consider the following characteristics:
1. They contain completely killed pathogens.
2. They require a booster dose for effective immunity.
3. They provide immediate immunity after administration.
4. They are generally safe for people with compromised immune systems.

How many of the given above characteristics is/are typically associated with inactivated vaccines?
(a) Only one
(b) Only two
(c) Only three
(d) All four

**44.** Consider the following diseases and the corresponding type of vaccines used to prevent them:

| | | |
|---|---|---|
| 1. | Tetanus | Toxoid Vaccine |
| 2. | Hepatitis B | Recombinant Vaccine |
| 3. | Measles | Live Attenuated Vaccine |
| 4. | Rabies | Inactivated Vaccine |

How many of the given above pairs is/are correctly matched?
(a) Only one (b) Only two
(c) Only three (d) All four

**45.** Which of the following diseases are being researched for DNA vaccine applications?
1. COVID-19
2. HPV (Human Papillomavirus)
3. Zika Virus
4. Tuberculosis

Select the correct answer using the codes given below:
(a) 1 and 3 only (b) 2 and 4 only
(c) 1, 2 and 3 only (d) 1, 2, 3 and 4

**46.** Consider the following diseases:

1. Measles
2. Hepatitis B
3. Japanese Encephalitis
4. Malaria

How many of the given above diseases is/are covered under Mission Indradhanush?

(a) Only one
(b) Only two
(c) Only three
(d) All four

**47.** With reference to the International Coordination Group (ICG) on Vaccine Provision, consider the following statements:

1. The ICG was established to manage emergency vaccine stockpiles for outbreak response.
2. The ICG primarily focuses on providing vaccines for diseases like measles, polio and cholera.
3. The ICG is a collaborative initiative involving multiple international organisations.

How many of the above statements is/are correct?

(a) Only one (b) Only two
(c) All three (d) None

**48.** Consider the following diseases:

1. Cholera 2. Yellow Fever
3. Meningitis 4. Tuberculosis

How many of the given above diseases is/are covered by the ICG for emergency vaccine stockpiling?

(a) Only one (b) Only two
(c) Only three (d) All four

**49.** With reference to GAVI, the Vaccine Alliance, consider the following statements:

1. GAVI focuses on increasing access to vaccines in low-income countries.
2. GAVI collaborates with global organisations like WHO, UNICEF and the World Bank.
3. GAVI primarily funds research and development for vaccine innovations in high-income countries.

How many of the above statements is/are correct?

(a) Only one (b) Only two
(c) All three (d) None

## Topic 4 : Diseases

**50.** Consider the following terms with their definitions:

| | Term | Definition |
|---|---|---|
| 1. | Endemic | A disease that spreads across multiple countries or continents |
| 2. | Epidemic | A disease constantly present in a specific region or population |
| 3. | Pandemic | A sudden increase in the number of cases of a disease in a specific area |

How many of the above pairs is/are correctly matched?

(a) Only one (b) Only two
(c) All three (d) None

**51.** Consider the following diseases with their correct classifications:

| | Disease | Classification |
|---|---|---|
| 1. | Tuberculosis | Infectious disease |
| 2. | Diabetes | Non-infectious disease |
| 3. | Cystic Fibrosis | Genetic disease |
| 4. | Influenza | Autoimmune disease |

How many of the above pairs is/are correctly matched?

(a) Only one (b) Only two
(c) Only three (d) All four

**52.** Which of the following diseases are classified as 'Infectious Diseases'?

1. Tuberculosis 2. Influenza
3. Hemophilia 4. Measles

Select the correct answer using the codes given below:

(a) 1, 2 and 4 only (b) 1 and 3 only
(c) 2, 3 and 4 only (d) 1, 2, 3 and 4

**53.** Which of the following are considered genetic diseases?
1. Sickle Cell Anemia
2. Cystic Fibrosis
3. Diabetes
4. Huntington's Disease

Select the correct answer using the codes given below:
(a) 1 and 3 only (b) 1, 2 and 4 only
(c) 2, 3 and 4 only (d) 1, 2, 3 and 4

**54.** Consider the following statements:
1. Diabetes is an endocrine disorder characterised by abnormal insulin regulation.
2. Anemia is a hematological disorder caused by low hemoglobin levels.
3. Hypothyroidism is a hematological disorder related to low thyroid hormone production.

How many of the above statements is/are correct?
(a) Only one (b) Only two
(c) All three (d) None

**55.** With reference to different disease types, consider the following statements:
1. Anemia is a hematological disease caused by low levels of hemoglobin.
2. Diabetes is an endocrine disease related to insulin production.
3. Epilepsy is a neurological disease characterised by recurrent seizures.

How many of the above statements is/are correct?
(a) Only one (b) Only two
(c) All three (d) None

**56.** Consider the following pairs of diseases and their classifications:
1. Sickle Cell Anemia-Hematological Disease
2. Parkinson's Disease- Neurological Disease
3. Asthma-Endocrine Disease
4. Hypothyroidism-Endocrine Disease

How many of the above pairs is/are correctly matched?
(a) Only one pair (b) Only two pairs
(c) Only three pairs (d) All four pairs

**57.** With reference to viral diseases, consider the following statements:
1. Influenza is caused by a virus that primarily affects the respiratory system.
2. Dengue is a viral disease transmitted by mosquitoes.
3. Tuberculosis is a viral disease that affects the lungs.

How many of the above statements is/are correct?
(a) Only one (b) Only two
(c) All three (d) None

**58.** Consider the following diseases:
1. Chickenpox 2. Malaria
3. Hepatitis B 4. Tetanus

How many of the given above diseases is/are caused by virus?
(a) Only one (b) Only two
(c) Only three (d) All four

**59.** Consider the following diseases with the correct mosquito species responsible for their transmission:

| | Disease Mosquito | Species |
|---|---|---|
| 1. | Dengue | Anopheles |
| 2. | Malaria | Aedes aegypti |
| 3. | Japanese Encephalitis | Culex |
| 4. | Zika Fever | Aedes albopictus |

How many of the above pairs is/are correctly matched?
(a) Only one pair (b) Only two pairs
(c) Only three pairs (d) All four pairs

**60.** Which of the following diseases are caused by 'Protozoa'?
1. Malaria
2. Tuberculosis
3. Amoebiasis
4. Typhoid

Select the correct answer using the codes given below:
(a) 1 and 3 only (b) 2 and 4 only
(c) 1, 2 and 4 only (d) 1, 2, 3 and 4

**61.** Consider the following diseases:
1. Tuberculosis 2. Influenza
3. Typhoid 4. Leprosy

How many of the given above diseases is/are caused by bacteria?
(a) Only one (b) Only two
(c) Only three (d) All four

**62.** With reference to the WHO Fungal Priority Pathogen List (FPPL), consider the following statements:
1. The FPPL includes only fungal pathogens that affect plants.
2. Candida auris is included in the FPPL due to its resistance to multiple antifungal drugs.
3. The FPPL aims to address the growing threat of fungal infections in humans.

How many of the above statements is/are correct?
(a) Only one
(b) Only two
(c) All three
(d) None

**63.** Consider the following fungi and identify how many of them are included in the WHO Fungal Priority Pathogen List (FPPL):
1. Candida albicans
2. Cryptococcus neoformans
3. Aspergillus fumigatus
4. Penicillium chrysogenum

Select the correct answer from the codes given below:
(a) Only one (b) Only two
(c) Only three (d) All four

**64.** With reference to 'Zoonotic Diseases', consider the following statements:
1. Rabies is a zoonotic disease transmitted through animal bites.
2. Tuberculosis is exclusively a human disease and cannot be transmitted from animals to humans.
3. Anthrax can be contracted by humans through contact with infected animals or animal products.

How many of the given above statements is/are correct?
(a) Only one (b) Only two
(c) All three (d) None

**65.** Consider the following diseases:
1. Rabies
2. HIV/AIDS
3. Salmonellosis
4. Lyme disease

How many of the given above diseases is/are zoonotic diseases?
(a) Only one
(b) Only two
(c) Only three
(d) All four

**66.** Consider the following minerals with the diseases or conditions caused by their deficiency:

| | Mineral Disease | Condition |
|---|---|---|
| 1. | Iron | Rickets |
| 2. | Iodine | Anemia |
| 3. | Calcium | Goiter |
| 4. | Phosphorus | Osteoporosis |

How many of the above pairs are correctly matched?
(a) Only two pairs (b) Only three pairs
(c) All four pairs (d) None

**67.** Consider the following diseases with the elements that cause them:

| | Disease | Element |
|---|---|---|
| 1. | Minamata disease | Mercury |
| 2. | Itai-itai disease | Lead |
| 3. | Plumbism | Cadmium |
| 4. | Blue Baby Syndrome | Nitrates |

How many of the above pairs is/are correctly matched?
(a) Only one pair
(b) Only two pairs
(c) Only three pairs
(d) All four pairs

**68.** Which of the following best describes the purpose of 'Chelation Therapy'?
(a) To increase the levels of essential minerals in the body
(b) To enhance immune function by stimulating white blood cell production
(c) To remove heavy metals from the bloodstream by binding to toxic metals
(d) To provide a source of antioxidants for the prevention of chronic diseases

**69.** With reference to the 'Neglected Tropical Diseases (NTDs)', consider the following statements:
1. NTDs primarily affect populations in tropical and subtropical regions.
2. Diseases like dengue, leprosy and river blindness are classified as NTDs.
3. NTDs are mainly caused by nutritional deficiencies.

How many of the above statements is/are correct?
(a) Only one (b) Only two
(c) All three (d) None

**70.** How many of them are classified as Neglected Tropical Diseases (NTDs)?
1. Chagas disease 2. Malaria
3. Lymphatic filariasis 4. Ebola

Select the correct answer from the codes given below:
(a) Only one (b) Only two
(c) Only three (d) All four

**71.** With reference to genetic disorders, consider the following statements:
1. Mendelian disorders are caused by mutations in a single gene.
2. Chromosomal disorders are typically caused by an abnormal number or structure of chromosomes.
3. Down syndrome is an example of a Mendelian disorder.

How many of the above statements is/are correct?
(a) Only one (b) Only two
(c) All three (d) None

**72.** Which of the following are Mendelian disorders?
1. Cystic fibrosis 2. Down syndrome
3. Hemophilia 4. Turner syndrome

Select the correct answer using the codes given below:
(a) 1 and 3 only (b) 2 and 4 only
(c) 1, 2 and 3 only (d) 1, 2, 3 and 4

**73.** Which of the following diseases are considered sexually transmitted diseases (STDs)?
1. Syphilis
2. Hepatitis B
3. Tuberculosis
4. Gonorrhea

Select the correct answer using the codes given below:
(a) 1 and 2 only (b) 1, 2 and 4 only
(c) 2 and 3 only (d) 1, 2, 3 and 4

## Topic 5 : Medicines

**74.** Consider the following drug types with their primary functions:

| | Drug Type | Function |
|---|---|---|
| 1. | Antiflatulents | Reduces fever |
| 2. | Antipyretics | Relieves pain |
| 3. | Analgesics | Eases gas and bloating |
| 4. | Antihistamines | Alleviates allergy symptoms |

How many of the above pairs is/are correctly matched?
(a) Only one pair (b) Only two pairs
(c) Only three pairs (d) All four pairs

**75.** Which of the following best describes the function of an antispasmodic?
(a) Reduces fever and inflammation
(b) Relieves muscle spasms, especially in the digestive tract
(c) Blocks pain signals to the brain
(d) Decreases histamine reactions in allergic responses

**76.** Which of the following best describes a 'Biosimilar'?
(a) A highly similar, but not identical, version of an approved biologic drug.
(b) A generic version of a synthetic small-molecule drug.
(c) A synthetic drug with the exact same chemical structure as the original biologic.
(d) A natural substance with no therapeutic effect.

**77.** Which of the following best describes a biologic medication?
(a) A small-molecule drug synthesised in a laboratory.
(b) A complex drug made from living cells or organisms.
(c) A drug with a simple, easily replicable chemical structure.
(d) An exact copy of another drug with the same therapeutic effects.

**78.** Which of the following medicines are included in the WHO Model List of Essential Medicines?
1. Paracetamol
2. Amoxicillin
3. Ibuprofen
4. Remdesivir

Select the correct answer using the codes given below:
(a) 1 and 2 only (b) 1, 2 and 3 only
(c) 2 and 4 only (d) 1, 2, 3 and 4

**79.** With reference to antimicrobial resistance (AMR), consider the following statements:
1. AMR occurs when bacteria, viruses, fungi and parasites evolve to resist the effects of medications.
2. Overuse of antibiotics in healthcare and agriculture contributes to AMR.
3. Vaccination has no role in controlling anti-microbial resistance.

How many of the above statements is/are correct?
(a) Only one (b) Only two
(c) All three (d) None

**80.** Which of the following factors contribute to the spread of anti-microbial resistance?
1. Overuse of antibiotics in healthcare settings
2. Improper disposal of expired medications
3. Lack of access to clean water and sanitation
4. Use of antibiotics for growth promotion in livestock

Select the correct answer using the codes given below:
(a) 1 and 2 only (b) 1, 3 and 4 only
(c) 2 and 4 only (d) 1, 2, 3 and 4

**81.** With reference to the initiatives in India to address anti-microbial resistance, consider the following statements:
1. The Red Line Campaign was launched to educate the public on the dangers of overusing antibiotics.
2. The Chennai Declaration was an AMR initiative led by the Indian government.
3. The Indian Council of Medical Research (ICMR) conducts AMR surveillance and research in India.

How many of the above statements is/are correct?
(a) Only one (b) Only two
(c) All three (d) None

**82.** Which of the following organisations publishes the GLASS report on Antimicrobial Resistance (AMR)?
(a) World Health Organisation (WHO)
(b) United Nations (UN)
(c) Food and Agriculture Organisation (FAO)
(d) Centers for Disease Control and Prevention (CDC)

**83.** Which of the following initiatives have been launched by the Ministry of AYUSH?
1. National AYUSH Mission
2. AYUSH Wellness Centres
3. Ayushman Bharat Yojana
4. International Day of Yoga

Select the correct answer using the codes given below:
(a) 1 and 3 only (b) 1, 2 and 4 only
(c) 2 and 3 only (d) 1, 2, 3 and 4

**84.** Where is the headquarters of the WHO Global Centre for Traditional Medicine located?
(a) Geneva, Switzerland
(b) Beijing, China
(c) New Delhi, India
(d) Jamnagar, India

# OMR SHEET

**Assessment Round**

| | | | | | | | |
|---|---|---|---|---|---|---|---|
| 1 | (a) (b) (c) (d) | 31 | (a) (b) (c) (d) | 61 | (a) (b) (c) (d) | 91 | (a) (b) (c) (d) |
| 2 | (a) (b) (c) (d) | 32 | (a) (b) (c) (d) | 62 | (a) (b) (c) (d) | 92 | (a) (b) (c) (d) |
| 3 | (a) (b) (c) (d) | 33 | (a) (b) (c) (d) | 63 | (a) (b) (c) (d) | 93 | (a) (b) (c) (d) |
| 4 | (a) (b) (c) (d) | 34 | (a) (b) (c) (d) | 64 | (a) (b) (c) (d) | 94 | (a) (b) (c) (d) |
| 5 | (a) (b) (c) (d) | 35 | (a) (b) (c) (d) | 65 | (a) (b) (c) (d) | 95 | (a) (b) (c) (d) |
| 6 | (a) (b) (c) (d) | 36 | (a) (b) (c) (d) | 66 | (a) (b) (c) (d) | 96 | (a) (b) (c) (d) |
| 7 | (a) (b) (c) (d) | 37 | (a) (b) (c) (d) | 67 | (a) (b) (c) (d) | 97 | (a) (b) (c) (d) |
| 8 | (a) (b) (c) (d) | 38 | (a) (b) (c) (d) | 68 | (a) (b) (c) (d) | 98 | (a) (b) (c) (d) |
| 9 | (a) (b) (c) (d) | 39 | (a) (b) (c) (d) | 69 | (a) (b) (c) (d) | 99 | (a) (b) (c) (d) |
| 10 | (a) (b) (c) (d) | 40 | (a) (b) (c) (d) | 70 | (a) (b) (c) (d) | 100 | (a) (b) (c) (d) |
| 11 | (a) (b) (c) (d) | 41 | (a) (b) (c) (d) | 71 | (a) (b) (c) (d) | 101 | (a) (b) (c) (d) |
| 12 | (a) (b) (c) (d) | 42 | (a) (b) (c) (d) | 72 | (a) (b) (c) (d) | 102 | (a) (b) (c) (d) |
| 13 | (a) (b) (c) (d) | 43 | (a) (b) (c) (d) | 73 | (a) (b) (c) (d) | 103 | (a) (b) (c) (d) |
| 14 | (a) (b) (c) (d) | 44 | (a) (b) (c) (d) | 74 | (a) (b) (c) (d) | 104 | (a) (b) (c) (d) |
| 15 | (a) (b) (c) (d) | 45 | (a) (b) (c) (d) | 75 | (a) (b) (c) (d) | 105 | (a) (b) (c) (d) |
| 16 | (a) (b) (c) (d) | 46 | (a) (b) (c) (d) | 76 | (a) (b) (c) (d) | 106 | (a) (b) (c) (d) |
| 17 | (a) (b) (c) (d) | 47 | (a) (b) (c) (d) | 77 | (a) (b) (c) (d) | 107 | (a) (b) (c) (d) |
| 18 | (a) (b) (c) (d) | 48 | (a) (b) (c) (d) | 78 | (a) (b) (c) (d) | 108 | (a) (b) (c) (d) |
| 19 | (a) (b) (c) (d) | 49 | (a) (b) (c) (d) | 79 | (a) (b) (c) (d) | 109 | (a) (b) (c) (d) |
| 20 | (a) (b) (c) (d) | 50 | (a) (b) (c) (d) | 80 | (a) (b) (c) (d) | 110 | (a) (b) (c) (d) |
| 21 | (a) (b) (c) (d) | 51 | (a) (b) (c) (d) | 81 | (a) (b) (c) (d) | 111 | (a) (b) (c) (d) |
| 22 | (a) (b) (c) (d) | 52 | (a) (b) (c) (d) | 82 | (a) (b) (c) (d) | 112 | (a) (b) (c) (d) |
| 23 | (a) (b) (c) (d) | 53 | (a) (b) (c) (d) | 83 | (a) (b) (c) (d) | 113 | (a) (b) (c) (d) |
| 24 | (a) (b) (c) (d) | 54 | (a) (b) (c) (d) | 84 | (a) (b) (c) (d) | 114 | (a) (b) (c) (d) |
| 25 | (a) (b) (c) (d) | 55 | (a) (b) (c) (d) | 85 | (a) (b) (c) (d) | 115 | (a) (b) (c) (d) |
| 26 | (a) (b) (c) (d) | 56 | (a) (b) (c) (d) | 86 | (a) (b) (c) (d) | 116 | (a) (b) (c) (d) |
| 27 | (a) (b) (c) (d) | 57 | (a) (b) (c) (d) | 87 | (a) (b) (c) (d) | 117 | (a) (b) (c) (d) |
| 28 | (a) (b) (c) (d) | 58 | (a) (b) (c) (d) | 88 | (a) (b) (c) (d) | 118 | (a) (b) (c) (d) |
| 29 | (a) (b) (c) (d) | 59 | (a) (b) (c) (d) | 89 | (a) (b) (c) (d) | 119 | (a) (b) (c) (d) |
| 30 | (a) (b) (c) (d) | 60 | (a) (b) (c) (d) | 90 | (a) (b) (c) (d) | 120 | (a) (b) (c) (d) |

## Calculate Your Score

| | |
|---|---|
| **Correct (✓)** | |
| **Incorrect (✓)** | |
| **Unattempted** | |
| **Total Score** | |
| **Accuracy (%)** | |

## Reasons for Incorrect Answers?

| | |
|---|---|
| 1. Lack of Knowledge/Existing Source Insufficient | |
| 2. Lack of Multiple Revision | |
| 3. Common Sense Mistakes | |

**Note :**

1. Calculate total score as correct answers carry 2 marks each 1/3rd marks will deducted for **Incorrect** Answers.
2. Calculate Accuracy (%) by dividing the number of correct answers to the total number of attempted questions.

## Past Learning

**1.** 'Wolbachia method' is sometimes talked about with reference to which one of the following? **(2023)**

(a) Controlling the viral diseases spread by mosquitoes.

(b) Converting crop residues into packing material.

(c) Producing biodegradable plastics.

(d) Producing biochar from thermochemical conversion of biomass.

**2.** In the context of vaccines manufactured to prevent COVID-19 pandemic, consider the following statements: **(2022)**

1. The Serum Institute of India produced COVID-19 vaccine named Covishield using mRNA platform.
2. Sputnik V vaccine is manufactured using vector-based platform.
3. COVAXIN is an inactivated pathogen-based vaccine.

Which of the statements given above are correct?

(a) 1 and 2 only (b) 2 and 3 only

(c) 1 and 3 only (d) 1, 2 and 3

**3.** In the context of hereditary diseases, consider the following statements: **(2021)**

1. Passing on mitochondrial diseases from parent to child can be prevented by mitochondrial replacement therapy either before or after in vitro fertilization of egg.
2. A child inherits mitochondrial diseases entirely from mother and not from father.

Which of the statements given above is/are correct?

(a) 1 only (b) 2 only

(c) Both 1 and 2 (d) Neither 1 nor 2

**4.** The term 'ACE2' is talked about in the context of: **(2021)**

(a) genes introduced in the genetically modified plants

(b) development of India's own satellite navigation system

(c) radio collars for wildlife tracking

(d) spread of viral diseases

**5.** With reference to recent developments regarding 'Recombinant Vector Vaccines', consider the following statements: **(2021)**

1. Genetic engineering is applied in the development of these vaccines.
2. Bacteria and viruses are used as vectors.

Which of the statements given above is/are correct?

(a) 1 only

(b) 2 only

(c) Both 1 and 2

(d) Neither 1 nor 2

**6.** Consider the following statements: **(2021)**

1. Adenoviruses have single-stranded DNA genomes whereas retroviruses have double-stranded DNA genomes.
2. Common cold is sometimes caused by an adenovirus whereas AIDS is caused by a retrovirus.

Which of the statements given above is/are correct?

(a) 1 only (b) 2 only

(c) Both 1 and 2 (d) Neither 1 nor 2

**7.** What is the importance of using Pneumococcal Conjugate Vaccines in India? **(2020)**

1. These vaccines are effective against pneumonia as well as meningitis and sepsis.
2. Dependence on antibiotics that are not effective against drug-resistant bacteria can be reduced.
3. These vaccines have no side effects and cause no allergic reactions.

Select the correct answer using the codes given below:

(a) 1 only (b) 1 and 2 only

(c) 3 only (d) 1, 2 and 3

**8.** Which one of the following statements is not correct? **(2019)**

(a) Hepatitis B virus is transmitted much like HIV.

(b) Hepatitis B, unlike Hepatitis C, does not have a vaccine.

(c) Globally, the numbers of people infected with Hepatitis B and C viruses are several times more than those infected with HIV.

(d) Some of those infected with Hepatitis B and C viruses do not show the symptoms for many years.

**9.** Which of the following are the reasons for the occurrence of multi-drug resistance in microbial pathogens in India? **(2019)**

1. Genetic predisposition of some people
2. Taking incorrect doses of antibiotics to cure diseases
3. Using antibiotics in livestock farming
4. Multiple chronic diseases in some people

Select the correct answer using the codes given below:

(a) 1 and 2 only (b) 2 and 3 only
(c) 1, 3 and 4 only (d) 2, 3 and 4 only

**10.** Consider the following statements: **(2017)**

1. In tropical regions, Zika virus disease is transmitted by the same mosquito that transmits dengue.
2. Sexual transmission of Zika virus disease is possible.

Which of the statements given above is/are correct?

(a) 1 only (b) 2 only
(c) Both 1 and 2 (d) Neither 1 nor 2

**11.** Which of the following statements is/are correct? **(2016)**

Viruses can infect:

1. Bacteria
2. Fungi
3. Plants

Select the correct answer using the codes given below:

(a) 1 and 2 only
(b) 3 only
(c) 1 and 3 only
(d) 1, 2 and 3

**12.** H1N1 virus is sometimes mentioned in the news with reference to which one of the following diseases? **(2015)**

(a) AIDS (b) Bird Flu
(c) Dengue (d) Swine Flu

**13.** Consider the following diseases: **(2014)**

1. Diphtheria
2. Chickenpox
3. Smallpox

Which of the above diseases has/have been eradicated in India?

(a) 1 and 2 only (b) 3 only
(c) 1, 2 and 3 (d) None of these

# Detailed Solutions

## Assessment Round

**1.** *(c)* Only three

- **Option 1 is correct: Vitamin C** is a **micronutrient** that supports immunity and acts as an antioxidant.
- **Option 2 is correct: Calcium** is a **micronutrient** (a mineral) essential for bone health and muscle function.
- **Option 3 is incorrect: Carbohydrates** are **macronutrients** that provide energy for bodily functions.
- **Option 4 is correct: Iron** is a **micronutrient** (a mineral) essential for oxygen transport and energy production.

**Thus, three of the listed nutrients are micronutrients, making the answer (c) Only three.**

**2.** *(b)* Only two

- **Statement 1 is correct: Macronutrients** include carbohydrates, proteins and fats, which are primarily required for **energy production, growth** and the maintenance of bodily functions. They are needed in large quantities to support essential physiological processes.
- **Statement 2 is correct: Micronutrients,** such as vitamins and minerals, are critical for **metabolic processes,** maintaining **immune function** and supporting overall health. For example, Vitamin C boosts immunity, while iron is essential for oxygen transport in the blood.
- **Statement 3 is incorrect:** Vitamins and minerals are classified as **micronutrients,** not macronutrients. Macronutrients include carbohydrates, proteins, fats and water, which are required in larger amounts.

**Thus, the correct answer is (b) Only two.**

**3.** *(b)* 1, 3 and 4 only

- **Option 1 is correct: Protein** is a **macronutrient** that provides energy and aids in tissue repair and muscle growth.
- **Option 2 is incorrect: Vitamin A** is a **micronutrient** (a vitamin) necessary for vision and immune function.
- **Option 3 is correct: Fiber** is a **macronutrient** component, often categorised as a carbohydrate, essential for digestion.
- **Option 4 is correct: Carbohydrates** are a **macronutrient** that serve as the primary energy source for the body.

**Thus, the correct answer is (b) 1, 3 and 4 only.**

**4.** *(b)* 1 and 3 only

- **Option 1 is correct: Vitamin A** is a **fat-soluble vitamin** and is stored in the liver. It plays an essential role in vision and immune health.
- **Option 2 is incorrect: Vitamin C** is a **water-soluble vitamin** and is not stored in the body, requiring regular intake through diet.
- **Option 3 is correct: Vitamin D** is a **fat-soluble vitamin** that helps in calcium absorption and bone health.
- **Option 4 is incorrect: Vitamin B12** is a **water-soluble vitamin** that supports nerve function and blood cell production.

**Thus, the correct answer is (b) 1 and 3 only.**

**5.** *(a)* 1 and 4 only

- **Option 1 is correct: Vitamin B1 (Thiamine)** is a **water-soluble vitamin** essential for energy metabolism and nerve function.
- **Option 2 is incorrect: Vitamin A** is a **fat-soluble vitamin** important for vision and immune health.
- **Option 3 is incorrect: Vitamin D** is a **fat-soluble vitamin** that supports bone health and calcium absorption.
- **Option 4 is correct: Vitamin B12** is a **water-soluble vitamin** necessary for red blood cell formation and neurological function.

**Thus, the correct answer is (a) 1 and 4 only.**

**6.** *(b)* Only two

- **Pair 1 is incorrect: Vitamin B1 (Thiamine)** deficiency leads to **Beriberi**, affecting the nervous and cardiovascular systems.
- **Pair 2 is incorrect:** Vitamin C deficiency causes **Scurvy**, which leads to symptoms such as bleeding gums and weakened immunity.
- **Pair 3 is correct: Vitamin D** deficiency causes **Rickets** in children, leading to weak bones and skeletal deformities.
- **Pair 4 is correct: Vitamin A** deficiency leads to **Night blindness** due to its role in vision health and eye function.

**Thus, only two pairs are correctly matched, making the answer (b) Only two.**

**7.** *(a)* 1 only

- **Option 1 is correct:** Vitamin K is directly responsible for the **activation of blood clotting factors.** Deficiency in Vitamin K can lead to **increased bleeding time and a risk of hemorrhagic disease**, especially in newborns and individuals with malabsorption issues.
- **Option 2 is incorrect: Vitamin D** is important for bone health and calcium absorption, but it does not play a direct role in blood clotting.
- **Option 3 is incorrect: Vitamin C** deficiency leads to scurvy and fragile blood vessels, but does not directly impact clotting.
- **Option 4 is incorrect: Vitamin A** is essential for vision and immune health, not blood clotting.

**Thus, the correct answer is (a) 1 only.**

**8.** *(d)* All four

- **Pair 1 is correct: Vitamin A is abundant in carrots, which are rich in beta-carotene.** Other sources of Vitamin A include sweet potatoes, spinach and fortified dairy products.
- **Pair 2 is correct: Vitamin C is found in high quantities in citrus fruits such as oranges, lemons and grapefruits.** Other sources include strawberries, kiwis and bell peppers.
- **Pair 3 is correct: Vitamin D is primarily found in fish oil, including cod liver oil.** Vitamin D can also be synthesised in the skin upon exposure to sunlight, with additional sources including fortified milk and fatty fish like salmon.
- **Pair 4 is correct: Vitamin K is present in leafy green vegetables such as spinach, kale and broccoli.** Fermented foods like natto are also rich in Vitamin K2.

**Thus, all four pairs are correctly matched, making the correct answer (d) All four.**

**9.** *(b)* Only two

- **Statement 1 is correct:** Proteins are large biomolecules composed of chains of **amino acids linked by peptide bonds.** These amino acids act as the building blocks of proteins and determine their structure and function.
- **Statement 2 is correct:** Proteins are crucial for **muscle growth and repair,** as well as for the maintenance of tissues. They play a structural and functional role in the body, including acting as enzymes, hormones and antibodies.
- **Statement 3 is incorrect:** Proteins are not stored in the body for long-term energy needs. Instead, the body primarily uses **carbohydrates and fats** for energy storage. Proteins are broken down for energy only under conditions of prolonged starvation or extreme physical stress.

**Thus, the correct answer is (b) Only two.**

**10.** *(b)* Only two

- **Pair 1 matches with (A): Enzymes** are proteins that act as **biological catalysts,** speeding up biochemical reactions in the body.
- **Pair 2 matches with (C): Antibodies** are proteins produced by the immune system to **support immune function** and fight pathogens.
- **Pair 3 matches with (B): Hemoglobin** is a protein that **transports oxygen in the blood.**
- **Pair 4 matches with (D): Structural proteins,** such as collagen, provide **structure and support to cells and tissues.**

**Thus, only two pairs are correctly matched, making the answer (b) Only two.**

**11.** *(b)* Only two

- **Statement 1 is correct:** Monounsaturated fats are considered healthy dietary fats because they can **help reduce bad cholesterol levels (LDL) and maintain good cholesterol levels (HDL).**
  - They are predominantly found in foods like olive oil, avocados, nuts, and seeds.
  - These fats are beneficial for heart health and may also play a role in reducing inflammation.
- **Statement 2 is correct:** Trans fats are artificially created through a **process called hydrogenation**, which solidifies liquid oils to extend shelf life and improve texture.
  - They are commonly found in processed foods like margarine, baked goods and fried items.
  - These fats have been linked to an increased risk of heart disease as they raise LDL cholesterol levels and lower HDL cholesterol levels, contributing to arterial blockages.
- **Statement 3 is incorrect: Omega-3 and Omega-6 fatty acids are not trans fats.** They are polyunsaturated fatty acids essential for the body and play vital roles in brain function, heart health and inflammation control.

**Thus, the correct answer is (b) Only two.**

**12.** *(b)* 1, 2 and 4 only

- **Statement 1 is correct: Saturated fats are typically solid at room temperature** because their chemical structure lacks double bonds, making them more tightly packed. Common sources include animal fats, butter and lard.
- **Statement 2 is correct: Unsaturated fats are generally considered healthier than saturated fats** as they are associated with reducing the risk of cardiovascular diseases. They are found in foods such as nuts, seeds and fish.
- **Statement 3 is incorrect:** Saturated fats are not **predominantly found in plant-based oils.** Instead, they are mostly found in animal-based products and some tropical oils like coconut and palm oil. Plantbased oils like olive oil and canola oil are typically rich in **unsaturated fats.**
- **Statement 4 is correct:** Unsaturated fats, particularly monounsaturated and polyunsaturated fats, can help **reduce bad cholesterol (LDL)** levels, thus **lowering the risk of heart disease and stroke.**

**Thus, the correct answer is (b) 1, 2 and 4 only.**

**13.** *(b)* It converts unsaturated fats into trans fats, which can increase the risk of heart disease.

Hydrogenation is a chemical process that adds hydrogen atoms to unsaturated fats, converting them into **trans fats** or saturated fats. This process improves the shelf life and texture of fats but increases the risk of heart disease by raising **LDL (bad cholesterol) and lowering HDL (good cholesterol).**

**Thus, option (b) is the correct answer.**

**14.** *(c)* Only three

- **Pair 1 is correct: Avocado** is rich in **Monounsaturated Fatty Acids (MUFAs),** particularly oleic acid, which supports heart health.
- **Pair 2 is correct:** Walnuts are high in **Polyunsaturated Fatty Acids (PUFAs),** specifically Omega-3 fatty acids.
- **Pair 3 is correct: Salmon** is a good source of **polyunsaturated fatty acids,** particularly Omega-3 like EPA and DHA, beneficial for heart, and brain health.
- **Pair 4 is incorrect: Coconut oil** is primarily composed of **saturated fats,** not monounsaturated fats.

**Thus, three pairs are correctly matched, making the answer (c) Only three.**

**15.** *(b)* Only two

- **Statement 1 is incorrect:** Cholesterol is not **only obtained from dietary sources; it is also synthesised by the liver.** While foods like meat, eggs and dairy products contribute dietary cholesterol, the liver produces enough cholesterol to meet the body's needs.
  - Cholesterol is an essential lipid used in the synthesis of hormones, Vitamin D and bile acids.
- **Statement 2 is correct: High-Density Lipoprotein (HDL) is considered 'good' cholesterol** because it helps transport cholesterol from the arteries to the liver,

where it can be processed and removed from the body.
  - Higher levels of HDL are associated with a reduced risk of cardiovascular diseases.
- **Statement 3 is correct: Low-Density Lipoprotein (LDL) is considered 'bad' cholesterol** because high levels can lead to the accumulation of cholesterol in the arterial walls, forming plaques.
  - This buildup can restrict blood flow and increase the risk of atherosclerosis, heart attack, and stroke.

**Thus, the correct answer is (b) Only two.**

**16.** *(b)* A thick layer of fat found in marine mammals.
- **Blubber** is a thick layer of **fat** found beneath the skin of marine mammals such as whales, seals and dolphins.
- It serves multiple important functions, including **insulation** to keep the animal warm in cold ocean waters, **energy storage** as a reserve of calories and **buoyancy** to help the animal stay afloat.
- Unlike other types of fat, blubber is uniquely adapted for the marine environment, providing essential protection against the cold depths of the ocean.

**Thus, option (b) is the correct answer.**

**17.** *(d)* None
- **Pair 1 is incorrect: Ischemia** is defined as the **reduction of blood flow to tissues,** which deprives the tissue of oxygen and nutrients.
- **Pair 2 is incorrect: Infarction** refers to the **death of tissue** due to a prolonged lack of blood supply, often caused by a blockage in a blood vessel.
- **Pair 3 is incorrect: Atherosclerosis** is the **narrowing of arteries** due to plaque buildup, which can restrict blood flow.

**Thus, none of the pairs are correctly matched, making the answer (d) None.**

**18.** *(c)* All three
- **Statement 1 is correct:** The Food Safety and Standards Authority of India (FSSAI) is indeed responsible for **setting standards for food safety in India.** Its role includes framing regulations, setting benchmarks for food quality and ensuring that food products meet these standards to ensure public health, and safety.
- **Statement 2 is correct:** FSSAI **operates under the Ministry of Health and Family Welfare, Government of India.** It was established under the Food Safety and Standards Act, 2006 and acts as a statutory body to oversee food safety regulations in the country.
- **Statement 3 is correct:** FSSAI has the authority to **conduct food safety inspections and issue licenses to food businesses.** It monitors compliance with food safety laws and has the power to take action against violations to ensure that food is safe for consumption.

**Thus, the correct answer is (c) All three.**

**19.** *(d)* All four
- **Function 1 is correct:** The organisation establishes standards and guidelines to ensure that food is safe for consumption, thereby promoting public health.
- **Function 2 is correct:** The authority sets safety standards for imported food products and ensures compliance with these standards. It also plays a role in certifying food exports based on international safety norms.
- **Function 3 is correct:** The authority funds and facilitates research to improve food safety practices and educates the public through campaigns like the 'Eat Right India' initiative.
- **Function 4 is correct:** It ensures that businesses comply with food safety standards by issuing licenses and conducting inspections to monitor adherence.

**Thus, all four functions are performed by FSSAI, making the correct answer (d) All four.**

**20.** *(c)* Only three
- **Statement 1 is correct:** The initiative aims to **reduce industrially produced trans fats in food products to less than 2%** to align with global health standards.
- **Statement 2 is correct: Promoting public awareness** about the health risks associated with trans fats, such as heart disease, is a major part of this initiative.

- **Statement 3 is correct:** The initiative encourages the **food industry to adopt healthier alternatives** to trans fats, like using unsaturated fats instead.
- **Statement 4 is incorrect:** The primary focus of this initiative is on domestic health improvement rather than increasing the export of trans fat-free products.

**Thus, three objectives are part of the initiative, making the answer (c) Only three.**

**21.** *(d)* All four

- **Option 1 is correct: Iron** is commonly added to staple foods like wheat flour to combat irondeficiency anemia.
- **Option 2 is correct: Vitamin A** is added to edible oils to improve vision health and reduce deficiency.
- **Option 3 is correct: Calcium** is fortified in some products, particularly milk and dairy alternatives, to support bone health.
- **Option 4 is correct: Iodine** is added to salt to prevent iodine deficiency and related thyroid issues.

**Thus, all four nutrients are commonly added, making the answer (d) All four.**

**22.** *(a)* 1 and 2 only

- **Statement 1 is correct: FSSAI has established standards** for fortifying wheat flour with iron, folic acid and other nutrients.
- **Statement 2 is correct: FSSAI mandates that fortified products must carry a specific logo (the '+F' logo) to help consumers easily identify fortified foods.**
- **Statement 3 is incorrect: FSSAI permits fortification for a variety of foods, including rice, milk and** edible oils, not just dairy products.

**Thus, the correct answer is (a) 1 and 2 only.**

**23.** *(b)* 1, 2, and 3 only

- **Option 1 is correct: Iron is a key nutrient added to fortified rice in India.** Iron deficiency is a leading cause of anaemia, particularly among children and women. Adding iron helps address this widespread nutritional challenge.
- **Option 2 is correct: Folic acid (a form of Vitamin B9) is included in fortified rice.** It plays a vital role in preventing neural tube defects in newborns and supports red blood cell formation, addressing folate deficiency-related anemia.
- **Option 3 is correct: Vitamin B12 is commonly added to fortified rice** as part of India's efforts to combat micronutrient deficiencies. It helps in nerve function, DNA synthesis and red blood cell production, especially for vegetarians who may lack dietary sources of Vitamin B12.
- **Option 4 is incorrect: Calcium is not typically added to fortified rice in India.** While it is an important nutrient, its supplementation is more common in products like milk or fortified cereals and not part of rice fortification programs.

**Thus, options 1, 2 and 3 are correct, making the correct answer (b) 1, 2 and 3 only.**

**24.** *(b)* 1, 3 and 4 only

- **Statement 1 is correct:** Antigens are **substances that can trigger an immune response.** When introduced into the body, they are recognised as **foreign by the immune system,** prompting the production of antibodies or activation of immune cells.
- **Statement 2 is incorrect:** Antigens are not always harmful to the body. While many antigens, such as those from pathogens, can cause disease, others, like **harmless proteins in vaccines, stimulate protective immune responses without harm.**
- **Statement 3 is correct: Each antigen is specific to a particular pathogen.** This specificity allows the immune system to identify and target specific invaders, ensuring a tailored response to infections.
- **Statement 4 is correct: Antigens can be composed of proteins, polysaccharides or toxins.** For example, bacterial cell walls contain polysaccharides, while toxins released by bacteria are proteinbased antigens.

**Thus, statements 1, 3 and 4 are correct, making the correct answer (b) 1, 3 and 4 only.**

**25.** *(c)* 1, 3 and 4 only

- **Statement 1 is correct: Antibodies neutralise pathogens by binding to their antigens.** This prevents the pathogen from attaching to host cells and spreading infection. For example, antibodies can block viruses from infecting cells by covering their surface antigens.
- **Statement 2 is incorrect:** Antibodies **do not directly destroy pathogens through phagocytosis.** Instead, they facilitate phagocytosis by marking the pathogens for immune cells such as macrophages and neutrophils, which then engulf and destroy the pathogens.
- **Statement 3 is correct:** Antibodies **mark pathogens for destruction by immune cells.** This process, known as **opsonisation,** involves coating pathogens with antibodies, making them more recognisable and easier for immune cells to destroy.
- **Statement 4 is correct:** Antibodies **provide long-term immunity after an infection.** This is achieved through the generation of memory B cells, which can quickly produce specific antibodies upon subsequent exposure to the same pathogen.

**Thus, statements 1, 3 and 4 are correct, making the correct answer (c) 1, 3 and 4 only.**

**26.** *(b)* 1, 2 and 4 only

- **Statement 1 is correct:** Antibodies bind to specific regions on antigens known as **epitopes.** An epitope is a particular part of the antigen recognised by the antibody, ensuring a **highly specific immune response.**
- **Statement 2 is correct:** When an antibody binds to an antigen, it forms an **antibody-antigen complex,** which helps neutralise the pathogen by either preventing its attachment to host cells, marking it for destruction by immune cells (opsonisation), or triggering complement-mediated lysis.
- **Statement 3 is incorrect:** Antibody-antigen interactions are **highly specific.** Antibodies are produced to recognise a specific epitope on an antigen, ensuring targeted immune recognition.
- **Statement 4 is correct:** The interaction between antigens and antibodies follows a **'lock-and-key' mechanism,** where the antibody fits precisely with the antigen's epitope, allowing accurate immune recognition and response.

**Thus, the correct answer is (b) 1, 2 and 4 only.**

**27.** *(b)* Protection from infectious diseases that occurs when a large percentage of a population is immune

**Herd immunity** occurs when a large portion of a community (the 'herd') becomes immune to an infectious disease, either through vaccination or previous infection, which helps prevent the spread of the disease. When a significant percentage of the population is immune, it reduces the likelihood of infection spreading, thus indirectly protecting those who are not immune, such as individuals who cannot get vaccinated due to medical reasons. Herd immunity is critical in controlling infectious diseases and protecting vulnerable individuals.

**Thus, option (b) is the correct answer.**

**28.** *(b)* 1, 2 and 3 only

- **Option 1 is correct:** T-cells are a key component of acquired immunity. They are **produced in the thymus and help fight specific pathogens** by either directly killing infected cells (cytotoxic T-cells) or assisting other immune cells (helper T-cells).
- **Option 2 is correct:** B-cells are another crucial component of acquired immunity. They are **responsible for producing antibodies that specifically target pathogens.** B-cells can differentiate into plasma cells, which secrete antibodies, or memory B-cells, which provide long-term immunity.
- **Option 3 is correct:** Antibodies, produced by B-cells, are a part of acquired immunity. They **specifically bind to antigens on pathogens,** neutralising them or marking them for destruction by immune cells. Antibodies play a significant role in long-term immune protection.

- **Option 4 is incorrect: Natural killer (NK) cells are a part of the innate immune system,** not acquired immunity. NK cells provide a rapid response to virus-infected cells and tumor formation, but do not specifically target antigens or develop immunological memory.

**Thus, statements 1, 2 and 3 are correct, making the correct answer (b) 1, 2 and 3 only.**

***29.*** *(a)* 1 and 3 only

- **Statement 1 is correct: Innate immunity** is the body's first line of defense and provides a **rapid and immediate response** to pathogens. It acts within hours of infection to neutralise or eliminate invading organisms.
- **Statement 2 is incorrect**: Innate immunity does not have **memory** and cannot adapt to specific pathogens over time. These characteristics are a part of **adaptive immunity**, which improves with repeated exposure to the same pathogen.
- **Statement 3 is correct**: Innate immunity includes **physical barriers** such as the **skin, mucous membranes** and chemical defenses like enzymes and antimicrobial peptides. These barriers prevent pathogens from entering the body.
- **Statement 4 is incorrect**: Innate immunity is **not highly specific** to particular pathogens. Instead, it recognises and responds to **broad patterns** associated with pathogens, such as lipopolysaccharides on bacterial surfaces or viral RNA.

**Thus, the correct answer is (a) 1 and 3 only.**

***30.*** *(d)* All four

- **Pair 1 is correct: Physical barriers,** such as the **skin and mucous membranes**, act as the first line of defense against pathogens by blocking entry.
- **Pair 2 is correct: Physiological barriers include stomach acid** and enzymes in tears and saliva, which help prevent pathogen infection by creating an inhospitable environment.
- **Pair 3 is correct: Cellular barriers** consist of immune cells like **macrophages and neutrophils** that engulf and destroy pathogens.
- **Statement 4 is correct: Cytokine barriers** involve proteins, called **cytokines,** that mediate immune responses and promote inflammation to combat infection.

**Thus, all four pairs are correctly matched, making the answer (d) All four.**

***31.*** *(d)* All four

- **Pair 1 is correct: Skin** is a **physical barrier** that prevents pathogens from entering the body.
- **Pair 2 is correct: Tears and saliva** contain enzymes (like lysozyme) that help break down bacterial cell walls, acting as a **physiological barrier.**
- **Pair 3 is correct: Neutrophils** are white blood cells that target and destroy pathogens, forming part of the **cellular barrier.**
- **Pair 4 is correct: Interferons** are signaling proteins that enhance immune response and belong to the **cytokine barrier.**

**Thus, all four pairs are correctly matched, making the answer (d) All four.**

***32.*** *(b)* Chemical signals produced by cells to modulate immune responses.

**Cytokine barriers** are part of the immune system's response to infection and involve chemical signals called cytokines. These are **proteins secreted** by immune cells in response to pathogens. Cytokines help **regulate the intensity and duration of immune responses** by signaling other cells to activate, multiply, or target pathogens. Cytokines play a crucial role in both **inflammation** and **cellular communication** in the immune response.

**Thus, option (b) is the correct answer.**

***33.*** *(b)* 1, 2 and 3 only

- **Statement 1 is correct: Helper T cells (CD4+ T cells)** play a crucial role in activating B **cells.** They interact with B cells and release cytokines, which stimulate B cells to differentiate into plasma cells, and produce antibodies against specific antigens.
- **Statement 2 is correct: B cells** can present antigens **to T cells** through **Major Histocompatibility Complex (MHC) molecules.** This interaction is essential for activating T cells and initiating an immune response.

- **Statement 3 is correct:** T cells produce **cytokines**, which are signaling proteins that regulate immune responses, including the activation and regulation of B cells. Cytokines help B cells proliferate and produce antibodies.
- **Statement 4 is incorrect:** B cells do not directly destroy infected cells. Their primary function is to produce antibodies. The destruction of infected cells is primarily carried out by **cytotoxic T cells (CD8+ T cells)** or other immune cells such as natural killer (NK) cells.

**Thus, the correct answer is (b) 1, 2 and 3 only.**

**34.** *(a)* Only one

- **Pair 1 is incorrect:** Inactivated vaccines contain **killed pathogens that cannot replicate, but still stimulate an immune response.** These vaccines are stable and safe for use in individuals with weakened immune systems. Examples include the **Polio** (IPV) and **Hepatitis A Vaccines.**
- **Pair 2 is incorrect:** Live attenuated vaccines contain **weakened forms of the virus or bacteria** that can replicate, but do not cause disease in healthy individuals. These vaccines provide long-lasting immunity. Examples include the **Measles, Mumps and Rubella (MMR) vaccine** and, **the Oral Polio Vaccine** (OPV).
- **Pair 3 is incorrect:** Sub-unit vaccines use **specific parts of the pathogen,** such as proteins, to stimulate an immune response. These vaccines reduce the risk of side effects since they do not include the entire pathogen. Examples include the **hepatitis B vaccine** and **Human Papillomavirus (HPV) Vaccine.**
- **Pair 4 is correct:** mRNA vaccines use **genetic material** (messenger RNA) to instruct the body's cells to produce viral proteins, which trigger an immune response. These vaccines have been widely used during the COVID-19 pandemic, such as the **Pfizer-BioNTech and Moderna vaccines.**

**Thus, only one pair is correctly matched, making the correct answer (a) Only one.**

**35.** *(c)* Only three

- **Pair 1 is incorrect:** The **Hepatitis B vaccine** is a sub-unit vaccine, not a live attenuated vaccine.
- **Pair 2 is correct:** The **Polio vaccine** (IPV) is an example of an inactivated vaccine, as it contains a killed version of the polio virus.
- **Pair 3 is correct: Influenza vaccine (Flu shot)** is a subunit vaccine, which contains parts of the virus to stimulate immunity.
- **Pair 4 is correct: COVID-19 vaccines (Pfizer-BioNTech, Moderna)** are examples of mRNA vaccines, which use genetic material to instruct cells to make viral proteins.

**Thus, three pairs are correctly matched, making the answer (c) Only three.**

**36.** *(b)* Viral vector vaccine

**iNCOVACC** is a **viral vector vaccine,** which means it uses a harmless virus (not the coronavirus) to deliver genetic material from the SARS-CoV-2 virus into the body. This genetic material instructs cells to produce a viral protein that stimulates an immune response. The nasal delivery allows iNCOVACC to activate the immune system in the respiratory tract, potentially providing both mucosal and systemic immunity.

**Thus, option (b) is the correct answer.**

**37.** *(b)* Only two

- **Statement 1 is correct: Toxoid vaccines** contain inactivated toxins (or 'toxoids') produced by bacteria, making the toxin harmless while still prompting an immune response.
- **Statement 2 is correct:** Toxoid vaccines target **bacterial toxins,** offering immunity against the effects of the toxin rather than directly against the bacteria.
- **Statement 3 is incorrect:** Toxoid vaccines are used primarily for bacterial infections (e.g., tetanus and diphtheria), not viral infections.

**Thus, two statements are correct, making the answer (b) Only two.**

**38.** *(c)* Both 1 and 2

- **Statement 1 is correct:** Conjugate vaccines are specifically designed to protect against **bacteria with polysaccharide outer coats, such as Haemophilus influenzae type b (Hib), Streptococcus pneumoniae and Neisseria meningitidis.**
  - These outer polysaccharide layers make it difficult for the immune system to recognise and mount a strong response. Conjugate vaccines overcome this limitation by enhancing the immune response to these bacteria.
- **Statement 2 is correct:** Conjugate vaccines are created by **attaching a weak antigen**, such as a bacterial polysaccharide, to a **strong carrier protein** (e.g., tetanus or diphtheria toxoid).
  - The carrier protein stimulates the immune system, leading to a more robust and long-lasting immune response against the weak antigen.

**Thus, the correct answer is (c) Both 1 and 2.**

**39.** *(b)* Only two

- **Option 1 is correct: Tetanus** is prevented by a toxoid vaccine, as it's a disease caused by bacterial toxin.
- **Option 2 is incorrect: Pertussis** is not typically prevented by a toxoid vaccine; it's prevented by a different vaccine type (whole-cell or acellular).
- **Option 3 is correct: Diphtheria** is also prevented by a toxoid vaccine, as the disease is primarily caused by a toxin.
- **Option 4 is incorrect: Influenza** is prevented by an inactivated or live-attenuated vaccine, not a toxoid vaccine.

**Thus, two diseases are commonly prevented by toxoid vaccines, making the answer (b) Only two.**

**40.** *(b)* Only two

- **Statement 1 is incorrect:** mRNA vaccines **do not contain a live or weakened virus.** Instead, they use a **synthetic strand of messenger RNA to provide genetic instructions** for cells to produce a specific viral protein. This distinguishes them from traditional vaccine types like live-attenuated or inactivated vaccines.
- **Statement 2 is correct:** mRNA vaccines instruct cells to produce a **viral protein,** usually a harmless spike protein found on the surface of a virus. The immune system **recognises this protein as foreign and produces antibodies against it,** building immunity to the actual virus.
- **Statement 3 is correct:** mRNA vaccines are known for their **rapid development and easy modification.** Since they use a synthetic process to create the mRNA sequence, vaccine development is faster than traditional methods. This adaptability was a key factor in the development of COVID-19 vaccines, like those by Pfizer-BioNTech and Moderna, in record time.

**Thus, only two statements are correct, making the correct answer (b) Only two.**

**41.** *(a)* 1 and 2 only

- **Option 1 is correct:** The **Pfizer-BioNTech COVID-19 vaccine** is an RNA vaccine that uses an mRNA to instruct cells to make the spike protein of the virus, triggering an immune response.
- **Option 2 is correct:** The **Moderna COVID-19 vaccine** is also an mRNA vaccine, using similar technology as Pfizer-BioNTech to produce an immune response.
- **Option 3 is incorrect: ZyCoV-D** is a **DNA vaccine** developed by Zydus Cadila, using plasmid DNA to generate an immune response.
- **Option 4 is incorrect:** The **Johnson & Johnson COVID-19 vaccine** is a viral vector vaccine, not an RNA vaccine.

**Thus, the correct answer is (a) 1 and 2 only.**

**42.** *(a)* 1 and 3 only

- **Statement 1 is correct:** DNA vaccines deliver **genetic material (DNA)** into cells, which then produce viral proteins to stimulate an immune response.
- **Statement 2 is incorrect:** DNA vaccines are generally more stable than RNA vaccines and do not always require specialised cold storage.

- **Statement 3 is correct: ZyCoV-D**, developed by Zydus Cadila, is a notable example of a **DNA vaccine.**
- **Statement 4 is incorrect:** DNA vaccines use **DNA, not mRNA** to generate an immune response.

**Thus, the correct answer is (a) 1 and 3 only.**

**43.** *(c)* Only three

- **Statement 1 is correct: Inactivated vaccines** are **made from pathogens (bacteria or viruses) that have been completely killed or inactivated using chemicals, heat or radiation.** As the pathogens are nonliving, they cannot replicate but still trigger an immune response.
- **Statement 2 is correct:** Inactivated vaccines typically require **booster doses to maintain immunity** because the **immune response** they generate is not as strong or long-lasting as that from live vaccines. Examples include the inactivated polio vaccine (IPV).
- **Statement 3 is incorrect:** Inactivated vaccines do not provide immediate immunity. Like other vaccines, they **require time for the immune system to recognise the antigen, produce antibodies** and mount an effective immune response. Immediate immunity is generally achieved through passive immunity, such as antibody therapy.
- **Statement 4 is correct:** Inactivated vaccines are generally **safe for people with compromised immune systems,** as they do not contain live pathogens and cannot cause infections in immunocompromised individuals.

**Thus, the correct answer is (c) Only three.**

**44.** *(d)* All four

- **Pair 1 is correct:** The **Tetanus vaccine** is a **toxoid vaccine** that uses an inactivated toxin to generate immunity.
- **Pair 2 is correct:** The **Hepatitis B vaccine** is a **recombinant vaccine,** using genetically engineered viral proteins.
- **Pair 3 is correct:** The **Measles vaccine** is a **live attenuated vaccine,** as part of the MMR (Measles, Mumps, Rubella) vaccine.
- **Pair 4 is correct:** The **Rabies vaccine** is an **inactivated vaccine,** as it uses a killed virus to stimulate an immune response.

**Thus, all four pairs are correctly matched, making the answer (d) All four.**

**45.** *(c)* 1, 2 and 3 only

- **Option 1 is correct:** COVID-19 has been targeted by **DNA vaccines** such as ZyCoV-D, which was the first DNA vaccine approved for emergency use in India.
- **Option 2 is correct: HPV vaccines,** like those targeting HPV-related cancers, use DNA-based platforms to deliver genetic material and stimulate immunity.
- **Option 3 is correct:** DNA vaccines are being researched for **Zika virus,** aiming to develop a stable, rapid vaccine response.
- **Option 4 is incorrect: Tuberculosis** does not currently utilise DNA vaccines; other vaccine approaches are typically used to address this bacterial infection.

**Thus, the correct answer is (c) 1, 2 and 3 only.**

**46.** *(c)* Only three

- **Option 1 is correct: Measles** is a target of Mission Indradhanush, as it is a vaccine-preventable disease.
- **Option 2 is correct: Hepatitis B** is included in the mission's immunisation program, aiming to reduce infection rates.
- **Option 3 is correct: Japanese Encephalitis** is targeted in specific high-risk areas under Mission Indradhanush.
- **Option 4 is incorrect: Malaria** is not covered by Mission Indradhanush, as it does not have a vaccine and is instead addressed through vector control measures.

**Thus, three diseases are covered by Mission Indradhanush, making the answer (c) Only three.**

**47.** *(b)* Only two

- **Statement 1 is correct:** The **International Coordination Group (ICG)** was established to manage **emergency vaccine stockpiles** to ensure timely responses to outbreaks of epidemic-prone diseases. The ICG coordinates the distribution of vaccines and medical supplies in crisis situations to prevent major outbreaks.

- **Statement 2 is incorrect:** The ICG focuses on managing vaccine stockpiles for specific diseases, primarily **meningitis, yellow fever, cholera** and **measles,** but **not polio.** Polio eradication and vaccine provisions are managed under separate global initiatives like the Global Polio Eradication Initiative (GPEI).
- **Statement 3 is correct:** The ICG is a **collaborative initiative** involving multiple international organisations, including the **World Health Organisation (WHO), UNICEF, Medecins Sans Frontieres (MSF), and the International Federation of Red Cross and Red Crescent Societies (IFRC). These organisations work together to maintain vaccine stockpiles and respond effectively to public health emergencies.**

**Thus, statements 1 and 3 are correct, making the correct answer (b) Only two.**

**48.** *(c)* Only three

- **Option 1 is correct: Cholera** is one of the diseases for which the ICG manages emergency vaccine stockpiles, especially due to its rapid spread in outbreaks.
- **Option 2 is correct: Yellow Fever** is included in the ICG's emergency vaccine stockpiles due to the disease's high potential for severe outbreaks in certain regions.
- **Option 3 is correct: Meningitis** is another disease targeted by the ICG, especially in Africa's meningitis belt, where outbreaks are recurrent.
- **Option 4 is incorrect: Tuberculosis** is not included in the ICG's stockpiling efforts, as its spread is more endemic and chronic rather than outbreak-based.

**Thus, three diseases are covered by the ICG, making the answer (c) Only three.**

**49.** *(b)* Only two

- **Statement 1 is correct:** GAVI works to **increase access to vaccines** in low- and middle-income countries, aiming to improve global immunisation coverage.
- **Statement 2 is correct:** GAVI collaborates with major global health organisations, including **WHO, UNICEF, the World Bank** and the Bill & Melinda Gates Foundation, to strengthen healthcare systems, and support immunisation programmes.
- **Statement 3 is incorrect:** GAVI does not primarily fund vaccine research for high-income countries; instead, it focuses on **providing vaccines and strengthening healthcare systems** in low-income countries to address preventable diseases.

**Thus, two statements are correct, making the answer (b) Only two.**

**50.** *(c)* All three

- **Pair 1 is correct: Endemic** refers to a disease that is constantly present in a particular region or population. For example, **malaria** is endemic in certain tropical regions.
- **Pair 2 is correct: Epidemic** refers to a sudden increase in the number of cases of a disease within a specific geographic area. For example, a seasonal outbreak of **influenza** in a city can be termed an epidemic.
- **Option 3 is correct: Pandemic** refers to an epidemic that has spread across multiple countries or continents, often affecting a large number of people. COVID-19 became a pandemic as it spread globally.

**Thus, all three pairs are correctly matched, making the answer (c) All three.**

**51.** *(c)* Only three

- **Pair 1 is correct: Tuberculosis** is an **infectious disease** caused by the Mycobacterium tuberculosis bacterium, spread through respiratory droplets.
- **Pair 2 is correct:** Diabetes is a **non-infectious disease** that results from either insufficient insulin production (Type 1) or ineffective insulin use by the body (Type 2). It is not caused by pathogens and is often linked to genetic predisposition, lifestyle factors, or auto-immune mechanisms.
- **Pair 3 is correct:** Cystic Fibrosis is a **genetic disease** caused by mutations in the CFTR (Cystic Fibrosis Transmembrane Conductance Regulator) gene.

- **Pair 4 is incorrect:** Influenza is not an auto-immune disease; it is an **infectious disease** caused by the influenza virus.

**Thus, three pairs are correctly matched, making the answer (c) Only three.**

**52.** *(a)* 1, 2 and 4 only

- **Option 1 (Tuberculosis) is correct:** Tuberculosis is an **infectious disease** caused by the bacterium Mycobacterium tuberculosis, spread through airborne droplets.
- **Option 2 (Influenza) is correct:** Influenza, commonly known as the flu, is an **infectious disease** caused by influenza viruses, transmitted *via* respiratory droplets.
- **Option 3 (Hemophilia) is incorrect:** Hemophilia is a **genetic disease**, inherited through mutations in genes that control blood clotting.
- **Option 4 (Measles) is correct:** Measles is an **infectious disease** caused by the measles virus, known for its high transmissibility.

**Thus, the correct answer is (a) 1, 2 and 4 only.**

**53.** *(b)* 1, 2 and 4 only

- **Option 1 is correct:** Sickle cell anemia is a **genetic disease** caused by mutations in the hemoglobin gene.
- **Option 2 is correct:** Cystic fibrosis is a **genetic disease** resulting from mutations in the CFTR gene, affecting respiratory and digestive systems.
- **Option 3 is incorrect:** While Type 2 diabetes has a genetic component, it is primarily classified as a **non-infectious disease** and often influenced by lifestyle factors.
- **Option 4 is correct:** Huntington's disease is a **genetic disorder** caused by mutations in the HTT gene.

**Thus, the correct answer is (b) 1, 2 and 4 only.**

**54.** *(b)* Only two

- **Statement 1 is correct: Diabetes** is an **endocrine disorder** that involves irregularities in insulin production or function, impacting blood sugar regulation.
- **Statement 2 is correct: Anemia** is a **hematological disorder** commonly caused by a deficiency in hemoglobin or red blood cells, leading to reduced oxygen-carrying capacity in the blood.
- **Statement 3 is incorrect: Hypothyroidism** is an **endocrine disorder,** not a hematological disorder. It occurs when the thyroid gland does not produce enough thyroid hormones, affecting metabolism.

**Thus, two statements are correct, making the answer (b) Only two.**

**55.** *(c)* All three

- **Statement 1 is correct: Anaemia** is a **haematological (blood-related) disease that occurs when there are insufficient levels of haemoglobin or red blood cells in the body.** It is often caused by iron deficiency, vitamin deficiencies, or chronic diseases.
- **Statement 2 is correct: Diabetes is an endocrine disorder caused by issues related to insulin production.** Type 1 diabetes results from the body's inability to produce insulin, while Type 2 diabetes occurs due to insulin resistance or insufficient insulin production.
- **Statement 3 is correct: Epilepsy is a neurological disease marked by recurrent seizures,** which are caused by abnormal electrical activity in the brain. It can be triggered by genetic factors, brain injury, or infections.

**Thus, all three statements are correct and the correct answer is (c) All three.**

**56.** *(c)* Only three pairs

- **Pair 1 is correct: Sickle Cell Anemia** is a **hematological disease** caused by a genetic mutation that results in abnormally shaped red blood cells.
- **Pair 2 is correct: Parkinson's Disease** is a **neurological disease** that affects movement and coordination due to the degeneration of dopamine-producing neurons.
- **Pair 3 is incorrect: Asthma** is a **respiratory disease**, not an endocrine disease.
- **Pair 4 is correct: Hypothyroidism** is an **endocrine disease** caused by insufficient thyroid hormone production, affecting the body's metabolism.

**Thus, three pairs are correctly matched, making the answer (c) Only three pairs.**

***57.*** *(b)* Only two

- **Statement 1 is correct: Influenza** is caused by the influenza virus and primarily affects the respiratory system, leading to symptoms such as fever, cough and body aches.
- **Statement 2 is correct: Dengue** is a viral disease transmitted by the **Aedes mosquito,** causing fever, joint pain and in severe cases, bleeding and shock.
- **Statement 3 is incorrect: Tuberculosis** is not a viral disease; it is caused by the bacterium Mycobacterium tuberculosis.

**Thus, two statements are correct, making the answer (b) Only two.**

***58.*** *(b)* Only two

- **Option 1 is correct: Chickenpox** is caused by the varicella-zoster virus, leading to an itchy rash and fever.
- **Option 2 is incorrect: Malaria** is caused by the Plasmodium parasite, not a virus and is transmitted by the Anopheles mosquito.
- **Option 3 is correct: Hepatitis B** is a viral infection that affects the liver and can lead to chronic liver disease.
- **Option 4 is incorrect: Tetanus** is caused by the bacterium Clostridium tetani, not a virus.

**Thus, two diseases are caused by viruses, making the answer (b) Only two.**

***59.*** *(b)* Only two pairs

- **Pair 1 is incorrect: Dengue** is transmitted by **Aedes aegypti** mosquitoes, not Anopheles. Aedes aegypti is a primary vector for dengue, chikungunya and yellow fever, thriving in urban areas and biting primarily during the day.
- **Pair 2 is incorrect: Malaria** is transmitted by **Anopheles** mosquitoes, specifically female Anopheles. This species acts as the primary vector for malaria, a parasitic disease caused by Plasmodium species.
- **Pair 3 is correct: Japanese Encephalitis** is transmitted by **Culex mosquitoes,** particularly Culex tritaeniorhynchus. These mosquitoes are found in rural areas, often breeding in rice paddies and other stagnant water sources.
- **Pair 4 is correct: Zika Fever** is primarily transmitted by **Aedes albopictus** (Asian tiger mosquito), along with Aedes aegypti. Both mosquito species are capable of spreading Zika virus due to their prevalence in tropical and subtropical regions.

**Thus, only two pairs are correctly matched, making the correct answer (b) Only two pairs.**

***60.*** *(a)* 1 and 3 only

- **Option 1 is correct: Malaria** is caused by the protozoan parasite Plasmodium, transmitted by the Anopheles mosquito.
- **Option 2 is incorrect: Tuberculosis** is caused by the bacterium *Mycobacterium tuberculosis,* not a protozoan.
- **Option 3 is correct: Amoebiasis** is caused by the protozoan *Entamoeba histolytica,* often through contaminated food or water.
- **Option 4 is incorrect: Typhoid** is caused by the bacterium *Salmonella typhi,* not a protozoan.

**Thus, the correct answer is (a) 1 and 3 only.**

***61.*** *(c)* Only three

- **Option 1 is correct: Tuberculosis** is a bacterial infection caused by *Mycobacterium tuberculosis.*
- **Option 2 is incorrect: Influenza** is caused by the influenza virus, not by bacteria.
- **Option 3 is correct: Typhoid** is caused by the bacterium *Salmonella typhi.*
- **Option 4 is correct: Leprosy** is caused by the bacterium *Mycobacterium leprae,* which affects the skin, nerves and mucous membranes.

**Thus, three diseases are caused by bacteria, making the answer (c) Only three.**

***62.*** *(b)* Only two

- **Statement 1 is incorrect:** The FPPL focuses on **fungal pathogens that affect human health,** not plants, to prioritise research and treatments for human fungal infections.
- **Statement 2 is correct: Candida auris** is on the FPPL as it is resistant to multiple antifungal drugs and poses a significant healthcare challenge, especially in hospitals.

- **Statement 3 is correct:** The FPPL aims to **address the increasing threat of fungal infections** in humans, particularly as resistance to antifungal medications grows.

**Thus, two statements are correct, making the answer (b) Only two.**

**63.** *(c)* Only three

- **Option 1 is correct:** ***Candida albicans*** is a common fungal pathogen included in the FPPL due to its potential to cause severe infections, especially in immuno compromised individuals.
- **Option 2 is correct:** ***Cryptococcus neoformans*** is included in the FPPL because it can cause life-threatening infections, such as cryptococcal meningitis, particularly in HIV/AIDS patients.
- **Option 3 is correct: Aspergillus fumigatus** is listed in the FPPL due to its association with high morbidity and mortality in respiratory infections.
- **Option 4 is incorrect: Penicillium chrysogenum** is not included in the FPPL; it is generally not considered a human pathogen and is known for its role in producing the antibiotic penicillin.

**Thus, three fungi are included in the FPPL, making the answer (c) Only three.**

**64.** *(b)* Only two

- **Statement 1 is correct: Rabies** is a zoonotic disease that is primarily transmitted to humans through the bites of infected animals, especially dogs.
- **Statement 2 is incorrect: Tuberculosis** can be zoonotic; it can be transmitted from animals to humans, particularly strains like Mycobacterium bovis, which is transmitted through infected cattle.
- **Statement 3 is correct: Anthrax** is a zoonotic disease caused by Bacillus anthracis, which humans can contract through contact with infected animals or contaminated animal products.

**Thus, two statements are correct, making the answer (b) Only two.**

**65.** *(c)* Only three

- **Option 1 is correct: Rabies** is a zoonotic disease primarily transmitted through the bites of infected animals, such as dogs and bats.
- **Option 2 is incorrect:** While **HIV/AIDS** is believed to have originated from cross-species *transmission* of the *Simian Immuno-deficiency Virus* (SIV) from primates to humans, **it is not classified as a zoonotic disease because it primarily spreads between humans through bodily fluids.**
- **Option 3 is correct: Salmonellosis** is a zoonotic bacterial infection that humans can acquire through consuming food contaminated with animal feces, such as undercooked poultry or eggs.
- **Statement 4 is correct: Lyme disease** is a zoonotic infection caused by Borrelia burgdorferi, transmitted to humans through the bite of infected ticks, which often acquire the bacteria from rodents or deer.

**Thus, three diseases are zoonotic, making the answer (c) Only three.**

**66.** *(d)* None

- **Pair 1 is incorrect: Iron deficiency** is a common cause of **anemia,** as iron is essential for producing hemoglobin, which carries oxygen in the blood.
- **Pair 2 is incorrect: Iodine deficiency** leads to **Goiter,** which is an enlargement of the thyroid gland due to inadequate iodine levels required for thyroid hormone production.
- **Pair 3 is incorrect: Calcium deficiency** can lead to **Osteoporosis,** a condition characterised by weakened bones and increased fracture risk.
- **Pair 4 is incorrect: Rickets** is caused by a deficiency in **Vitamin D, calcium,** or **phosphate,** not phosphorus alone and it affects bone development in children.

**Thus, none of the pairs are correctly matched, making the answer (d) None.**

**67.** *(b)* Only two pairs

- **Pair 1 is correct: Minamata disease** is caused by **mercury poisoning** due to industrial pollution in Minamata Bay, Japan. It leads to severe neurological symptoms, including tremors, vision loss and cognitive impairment.
- **Pair 2 is incorrect: Itai-itai disease** was caused by **cadmium poisoning** from mining pollution in Japan. It leads to bone pain, fractures and kidney damage.
- **Pair 3 is incorrect: Plumbism** is another term for **lead poisoning**, which can cause anaemia, neurological damage and cognitive impairments, particularly in children.
- **Pair 4 is correct: Blue Baby Syndrome** is caused by **nitrate contamination** in drinking water, leading to methemoglobinemia, where the blood's ability to carry oxygen is reduced, giving a bluish skin tint in infants.

**Thus, only two pairs are correctly matched, making the answer *(b)* Only two pairs.**

**68.** *(c)* To remove heavy metals from the bloodstream by binding to toxic metals

- Chelation therapy involves the use of chelating agents, which are chemicals that **bind to heavy metals** such as lead, mercury, arsenic and cadmium in the bloodstream.
- This process allows these toxic metals to be safely excreted from the body through urine. **Chelating agents** commonly used in chelation therapy include EDTA (ethylenediaminetetraacetic acid), DMPS (dimercaptopropanesulfonic acid) and DMSA (dimercaptosuccinic acid).
- This treatment is particularly effective for **heavy metal poisoning**, but is not designed to boost immune function, increase minerals, or act as an antioxidant.

**Thus, option (c) is the correct answer.**

**69.** *(b)* Only two

- **Statement 1 is correct: Neglected Tropical Diseases** (NTDs) predominantly affect low-income populations in tropical and subtropical areas, where access to healthcare and sanitation may be limited.
- **Statement 2 is correct: Dengue, leprosy and river blindness (onchocerciasis)** are among the diseases classified as NTDs by the World Health Organisation (WHO).
- **Statement 3 is incorrect**: NTDs are not primarily caused by nutritional deficiencies, instead, they are typically caused by pathogens such as **viruses, bacteria, protozoa and parasites.**

**Thus, two statements are correct, making the answer (b) Only two.**

**70.** *(c)* Only three

- **Option 1 is correct: Chagas disease** is a parasitic disease transmitted by the triatomine bug and is classified as an NTD by the WHO.
- **Option 2 is incorrect**: While **malaria** is a major global health issue, it is **not categorised as an NTD**; it has separate, large-scale global health programmes.
- **Option 3 is correct: Lymphatic filariasis is an NTD** caused by parasitic worms and is spread by mosquitoes.
- **Option 4 is correct: Ebola is classified as an NTD**; it is a viral hemorrhagic fever with separate control programs due to its high fatality rate and epidemic potential.

**Thus, three diseases are classified as NTDs, making the answer (c) Only three.**

**71.** *(b)* Only two

- **Statement 1 is correct**: Mendelian disorders are genetic disorders caused by mutations in a single gene. These disorders follow Mendelian inheritance patterns, such as autosomal dominant, autosomal recessive, or X-linked inheritance. Examples of Mendelian disorders include **sickle cell anaemia, thalassemia and cystic fibrosis.**
- **Statement 2 is correct**: Chromosomal disorders occur due to abnormalities in the number or structure of chromosomes. These disorders often result from non-disjunction or chromosomal mutations. Examples include **Down syndrome** (caused by trisomy 21), **Turner syndrome** (monosomy X) and **Klinefelter syndrome** (XXY).

- **Statement 3 is incorrect:** Down syndrome is **not a Mendelian disorder but a chromosomal disorder** caused by the presence of an extra copy of chromosome 21 (trisomy 21). It results from a chromosomal abnormality rather than a single gene mutation, distinguishing it from Mendelian disorders.

**Thus, the correct answer is (b) Only two.**

**72.** *(a)* 1 and 3 only

- **Option 1 is correct: Cystic fibrosis** is a Mendelian disorder caused by a mutation in the CFTR gene and follows an autosomal recessive inheritance pattern.
- **Option 2 is incorrect: Down syndrome** is a chromosomal disorder caused by an extra copy of chromosome 21 (trisomy 21).
- **Option 3 is correct: Hemophilia** is a Mendelian disorder, often X-linked recessive, caused by mutations in genes responsible for blood clotting.
- **Option 4 is incorrect: Turner syndrome** is a chromosomal disorder that occurs when one of the X chromosomes is partially or completely missing in females.

**Thus, the correct answer is (a) 1 and 3 only.**

**73.** *(b)* 1, 2 and 4 only

- **Option 1 is correct: Syphilis** is a bacterial STD caused by *Treponema pallidum*. It can cause long-term complications if untreated, and it spreads through sexual contact.
- **Option 2 is correct: Hepatitis B** is a viral infection that can be sexually transmitted, in addition to transmission through blood and bodily fluids. Chronic infection can lead to liver disease and cancer.
- **Option 3 is incorrect: Tuberculosis** (TB) is not an STD, it is an airborne infection caused by *Mycobacterium tuberculosis,* spread through respiratory droplets.
- **Option 4 is correct: Gonorrhea** is a bacterial STD caused by *Neisseria gonorrhoeae,* which infects mucous membranes of the reproductive tract and can cause severe complications if untreated.

**Thus, the correct answer is (b) 1, 2 and 4 only.**

**74.** *(a)* Only one pair

- **Pair 1 is incorrect: Antiflatulents** are medications that help alleviate gas and bloating by breaking down gas bubbles in the digestive system.
- **Pair 2 is incorrect: Antipyretics** are used to **reduce fever** by acting on the body's temperature regulating center in the brain.
- **Pair 3 is incorrect: Analgesics** are drugs that **relieve pain** without causing a loss of consciousness. Common examples include aspirin and acetaminophen.
- **Pair 4 is correct: Antihistamines** block histamine receptors to relieve **allergy symptoms** such as sneezing, itching and runny nose.

**Thus, only one pair is correctly matched, making the answer (a) Only one pair.**

**75.** *(b)* Relieves muscle spasms, especially in the digestive tract.

- Antispasmodic medications are primarily used to **relieve muscle spasms,** particularly in smooth muscles, such as those in the gastrointestinal (GI) tract.
- These drugs help reduce abdominal cramping and discomfort associated with conditions like irritable bowel syndrome (IBS) and other GI disturbances.
- They work by relaxing the muscles, preventing spasms and allowing for smoother digestive function. Unlike anti-inflammatory drugs (choice a), analgesics (choice c), or antihistamines (choice d), antispasmodics specifically target muscle spasms.

**Thus, option (b) is the correct answer.**

**76.** *(a)* A highly similar, but not identical, version of an approved biologic drug.

A **biosimilar** is a **biologic medical product** that is highly similar to an already approved biologic drug (referred to as the 'reference product') but not identical. Unlike small-molecule generic drugs, which are exact chemical copies, biosimilars may have minor differences due to the complexity of biologic manufacturing processes, which involve living organisms. However, biosimilars are required to demonstrate no clinically meaningful differences in terms of safety, purity and effectiveness compared to the reference biologic.

**Thus, option (a) is the correct answer.**

**77.** *(b)* A complex drug made from living cells or organisms.

A **biologic** is a **complex drug** that is produced from **living cells or organisms.** Examples include monoclonal antibodies, vaccines and recombinant proteins. Biologics have larger and more intricate molecular structures than traditional small-molecule drugs, making them challenging to manufacture and replicate. This complexity also contributes to why exact copies, or 'generics,' of biologics are not feasible, leading to the development of **biosimilars** instead. Biosimilars are highly similar versions but may have minor differences that do not affect therapeutic function.

**Thus, option (b) is the correct answer.**

**78.** *(b)* 1, 2 and 3 only

- **Option 1 is correct: Paracetamol** is included in the WHO Model List of Essential Medicines as an analgesic and antipyretic for relieving pain and reducing fever.
- **Option 2 is correct: Amoxicillin** is an essential antibiotic widely used to treat bacterial infections.
- **Option 3 is correct: Ibuprofen** is an essential medicine used as an analgesic and anti-inflammatory drug.
- **Option 4 is incorrect:** Although **Remdesivir** was used for COVID-19 treatment, it is not included in the WHO's list of essential medicines.

**Thus, the correct answer is (b) 1, 2 and 3 only.**

**79.** *(b)* Only two

- **Statement 1 is correct:** Anti-microbial resistance (AMR) occurs when **micro-organisms such as bacteria, viruses, fungi and parasites evolve mechanisms to resist the effects of antimicrobial medications** like antibiotics, antivirals and antifungals. This makes infections harder to treat and increases the risk of disease spread, severe illness and death.
- **Statement 2 is correct: Overuse and misuse of antibiotics in healthcare (e.g., unnecessary prescriptions), and agriculture (e.g., as growth promoters in livestock)** are major contributors to the development of AMR. This misuse provides selective pressure that allows resistant strains to thrive and multiply.
- **Statement 3 is incorrect:** Vaccination plays a significant role in controlling AMR. **By preventing bacterial and viral infections, vaccines reduce the need for antimicrobial use,** thereby limiting opportunities for resistance to develop. For example, vaccines against pneumococcal disease and influenza indirectly help reduce the use of antibiotics.

**Thus, the correct answer is (b) Only two.**

**80.** *(d)* 1, 2, 3 and 4

- **Statement 1 is correct:** Overuse of antibiotics in healthcare, especially without a prescription, leads to the development of resistant strains.
- **Statement 2 is correct:** Improper disposal of antibiotics can introduce these drugs into the environment, promoting resistance.
- **Statement 3 is correct:** Lack of **clean water and sanitation** can lead to the spread of resistant infections, as poor hygiene facilitates transmission.
- **Statement 4 is correct: Antibiotics used in livestock** for growth promotion can lead to resistance, which can spread to humans.

**Thus, the correct answer is (d) 1, 2, 3 and 4.**

**81.** *(b)* Only two

- **Statement 1 is correct:** The **Red Line Campaign** was launched to create awareness among the public about the responsible use of antibiotics. Antibiotics packaged with a red line indicate that they should only be taken with a doctor's prescription.
- **Statement 2 is incorrect:** The **Chennai Declaration** was a national initiative developed by a group of doctors in 2012 to promote antibiotic stewardship in hospitals, it was not directly led by the government.

- **Statement 3 is correct:** The **Indian Council of Medical Research (ICMR)** conducts AMR surveillance and research to monitor resistance patterns and develop strategies for AMR control.

**Thus, two statements are correct, making the answer (b) Only two.**

***82.*** *(a)* World Health Organisation (WHO)

The **GLASS report**, or **Global Anti-microbial Resistance Surveillance System report,** is published by the **World Health Organisation** (WHO). GLASS was launched in 2015 to provide a standardised approach to collecting, analysing and sharing data on anti-microbial resistance at a global level. The purpose of the report is to track the spread of AMR worldwide and identify patterns that can inform public health actions, and policy decisions.

**Thus, option (a) is the correct answer.**

***83.*** *(b)* 1, 2 and 4 only

- **Option 1 is correct:** The **National AYUSH Mission** was launched to strengthen and promote AYUSH systems of healthcare across India.
- **Option 2 is correct: AYUSH Wellness Centers** have been established to provide holistic AYUSH based healthcare services.
- **Option 3 is incorrect: Ayushman Bharat Yojana** is a government health scheme, but falls under the Ministry of Health and Family Welfare, not the Ministry of AYUSH.
- **Statement 4 is correct:** The **International Day of Yoga** on 21st June was established with the Ministry of AYUSH's active involvement to promote yoga worldwide.

**Thus, the correct answer is (b) 1, 2 and 4 only.**

***84.*** *(d)* Jamnagar, India

The **WHO Global Centre for Traditional Medicine** is headquartered in **Jamnagar, Gujarat, India.** Established in collaboration between the **World Health Organisation** (WHO) and the **Government of India,** this center is the first of its kind globally and aims to harness the potential of traditional medicine by supporting research, innovation and data collection on traditional practices. The center's objectives include promoting safe and effective traditional medicine worldwide, integrating traditional medicine with modern health systems and ensuring access to quality traditional health practices. By situating the headquarters in India, WHO leverages the country's rich heritage in traditional practices such as Ayurveda, Yoga and Naturopathy, aligning with India's growing role in global health initiatives.

**Thus, option (d) is the correct answer.**

## Past Learning (Answers)

| | | | | | | | | | |
|---|---|---|---|---|---|---|---|---|---|
| 1 (a) | 2 (b) | 3 (c) | 4 (d) | 5 (c) | 6 (b) | 7 (b) | 8 (b) | 9 (b) | 10 (c) |
| 11 (d) | 12 (d) | 13 (b) | | | | | | | |

# CHAPTER 07 Biotechnology

## Assessment Round

### Topic 1 : Cellular Biology

**1.** With reference to the contributions for cell theory, consider the following statements:

1. Robert Hooke was the first to use the term 'cell' to describe the basic unit of life.
2. Robert Brown is credited with discovering the nucleus in plant cells.
3. Matthias Schleiden and Theodor Schwann jointly proposed the cell theory stating that all organisms are composed of cells.

How many of the given above statements is/are correct?

(a) Only one
(b) Only two
(c) All three
(d) None

**2.** Consider the following differences between 'Diffusion' and 'Osmosis':

1. Osmosis only involves the movement of solvent (water), while diffusion can involve solutes or solvents.
2. Osmosis requires a membrane, while diffusion does not.
3. Osmosis occurs from low to high concentration of solutes, while diffusion occurs from high to low concentration of particles.

How many of the given above statements is/are correct?

(a) Only one
(b) Only two
(c) All three
(d) None

**3.** With reference to the cellular boundaries, consider the following statements:

1. The plasma membrane is composed primarily of a lipid bilayer, while the cell wall is made up of cellulose in plant cells.
2. Both the plasma membrane and cell wall are found in all types of cells.
3. The plasma membrane plays a role in communication and signaling, while the cell wall is more involved in structural support.

How many of the given above statements is/are correct?

(a) Only one (b) Only two
(c) All three (d) None

**4.** Which of the following best describes 'Plasmolysis'?

(a) The process of water entering a cell, causing it to swell.
(b) The process of water leaving a cell, causing the cell membrane to pull away from the cell wall.
(c) The rupture of a cell due to excessive internal pressure.
(d) The intake of solute molecules by active transport.

**5.** Which of the following conditions would most likely lead to plasmolysis in a plant cell?

(a) Placing the cell in distilled water
(b) Placing the cell in a hypertonic solution, like a strong salt solution
(c) Placing the cell in an isotonic solution
(d) Exposing the cell to high temperature without changing the solution

**6.** Consider the following statements with respect to 'Reverse Osmosis':
1. It requires a semi-permeable membrane.
2. In reverse osmosis, water moves from an area of high solute concentration to low solute concentration.
3. It requires external pressure to overcome natural osmotic pressure.
4. It can remove most dissolved salts and impurities from water.

How many of the given above statements is/are correct?
(a) Only one (b) Only two
(c) Only three (d) All four

**7.** Consider the following applications:
1. Desalination of seawater
2. Filtration of large particles like sand and silt
3. Purification of drinking water
4. Industrial wastewater treatment

How many of the given above is/are correct applications of the reverse osmosis process?
(a) Only one
(b) Only two
(c) Only three
(d) All four

**8.** With reference to cellular structures, consider the following statements:
1. The nucleoid is present in prokaryotic cells and contains circular DNA.
2. The nucleolus is involved in ribosome synthesis in eukaryotic cells.
3. Chromatin material consists of DNA and proteins and is found in the nucleus of eukaryotic cells.

How many of the statements given above is/are correct?
(a) Only one (b) Only two
(c) All three (d) None

**9.** Consider the following components of cells:
1. Nucleoid
2. Nucleolus
3. Chromatin material
4. Ribosomes

How many of the given above is/are found in both prokaryotic and eukaryotic cells?
(a) Only one
(b) Only two
(c) Only three
(d) All four

**10.** With reference to chromatin material in eukaryotic cells, consider the following statements:
1. Chromatin consists of DNA and proteins, mainly histones.
2. Chromatin condenses to form chromosomes during cell division.
3. Chromatin is located in both the nucleoid and nucleus.

How many of the given above statements is/are correct?
(a) Only one (b) Only two
(c) All three (d) None

**11.** Consider the following cellular structures:
1. Nucleoid
2. Nucleolus
3. Chromatin material
4. Ribosomes

How many of the given above structures is/are involved in genetic information storage or expression?
(a) Only one (b) Only two
(c) Only three (d) All four

**12.** With reference to cellular organelles, consider the following statements:
1. Mitochondria are known as the 'powerhouses' of the cell because they generate ATP.
2. The endoplasmic reticulum helps in protein and lipid synthesis.
3. The Golgi apparatus is involved in modifying, packaging and transporting proteins.

How many of the statements given above is/are correct?
(a) Only one (b) Only two
(c) All three (d) None

**13.** Consider the following functions:
1. Protein modification and packaging
2. Lipid synthesis
3. Formation of lysosomes
4. Energy production through ATP synthesis

How many of above statements is/are correctly associated with the Golgi apparatus?
(a) Only one (b) Only two
(c) Only three (d) All four

**14.** Which of the following cell organelles is known as the 'suicidal bag' of the cell?
(a) Nucleus
(b) Lysosome
(c) Mitochondria
(d) Golgi apparatus

**15.** Consider the following statements about cellular organelles:
1. Plastids are present only in plant cells and are involved in photosynthesis and storage.
2. Vacuoles help maintain turgor pressure in plant cells.
3. Centrioles play a role in cell division in animal cells.

How many of the statements given above is/are correct?
(a) Only one
(b) Only two
(c) All three
(d) None

**16.** Which of the following is a primary function of centrioles in animal cells?
(a) Protein synthesis
(b) Photosynthesis
(c) Organising spindle fibers during cell division
(d) Energy production through cellular respiration

**17.** Consider the following features:
1. Mitochondria have a double membrane structure.
2. Mitochondria are involved in photosynthesis.
3. Mitochondria contain their own DNA and ribosomes.
4. The inner membrane of mitochondria has folds called cristae

How many of given above is/are features of mitochondria?
(a) Only one (b) Only two
(c) Only three (d) All four

**18.** What is the primary function of vacuoles in plant cells?
(a) ATP production
(b) Storage of genetic information
(c) Maintenance of turgor pressure
(d) Protein synthesis

**19.** With reference to cell structure, consider the following statements:
1. Plant cells have a cell wall, while animal cells do not.
2. Animal cells have small vacuoles, while plant cells have a large central vacuole.
3. Chloroplasts are present in plant cells but absent in animal cells.

How many of the given statements is/are correct?
(a) Only one
(b) Only two
(c) All three
(d) None

**20.** Consider the following cellular structures:
1. Cell wall
2. Chloroplasts
3. Mitochondria
4. Large central vacuole

How many of statements given above can be found in the plant cells?
(a) Only one (b) Only two
(c) Only three (d) All four

**21.** Consider the following statements:
1. Prokaryotic cells have smaller ribosomes compared to eukaryotic cells.
2. Eukaryotic cells divide by mitosis, while prokaryotic cells divide by binary fission.
3. Both cell types have mitochondria for energy production.

How many of the given above statements is/are correct?
(a) Only one (b) Only two
(c) All three (d) None

**22.** Consider the following statements with reference to the genetic material:

1. Prokaryotic DNA is circular while eukaryotic DNA is linear.
2. Eukaryotic DNA is associated with histone proteins but prokaryotic DNA is not.
3. Both cell types have their genetic material located in the nucleus.

How many of the statements given above is/are correct?

(a) Only one (b) Only two
(c) All three (d) None

**23.** Consider the following statements with reference to cell division:

1. Mitosis results in two genetically identical daughter cells, while meiosis results in four genetically diverse cells.
2. Mitosis occurs in somatic cells, whereas meiosis occurs in germ cells.
3. Crossing over, which increases genetic diversity, occurs during mitosis but not during meiosis.

How many of the given above statements is/are correct?

(a) Only one (b) Only two
(c) All three (d) None

**24.** Consider the following characteristics:

1. Diploid chromosome number
2. Involvement in growth and tissue repair
3. Production of genetically diverse cells
4. Undergoing mitosis

How many of the given above characteristics is/are specific to somatic cells?

(a) Only one (b) Only two
(c) Only three (d) All four

## Topic 2 : Genetics

**25.** Which of the following statements are differences between DNA and RNA?

1. DNA contains the sugar deoxyribose, while RNA contains the sugar ribose.
2. DNA is typically double-stranded, whereas RNA is usually single-stranded.
3. DNA uses the base thymine, while RNA uses uracil instead of thymine.

Select the correct answer using the codes below:

(a) 1 and 2 only (b) 1 and 3 only
(c) 2 and 3 only (d) 1, 2 and 3

**26.** Which of the following functions or characteristics are unique to DNA rather than RNA?

1. Long-term storage of genetic information
2. Catalytic activity in the cell
3. Double-helix structure
4. Use of thymine as a base

Select the correct answer using the codes given below:

(a) 1 and 3 only
(b) 1, 3 and 4 only
(c) 2 and 3 only
(d) 1, 2, 3 and 4

**27.** Consider the following properties:

1. Presence of thymine
2. Pairing of adenines with uracil
3. Double-stranded structure with complementary base pairing
4. Use of deoxyribose sugar

How many of the statements given above is/are exclusive to DNA?

(a) Only one
(b) Only two
(c) Only three
(d) All four

**28.** With reference to RNA, consider the following statements:

1. RNA contains ribose sugar, which is more reactive than deoxyribose.
2. RNA uses uracil as a base instead of thymine.
3. RNA is usually found as a double-stranded molecule in cells.

How many of the given above statements is/are correct?

(a) Only one (b) Only two
(c) All three (d) None

**29.** Consider the following pairs regarding types of RNA and their functions:

| RNA Type | Function |
|---|---|
| 1. mRNA | Carries genetic code from DNA to ribosomes |
| 2. rRNA | Transfers amino acids to the ribosome for protein assembly |
| 3. tRNA | Forms the structural and functional core of ribosomes |

How many of the given above pairs is/are correctly matched?
(a) Only one pair
(b) Only two pairs
(c) All three pairs
(d) None

**30.** What is 'Dark DNA' in the context of genetic research?
(a) DNA that does not code for proteins, so it is not detected in sequencing
(b) DNA segments with high mutation rates or unusual sequences, making them hard to detect in standard sequencing
(c) DNA present only in extinct species, making it undetectable in modern studies
(d) DNA that consists entirely of repetitive sequences and is therefore ignored in genome sequencing

**31.** Consider the following statements with reference to chromosomal disorders:
1. Down Syndrome is caused by an extra copy of chromosome 21.
2. Klinefelter Syndrome occurs in males with an additional X chromosome (XXY).
3. Turner Syndrome affects only females and is characterised by the presence of a single X chromosome (45, X).

How many of the statements given above is/are correct?
(a) Only one
(b) Only two
(c) All three
(d) None

## Topic 3 : Blood Cells

**32.** Consider the following characteristics:
1. Carry blood away from the heart
2. Contain valves to regulate blood flow
3. Have thicker, more muscular walls

How many of the given above characteristics is/are true for arteries?
(a) Only one
(b) Only two
(c) All three
(d) None

**33.** Consider the following pairs about the types of plasma proteins and their functions:

| Plasma Protein | Function |
|---|---|
| 1. Fibrinogen | Essential for blood clotting |
| 2. Globulin | Helps in maintaining blood pressure |
| 3. Albumin | Regulates osmotic pressure in blood |

How many of the pairs given above is/are correctly matched?
(a) Only one pair
(b) Only two pairs
(c) All three pairs
(d) None

**34.** With reference to the functions of blood cells, consider the following statements:
1. Red blood cells are primarily responsible for transporting oxygen throughout the body.
2. White blood cells protect the body from infections and foreign invaders.
3. Red blood cells have a nucleus, while white blood cells do not.

How many of the given above statements is/are correct?
(a) Only one
(b) Only two
(c) All three
(d) None

**35.** Consider the following characteristics:
1. Lack of a nucleus
2. Presence of hemoglobin
3. Phagocytic activity
4. Biconcave shape

How many of the statements given above is/are correct about red blood cells (RBCs)?
(a) Only one (b) Only two
(c) Only three (d) All four

**36.** With reference to the characteristics of red blood cells, consider the following statements:
1. White blood cells are more numerous than red blood cells in human blood.
2. Red blood cells are involved in gas exchange, while white blood cells are involved in immune defense.
3. White blood cells are produced in the bone marrow.

How many of the statements given above is/are correct?
(a) Only one (b) Only two
(c) All three (d) None

**37.** Which of the following statements differentiate red blood cells (RBCs) from white blood cells (WBCs)?
1. RBCs have a biconcave shape that maximises surface area for oxygen exchange, while WBCs have varied shapes depending on their type.
2. RBCs have a longer lifespan than WBCs.
3. RBCs help in oxygen transport, while WBCs help in fighting infections.
4. WBCs can move in and out of blood vessels to reach infection sites, but RBCs cannot.

Select the correct answer using the codes given below:
(a) 1 and 3 only (b) 1, 3 and 4 only
(c) 2 and 4 only (d) 1, 2, 3 and 4

**38.** What is the primary function of 'megakaryocytes' in the human body?
(a) To produce red blood cells
(b) To produce white blood cells
(c) To produce platelets for blood clotting
(d) To produce antibodies for immune defense

**39.** Which of the following are the functions of lymphatic system?
1. Transporting excess tissue fluid back to the bloodstream
2. Absorbing fats from the digestive system
3. Filtering blood to remove old red blood cells
4. Providing immune defense by transporting lymphocytes

Select the correct answer using the codes given below:
(a) 1 and 3 only
(b) 1, 2 and 4 only
(c) 2 and 4 only
(d) 1, 2, 3 and 4

**40.** With reference to the ABO blood group system, consider the following statements:
1. Blood group A has A antigens on the red blood cells and anti-B antibodies in the plasma.
2. Blood group O has no antigens on red blood cells but contains both anti-A and anti-B antibodies in the plasma.
3. Blood group AB has both A and B antigens on red blood cells and no antibodies in the plasma.

How many of the statements given above is/are correct?
(a) Only one
(b) Only two
(c) All three
(d) None

**41.** Consider the following characteristics of a blood group:
1. It is considered a universal donor for red blood cell transfusions.
2. It contains both A and B antigens on the red blood cells.
3. It has anti-A and anti-B antibodies in the plasma.
4. It is a universal recipient in plasma transfusions.

How many of the given above statements is/are correct about 'Blood group O'?
(a) Only one (b) Only two
(c) Only three (d) All four

**42.** With reference to blood transfusions, consider the following statements:

1. Individuals with blood group AB can receive red blood cells from any ABO group.
2. Individuals with blood group A can only donate to A and AB blood groups.
3. Blood group B has anti-A antibodies, so it cannot receive blood from groups A or AB.

How many of the statements given above is/are correct?

(a) Only one (b) Only two
(c) All three (d) None

**43.** With reference to the Rh blood group system, consider the following statements:

1. Individuals who have the Rh antigen on their red blood cells are considered Rh-positive.
2. Rh-negative individuals can safely receive Rh-positive blood without any complications.
3. The Rh factor is crucial during pregnancy as it can affect the health of the fetus.

How many of the statements given above is/are correct?

(a) Only one (b) Only two
(c) All three (d) None

**44.** With reference to blood transfusion compatibility, consider the following statements:

1. Individuals with blood type AB+ can receive blood from any ABO and Rh type.
2. Individuals with blood type O- can donate blood to any ABO and Rh type.
3. Individuals with blood type A- can receive blood from donors with blood type A+ or O+.

How many of the statements given above is/are correct?

(a) Only one (b) Only two
(c) All three (d) None

**45.** Consider the following statements with respect to the ABO blood group system:

1. Blood group A has A antigens on the red blood cells.
2. Blood group A has anti-B antibodies in the plasma.
3. Blood group A can receive blood from blood groups A and AB.

How many of the statements given above is/are true regarding blood group A?

(a) Only one
(b) Only two
(c) All three
(d) None

**46.** Consider the following characteristics for blood group O:

1. Blood group O has no antigens on the red blood cells.
2. Blood group O has both anti-A and anti-B antibodies in the plasma.
3. Blood group O can receive blood from any ABO group due to the absence of antigens.

How many of the above statements is/are true for blood group O?

(a) Only one
(b) Only two
(c) All three
(d) None

## Topic 4 : Biotechnology

**47.** Which of the following are applications of biotechnology in the field of medicine?

1. Production of insulin for diabetes treatment
2. Development of vaccines using recombinant DNA technology
3. Gene therapy for genetic disorders
4. Creation of hybrid crops with improved resistance to pests

Select the correct answer using the codes given below:

(a) 1 and 3 only (b) 1, 2 and 3 only
(c) 2 and 4 only (d) 1, 2, 3 and 4

**48.** Who coined the term 'biotechnology'?

(a) Louis Pasteur
(b) Karl Ereky
(c) Gregor Mendel
(d) Alexander Fleming

**49.** With reference to recombinant DNA technology, consider the following statements:

1. Recombinant DNA technology involves combining DNA from two different organisms.
2. The CRISPR-Cas9 system is an example of a tool used in gene editing *via* recombinant DNA technology.
3. Recombinant DNA technology has been used to produce synthetic insulin.

How many of the statements given above is/are correct?

(a) Only one (b) Only two
(c) All three (d) None

**50.** Consider the following pairs of biotechnology colours matched with their fields of application :

| Colour | Field of Application |
|---|---|
| 1. Red | Healthcare and pharmaceuticals |
| 2. Green | Environmental conservation and remediation |
| 3. White | Industrial processes, such as production and energy |

How many of the given pairs is/are correctly matched?

(a) Only one (b) Only two
(c) All three (d) None

**51.** With reference to 'Bio-informatics', consider the following statements:

1. Bioinformatics involves the use of computational tools to analyse biological data.
2. One of the primary applications of bioinformatics is in the development of new medications.
3. Bioinformatics only focuses on the analysis of genetic sequences and does not include protein structures.

How many of the statements given above is/are correct?

(a) Only one (b) Only two
(c) All three (d) None

**52.** What is purple biotechnology?

(a) Biotechnology focused on healthcare applications
(b) Biotechnology related to agricultural and food production
(c) Biotechnology that addresses bioethical, legal, and social issues
(d) Biotechnology involving marine and aquatic applications

**53.** Which of the following statements differentiate 'Gene Editing' from 'Genetic Engineering'?

1. Gene editing involves making precise changes to an organism's DNA, whereas genetic engineering may involve introducing new DNA from other organisms.
2. Gene editing tools like CRISPR can target specific locations in the genome without adding foreign DNA.
3. Genetic engineering focuses on altering genetic material only within the organism's natural gene pool.
4. Genetic engineering often involves the creation of genetically modified organisms (GMOs) with entirely new traits.

Select the correct answer using the codes below:

(a) 1 and 3 only
(b) 1, 2 and 4 only
(c) 2 and 3 only
(d) 1, 2, 3 and 4

**54.** Consider the following applications:

1. Production of biofuels using microbial fermentation
2. Wastewater treatment by using biological processes
3. Genetically modifying plants for higher crop yield
4. Production of single-cell protein for food supplements

How many of the statements given above is/are correct for bioprocess engineering?

(a) Only one
(b) Only two
(c) Only three
(d) All four

**55.** What is the primary function of plasmid DNA in bacterial cells?

(a) Carrying genetic information essential for bacterial survival

(b) Providing antibiotic resistance or other advantageous traits

(c) Encoding ribosomal RNA and proteins for protein synthesis

(d) Serving as the main source of energy production in cells

**56.** With reference to restriction enzymes, consider the following statements:

1. Restriction enzymes cut DNA at specific sequences known as recognition sites.
2. They are naturally found in bacteria, where they provide defense against viral infections.
3. Restriction enzymes always cut DNA in a straight, linear manner.

How many of the statements given above is/are correct?

(a) Only one
(b) Only two
(c) All three
(d) None

**57.** Consider the following applications:

1. DNA fingerprinting in forensic science
2. Creation of recombinant DNA for gene cloning
3. Sequencing of entire genomes
4. Detection of specific genetic mutations

How many of the given above is/are application of restriction enzymes?

(a) Only one
(b) Only two
(c) Only three
(d) All four

**58.** What is a palindromic sequence in the context of DNA?

(a) A sequence of DNA that reads the same forward and backward on the same strand.

(b) A sequence of DNA that is identical on both strands when read in opposite directions.

(c) A repeating sequence of nucleotides that forms a loop structure.

(d) A DNA sequence that does not allow restriction enzymes to bind.

**59.** Which of the following are commonly used techniques for gene-editing?

1. CRISPR-Cas9
2. TALENs (Transcription Activator-Like Effector Nucleases)
3. RNA Interference (RNAi)
4. ZFNs (Zinc Finger Nucleases)

Select the correct answer using the codes given below:

(a) 1 and 3 only
(b) 1, 2 and 4 only
(c) 2 and 3 only
(d) All four

**60.** What is the primary function of TALENs in genetic engineering?

(a) To silence gene expression by degrading mRNA

(b) To cut DNA at specific sites for gene editing

(c) To replicate DNA sequences in a cell

(d) To serve as a vector for gene transfer

**61.** Consider the following statements about the structure and function of 'Zinc Finger Nucleases (ZFNs)':

1. ZFNs consist of a DNA-binding domain made up of zinc finger proteins.
2. ZFNs use a FokI nuclease domain to cleave DNA at targeted sites.
3. These are naturally occurring enzymes found in bacterial cells.
4. ZFNs can be customised to target specific DNA sequences.

How many of the statements given above is/are correct?

(a) Only one
(b) Only two
(c) Only three
(d) All four

**62.** With reference to CRISPR technology, consider the following statements:

1. It is a naturally occurring defense mechanism found in bacteria.
2. CRISPR-Cas9 can be used to edit specific DNA sequences in any organism.
3. CRISPR technology requires inserting foreign genes into the organism being edited.

How many of the statements given above is/are correct?

(a) Only one (b) Only two
(c) All three (d) None

**63.** Which of the following are applications of genome sequencing?

1. Identifying genetic mutations that cause diseases
2. Tracing ancestry and human evolution
3. Developing pest-resistant crops
4. Producing energy by breaking down plant matter

Select the correct answer using the codes given below:

(a) 1 and 3 only (b) 1, 2 and 3 only
(c) 2 and 4 only (d) 1, 2, 3 and 4

**64.** Which of the following types of Assisted Reproductive Technology (ART) specifically involves placing both eggs and sperm into the fallopian tube for fertilisation within the body?

(a) In Vitro Fertilisation (IVF)
(b) Gamete Intrafallopian Transfer (GIFT)
(c) Zygote Intrafallopian Transfer (ZIFT)
(d) Intracytoplasmic Sperm Injection (ICSI)

**65.** Which of the following are common applications of Assisted Reproductive Technology (ART)?

1. Treating infertility in both males and females
2. Allowing same-sex couples to have biologically related children
3. Enhancing genetic characteristics in offspring
4. Facilitating embryo research and genetic screening

Select the correct answer using the codes given below:

(a) 1 and 2 only (b) 1, 2 and 4 only
(c) 2 and 4 only (d) 1, 2, 3 and 4

**66.** With reference to the applications of 'Gene Therapy', consider the following statements:

1. It can be used to treat certain types of inherited genetic disorders.
2. It is only effective for diseases caused by single-gene mutations.
3. It has potential applications in enhancing immune responses against cancer.

How many of the statements given above is/are correct?

(a) Only one
(b) Only two
(c) All three
(d) None

**67.** Which of the following best describes a phenotype?

(a) The genetic makeup of an organism responsible for specific traits.
(b) The observable characteristics of an organism resulting from the interaction of its genotype and environment.
(c) A sequence of DNA that codes for a protein responsible for a trait.
(d) The cellular structure and composition of an organism.

**68.** Which of the following best describes the difference between sexual and asexual reproduction?

(a) Sexual reproduction involves the fusion of gametes, resulting in genetic variation, whereas asexual reproduction produces genetically identical offspring.
(b) Sexual reproduction requires one parent, while asexual reproduction requires two parents.
(c) Asexual reproduction occurs only in unicellular organisms, while sexual reproduction occurs only in multicellular organisms.
(d) Asexual reproduction leads to greater genetic diversity compared to sexual reproduction.

**69.** Consider the following:
1. Binary fission
2. Budding
3. Sporulation
4. Fertilisation

How many of the given above is/are methods of 'Asexual Reproduction'?
(a) Only one
(b) Only two
(c) Only three
(d) All four

**70.** Which of the following techniques are commonly used in genetic engineering?
1. CRISPR-Cas9
2. Gene Cloning
3. Polymerase Chain Reaction (PCR)
4. Crossbreeding

Select the correct answer using the codes given below:
(a) 1, 2 and 3 only
(b) 2, 3 and 4 only
(c) 1 and 4 only
(d) 1, 2, 3 and 4

**71.** Which of the following best describes 'Transgenic Animals'?
(a) Animals bred using traditional crossbreeding techniques to enhance specific traits.
(b) Animals whose genome has been altered by introducing foreign DNA to express a desired trait.
(c) Animals that are cloned using the DNA of another organism.
(d) Animals that develop genetic mutations naturally due to environmental factors.

**72.** Which of the following applications can be treated using 'Stem Cell Therapy (SCT)'?
1. Leukemia and other blood-related disorders
2. Parkinson's disease
3. Diabetes
4. Heart disease
5. Genetic disorders like sickle cell anaemia

Select the correct answer from the codes given below:
(a) 1, 2 and 4 only
(b) 1, 2, 3 and 4 only
(c) 1, 3 and 5 only
(d) 1, 2, 3, 4 and 5

**73.** With reference to Somatic Gene Therapy and Germline Gene Therapy, consider the following statements:
1. Somatic gene therapy targets non-reproductive cells and its effects are not heritable.
2. Germline gene therapy targets reproductive cells and the changes are passed on to future generations.
3. Both somatic and germline gene therapy are equally accepted in human medical practices worldwide.

Which of the statements given above is/are correct?
(a) 1 only (b) 1 and 2 only
(c) 2 and 3 only (d) 1, 2 and 3

**74.** Match the following types of stem cells with their descriptions:

| Stem Cell Type | | Description |
|---|---|---|
| 1. Totipotent | A. | Can differentiate into any cell type within the body, excluding extra-embryonic tissues. |
| 2. Pluripotent | B. | Can differentiate into any cell type, including extra-embryonic tissues like the placenta. |
| 3. Multipotent | C. | Can differentiate into a limited range of related cell types, typically within a specific tissue or organ. |

Select the correct matching pairs using the codes given below:
(a) 1-A, 2-B, 3-C (b) 1-B, 2-A, 3-C
(c) 1-C, 2-A, 3-B (d) 1-B, 2-C, 3-A

**75.** With reference to the Somatic Stem Cells and Embryonic Stem Cells, consider the following statements:

1. Somatic stem cells are multipotent while embryonic stem cells are pluripotent.
2. Embryonic stem cells are derived from adult tissues whereas somatic stem cells are obtained from early-stage embryos.
3. Somatic stem cells are typically used for regenerative therapies while embryonic stem cells are used primarily in research.

Which of the statements given above is/are correct?

(a) 1 only (b) 1 and 3 only
(c) 2 and 3 only (d) 1, 2 and 3

**76.** With reference to the 'National Organ Transplantation Guidelines' in India, consider the following practices:

1. Allocation of organs based on the 'first-come, first-serve' principle.
2. Mandatory registration of both donors and recipients with the National Organ and Tissue Transplant Organisation (NOTTO).
3. Legal acceptance of both living and deceased donors.

How many of the above practices is/are in line with the guidelines?

(a) Only one
(b) Only two
(c) All three
(d) None

**77.** Which of the following is considered the first written evidence of transplantation or reconstruction?

(a) The Edwin Smith Papyrus
(b) Hippocratic Corpus
(c) Sushruta Samhita
(d) De Humani Corporis Fabrica

**78.** Which of the following best defines 'Xenotransplantation'?

(a) The transplantation of organs or tissues between genetically identical individuals.
(b) The transplantation of organs or tissues from one species to another.
(c) The transplantation of organs or tissues from deceased humans to living humans.
(d) The use of 3D-printed synthetic organs for transplantation.

**79.** With reference to CAR-T (Chimeric Antigen Receptor T) cell therapy, consider the following statements:

1. CAR-T cell therapy involves genetically engineering a patient's T-cells to recognise and destroy cancer cells.
2. It is an effective treatment for all types of cancers, including solid tumors.
3. CAR-T cell therapy is a personalised treatment that uses the patient's own immune cells.

Which of the above statements are correct?

(a) 1 and 2 only
(b) 1 and 3 only
(c) 2 and 3 only
(d) 1, 2 and 3

**80.** Which of the following benefits can be attributed to the adoption of 'Genetically Modified (GM)' crops?

1. Increased resistance to pests and diseases.
2. Enhanced nutritional content of food crops.
3. Reduced use of chemical fertilisers.
4. Increased crop yield under unfavourable climatic conditions.

Select the correct answer using the codes given below:

(a) 1 and 2 only (b) 1, 2 and 4 only
(c) 2, 3 and 4 only (d) 1, 2, 3 and 4

**81.** How many of the following techniques can be used for the genetic modification in crops?

1. CRISPR-Cas9
2. Agrobacterium-mediated transfer
3. Hydroponics
4. Particle Bombardment (Gene Gun)

Select the correct answer from the codes given below:

(a) Only one (b) Only two
(c) Only three (d) All four

**82.** The Genetic Engineering Appraisal Committee (GEAC) is constituted under which of the following Acts?
(a) Environment (Protection) Act, 1986
(b) Biological Diversity Act, 2002
(c) Indian Patent Act, 1970
(d) Protection of Plant Varieties and Farmers' Rights Act, 2001

**83.** With reference to the status of GM crops in India, consider the following statements:
1. Bt cotton is the only commercially approved genetically modified crop in India.
2. India has allowed the import of GM soybean and canola oil for edible purposes.
3. The cultivation of GM mustard (DMH-11) has been approved for commercial release in India.

Which of the statements given above are correct?
(a) 1 and 2 only
(b) 2 and 3 only
(c) 1 and 3 only
(d) 1, 2 and 3

**84.** With reference to DMH-11, a genetically modified crop in India, consider the following statements:
1. It is a genetically modified variety of mustard developed to increase yield through hybridisation.
2. The crop has been developed by the Indian Agricultural Research Institute (IARI).
3. DMH-11 employs a 'Barnase-Barstar' genetic modification system to promote hybrid seed production.

How many of the given above statements is/are correct?
(a) Only one
(b) Only two
(c) All three
(d) None

**85.** Consider the following categories of data:
1. Genomic sequences
2. Clinical trial results
3. Financial data of pharmaceutical companies
4. Protein structures

How many of the given above come under 'Biological Data'?
(a) Only one
(b) Only two
(c) Only three
(d) All four

**86.** Consider the following benefits of biopesticides over conventional pesticides:
1. They are biodegradable and environmentally friendly.
2. They are more effective in controlling all types of pests, including non-target species.
3. They reduce the chances of pests developing resistance.
4. They leave minimal toxic residues on crops.

How many of the given above statements is/are correct?
(a) Only one
(b) Only two
(c) Only three
(d) All four

**87.** Consider the following Assisted Reproductive Technology (ART) methods:
1. In-Vitro Fertilisation (IVF)
2. Intracytoplasmic Sperm Injection (ICSI)
3. Surrogacy
4. Artificial Insemination (AI)

How many of the above is/are considered ART methods?
(a) Only one
(b) Only two
(c) Only three
(d) All four

**88.** Arrange the following steps involved in the In-Vitro Fertilisation (IVF) process in the correct sequence:
1. Fertilisation of eggs in a laboratory.
2. Hormonal stimulation of the ovaries.
3. Transfer of the embryo to the uterus.
4. Retrieval of eggs from the ovaries.

Choose the correct order using the codes given below:
(a) 2-4-1-3 (b) 4-1-2-3
(c) 1-2-3-4 (d) 3-2-4-1

**89.** With reference to the Surrogacy (Regulation) Act, 2021, consider the following statements:

1. The Act permits only altruistic surrogacy and prohibits commercial surrogacy in India.
2. The intending couple must be married for at least five years to avail of surrogacy.
3. Foreign nationals are eligible to opt for surrogacy in India under this Act.

Which of the statements given above is/are correct?

(a) 1 only
(b) 1 and 2 only
(c) 2 and 3 only
(d) 1, 2 and 3

**90.** Consider the following statements about the 'Surrogacy (Regulation) Act, 2021':

1. The surrogate mother must be a close relative of the intending couple.
2. The Act establishes a National Surrogacy Board to oversee implementation.
3. Surrogacy is permitted for couples with biological children.

Which of the statements given above is/are correct?

(a) 1 and 2 only
(b) 2 only
(c) 1 and 3 only
(d) 1, 2 and 3

**91.** Consider the following diseases:

1. Leigh syndrome
2. Kearns-Sayre syndrome
3. Hemophilia
4. MELAS (Mitochondrial Encephalomyopathy, Lactic Acidosis and Stroke-like episodes)

How many of the given above is/are 'Mitochondrial Diseases'?

(a) Only one
(b) Only two
(c) Only three
(d) All four

**92.** Consider the following:

1. Genes
2. Whole organisms
3. Organs
4. Tissues

How many of the above can be cloned using current scientific techniques?

(a) Only one (b) Only two
(c) Only three (d) All four

**93.** With reference to the 'Mitochondrial Replacement Therapy (MRT)', consider the following statements:

1. It is a genetic engineering technique that replaces faulty mitochondrial DNA (mtDNA) in embryos with healthy mtDNA from a donor.
2. It is used to prevent the transmission of mitochondrial diseases from mother to offspring.
3. MRT allows for the modification of nuclear DNA to correct genetic disorders.

Which of the statements given above are correct?

(a) 1 and 2 only
(b) 2 and 3 only
(c) 1 and 3 only
(d) 1, 2 and 3

**94.** Which of the following statements are correct about the '3 Parent Baby' technique?

1. It is aimed at preventing the transmission of mitochondrial diseases.
2. It involves the use of nuclear DNA from the father and mother and mitochondrial DNA from a donor.
3. It replaces faulty nuclear DNA with healthy nuclear DNA from a donor.
4. It results in a child with genetic material from three individuals.

Select the correct answer using the codes given below:

(a) 1, 2 and 4 only (b) 1 and 3 only
(c) 2, 3 and 4 only (d) 1, 2, 3 and 4

**95.** Which of the following best describes 'Therapeutic Cloning'?

(a) A process to create genetically identical organisms for organ transplantation.

(b) A technique used to clone entire organs using somatic cell nuclear transfer (SCNT).

(c) A process to produce embryonic stem cells for regenerative medicine and treating diseases.

(d) A cloning technique used exclusively in animal reproduction experiments.

**96.** Which of the following are applications of 'Therapeutic Cloning'?

1. Generating patient-specific embryonic stem cells.
2. Repairing damaged tissues and organs.
3. Cloning entire humans for experimental purposes.
4. Treating neurodegenerative diseases.

Select the correct answer using the codes given below:

(a) 1 and 2 only (b) 1, 2 and 4 only

(c) 2, 3 and 4 only (d) 1, 2, 3 and 4

**97.** Which of the following best describes the purpose of Somatic Cell Nuclear Transfer (SCNT)?

(a) To transfer genetic material from one somatic cell to another.

(b) To create genetically identical organisms or embryonic stem cells by transferring the nucleus of a somatic cell into an enucleated egg cell.

(c) To modify specific genes in somatic cells for medical research.

(d) To facilitate the fusion of gametes in reproductive cloning.

**98.** With reference to the Genetic Engineering Appraisal Committee (GEAC), consider the following statements:

1. It is the apex body under the Ministry of Science and Technology for approving genetically modified crops in India.
2. It is responsible for regulating the import, export, and manufacture of genetically engineered organisms.
3. The GEAC's recommendations are legally binding on the government.

Which of the statements given above is/are correct?

(a) 1 only (b) 2 and 3 only

(c) 1 and 2 only (d) 2 only

**99.** Which of the following best describes the primary purpose of a gene bank in India?

(a) To conserve and store seeds, plants and genetic material of animals for biodiversity preservation and agricultural research.

(b) To genetically modify crops for increased yield and resistance to pests.

(c) To provide immediate agricultural loans to farmers in times of crisis.

(d) To create hybrid species through genetic engineering for commercial purposes.

**100.** With reference to the National Bureau of Plant Genetic Resources (NBPGR), consider the following statements:

1. It is responsible for conserving the genetic diversity of plant species in India.
2. It operates under the Ministry of Environment, Forest and Climate Change.
3. NBPGR maintains a gene bank that stores seeds, tissues and DNA of various crop species.

Which of the statements given above is/are correct?

(a) 1 only (b) 1 and 3 only

(c) 2 and 3 only (d) 1, 2 and 3

**101.** Which of the following are features of India's Seed Vault in Ladakh?

1. It is located at high altitudes to ensure natural refrigeration.
2. The vault stores seeds of both indigenous and commercially important crops.
3. It is managed by the National Bureau of Plant Genetic Resources (NBPGR).
4. The facility operates independently without any connection to global seed banks.

Select the correct answer using the codes given below:

(a) 1, 2 and 3 only (b) 1 and 4 only

(c) 2, 3 and 4 only (d) 1, 2, 3 and 4

# OMR SHEET

**Assessment Round**

| | | | | | | | |
|---|---|---|---|---|---|---|---|
| 1 | a b c d | 31 | a b c d | 61 | a b c d | 91 | a b c d |
| 2 | a b c d | 32 | a b c d | 62 | a b c d | 92 | a b c d |
| 3 | a b c d | 33 | a b c d | 63 | a b c d | 93 | a b c d |
| 4 | a b c d | 34 | a b c d | 64 | a b c d | 94 | a b c d |
| 5 | a b c d | 35 | a b c d | 65 | a b c d | 95 | a b c d |
| 6 | a b c d | 36 | a b c d | 66 | a b c d | 96 | a b c d |
| 7 | a b c d | 37 | a b c d | 67 | a b c d | 97 | a b c d |
| 8 | a b c d | 38 | a b c d | 68 | a b c d | 98 | a b c d |
| 9 | a b c d | 39 | a b c d | 69 | a b c d | 99 | a b c d |
| 10 | a b c d | 40 | a b c d | 70 | a b c d | 100 | a b c d |
| 11 | a b c d | 41 | a b c d | 71 | a b c d | 101 | a b c d |
| 12 | a b c d | 42 | a b c d | 72 | a b c d | 102 | a b c d |
| 13 | a b c d | 43 | a b c d | 73 | a b c d | 103 | a b c d |
| 14 | a b c d | 44 | a b c d | 74 | a b c d | 104 | a b c d |
| 15 | a b c d | 45 | a b c d | 75 | a b c d | 105 | a b c d |
| 16 | a b c d | 46 | a b c d | 76 | a b c d | 106 | a b c d |
| 17 | a b c d | 47 | a b c d | 77 | a b c d | 107 | a b c d |
| 18 | a b c d | 48 | a b c d | 78 | a b c d | 108 | a b c d |
| 19 | a b c d | 49 | a b c d | 79 | a b c d | 109 | a b c d |
| 20 | a b c d | 50 | a b c d | 80 | a b c d | 110 | a b c d |
| 21 | a b c d | 51 | a b c d | 81 | a b c d | 111 | a b c d |
| 22 | a b c d | 52 | a b c d | 82 | a b c d | 112 | a b c d |
| 23 | a b c d | 53 | a b c d | 83 | a b c d | 113 | a b c d |
| 24 | a b c d | 54 | a b c d | 84 | a b c d | 114 | a b c d |
| 25 | a b c d | 55 | a b c d | 85 | a b c d | 115 | a b c d |
| 26 | a b c d | 56 | a b c d | 86 | a b c d | 116 | a b c d |
| 27 | a b c d | 57 | a b c d | 87 | a b c d | 117 | a b c d |
| 28 | a b c d | 58 | a b c d | 88 | a b c d | 118 | a b c d |
| 29 | a b c d | 59 | a b c d | 89 | a b c d | 119 | a b c d |
| 30 | a b c d | 60 | a b c d | 90 | a b c d | 120 | a b c d |

## Calculate Your Score

| | |
|---|---|
| **Correct (✓)** | |
| **Incorrect (✓)** | |
| **Unattempted** | |
| **Total Score** | |
| **Accuracy (%)** | |

## Reasons for Incorrect Answers?

| | |
|---|---|
| 1. Lack of Knowledge/Existing Source Insufficient | |
| 2. Lack of Multiple Revision | |
| 3. Common Sense Mistakes | |

**Note :**

1. Calculate total score as correct answers carry 2 marks each 1/3rd marks will deducted for **Incorrect** Answers.
2. Calculate Accuracy (%) by dividing the number of correct answers to the total number of attempted questions.

## Past Learning

**1.** Which one of the following is synthesised in human body that dilates blood vessels and increases blood flow? **(2024)**

(a) Nitric oxide
(b) Nitrous oxide
(c) Nitrogen dioxide
(d) Nitrogen pentoxide

**2.** 'Microsatellite DNA' is used in the case of which one of the following? **(2023)**

(a) Studying evolutionary relationships among various species of fauna
(b) Stimulating stem cells transform into diverse functional tissues
(c) Promoting clonal propagation of horticultural plant
(d) Assessing the efficacy of drugs by conducting series of drug trials in a population

**3.** Aerial metagenomics best refers to which one of the following situations? **(2023)**

(a) Collecting DNA samples from air in a habitat at one go
(b) Understanding the genetic makeup of avian species of a habitat
(c) Using air-borne devices to collect blood samples from moving animals
(d) Sending drones to inaccessible areas to collect plant and animal samples from land surfaces and water bodies

**4.** Consider the following statements: **(2022)**

1. Biofilms can form on medical implants within human tissues.
2. Biofilms can form on food and food processing surfaces.
3. Biofilms can exhibit antibiotic resistance.

Which of the statements given above are correct?

(a) 1 and 2 only
(b) 2 and 3 only
(c) 1 and 3 only
(d) 1, 2 and 3

**5.** Consider the following statements: **(2022)**

DNA Barcoding can be a tool to:

1assess the age of a plant or animal.
2distinguish among species that look alike.
3. identify undesirable animal or plant materials in processed foods.

Which of the statements given above is/are correct?

(a) 1 only (b) 3 only
(c) 1 and 2 (d) 2 and 3

**6.** Bollgard I and Bollgard II technologies are mentioned in the context of: **(2021)**

(a) clonal propagation of crop plants
(b) developing genetically modified crop plants
(c) production of plant growth substances
(d) production of biofertilisers

**7.** In the context of recent advances in human reproductive technology, 'Pronuclear Transfer' is used for: **(2020)**

(a) fertilisation of egg in vitro by the donor sperm
(b) genetic modification of sperm producing cells
(c) development of stem cells into functional embryos
(d) prevention of mitochondrial diseases in offspring

**8.** Consider the following statements: **(2020)**

1. Genetic changes can be introduced in the cells that produce eggs or sperms of a prospective parent.
2. A person's genome can be edited before birth at the early embryonic stage.
3. Human-induced pluripotent stem cells can be injected into the embryo of a pig.

Which of the statements given above is/are correct?

(a) 1 only (b) 2 and 3 only
(c) 2 only (d) 1, 2 and 3

**9.** With reference to the recent developments in science, which one of the following statements is not correct? **(2019)**

(a) Functional chromosomes can be created by joining segments of DNA taken from cells of different species.

(b) Pieces of artificial functional DNA can be created in labouratories.

(c) A piece of DNA taken out from an animal cell can be made to replicate outside a living cell in a labouratory.

(d) Cells taken out from plants and animals can be made to undergo cell division in labouratory petri dishes.

**10.** What is Cas9 protein that is often mentioned in news? **(2019)**

(a) A molecular scissors used in targeted gene editing

(b) A biosensor used in the accurate detection of pathogens in patients

(c) A gene that makes plants pest-resistant

(d) A herbicidal substance synthesized in genetically modified crops

**11.** 'RNA interference (RNAi)' technology has gained popularity in the last few years. Why?

1. It is used in developing gene silencing therapies. **(2019)**
2. It can be used in developing therapies for the treatment of cancer.
3. It can be used to develop hormone replacement therapies.
4. It can be used to produce crop plants that are resistant to viral pathogens.

Select the correct answer using the codes given below:

(a) 1, 2 and 4
(b) 2 and 3 only
(c) 1 and 3 only
(d) 1 and 4 only

**12.** Consider the following techniques/ phenomena: **(2019)**

1. Budding and grafting in fruit plants
2. Cytoplasmic male sterility
3. Gene silencing

Which of the above is/are used to create transgenic crops?

(a) 1 only
(b) 2 and 3 only
(c) 1 and 3 only
(d) None

**13.** With reference to the Genetically Modified mustard (GM mustard developed in India), consider the following statements: **(2018)**

1. GM mustard has the genes of a soil bacterium that give the plant the property of pest-resistance to a wide variety of pests.
2. GM mustard has the genes that allow the plant cross-pollination and hybridization.
3. GM mustard has been developed jointly by the IARI and Punjab Agricultural University.

Which of the statements given above is/are correct?

(a) 1 and 3 only  (b) 2 only
(c) 2 and 3 only  (d) 1, 2 and 3

**14.** What is the application of Somatic Cell Nuclear Transfer Technology? **(2017)**

(a) Production of bio-larvicides
(b) Manufacture of biodegradable plastics
(c) Reproductive cloning of animals
(d) Production of organisms free of diseases

**15.** With reference to agriculture in India, how can the technique of 'genome sequencing', often seen in the news, be used in the immediate future? **(2017)**

1. Genome sequencing can be used to identify genetic markers for disease resistance and drought tolerance in various crop plants.
2. This technique helps in reducing the time required to develop new varieties of crop plants.
3. It can be used to decipher the host-pathogen relationship in crops.

Select the correct answer using the codes given below:

(a) 1 only
(b) 2 and 3 only
(c) 1 and 3 only
(d) 1, 2 and 3

**16.** In the context of the developments in Bioinformatics, the term 'transcriptome',sometimes seen in the news, refers to: **(2016)**

(a) a range of enzymes used in genome editing

(b) the full range of mRNA molecules expressed by an organism

(c) the description of the mechanism of gene expression

(d) a mechanism of genetic mutations taking place in cells

**17.** Mycorrhizal biotechnology has been used in rehabilitating degraded sites because mycorrhiza enables the plants to: **(2013)**

1. Resist drought and increase absorptive area
2. Tolerate extremes of pH
3. Resist disease infestation

Select the correct answer using the codes given below:

(a) 1 only (b) 2 and 3 only

(c) 1 and 3 only (d) 1, 2 and 3

# Detailed Solutions

## Assessment Round

**1.** *(c)* All three

- **Statement 1 is correct: Robert Hooke** was the first to use the term 'cell' in 1665 after observing a thin slice of cork under a microscope. He noted that the structure resembled small, empty rooms or 'cells,' leading to the term we use today.
- **Statement 2 is correct: Robert Brown**, a Scottish botanist, discovered the **nucleus** in plant cells in 1831. His work highlighted the importance of the nucleus in cellular structure and function.
- **Statement 3 is correct: Matthias Schleiden** (a botanist) and **Theodor Schwann** (a zoologist) jointly proposed the **cell theory** in 1838-1839. Schleiden concluded that plants were composed of cells, while Schwann extended this idea to animals, proposing that all organisms are made of cells.

**Therefore, all three statements are correct, making the answer (c) All three.**

**2.** *(b)* Only two

- **Osmosis** is the movement of a **solvent**, usually water, through a **semi-permeable membrane** from a region of **low solute concentration** to a region of **high solute concentration.** Example: Water entering plant roots from the soil.
- **Diffusion** is the movement of **particles (solutes or gases)** from a region of **higher concentration** to a region of **lower concentration** until equilibrium is achieved. Example: Perfume spreading in a room or oxygen moving into cells from the bloodstream.
- **Statement 1 is correct: Osmosis** involves the movement of **water** (solvent) across a membrane, while diffusion can involve any particle, including solutes.
- **Statement 2 is incorrect: Osmosis** specifically requires a semi-permeable membrane, whereas **diffusion** does not.
- **Statement 3 is correct:** In **osmosis**, water moves toward the area with a higher solute concentration to balance concentrations on both sides of the membrane.

**Thus, two statements correctly differentiate osmosis from diffusion, making the answer (b) Only two.**

**3.** *(b)* Only two

- **Statement 1 is correct:** The **plasma membrane** is primarily composed of a **phospholipid bilayer** with embedded proteins, which provides flexibility and selectively permeable properties. In plant cells, the **cell wall** is composed of **cellulose**, a polysaccharide that provides strength and rigidity. Fungal cell walls are made of chitin, while bacterial cell walls contain peptidoglycan.
- **Statement 2 is incorrect:** The **plasma membrane** is found in **all cell types** (including plant, animal, bacterial, and fungal cells), serving as the cell's outer boundary. However, the **cell wall** is not universal and is absent in **animal cells**; it is primarily found in plant cells, fungi and prokaryotes.
- **Statement 3 is correct:** The **plasma membrane** plays a key role in **cellular communication and signaling,** with receptors on its surface that interact with signaling molecules, allowing cells to respond to environmental changes. The **cell wall** is more involved in **structural support,** maintaining cell shape and providing a rigid framework for plants.

**Thus, two statements are correct, making the answer (b) Only two.**

**4.** *(b)* The process of water leaving a cell, causing the cell membrane to pull away from the cell wall

- **Plasmolysis** is the process in which a plant cell **loses water** when placed in a **hypertonic solution** (a solution with a higher solute concentration than the cell's cytoplasm).

- During plasmolysis, water moves out of the cell by osmosis, causing the cell to shrink. As a result, the **cell membrane detaches from the cell wall** and pulls inward, leaving a gap between the cell membrane and cell wall. Plasmolysis typically occurs in plant cells because of the rigid cell wall, which remains intact as the membrane shrinks.
- This process does not involve rupture or solute intake by active transport. It highlights the effects of osmotic pressure and the importance of water balance in maintaining cell structure.

**Thus, option (b) is the correct answer.**

**5.** *(b)* Placing the cell in a hypertonic solution, like a strong salt solution

- Plasmolysis occurs when a plant cell is placed in a **hypertonic solution**, such as a strong salt or sugar solution. In this environment, the solute concentration outside the cell is higher than inside the cell, causing **water to move out** of the cell *via* osmosis.
- As water leaves, the **cell membrane shrinks away from the cell wall,** leading to plasmolysis. If the cell is placed in distilled water (choice a), which is a hypotonic solution, water would move into the cell, potentially causing it to swell instead.
- In an isotonic solution (choice c), water movement would be balanced, preventing plasmolysis.
- High temperatures alone (choice d) do not cause plasmolysis, as plasmolysis specifically results from osmotic pressure changes in a hypertonic environment.

**Thus, option (b) is the correct answer.**

**6.** *(c)* Only three

- **Reverse Osmosis** (RO) is a water purification process in which water is forced through a **semi-permeable membrane** under high pressure to remove contaminants such as dissolved salts, impurities and microorganisms. The process is the reverse of natural osmosis, where water naturally moves from a region of low solute concentration to high solute concentration.
- **Statement 1 is correct**: In **reverse osmosis,** a **semi-permeable membrane** is essential. This membrane allows only water molecules to pass through while blocking dissolved salts, impurities and other contaminants.
- **Statement 2 is incorrect**: In reverse osmosis, water moves from an area of **low solute concentration to high solute concentration.** This movement is opposite to natural osmosis, hence the term 'reverse osmosis.'
- **Statement 3 is correct: External pressure** is applied in reverse osmosis to push water through the membrane, overcoming the natural osmotic pressure that would normally drive water in the opposite direction.
- **Statement 4 is correct: Reverse osmosis** is widely used for water purification because it effectively removes **dissolved salts, impurities and other contaminants,** producing clean water.

**Therefore, three statements are correct, making the answer (c) Only three.**

**7.** *(c)* Only three

- **Statement 1 is correct: Reverse osmosis** is commonly used in **desalination** to remove salts from seawater, making it suitable for drinking and irrigation.
- **Statement 2 is incorrect: Reverse osmosis membranes** are designed to filter out dissolved salts and smaller impurities, not larger particles like sand and silt. Pre-filtration systems are usually needed to remove such larger particles before water enters the RO system.
- **Statement 3 is correct: RO systems** are frequently used to purify drinking water by removing contaminants, including dissolved salts, heavy metals and pathogens.
- **Statement 4 is correct: Reverse osmosis** is used in **industrial wastewater treatment** to remove contaminants from wastewater before discharge or reuse.

**Thus, three applications are correct, making the answer (c) Only three.**

**8.** *(c)* All three

- Cells are the **basic structural and functional units of life.** Cellular structures, also known as organelles, perform specific functions essential for the survival and functioning of the cell. These structures vary between **prokaryotic** and **eukaryotic** cells.

- **Statement 1 is correct:** The **nucleoid** is an irregularly-shaped region in prokaryotic cells where **circular DNA** is located. Unlike eukaryotic cells, prokaryotes lack a true nucleus, so their genetic material is not enclosed in a membrane but rather exists in the nucleoid region.
- **Statement 2 is correct:** The **nucleolus** is a dense structure within the nucleus of **eukaryotic cells** responsible for **ribosome synthesis.** It assembles ribosomal RNA (rRNA) and combines it with proteins to form ribosomal subunits.
- **Statement 3 is correct: Chromatin material** is composed of **DNA and associated proteins** (mainly histones) and is found within the nucleus of eukaryotic cells. Chromatin condenses to form chromosomes during cell division.

**Thus, all three statements are correct, making the answer (c) All three.**

**9.** *(a)* Only one

- **Option 1 is incorrect: Nucleoid** is found only in **prokaryotic cells.** The nucleoid contains the circular DNA in prokaryotes but does not exist in eukaryotic cells, where DNA is enclosed within a nucleus.
- **Option 2 incorrect: Nucleolus** is found only in **eukaryotic cells.** The nucleolus is a structure within the nucleus that synthesises ribosomes, and since prokaryotes lack a true nucleus, they do not have a nucleolus.
- **Option 3 is incorrect: Chromatin material** is specific to **eukaryotic cells.** In eukaryotes, DNA is packaged with proteins to form chromatin within the nucleus. Prokaryotes, however, have naked circular DNA without chromatin structure.
- **Option 4 is correct: Ribosomes** are found in **both prokaryotic and eukaryotic cells** and are responsible for protein synthesis. In eukaryotes, ribosomes are found in the cytoplasm and attached to the endoplasmic reticulum, while in prokaryotes, ribosomes are free-floating in the cytoplasm.

**Thus, only one component (ribosomes) is found in both cell types, making the answer (a) Only one.**

**10.** *(b)* Only two

- **Statement 1 is correct: Chromatin** is composed of **DNA and proteins,** primarily histones, which help to organise and package the DNA into a compact, manageable form within the nucleus of eukaryotic cells.
- **Statement 2 is correct:** During **cell division,** chromatin condenses and becomes visible as chromosomes. This structural change enables the even distribution of genetic material to daughter cells.
- **Statement 3 is incorrect:** Chromatin is found only in the **nucleus of eukaryotic cells.** In prokaryotic cells, DNA exists in the nucleoid as circular DNA without forming chromatin, as prokaryotes lack histones and a nuclear membrane.

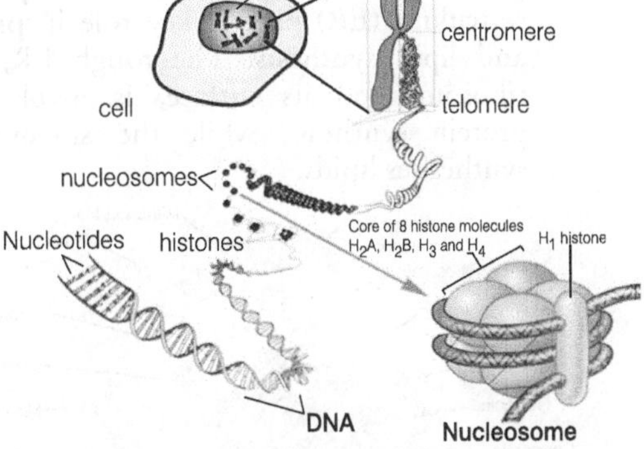


**Hence, two statements are correct, making the answer (b) Only two.**

**11.** *(c)* Only three

- **Option 1 is correct: Nucleoid** is involved in **genetic information storage** in prokaryotes. The nucleoid contains the cell's genetic material in the form of circular DNA, which carries genetic information for cellular functions.
- **Option 2 is correct: Nucleolus** is involved in **genetic expression,** as it synthesises ribosomal RNA (rRNA) necessary for ribosome formation, which plays a central role in protein synthesis.
- **Option 3 is correct: Chromatin material** is involved in **genetic information storage** in eukaryotes. Chromatin contains DNA,

which holds the cell's genetic information, and the associated proteins help regulate gene expression.

- **Option 4 is incorrect: Ribosomes** are not directly involved in genetic expression, as they are the sites of **protein synthesis,** translating genetic information from mRNA into functional proteins.

**Thus, three components (Nucleoid, Nucleolus, and Chromatin) are involved in genetic information storage and expression, making the answer (c) Only three.**

***12.*** *(c)* All three

- **Statement 1 is correct: Mitochondria** are often referred to as the **powerhouses of the cell** because they generate ATP (adenosine triphosphate) through cellular respiration, providing energy for cellular processes.
- **Statement 2 is correct**: The **endoplasmic reticulum** (ER) plays a key role in **protein and lipid synthesis**. The rough ER, with ribosomes on its surface, is involved in protein synthesis, while the smooth ER synthesises lipids.

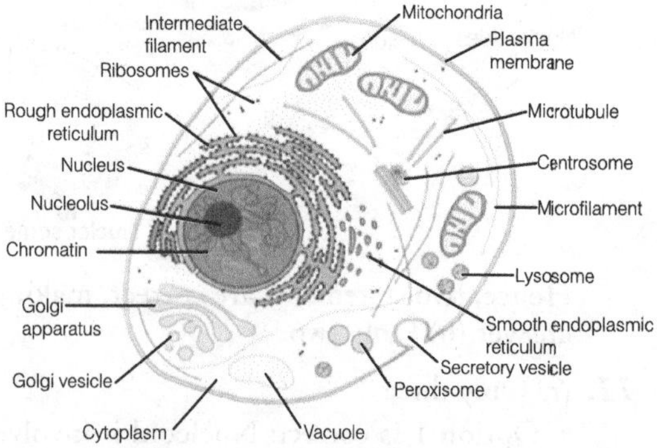


- **Statement 3 is correct**: The **Golgi apparatus** modifies, sorts, and packages proteins received from the ER and then transports them to their destination within or outside the cell.

**Therefore, all three statements are correct, making the answer (c) All three.**

***13.*** *(b)* Only two

- The **Golgi apparatus,** also known as the Golgi body, is an essential organelle in eukaryotic cells. It plays a central role in the processing, packaging, and transport of cellular molecules.
- **Statement 1 is correct**: The **Golgi apparatus** modifies, sorts and packages proteins for transport within or outside the cell.
- **Statement 2 is incorrect: Lipid synthesis** primarily occurs in the **smooth endoplasmic reticulum (ER),** not in the Golgi apparatus.
- **Statement 3 is correct**: The **Golgi apparatus** is involved in the formation of **lysosomes,** which contain digestive enzymes for breaking down cellular waste.
- **Statement 4 is incorrect: Adenosine Triphosphate (ATP)** is the primary energy currency of the cell. ATP synthesis refers to the biochemical processes by which cells generate ATP, providing energy for various cellular activities. **ATP synthesis** occurs in the **mitochondria,** not in the Golgi apparatus.

**Thus, two functions are correctly associated with the Golgi apparatus, making the answer (b) Only two.**

***14.*** *(b)* Lysosome

- The **lysosome** is often referred to as the **'suicidal bag'** or **'suicide organelle'** of the cell due to its ability to break down cellular components.
- Lysosomes contain powerful **hydrolytic enzymes** capable of digesting cellular waste, damaged organelles and even the entire cell if it becomes damaged or dysfunctional.
- These enzymes, including proteases, lipases, and nucleases, are normally contained within the lysosome's membrane. If the membrane of the lysosome were to rupture, these enzymes could be released into the cytoplasm, leading to the **self-digestion of the cell** or autolysis.

- This process is important in **cellular turnover** and **development**, and is crucial for **recycling cellular components** in eukaryotic cells, especially animal cells.

**Thus, option (b) is the correct answer.**

***15.*** *(c)* All three

- **Statement 1 is correct: Plastids** are organelles found only in **plant cells** and certain algae. They include chloroplasts, which are involved in **photosynthesis**, and other types that store pigments and starch.
- **Statement 2 is correct: Vacuoles** are large fluid-filled structures in plant cells that help maintain **turgor pressure** (internal pressure against the cell wall), which is essential for keeping the plant upright and firm.
- **Statement 3 is correct: Centrioles** are involved in **cell division** in animal cells. They help in forming the spindle fibers that separate chromosomes during mitosis and meiosis.

**Thus, all three statements are correct, making the answer (c) All three.**

***16.*** *(c)* Organising spindle fibers during cell division

- **Centrioles** are cylindrical structures made of **microtubules** arranged in a specific pattern of nine triplets. They are found primarily in animal cells and play a crucial role in **cell division.** During cell division, centrioles help in forming the **spindle fibers** required to separate chromosomes, ensuring accurate distribution of genetic material to the daughter cells.

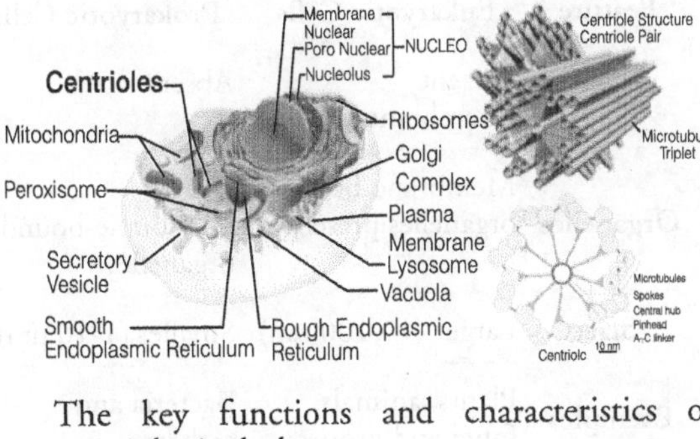


The key functions and characteristics of centrioles include:

1. **Formation of Spindle Fibers:** Centrioles organise and anchor spindle fibers, which attach to chromosomes, and help pull them apart during mitosis and meiosis. This is essential for accurate chromosomal segregation.
2. **Structure:** Each centriole is composed of **nine sets of microtubule triplets** arranged in a circular pattern, which provides structural integrity and the ability to generate and organise spindle fibers effectively.
3. **Role in Animal Cells:** Centrioles are typically absent in most plant cells and are mainly present in **animal cells.** Plant cells often rely on other microtubule organising centers for cell division.
4. **Involvement in Cilia and Flagella Formation:** In certain cells, centrioles also play a role in forming the **basal bodies** that give rise to **cilia and flagella,** structures responsible for cell movement and fluid movement across cell surfaces.

**Thus, option (c) is the correct answer.**

***17.*** *(c)* Only three

- **Mitochondria** are double membraned organelles found in most eukaryotic cells. They are often referred to as the **powerhouses of the cell** because they produce the majority of the cell's **adenosine triphosphate** (ATP), the energy currency of the cell.
- **Statement 1 is correct: Mitochondria** have a **double membrane** structure with an outer membrane and a highly folded inner membrane.
- **Statement 2 is incorrect:** Photosynthesis occurs in **chloroplasts** in plant cells, not in mitochondria. Mitochondria are responsible for cellular respiration and energy production.
- **Statement 3 is correct: Mitochondria** have their own **DNA and ribosomes,** allowing them to produce some of their own proteins.
- **Statement 4 is correct:** The **inner membrane** of mitochondria has folds called **cristae,** which increase the surface area for ATP production during cellular respiration.

**Therefore, the correct option is (c) Only three.**

**18.** *(c)* Maintenance of turgor pressure

**Vacuoles** are large, membrane-bound organelles present in **plant cells** (and some animal and fungal cells, though typically smaller). In plant cells, vacuoles serve a variety of crucial functions, with one of the most important being the **maintenance of turgor pressure.**

Key characteristics and functions of vacuoles include:

1. **Maintenance of Turgor Pressure**: Vacuoles store **water,** and by doing so, they maintain **turgor pressure** (the internal pressure exerted by the vacuole against the cell wall). This pressure helps the plant cell stay rigid and supports the plant's structure, keeping leaves, and stems upright.
2. **Storage of Nutrients and Waste**: Vacuoles act as storage sites for **nutrients, ions, pigments** and **waste products**. This ability allows the plant cell to store necessary compounds and isolate potentially harmful substances.
3. **Regulation of pH and Osmosis**: Vacuoles help regulate the cell's **pH** by storing acidic or basic ions and play a role in osmoregulation (water balance), which helps maintain a stable internal environment.
4. **Support for Plant Growth**: By filling with water, vacuoles can expand, allowing plant cells to grow larger without having to produce more cytoplasm. This expansion is energy-efficient and essential for the overall growth of the plant.

**Thus, option (c) is the correct answer.**

**19.** *(c)* All three

- **Statement 1 is correct: Plant cells** have a **cell wall** composed of cellulose that provides structure and support, whereas **animal cells** do not have a cell wall.
- **Statement 2 is correct: Plant cells** typically have a large, central **vacuole** that helps maintain turgor pressure, while animal cells may have smaller, scattered vacuoles.
- **Statement 3** is correct: **Chloroplasts**, the organelles responsible for photosynthesis, are present in plant cells but absent in animal cells, as animals do not perform photosynthesis.

**Thus, all three statements are correct, making the answer (c) All three.**

**20.** *(d)* All four

- **Option 1 is correct**: The **cell wall** is specific to **plant cells** (and some fungi and bacteria) but absent in animal cells.
- **Option2 is correct: Chloroplasts** are present in plant cells for photosynthesis but are absent in animal cells.
- **Option 3 is correct: Mitochondria** are found in both **plant and animal cells** as they are essential for energy production.
- **Option 4 is correct**: While vacuoles are present in both plant and animal cells, but a **large central vacuole is characteristic of plant cells,** helping with storage, waste disposal and maintaining cell structure.

**Therefore, all four structures are found in plant cells so, the correct answer is (d) All four.**

**21.** *(b)* Only two

- **Statement 1 is correct: Prokaryotic ribosomes are** 70S in size, which is smaller than the **80S ribosomes** found in eukaryotic cells.
- **Statement 2 is correct: Eukaryotic cells** divide by **mitosis** (and meiosis for reproductive cells), while **prokaryotic cells** divide by **binary fission**, a simpler process that does not involve a mitotic spindle.
- **Statement 3 is incorrect: Mitochondria** are present **only in eukaryotic cells** for ATP production. **Prokaryotes** lack mitochondria and instead perform cellular respiration in the cell membrane.

| Feature | Eukaryotic Cells | Prokaryotic Cells |
|---|---|---|
| Nucleus | Present (membrane-bound) | Absent |
| Organelles | Membrane-bound organelles present | No membrane-bound organelles |
| Size | Larger (10-100 μm) | Smaller (1-10 μm) |
| Examples | Plants, animals, fungi and protists | Bacteria and archaea |

**Thus, two statements are correct, making the answer (b) Only two.**

**22.** *(b)* Only two

- **Statement 1 is correct: Prokaryotic DNA** is **circular** and free-floating within the cell, while **eukaryotic DNA** is **linear** and organised into chromosomes.
- **Statement 2 is correct: Eukaryotic DNA** is associated with **histone proteins** that help in organising and packing DNA, while **prokaryotic DNA** lacks histones.
- **Statement 3 is incorrect:** Only **eukaryotic** cells have a **nucleus** where DNA is enclosed. **Prokaryotic cells** lack a nucleus and have their genetic material in the nucleoid region.

**Thus, two statements are correct, making the answer (b) Only two.**

**23.** *(b)* Only two

- **Statement 1 is correct:** Mitosis produces **two genetically identical daughter cells**, each with the same chromosome number as the parent cell (diploid). **Meiosis**, on the other hand, produces **four genetically diverse cells** (haploid), which contain half the chromosome number of the original cell.
- **Statement 2 is correct: Mitosis** occurs in **somatic (body) cells**, which are responsible for growth, repair and maintenance. **Meiosis** occurs only in **germ cells** (reproductive cells), leading to the formation of gametes (sperm and egg cells).
- **Statement 3 is incorrect: Crossing over** occurs during **meiosis (specifically in Prophase I)**, where homologous chromosomes exchange genetic material to increase genetic diversity. Crossing over does not occur in mitosis, as it is primarily concerned with creating identical cells.

**Therefore, two statements are correct, making the answer (b) Only two.**

**24.** *(c)* Only three

- **Statement 1 is correct: Diploid chromosome number** is specific to **somatic cells**, which are generally diploid, meaning they contain two sets of chromosomes. Germ cells are also diploid but produce haploid gametes.
- **Statement 2 is correct: Involvement in growth and tissue repair** is specific to **somatic cells**, as they are responsible for growth, repair and maintenance of tissues.
- **Statement 3 is incorrect: Production of genetically diverse cells** is not specific to somatic cells. Genetic diversity results from meiosis in germ cells, not from mitosis in somatic cells, which produces genetically identical cells.
- **Statement 4 is correct: Undergoing mitosis** is specific to **somatic cells,** as they divide through mitosis to produce identical daughter cells.

**Hence, three characteristics are specific to somatic cells, making the answer (c) Only three.**

**25.** *(d)* 1, 2 and 3

- **Statement 1 is correct:** DNA contains **deoxyribose** as its sugar, which lacks one oxygen atom compared to **ribose**, the sugar in **RNA**. This structural difference helps make DNA more stable, suitable for long-term genetic storage, while ribose in RNA makes it more reactive and suitable for temporary functions.
- **Statement 2 is correct:** DNA is generally **double-stranded**, forming a double helix structure, which provides stability for storing genetic information. In contrast, **RNA** is typically **single-stranded** and functions in protein synthesis, and other cellular processes.
- **Statement 3 is correct:** DNA contains the nitrogenous base **thymine** (T), while RNA contains **uracil** (U) in place of thymine. This substitution allows RNA to carry out its roles in gene expression and protein synthesis more efficiently.

**Thus, all three statements are correct, making the answer (d) 1, 2 and 3.**

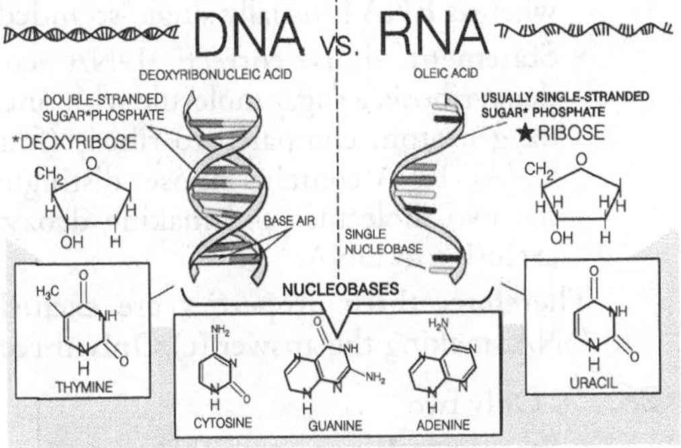

**26.** *(b)* 1, 3 and 4 only

- **Statement 1 is correct: Long-term storage of genetic information** is correct for **DNA,** which serves as the cell's permanent blueprint, storing genetic information that can be passed to future generations. **RNA** primarily functions as a temporary copy of DNA's instructions.
- **Statement 2 is incorrect:** Catalytic activity in cells refers to the role of enzymes, which are biological catalysts that speed up chemical reactions necessary for cellular processes. **Catalytic activity in the cell is not unique to DNA** and in fact it lacks catalytic function. However, certain **RNAs** (like ribozymes) have catalytic properties and can accelerate biochemical reactions.
- **Statement 3 is correct:** DNA is typically found in a stable **double-helix form,** whereas RNA is usually single-stranded.
- **Statement 4 is correct: Use of thymine as a base** is also specific to **DNA. RNA** uses uracil instead of thymine.

**Therefore, 1, 3 and 4 are unique to DNA, making the answer (b) 1, 3 and 4 only.**

**27.** *(c)* Only three

- **Statement 1 is correct: Presence of thymine** is specific to **DNA.** Thymine is a base found only in DNA; RNA uses uracil in its place.
- **Statement 2 is incorrect: Pairing of adenine with uracil** is not in DNA. This pairing occurs in RNA, where adenine pairs with uracil instead of thymine.
- **Statement 3 is correct:** DNA is typically double-stranded, with bases pairing complementarily across the two strands, whereas RNA is usually single-stranded.
- **Statement 4 is correct:** DNA contains **deoxyribose,** a sugar molecule with one fewer oxygen atom compared to ribose (found in RNA). RNA contains **ribose,** distinguishing the two molecules and making deoxyribose exclusive to DNA.

**Therefore, three properties are exclusive to DNA, making the answer (c) Only three.**

**28.** *(b)* Only two

- **Statement 1 is correct:** RNA contains **ribose** as its sugar, which has one more oxygen atom than deoxyribose in DNA, making RNA more chemically reactive and less stable than DNA. This reactivity suits RNA's temporary functions within cells.
- **Statement 2 is correct: RNA** uses **uracil** (U) instead of thymine as one of its nitrogenous bases. This difference in bases distinguishes RNA from DNA, which uses thymine instead of uracil.
- **Statement 3 is incorrect:** RNA is typically **single-stranded** in cells, allowing it to function flexibly in processes like protein synthesis and catalysis. Only in some viruses is RNA found as a double-stranded molecule.

**Therefore, two statements are correct, making the answer (b) Only two.**

**29.** *(a)* Only one pair

- **Pair 1 is correct: Messenger RNA (mRNA)** is responsible for carrying the **genetic code** from DNA in the nucleus to the ribosomes in the cytoplasm. This code provides instructions for assembling amino acids into proteins. mRNA is transcribed from DNA and contains codons, which specify the sequence of amino acids.
- **Pair 2 is incorrect: Ribosomal RNA (rRNA)** does not transfer amino acids; instead, it is a component of the ribosome itself. rRNA makes up the ribosome's structural and catalytic core, providing a site for **protein synthesis** by facilitating the binding of mRNA and tRNA. The ribosome's rRNA helps position the mRNA and catalyses the formation of peptide bonds between amino acids.
- **Pair 3 is incorrect:** Transfer RNA (tRNA) is responsible for **bringing specific amino acids** to the ribosome during protein synthesis, not forming the structure of the ribosome. Each tRNA molecule has an anticodon that pairs with a complementary codon on the mRNA, ensuring that amino acids are added in the correct sequence to build the protein.

**Therefore, only Pair 1 is correctly matched, making the answer (a) Only one pair.**

**30.** *(b)* DNA segments with high mutation rates or unusual sequences, making them hard to detect in standard sequencing.

- **Dark DNA** refers to segments of DNA that are challenging to detect in genome sequencing due to characteristics like **high mutation rates, repetitive sequences** or other unique features.
- These regions may play a role in gene regulation or evolution but are often missing in sequencing results because they do not align well with known reference genomes.
- Dark DNA is significant as it may contain genetic information essential for adaptation and biological function, yet it remains elusive in standard genetic studies.

**Thus, option (b) is the correct answer.**

**31.** *(c)* All three

- **Chromosomal disorders** are genetic conditions caused by abnormalities in the structure or number of chromosomes. Such disorders occur due to errors during cell division (meiosis or mitosis), resulting in missing, extra, or rearranged chromosomes. These abnormalities can lead to developmental, physical and cognitive challenges.
- **Statement 1 is correct: Down Syndrome** is caused by **trisomy 21**, where there is an **extra copy of chromosome 21**. This leads to various physical and intellectual characteristics such as distinct facial features and developmental delays.
- **Statement 2 is correct: Klinefelter Syndrome** occurs in **males** with an **additional X chromosome**, resulting in an XXY karyotype. This extra chromosome can lead to symptoms like reduced muscle mass, low testosterone levels, and potential infertility.
- **Statement 3 is correct: Turner Syndrome** affects **only females** and is characterised by a **missing X chromosome** (45, X). Symptoms may include short stature, lack of ovarian development and other physical characteristics.

**Therefore, all three statements are correct, making the answer (c) All three.**

**32.** *(b)* Only two

- **Statement 1 is correct**: Arteries carry blood away from the heart to various parts of the body. For example: **Systemic arteries** (like the aorta) carry oxygen-rich blood from the heart to tissues. **Pulmonary arteries** carry oxygen-poor blood from the heart to the lungs for oxygenation.
- **Statement 2 is incorrect**: Valves prevent the backflow of blood due to lower pressure and the effect of gravity. Unlike veins, **arteries do not typically have valves** because blood flow in arteries is driven by the high pressure generated by the heart's pumping action.
- **Statement 3 is correct**: Arteries have thicker walls composed of smooth muscle and elastic tissue to withstand the high pressure of blood pumped from the heart.

**Thus, two characteristics are true for arteries, making the answer (b) Only two.**

**33.** *(b)* Only two pairs

- **Pair 1 is correct: Fibrinogen** is a plasma protein that plays a crucial role in **blood clotting**. When there is an injury to a blood vessel, fibrinogen is converted to fibrin, which forms a mesh that helps stop bleeding by trapping blood cells and forming a clot.
- **Pair 2 is incorrect: Globulin** does not primarily help in maintaining blood pressure. Instead, globulins are a diverse group of proteins involved in **immune response**, acting as antibodies, and in transport functions for various substances, including lipids and hormones.
- **Pair 3 is correct: Albumin** is the most abundant plasma protein and is essential in **maintaining osmotic pressure** in the blood, which helps regulate the balance of fluid between blood vessels and body tissues. This prevents excessive fluid leakage from blood vessels into tissues.

**Therefore, only two pairs are correctly matched, making the answer (b) Only two pairs.**

**34.** *(b)* Only two

- **Statement 1 is correct: Red blood cells (RBCs)** are primarily responsible for **transporting oxygen** from the lungs to the body's tissues and bringing carbon dioxide back to the lungs for exhalation. Hemoglobin, an oxygen-carrying molecule, is abundant in RBCs and enables this function.

- **Statement 2 is correct: White blood cells (WBCs)** are part of the **immune system** and help defend the body against infections, foreign invaders, and pathogens such as bacteria and viruses.
- **Statement 3 is incorrect: Red blood cells lack a nucleus** to allow more room for hemoglobin, which maximises their oxygen-carrying capacity. In contrast, **most white blood cells contain a nucleus**, which is necessary for their immune functions.

**Thus, two statements are correct, making the answer (b) Only two.**

**35.** *(c)* Only three

- **Statement 1 is correct: Red blood cells (RBCs)** in mammals **lack a nucleus,** allowing more space for hemoglobin, which maximises oxygen transport capacity.
- **Statement 2 is correct**: RBCs contain **hemoglobin**, an iron-containing protein that binds to oxygen in the lungs and transports it to tissues, while also carrying carbon dioxide back to the lungs.
- **Statement 3 is incorrect: Phagocytic activity** is not specific to red blood cells. Phagocytic activity is a characteristic of certain white blood cells, such as neutrophils and macrophages, which engulf and destroy pathogens.
- **Statement 4 is correct: Biconcave shape** is specific to **red blood cells.** This shape increases the surface area for gas exchange and enables RBCs to travel easily through capillaries.

**Therefore, three characteristics are specific to red blood cells, making the answer (c) Only three.**

**36.** *(b)* Only two

- **Statement 1 is incorrect: Red blood cells** are far more numerous than white blood cells in human blood. RBCs make up about 40-45% of blood volume, whereas WBCs are present in much smaller numbers, around 1% of blood volume.
- **Statement 2 is correct: Red blood cells** are involved in **gas exchange**, carrying oxygen from the lungs to tissues and carbon dioxide back to the lungs. **White blood cells** are part of the immune system and defend the body against infections.
- **Statement 3 is correct**: Both **red and white blood cells** are produced in the bone marrow. The **bone marrow** is a primary site of blood cell production, where stem cells differentiate into RBCs, WBCs and platelets.

**Thus, two statements are correct, making the answer (b) Only two.**

**37.** *(b)* 1, 3 and 4 only

- **Statement 1 is correct: RBCs have a biconcave shape** that increases their surface area, allowing for efficient oxygen exchange across cell membranes. WBCs, on the other hand, have **varied shapes** depending on their type (e.g., lymphocytes, neutrophils, monocytes), which suit their specific immune functions.
- **Statement 2 is incorrect**: RBCs have a lifespan of about **120 days**, while the lifespan of **WBCs** is generally shorter, ranging from a few hours to a few days, depending on the type. Some WBCs, like neutrophils, may live only a few hours to days, while others, like lymphocytes, can live for years. Therefore, not all WBCs have shorter lifespans than RBCs.
- **Statement 3 is correct**: RBCs are specialised for **oxygen transport**, while WBCs play a critical role in **immune defense** by identifying and eliminating pathogens.
- **Statement 4 is correct: WBCs have the ability to move in and out of blood vessels** (a process known as diapedesis) to reach tissues where infections or inflammation are present. This mobility enables them to respond to infections throughout the body, whereas RBCs remain within blood vessels.

**Therefore, statements 1, 3 and 4 are correct, making the answer (b) 1, 3 and 4 only.**

**38.** *(c)* To produce platelets for blood clotting

- **Megakaryocytes** are large bone marrow cells responsible for producing platelets (thrombocytes), which are essential for blood clotting.
- During the maturation process, megakaryocytes extend long protrusions called proplatelets into the blood vessels within the bone marrow.

- These proplatelets fragment, releasing platelets into the bloodstream. Platelets play a critical role in **hemostasis** (stopping bleeding) by aggregating at sites of vascular injury to form a temporary plug, preventing excessive blood loss. Unlike other blood cells, platelets are **not complete cells** but rather small cell fragments derived from megakaryocytes.

**Thus, option (c) is the correct answer.**

***39.*** *(d)* 1, 2, 3 and 4

- The **lymphatic system** is a network of vessels, nodes, and organs that play a vital role in maintaining fluid balance, defending the body against infections and supporting the circulatory system. It is a critical part of the immune system.
- **Statement 1 is correct**: One of the primary functions of the **lymphatic system** is to **transport excess tissue fluid back to the bloodstream.** Fluid leaks from the capillaries into surrounding tissues and, if not returned, can cause swelling (edema). The lymphatic system collects this excess fluid as lymph and returns it to the circulatory system.
- **Statement 2 is correct**: The lymphatic system plays a crucial role in **absorbing fats from the digestive system.** Specialised lymphatic vessels called **lacteals** in the small intestine absorb dietary fats, which are transported as chyle (a milky fluid) through the lymphatic system and eventually enter the bloodstream.
- **Statement 3 is correct**: Filtering blood to remove old red blood cells is a function of the spleen, which is the largest organ of lymphatic system. The spleen filters blood and removes unhealthy, old or damaged red blood cells.
- **Statement 4 is correct**: The lymphatic system provides **immune defense** by transporting **lymphocytes** (white blood cells) and other immune cells to areas of infection or injury. Lymph nodes filter lymph and trap pathogens, where immune cells can respond to infections and provide defense.

**Hence, the correct answer is (d) 1, 2, 3 and 4.**

***40.*** *(c)* All three

- **Antigens** are the proteins or carbohydrate molecules found on the **surface of red blood cells (RBCs)** and **Antibodies** are the proteins produced by the **immune system** that recognise and bind to specific antigens.

| | Group A | Group B | Group AB | Group O |
|---|---|---|---|---|
| Red blood cell type | 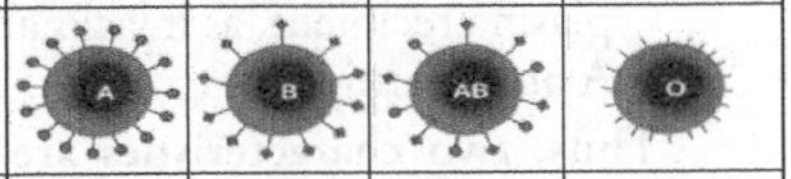 | | | |
| Antibodies in Plasma | Anti-B | Anti-A | None | Anti-A and Anti-B |
| Antigens in Red Blood Cell | A antigen | B antigen | A and B antigens | None |

- **Statement 1 is correct: In blood group A,** red blood cells have **A antigens** on their surface, and the plasma contains **anti-B antibodies,** which will attack B antigens if encountered in a transfusion.
- **Statement 2 is correct: Blood group O** has **no antigens** on the red blood cells, making it a universal donor type in terms of antigen compatibility. However, it contains both **anti-A and anti-B antibodies** in the plasma, meaning it can only receive blood from other group O individuals.
- **Statement 3 is correct: Blood group AB** has **both A and B antigens** on red blood cells and no antibodies in the plasma, making it a universal recipient in terms of plasma compatibility as it can accept any blood type without an immune reaction.

**Therefore, all three statements are correct, making the answer (c) All three.**

***41.*** *(b)* Only two

- **Statement 1 is correct: Universal donor for red blood cells** is true for **blood group O.** Since it has no A or B antigens, it can be donated to individuals with any blood type without risking an antigen-antibody reaction.
- **Statement 2 is incorrect**: Blood group O **lacks A and B antigens** on the surface of red blood cells. This absence is what allows it to be used as a universal donor in terms of red blood cell transfusions.
- **Statement 3 is correct: Anti-A and anti-B antibodies in plasma** is true for **blood group** O. That is people with this blood group produce both anti-A and anti-B antibodies, which is why they cannot receive blood from groups A, B or AB.

- **Statement 4 is incorrect:** Blood group O is **not a universal recipient** for plasma transfusions. **Blood group AB** is the universal plasma recipient, as it lacks antibodies against A and B antigens.

**Thus, two characteristics are true for blood group O, making the answer (b) Only two.**

**42.** *(c)* All three

- **Statement 1 is correct: Individuals with blood group AB** are considered **universal recipients** for red blood cell transfusions because they have **both A and B antigens** on their red blood cells, and no anti-A or anti-B antibodies in their plasma. This allows them to receive blood from any ABO group without a reaction.
- **Statement 2 is correct: Individuals with blood group A** can only donate to blood groups A and AB. Since they have **A antigens,** they cannot donate to group B or O individuals, as these would react to the A antigens.
- **Statement 3 is correct: Individuals with blood group B** produce **anti-A antibodies** in their plasma, so they cannot receive blood from individuals with blood group A or AB, as this would trigger an immune response.

**Thus, all three statements are correct, making the answer (c) All three.**

**43.** *(b)* Only two

- The **Rh factor** is a protein found on the surface of red blood cells. It is a significant component of blood typing, along with the **ABO system.** People either have the Rh factor **(Rh-positive)** or do not have it **(Rh-negative). That is Rh Factor** is an additional protein **(Rhesus antigen)** found on the surface of RBCs. Blood is classified as **Rh-positive** if the Rh factor is present and **Rh-negative** if absent.
- **Statement 1 is correct: Rh-positive individuals** have the **Rh antigen** (also known as the D antigen) on the surface of their red blood cells. If the Rh antigen is absent, the individual is considered **Rh-negative.**
- **Statement 2 is incorrect: Rh-negative individuals cannot safely receive Rh-positive blood.** If a Rh-negative person is given Rh-positive blood, their immune system may recognize the Rh antigen as foreign and produce anti-Rh antibodies, leading to an immune response. This reaction can cause hemolysis (destruction of red blood cells), which is dangerous.
- **Statement 3 is correct:** The **Rh factor** is **particularly important during pregnancy.** If a Rh-negative mother is carrying a Rh-positive fetus, her immune system may produce anti-Rh antibodies that can cross the placenta and attack the fetal red blood cells. This condition is known as **hemolytic disease of the newborn (HDN)** or **erythroblastosis fetalis** and it can cause severe anemia in the fetus.

**Therefore, two statements are correct, making the answer (b) Only two.**

**44.** *(b)* Only two

- **Statement 1 is correct: AB+ individuals** are considered **universal recipients** because they have both A and B antigens on their red blood cells and do not produce anti-A, anti-B, or anti-Rh antibodies. Therefore, they can receive blood from any ABO and Rh type without an immune response.
- **Statement 2 is correct: O- individuals** are considered **universal donors** because their blood lacks A, B, and Rh antigens, making it compatible with all ABO, and Rh types. Thus, O- blood can be donated to any blood type without risk of an antigen-antibody reaction.
- **Statement 3 is incorrect: A- individuals** can only receive blood from **A- or O-** donors because they produce anti-Rh antibodies and cannot safely receive Rh-positive blood.

**Thus, two statements are correct, making the answer (b) Only two.**

**45.** *(b)* Only two

- **Statement 1 is correct: Blood group A** has **A antigens** on the surface of red blood cells. These antigens define the blood group and determine compatibility for transfusions.
- **Statement 2 is correct:** Blood group A has **anti-B antibodies** in the plasma, which will attack B antigens if present. This is why blood group A individuals cannot safely receive blood from group B or AB.

- **Statement 3 is incorrect**: Blood group A can receive blood from **group A and group O**, but not from group AB. The anti-B antibodies in group A plasma would react with the B antigens in group AB blood, making it incompatible.

**Therefore, two statements are correct, making the answer (b) Only two.**

**46.** *(b)* Only two

- **Statement 1 is correct**: **Blood group O** has **no A or B antigens** on its red blood cells, which is why it is often referred to as the universal donor for red blood cells.
- **Statement 2 is correct**: Blood group O has **both anti-A and anti-B antibodies** in the plasma. These antibodies make it incompatible with blood types A, B and AB, as they would react with their respective antigens.
- **Statement 3 is incorrect**: Blood group O **cannot receive blood from any ABO group** due to the presence of anti-A and anti-B antibodies in its plasma. It can **only receive blood from other group O** donors.

**Therefore, two characteristics are true for blood group O, making the answer** (b) **Only two.**

**47.** *(b)* 1, 2 and 3 only

- **Biotechnology** is a field that harnesses the **power of living organisms** and biological processes to create solutions for real-world problems. It has applications in the field like medicine, agriculture, industrial processes and environmental management.
- **Statement 1 is correct**: Biotechnology has enabled the **production of insulin** through recombinant DNA technology. By inserting the human insulin gene into bacteria, scientists can produce large quantities of insulin, which is used in treating diabetes.
- **Statement 2 is correct**: The **development of vaccines** using recombinant DNA technology is another critical application of biotechnology in medicine. For example, the hepatitis B vaccine is produced by inserting a portion of the hepatitis B virus DNA into yeast cells to create a safe and effective vaccine.
- **Statement 3 is correct: Gene therapy** is an emerging field in biotechnology that aims to treat genetic disorders by replacing, inactivating, or introducing new genes to correct genetic defects.
- **Statement 4 is incorrect**: The creation of hybrid crops with improved resistance to pests falls under agricultural biotechnology rather than a direct medical application.

**Hence, 1, 2 and 3 are applications of biotechnology in medicine, making the answer (b) 1, 2 and 3 only.**

**48.** *(b)* Karl Ereky

- The term **biotechnology** was coined by **Karl Ereky**, a Hungarian engineer, in 1919. Ereky envisioned biotechnology as a process through which raw materials could be biologically converted into useful products on an industrial scale. His pioneering vision laid the foundation for what we now know as biotechnology, encompassing a wide range of applications in fields such as medicine, agriculture and environmental science.

**About Karl Ereky:**

- Ereky described biotechnology as a combination of biological and technological processes aimed at transforming living organisms to meet human needs.
- He foresaw the use of biological systems and organisms to produce goods and solve problems, an idea that has expanded tremendously over the past century.

**Thus, option (b) is the correct answer.**

**49.** *(c)* All three

- **Statement 1 is correct**: Recombinant DNA technology is a process where **DNA from two different sources** is combined to form new genetic combinations. This technique allows scientists to manipulate genes for various applications.

- **Statement 2 is correct:** **CRISPR-Cas9** is a modern tool used in gene editing, allowing precise alterations in DNA sequences. It's often used in recombinant DNA applications to modify genes in research and medicine.
- **Statement 3 is correct:** One of the earliest applications of recombinant DNA technology was the production of **synthetic insulin**. Scientists inserted the human insulin gene into bacteria, which then produced insulin that could be used to treat diabetes.

**Therefore, all three statements are correct, making the answer (c) All three.**

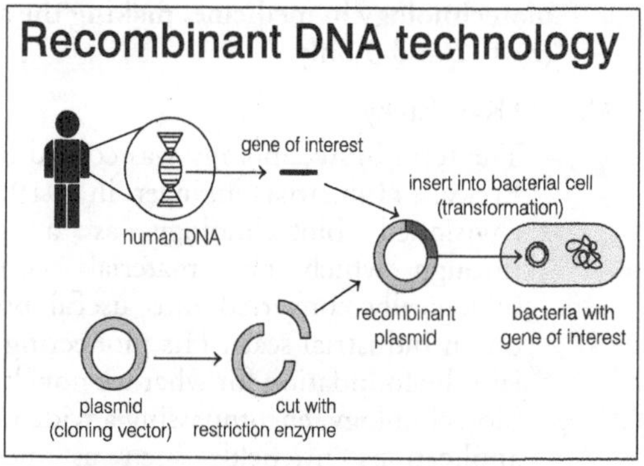


**50.** *(b)* Only two

- **Pair 1 is correct: Red biotechnology** is dedicated to the field of **healthcare and pharmaceuticals**. It involves the development of medical treatments, vaccines, gene therapies and pharmaceutical drugs.
- **Pair 2 is incorrect: Green biotechnology** actually refers to **agricultural applications**, such as the development of genetically modified crops, biofertilisers and biopesticides aimed at improving crop yields, and reducing environmental impact in agriculture.
- **Pair 3 is correct: White biotechnology** focuses on **industrial applications**. It includes the use of microorganisms and enzymes to create bio-based products, biofuels, and bioplastics, reducing reliance on chemical processes, and promoting sustainability in industrial production.

**Therefore, two pairs are correctly matched, making the answer (b) Only two.**

**51.** *(b)* Only two

- **Statement 1 is correct: Bioinformatics** is an interdisciplinary field that **combines biology, computer science, and mathematics** to analyse, and interpret biological data. It uses computational tools to manage and analyse vast amounts of data, such as genetic sequences, and protein structures.
- **Statement 2 is correct:** Bioinformatics has applications in various fields, including the **development of new medications.** By analysing genetic data and protein interactions, bioinformatics can help identify potential drug targets, and predict how different compounds will interact with biological molecules, speeding up the drug discovery process.
- **Statement 3 is incorrect:** Bioinformatics encompasses a broad range of studies, including **genetic sequences** (like DNA and RNA) as well as **protein structures.** It is not limited to genetic analysis but also includes other biomolecular data essential for understanding biological processes.

**Therefore, two statements are correct, making the answer (b) Only two.**

**52.** *(c)* Biotechnology that addresses bioethical, legal and social issues

**Purple biotechnology** is a branch of biotechnology focused on the **bioethical, legal and social issues** related to the advancements in biotechnology. As biotechnology progresses in areas such as genetic engineering, cloning, gene therapy, and synthetic biology, it raises significant ethical, and legal questions that need careful consideration. Purple biotechnology addresses these concerns by examining the moral and societal implications of using biotechnological tools, ensuring that the technology is developed and applied responsibly and ethically.

**Thus, option (c) is the correct answer.**

**53.** *(b)* 1, 2 and 4 only

- **Statement 1 is correct: Gene editing** involves making precise, targeted changes to an organism's existing DNA, such as modifying a single gene. In contrast, **genetic engineering** can involve **introducing new** DNA from other organisms, often resulting in more significant modifications.

- **Statement 2 is correct: Gene editing tools** like CRISPR-Cas9 can precisely target specific locations in the genome and make edits without introducing foreign DNA. This precision allows gene editing to make modifications while maintaining the organism's native DNA composition.
- **Statement 3** is **incorrect**: Genetic engineering often involves introducing genes from **outside an organism's natural gene pool**, such as adding bacterial genes to plants to confer resistance to pests. Gene editing, on the other hand, typically focuses on modifying genes already present in the organism.

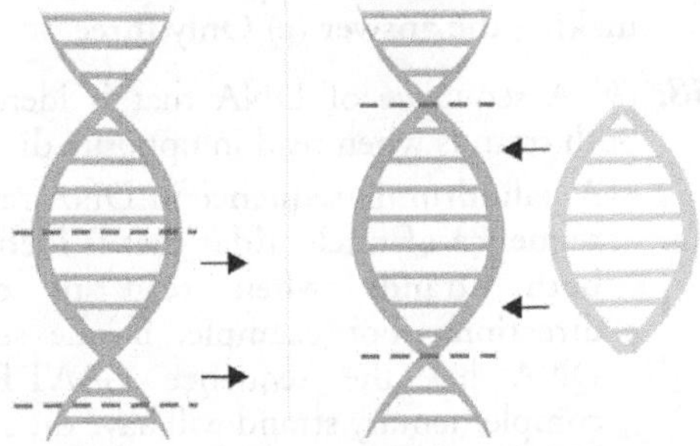


- **Statement 4 is correct**: Genetic engineering often leads to the creation of **genetically modified organisms** (**GMOs**) with new traits, such as pest resistance or enhanced nutritional content. These new traits result from adding or altering genes, sometimes from different species.

**Therefore, statements 1, 2 and 4 are correct, making the answer (b) 1, 2 and 4 only.**

**54.** *(c)* Only three

- **Bioprocess Engineering** is a branch of biotechnology that combines **biological processes** with **engineering principles** to design and develop processes for the large-scale production of products derived from living organisms or biological systems. For example, fermentation processes for yogurt, cheese and alcohol.
- **Statement 1 is correct**: Bioprocess engineering is widely used in the **production of biofuels**, such as ethanol and biodiesel, through **microbial fermentation** processes. These biofuels serve as renewable energy sources, reducing dependence on fossil fuels.
- **Statement 2 is correct**: Bioprocess engineering techniques are applied in **wastewater treatment**. Biological processes are used to degrade organic pollutants in wastewater, making it safer to release into the environment.
- **Statement 3 is incorrect**: Genetically modifying plants for higher crop yield is an application of genetic **engineering and agricultural biotechnology**, not bioprocess engineering. Bioprocess engineering is more focused on designing processes and systems rather than modifying plant genetics.
- **Statement 4 is correct**: The **production of single-cell protein** involves cultivating microorganisms like algae, yeast or bacteria as protein-rich food supplements, which is part of bioprocess engineering.

**Therefore, three applications are correct, making the answer (c) Only three.**

**55.** *(b)* Providing antibiotic resistance or other advantageous traits

- **Plasmid DNA** is an extra-chromosomal, **circular DNA molecule** commonly found in bacterial cells. Unlike the chromosomal DNA, which contains essential genes for the basic functions and survival of the cell, plasmid DNA often carries genes that confer specific advantages, such as antibiotic resistance, heavy metal tolerance or the ability to metabolise unusual substances.
- **Antibiotic Resistance**: Plasmids often carry genes that allow bacteria to survive in the presence of antibiotics, making them significant in medical and pharmaceutical studies due to their role in antibiotic resistance.
- **Non-Essential for Survival:** Plasmid DNA is not essential for the cell's survival but provides additional functions that can benefit the cell in specific environments.

- Plasmids are widely used in biotechnology and genetic engineering for **cloning, gene expression, and protein production**, as they can replicate independently and be manipulated to carry foreign genes.

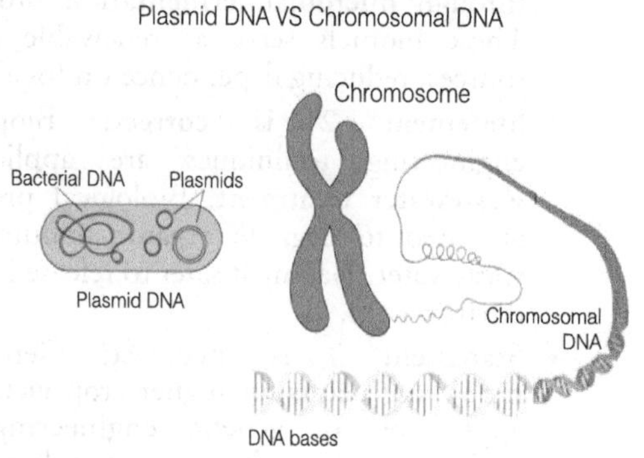


**Thus, option (b) is the correct answer.**

**56.** *(b)* Only two

- **Statement 1 is correct: Restriction enzymes** recognise specific DNA sequences known as **recognition sites** and cut the DNA at or near these sites. Each type of restriction enzyme has a unique recognition sequence, making them valuable tools in molecular biology for gene cloning and DNA analysis.
- **Statement 2 is correct**: Restriction enzymes are **naturally found in bacteria.** They function as a defense mechanism by cutting up the DNA of invading viruses (bacteriophages), preventing the virus from replicating within the bacterial cell.
- **Statement 3 is incorrect**: Restriction enzymes do not always cut DNA in a straight line. Some restriction enzymes make **staggered cuts**, creating 'sticky ends' with single-stranded overhangs, while others make **blunt cuts** with no overhangs. The type of cut depends on the specific enzyme.

**Therefore, two statements are correct, making the answer (b) Only two.**

**57.** *(c)* Only three

- **Statement 1 is correct**: Restriction enzymes are essential in **DNA fingerprinting**, as they cut DNA into fragments based on specific sequences. The resulting fragments are separated by gel electrophoresis, creating a unique pattern that can be used in forensic identification.
- **Statement 2 is correct: Recombinant DNA technology** often utilises restriction enzymes to cut both the DNA to be cloned and the plasmid vector, creating compatible ends that can be joined to produce recombinant DNA. This technique is fundamental in genetic engineering.
- **Statement 3 is incorrect**: While restriction enzymes are useful in DNA analysis, **sequencing entire genomes** typically involves other methods, such as high-throughput sequencing technologies, rather than using restriction enzymes alone.
- **Statement 4 is correct**: Restriction enzymes can aid in **detecting specific genetic mutations** by cutting at known recognition sites. If a mutation disrupts a restriction site, it can be detected by the presence or absence of certain DNA fragments after digestion.

**Therefore, three applications are correct, making the answer (c) Only three.**

**58.** *(b)* A sequence of DNA that is identical on both strands when read in opposite directions.

- A **palindromic sequence** in DNA refers to a **sequence of nucleotides** that is **identical on both strands when read in opposite directions**. For example, if one strand of DNA has the sequence **GAATTC,** the complementary strand will have the sequence **CTTAAG.** When read in the 5' to 3' direction on both strands, the sequence is the same, making it a palindrome.

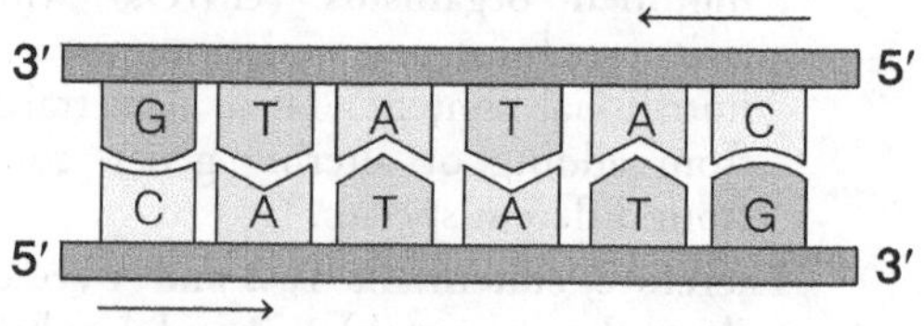


**Thus, option (b) is the correct answer.**

**59.** *(b)* 1, 2 and 4 only

- **Option 1 is correct: CRISPR-Cas9 (Clustered Regularly Interspaced Short Palindromic Repeats) is a revolutionary gene-editing technology** that uses a **guide RNA** to direct the **Cas9 enzyme** to a specific DNA sequence, where it makes a precise cut.

This technology allows scientists to add, delete, or replace specific genes with high accuracy.

- **Option 2 is correct: TALENs (Transcription Activator-Like Effector Nucleases)** are engineered enzymes that can bind to specific DNA sequences and introduce double-strand breaks at targeted sites. Each TALEN is designed to recognise a particular DNA sequence, making this technique precise for targeted gene editing.
- **Option 3 is incorrect: RNA Interference (RNAi)** is **not a gene-editing technique** in the traditional sense; rather, it is a process that silences gene expression by degrading specific messenger RNA (mRNA) molecules. It does not alter DNA directly.
- **Option 4 is correct: Zinc Finger Nucleases (ZFNs)** are synthetic proteins that combine a DNA-binding domain (zinc finger) with a DNA-cleaving enzyme (nuclease). They can be engineered to target specific genes for editing, allowing precise modifications to the DNA.

**Therefore, the correct answer is (b) 1, 2 and 4 only.**

**60.** *(b)* To cut DNA at specific sites for gene editing

- **TALENs (Transcription Activator-Like Effector Nucleases)** are engineered enzymes designed to **cut DNA at specific sites** for targeted gene editing. Each TALEN molecule is customised to recognise a particular DNA sequence, allowing precise cuts in the DNA at specific locations. The TALEN consists of two main parts:
  - **DNA-binding domain:** Composed of transcription activator-like effector (TALE) proteins that can be engineered to recognise and bind specific DNA sequences.
  - **Nuclease domain**: Typically derived from the FokI nuclease, this domain cleaves the DNA at the targeted site, enabling precise modifications.

Once the DNA is cut, cellular repair mechanisms can be harnessed to add, delete or alter specific genes. TALENs are especially valuable in gene therapy, research, and the development of genetically modified organisms due to their high specificity.

**Thus, option (b) is the correct answer.**

**61.** *(c)* Only three

- **Statement 1 is correct: Zinc Finger Nucleases (ZFNs)** have a **DNA-binding domain composed of zinc finger proteins.** Each zinc finger can recognise a specific three-base DNA sequence, and by combining several zinc fingers, ZFNs can be engineered to bind to specific DNA sequences.
- **Statement 2 is correct:** ZFNs use a **Fokl nuclease domain** as the cutting mechanism. Fokl is an endonuclease that cuts DNA only when two Fokl domains are brought together, allowing ZFNs to introduce double-strand breaks at the target site.
- **Statement 3 is incorrect:** ZFNs are **not naturally occurring enzymes;** they are engineered in labouratories for gene-editing purposes. They are created by combining zinc finger proteins with the Fokl nuclease to enable precise DNA targeting and cutting.
- **Statement 4 is correct:** ZFNs can be **customised to target specific DNA sequences** by designing zinc finger arrays that recognise the desired DNA sequences. This ability to target specific sequences makes ZFNs valuable in genetic engineering and gene therapy.

**Therefore, three statements are correct, making the answer (c) Only three.**

**62.** *(b)* Only two

- **Statement 1 is correct: CRISPR** (Clustered Regularly Interspaced Short Palindromic Repeats) is indeed a **naturally occurring immune system** found in bacteria. It helps bacteria defend against viral infections by using RNA molecules to guide the Cas9 protein to specific DNA sequences, which it then cuts to disable the invading virus.
- **Statement 2 is correct: CRISPR-Cas9** is a revolutionary gene-editing tool that can target and modify **specific DNA sequences in various organisms**, from bacteria to plants, animals, and even humans. This flexibility has made CRISPR a powerful tool for research, medicine, and biotechnology.

- **Statement 3 is incorrect:** Unlike some gene-editing techniques, CRISPR does not necessarily require the insertion of foreign genes into the organism. It typically involves making precise cuts in the DNA, which can then be edited by either removing, inserting, or replacing specific sequences.

**Therefore, two statements are correct, making the answer (b) Only two.**

## DNA editing

A DNA editing technique, called CRISPR/CAS9, works like a biological version of a word-processing programme's "find and replace" function.

HOW THE TECHNIQUE WORKS

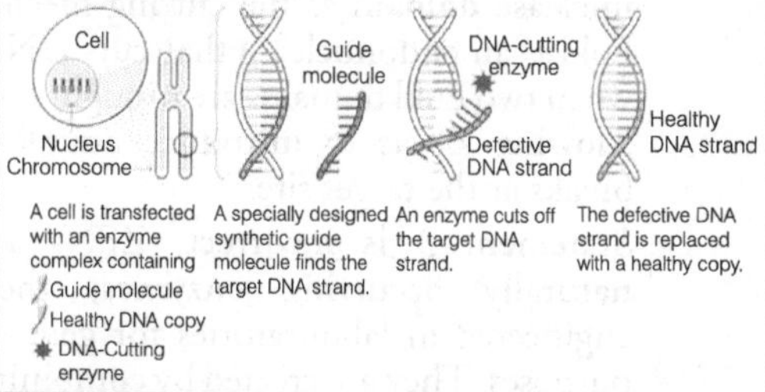


**63.** *(b)* 1, 2 and 3 only

- **Statement 1 is correct: Genome sequencing** allows for the **identification of mutations** associated with various genetic disorders. By analysing an individual's entire genome, researchers can pinpoint the exact location and nature of genetic alterations responsible for diseases, which can aid in diagnosis, treatment planning and personalised medicine.
- **Statement 2 is correct:** Genome sequencing provides valuable insights into **human ancestry and evolutionary history.** By comparing DNA sequences from different populations, scientists can trace lineage and understand how human species have migrated, and evolved over time.
- **Statement 3 is correct:** Genome sequencing is crucial in **agricultural biotechnology.** By understanding the genetic makeup of crops, scientists can develop pest-resistant or drought-tolerant varieties, improving crop yield and sustainability.
- **Statement 4 is incorrect:** While genome sequencing can help in understanding the metabolic pathways of certain microorganisms that break down plant material, genome sequencing itself is **not directly used to produce energy.** This application would require metabolic engineering or biofuel production techniques, not sequencing alone.

**Hence, statements 1, 2 and 3 are correct, making the answer (b) 1, 2 and 3 only.**

**64.** *(b)* Gamete Intrafallopian Transfer (GIFT)

- **Assisted Reproductive Technology (ART)** refers to medical procedures and techniques used to address infertility by manipulating eggs, sperm, or embryos to achieve pregnancy. These methods involve handling reproductive cells (gametes) or embryos outside the human body to assist individuals or couples in conceiving.
- **Gamete Intrafallopian Transfer (GIFT)** involves placing both **eggs and sperm into the fallopian tube,** so that fertilisation occurs **within the body,** not in a lab setting. This is **distinct from IVF,** where fertilisation takes place in a lab, and the embryo is then transferred to the uterus.
- **In Vitro Fertilization (IVF)** involves fertilising an egg outside the body in a labouratory setting before transferring the embryo into the uterus.
- **Zygote Intrafallopian Transfer (ZIFT)** involves fertilising an egg outside the body, like in IVF, but the resulting zygote is then placed in the fallopian tube instead of the uterus.
- **Intracytoplasmic Sperm Injection (ICSI)** is a technique used in IVF where a single sperm is injected directly into an egg to facilitate fertilisation in cases of male infertility.

**Thus, the correct answer is (b) Gamete Intrafallopian Transfer (GIFT).**

**65.** *(b)* 1, 2 and 4 only

- **Statement 1 is correct:** ART is widely used to **treat infertility** in both males and females. Techniques like IVF, ICSI and IUI help couples overcome various reproductive challenges.
- **Statement 2 is correct:** ART methods such as surrogacy and IVF are used to assist **same-sex couples** in having biologically related children, often using donor eggs or sperm and a surrogate if needed.

- **Statement 3 is incorrect:** ART does not focus on **enhancing genetic characteristics** in offspring. Its primary purpose is to aid reproduction and address infertility. Genetic enhancement or selection would fall under genetic engineering or designer baby concepts, which are not typical applications of ART.
- **Statement 4 is correct:** ART also facilitates **embryo research** and **genetic screening**, such as Preimplantation Genetic Testing (PGT), to identify genetic disorders before embryo implantation.

**Therefore, statements 1, 2 and 4 are correct, making the answer (b) 1, 2 and 4 only.**

**66.** *(b)* Only two

- **Statement 1 is correct:** Gene therapy is commonly used to treat **inherited genetic disorders** caused by specific **genetic mutations.** By inserting or correcting defective genes, gene therapy can potentially cure or alleviate the symptoms of genetic conditions like cystic fibrosis, hemophilia, and sickle cell anemia.
- **Statement 2 is incorrect:** Although gene therapy is often applied to **single-gene (monogenic)** disorders, it is **not limited** to such conditions. It can also be used for complex diseases like cancer, where genes are modified to enhance immune cells' ability to target cancer cells or to introduce genes that produce anti-cancer proteins.
- **Statement 3 is correct:** Gene therapy has applications in **cancer immunotherapy.** Techniques such as CAR-T cell therapy involve modifying a patient's immune cells to enhance their ability to recognise and destroy cancer cells, offering promising treatment options for certain cancers.

**Therefore, two statements are correct, making the answer (b) Only two.**

**67.** *(b)* The observable characteristics of an organism resulting from the interaction of its genotype and environment.

A **phenotype** refers to the **observable traits or characteristics** of an organism, such as its physical appearance, behaviour or physiological features. These characteristics result from the **interaction of the organism's genotype (genetic makeup) with the environment.** For example, a plant's height is influenced by its genetic code and environmental factors like sunlight, and water availability.

**Thus, option (b) is the correct answer.**

**68.** *(a)* Sexual reproduction involves the fusion of gametes, resulting in genetic variation, whereas asexual reproduction produces genetically identical offspring.

**Sexual reproduction** involves the **fusion of male and female gametes** (e.g., sperm and egg), which results in offspring with **genetic variation** due to the combination of genetic material from two parents. On the other hand, **asexual reproduction** does not involve gametes and produces offspring that are **genetically identical to the parent**, ensuring uniformity. Examples include **binary fission** in bacteria and **budding** in hydra.

**Thus, option (a) is the correct answer.**

**69.** *(c)* Only three

- **Binary fission:** A method of asexual reproduction where a single organism divides into two identical daughter organisms. It is common in bacteria and some protists.
- **Budding:** In budding, a new organism grows from a particular site on the parent's body and detaches when mature. Examples include hydra and yeast.
- **Sporulation:** Sporulation involves the production of spores, which develop into new organisms under favourable conditions. This method is common in fungi and some bacteria.
- **Fertilisation:** Fertilisation is a characteristic of **sexual reproduction**, involving the fusion of male and female gametes.

**Thus, the correct answer is (c) Only three.**

**70.** *(a)* 1, 2 and 3 only

- **Statement 1 is correct: CRISPR-Cas9** is a revolutionary tool in genetic engineering that allows for precise editing of DNA sequences. It enables targeted gene editing by introducing or correcting mutations, making it a widely used and powerful technique in genetic research.

- **Statement 2 is correct: Gene Cloning** involves isolating a specific gene and creating multiple copies of it. This technique is fundamental in genetic engineering for studying gene functions, producing proteins, or transferring genes into organisms.
- **Statement 3 is correct: Polymerase Chain Reaction (PCR)** is a method used to amplify specific DNA sequences. It plays a crucial role in genetic engineering by allowing scientists to generate millions of copies of a target DNA sequence for analysis, cloning or modification.
- **Statement 4 is incorrect: Crossbreeding** is a traditional breeding method used in agriculture and animal husbandry to combine desirable traits from different species or breeds. It does not involve manipulating DNA directly and is not considered a genetic engineering technique.

**Thus, the correct answer is (a) 1, 2 and 3 only.**

**71.** *(b)* Animals whose genome has been altered by introducing foreign DNA to express a desired trait.

Transgenic animals are created by introducing **foreign DNA** into their genome using genetic engineering techniques. These modifications allow the animal to express a **desired trait** or produce a specific protein, such as insulin in transgenic cows or disease resistance in transgenic mice.

**Thus, option (b) is the correct answer.**

**72.** *(d)* 1, 2, 3, 4 and 5

- **Option 1 is correct**: Stem cell therapy, particularly hematopoietic stem cells (HSCs), is extensively used to treat leukaemia and other blood-related disorders by replenishing the bone marrow with healthy stem cells.
- **Option 2 is correct**: Neural stem cells have shown promise in treating neurodegenerative diseases like Parkinson's disease by replacing damaged neurons.
- **Option 3 is correct**: Research in diabetes has shown that stem cells can help regenerate insulin-producing beta cells in the pancreas, aiding Type 1 and potentially Type 2 diabetes management.
- **Option 4 is correct**: Mesenchymal stem cells (MSCs) are used in cardiac repair to regenerate damaged heart tissues following heart attacks.
- **Option 5 is correct**: Genetic disorders like sickle cell anaemia can be treated using stem cell transplants to produce healthy red blood cells.

**Thus, the correct answer is (d) 1, 2, 3, 4 and 5.**

**73.** *(b)* 1 and 2 only

- **Statement 1 is correct: Somatic gene therapy involves modifications to non-reproductive cells (e.g., skin, muscle or blood cells)** and affects only the treated individual. These changes are **not heritable** and are confined to the patient.
- **Statement 2 is correct: Germline gene therapy** involves **altering the genetic material in reproductive cells (sperm, eggs or embryos)**. The changes are **heritable** and passed on to future generations, raising ethical and safety concerns.
- **Statement 3 is incorrect**: Germline gene therapy is **highly controversial** and **is largely restricted or banned in humans** due to ethical, safety, and societal implications. Somatic gene therapy, however, is widely accepted and practiced.

**Thus, the correct answer is (b) 1 and 2 only.**

**74.** *(b)* 1-B, 2-A, 3-C

- **Totipotent cells,** such as zygotes, can differentiate into any cell type, including embryonic and extra-embryonic tissues like the placenta.
- **Pluripotent cells,** like embryonic stem cells, can develop into any cell type within the body but cannot form extra-embryonic tissues.
- **Multipotent cells,** such as hematopoietic stem cells, are specialised and can only differentiate into related cell types within a specific tissue or organ.

**Thus, option (b) is the correct answer.**

**75.** *(b)* 1 and 3 only

- **Statement 1 is correct: Somatic stem cells** (also known as adult stem cells) are **multipotent**, meaning they can differentiate into a limited range of cell types. In contrast, **embryonic stem cells** are **pluripotent,** meaning they can develop into almost any cell type in the body.

- **Statement 2 is incorrect**: Embryonic stem cells are derived from **early-stage embryos,** whereas somatic stem cells are found in **adult tissues** such as bone marrow, fat or skin.
- **Statement 3 is correct: Somatic stem cells are used for regenerative therapies,** such as treating blood-related disorders and repairing damaged tissues. **Embryonic stem cells** are primarily used in research to study cell differentiation and for developing new treatments.

**Thus, the correct answer is (b) 1 and 3 only.**

**76.** *(b)* Only two

- **Statement 1 is incorrect**: The allocation of organs is not based on the 'first-come, first-serve' principle but rather on a transparent and ethical system, prioritising medical urgency, compatibility, and time on the waiting list.
- **Statement 2 is correct**: The guidelines mandate registration of both donors and recipients with NOTTO to ensure transparency, and prevent illegal organ trade.
- **Statement 3 is correct**: Both living and deceased donors are legally accepted under the Transplantation of Human Organs, and Tissues Act, 1994, provided the donation is ethical, and voluntary.

**Thus, the correct answer is (b) Only two.**

**77.** *(c)* Sushruta Samhita

- The **Sushruta Samhita,** written by the ancient Indian surgeon Sushruta around the 6th century BCE, is considered the **first written evidence of transplantation or reconstruction** in medical history.
- It contains detailed descriptions of surgical techniques, including skin grafts and reconstruction of the nose (rhinoplasty).
- Sushruta's pioneering techniques laid the foundation for modern plastic surgery and reconstructive medicine.

**Thus, option (c) is the correct answer.**

**78.** *(b)* The transplantation of organs or tissues from one species to another

- **Xenotransplantation:** It involves **transplanting organs, tissues, or cells from one species to another,** such as from pigs to humans. This approach is being explored to address the shortage of human organs for transplantation.
- **Applications:** The most notable application is the use of **pig hearts, kidneys and pancreatic cells** in humans. Pig organs are preferred due to their similarity in size and function to human organs.

**Thus, option (b) is the correct answer.**

**79.** *(b)* 1 and 3 only

- **Statement 1 is correct**: CAR-T cell therapy involves extracting a patient's T-cells and modifying them in a lab to express chimeric antigen receptors (CARs). These receptors enable the T-cells to target and kill cancer cells effectively.
- **Statement 2 is incorrect**: CAR-T cell therapy is highly effective for certain types of blood cancers like leukemia and lymphoma, but has limited success with solid tumors due to challenges like the tumor microenvironment.
- **Statement 3 is correct**: This therapy is highly personalised, as the patient's own T-cells are engineered and infused back into their body.

**Thus, the correct answer is (b) 1 and 3 only.**

**80.** *(b)* 1, 2 and 4 only

- **Statement 1 is correct**: GM crops like Bt cotton and **Bt brinjal are genetically modified to resist pests** such as bollworms and fruit borers, reducing the need for chemical pesticides.
- **Statement 2 is correct**: Some GM crops, such as Golden Rice, are engineered to have enhanced nutritional value, such as **increased levels of Vitamin A,** addressing malnutrition issues.
- **Statement 3 is incorrect**: GM crops may help reduce pesticide use but are not directly linked to reducing chemical fertilisers, as soil nutrient requirements remain the same.
- **Statement 4 is correct**: Certain GM crops are engineered to withstand drought, salinity and extreme temperatures, making them more resilient to adverse climatic conditions and improving yield stability.

**Thus, the correct answer is (b) 1, 2 and 4 only.**

**81.** *(c)* Only three

- **CRISPR-Cas9 is used:** It is an advanced genome-editing tool that enables precise alterations in the genetic makeup of crops, allowing targeted improvements such as disease resistance and stress tolerance.
- **Agrobacterium-mediated transfer is used:** This technique utilises the natural ability of Agrobacterium tumefaciens to transfer DNA into plant cells, allowing genetic modification. It is widely used for inserting desired traits into plants.
- **Hydroponics is not used:** This is a soil-less cultivation method, not a genetic modification technique.
- **Particle Bombardment (Gene Gun) is used:** This technique involves using high-velocity microprojectiles to deliver foreign DNA into plant cells, making it an effective method for genetically modifying crops.

**Thus, the correct answer is (c) Only three.**

**82.** *(a)* Environment (Protection) Act, 1986

- The **Genetic Engineering Appraisal Committee** (GEAC) is the apex body responsible for the regulation of activities related to genetically modified organisms (GMOs) and products derived from them, including field trials.
- **Constitutional Basis:** It is established under the **Environment (Protection) Act, 1986,** specifically under Rule 4 of the 1989 'Rules for the Manufacture, Use/Import/Export, and Storage of Hazardous Microorganisms/ Genetically Engineered Organisms or Cells.'
- The primary role of GEAC includes approving the release of GMOs and ensuring biosafety for both environmental, and human health.

**Thus, option (a) is the correct answer.**

**83.** *(a)* 1 and 2 only

- **Statement 1 is correct:** As of now, **Bt cotton** is the only genetically modified crop that has been commercially approved for cultivation in India. It was introduced in 2002 to improve resistance to bollworm pests.
- **Statement 2 is correct:** India permits the **import of GM soybean and canola oil,** but only as refined edible oil and not for cultivation purposes.
- **Statement 3 is incorrect:** The Government has **approved the environmental release of Genetically Modified (GM) Mustard hybrid** DMH-11 and its parental lines during 147th meeting of Genetic Engineering Appraisal Committee (GEAC) on 18th October, 2022 for its seed production, and testing as per existing ICAR guidelines.
  - **Its commercial cultivation has not yet been fully approved** due to legal and public concerns.

**Thus, the correct answer is (a) 1 and 2 only.**

**84.** *(b)* Only two

- **Statement 1 is correct:** DMH-11 is a genetically modified (GM) variety of mustard developed to increase yield through hybridisation. It is intended to address India's demand for edible oil by boosting domestic mustard production.
- **Statement 2 is incorrect:** DMH-11 has been developed by the **Centre for Genetic Manipulation of Crop Plants (CGMCP)** at the University of Delhi, not IARI.
- **Statement 3 is correct:** The crop uses the **Barnase-Barstar system,** which involves genetic modifications that ensure effective hybridisation by preventing self-pollination and facilitating cross-pollination.

**Thus, the correct answer is (b) Only two.**

**85.** *(c)* Only three

- **Genomic sequences:** This is **biological data** used to study genes, genetic variations and their relationships with diseases.
- **Clinical trial results:** These are considered **biological data** as they provide insights into the effects of drugs and treatments on living organisms.
- **Financial data of pharmaceutical companies:** This is not biological data; it falls under financial or economic data.
- **Protein structures:** Protein structures are **biological data** essential for understanding biochemical processes and drug design.

**Thus, the correct answer is (c) Only three.**

**86.** *(c)* Only three

Biopesticides are developed from **natural sources** like plant extracts, beneficial microbes (e.g., Bacillus thuringiensis) and minerals.

- **Statement 1 is correct:** Biopesticides are typically **biodegradable and have minimal impact** on the environment compared to conventional pesticides.
  - They generally have a **faster degradation rate,** reducing their environmental persistence compared to chemical pesticides.
- **Statement 2 is incorrect:** Biopesticides are often **specific to target pests** and are less likely to affect non-target species, unlike conventional pesticides that can harm beneficial organisms.
- **Statement 3 is correct:** Biopesticides have mechanisms of action that make it harder for pests to develop **resistance,** a common issue with chemical pesticides.
- **Statement 4 is correct:** Biopesticides **leave minimal toxic residues on crops,** making them safer for consumers and export markets.

**Thus, the correct answer is (c) Only three.**

**87.** *(d)* All four

**ART refers to the fertility treatments and procedures.**

- **In-Vitro Fertilisation (IVF):** A widely used ART method where eggs are fertilised with sperm in a labouratory and then transferred to the uterus.
- **Intracytoplasmic Sperm Injection (ICSI):** A technique where a single sperm is injected directly into an egg to achieve fertilisation, often used when male infertility is a factor.
- **Surrogacy:** Surrogacy involves implanting a fertilised embryo into another woman's uterus, making it part of ART.
- **Artificial Insemination (AI):** It is an ART method where sperm is directly introduced into the reproductive tract to facilitate fertilisation.

**Thus, the correct answer is (d) All four.**

**88.** *(a)* 2-4-1-3

- **Step 1: Hormonal stimulation of the ovaries** (2): Fertility hormones are administered to stimulate the ovaries to produce multiple eggs.
- **Step 2: Retrieval of eggs from the ovaries** (4): Mature eggs are retrieved using a minimally invasive procedure.
- **Step 3: Fertilisation of eggs in a laboratory** (1): The retrieved eggs are fertilised with sperm in a controlled laboratory environment.
- **Step 4: Transfer of the embryo to the uterus** (3): The resulting embryos are transferred to the uterus to establish a pregnancy.

**Thus, the correct order is (a) 2-4-1-3.**

**89.** *(b)* 1 and 2 only

- **Statement 1 is correct:** The Surrogacy (Regulation) Act, 2021, **permits only altruistic surrogacy,** where the surrogate mother receives no monetary compensation apart from medical expenses. **Commercial surrogacy is strictly prohibited under the Act.**
- **Statement 2 is correct:** The Act mandates that the **intending couple must be married for at least five years** and must have a medical certificate indicating their inability to conceive naturally.
- **Statement 3 is incorrect: Foreign nationals are not eligible for surrogacy in India.** Only Indian citizens are permitted to avail of surrogacy under the provisions of this Act.

**Thus, the correct answer is (b) 1 and 2 only.**

**90.** *(a)* 1 and 2 only

- **Statement 1 is correct:** The Act specifies that the **surrogate mother must be a close relative** of the intending couple, ensuring familial ties and minimising exploitation.
- **Statement 2 is correct:** The Act provides for the establishment of a **National Surrogacy Board** at the central level and state Surrogacy Boards to oversee regulation, and implementation.
- **Statement 3 is incorrect:** Surrogacy is not permitted for couples who already have **biological or adopted children,** except in cases where the child suffers from life-threatening illnesses or is deceased.

**Thus, the correct answer is (a) 1 and 2 only.**

**91.** *(c)* Only three

- **Leigh syndrome**: A mitochondrial disorder that affects the central nervous system, leading to developmental delays and progressive neurological issues.
- **Kearns-Sayre syndrome**: A mitochondrial disorder characterised by progressive weakness in muscles, heart conduction block, and other systemic symptoms.
- **Hemophilia**: Not a mitochondrial disease; it is a genetic disorder caused by mutations on the X chromosome affecting blood clotting.
- **MELAS**: A mitochondrial disorder characterised by neurological and muscular problems, including strokes, seisures, and muscle weakness.

**Thus, the correct answer is (c) Only three.**

**92.** *(c)* Only three

- **Statement 1 is correct: Genes can be cloned** through molecular cloning techniques. This involves isolating a specific DNA sequence, inserting it into a vector, and replicating it in host organisms like bacteria. This method is widely used in genetic research and biotechnology.
- **Statement 2 is correct: Whole organisms** have been cloned successfully using techniques like **somatic cell nuclear transfer** (SCNT). Examples include Dolly the sheep, the first mammal cloned from an adult somatic cell, demonstrating the feasibility of organism cloning.
- **Statement 3 is incorrect: Cloning entire organs** directly is not yet possible with current scientific techniques. Research is ongoing in the field of tissue engineering and regenerative medicine to grow functional organs using stem cells.
- **Statement 4 is correct: Tissues can be cloned** or grown in laboratories through tissue engineering techniques. Scientists use scaffolds and growth factors to regenerate tissues for research or therapeutic purposes.

**Thus, the correct answer is (c) Only three.**

**93.** *(a)* 1 and 2 only

- **Statement 1 is correct: Mitochondrial** Replacement Therapy (MRT) is a technique used to replace faulty **mitochondrial DNA (mtDNA)** in an embryo with healthy mtDNA from a donor. This process involves transferring nuclear genetic material from an egg or embryo with defective mitochondria into a healthy donor egg or embryo with intact mitochondria.
- **Statement 2 is correct:** MRT is primarily aimed at **preventing the transmission of mitochondrial diseases** from mother to offspring. These diseases result from mutations in mtDNA, which are exclusively inherited from the mother.
- **Statement 3 is incorrect:** MRT focuses on **mtDNA replacement** and does not involve the **modification of nuclear DNA**, which contains the majority of the genetic material responsible for inherited traits and other genetic disorders.

**Thus, the correct answer is (a) 1 and 2 only.**

**94.** *(a)* 1, 2 and 4 only

- **Statement 1 is correct:** The **3 Parent Baby technique**, also known as **Mitochondrial Replacement Therapy (MRT)**, is specifically designed to **prevent the transmission of mitochondrial diseases** from the mother to her child. These diseases are caused by mutations in the mitochondrial DNA, which is inherited exclusively from the mother.
- **Statement 2 is correct:** The technique involves transferring **nuclear DNA from the biological parents (father and mother)** into an egg from which defective mitochondrial DNA has been removed, and which contains **healthy mitochondrial DNA from a donor.**
- **Statement 3 is incorrect:** The process does not involve replacing faulty nuclear DNA. It focuses solely on replacing defective **mitochondrial DNA** to prevent mitochondrial disorders. The nuclear DNA remains unchanged and is entirely from the biological parents.
- **Statement 4 is correct:** The resulting child inherits **nuclear DNA from the biological parents** and **mitochondrial DNA from the donor**, effectively having genetic material from three individuals.

**Thus, the correct answer is (a) 1, 2 and 4 only.**

**95.** *(c)* A process to produce embryonic stem cells for regenerative medicine and treating diseases.

**Therapeutic cloning** involves the use of **somatic cell nuclear transfer** (SCNT) to create embryonic stem cells that can develop into various cell types. These cells are used in **regenerative medicine** to treat conditions like Parkinson's disease, diabetes and spinal cord injuries.

**Thus, option (c) is the correct answer.**

**96.** *(b)* 1, 2 and 4 only

- **Statement 1 is correct**: Therapeutic cloning generates **embryonic stem cells** that are genetically identical to the patient, reducing the risk of immune rejection during treatments.
- **Statement 2 is correct**: Embryonic stem cells derived through therapeutic cloning can be used to **repair damaged tissues** or develop new tissues and organs for transplantation.
- **Statement 3 is incorrect**: Therapeutic cloning does not involve cloning entire humans; its focus is strictly on stem cell production for therapeutic purposes.
- **Statement 4 is correct**: Therapeutic cloning shows promise in treating **neurodegenerative diseases** like Parkinson's and Alzheimer's by replacing damaged cells with healthy ones derived from stem cells.

**Thus, the correct answer is (b) 1, 2 and 4 only.**

**97.** *(b)* To create genetically identical organisms or embryonic stem cells by transferring the nucleus of a somatic cell into an enucleated egg cell.

SCNT is a cloning technique in which the nucleus of a somatic cell is inserted into an egg cell that has had its nucleus removed. This process can be used for **reproductive cloning** (e.g., creating a clone of an organism) or **therapeutic cloning** (e.g., generating embryonic stem cells for medical purposes).

**Thus, option (b) is the correct answer.**

**98.** *(d)* 2 only

- **Statement 1 is incorrect**: The **Genetic Engineering Appraisal Committee (GEAC)** operates under the **Ministry of Environment, Forest and Climate Change (MoEFCC)**, not the Ministry of Science and Technology.
  - It evaluates the proposal for the **commercial release** of genetically modified organisms, ensuring compliance with biosafety standards.
  - GEAC operates under the **Environment (Protection) Act, 1986,** which provides the legal framework for its functions.
  - It ensures compliance with **global biosafety protocols**, including the **Cartagena Protocol** on **Biosafety**, to which India is a signatory.
- **Statement 2 is correct**: GEAC is responsible for regulating the **import, export, transport, manufacture, and use of genetically engineered organisms** in India, ensuring environmental and human safety.
- **Statement 3 is incorrect**: GEAC's recommendations are **not legally binding** but advisory in nature. The final decision often rests with the government.

**Thus, the correct answer is (d) 2 only.**

**99.** *(a)* To conserve and store seeds, plants, and genetic material of animals for biodiversity preservation and agricultural research.

- A **gene bank** is a facility dedicated to **storing genetic material**, such as seeds, plants and genetic resources of animals, to preserve biodiversity, and support agricultural research.
- In India, facilities like the **National Bureau of Plant Genetic Resources** (**NBPGR**) ensure the long-term conservation of genetic diversity.

**Thus, option (a) is the correct answer.**

**100.** *(b)* 1 and 3 only

- **Statement 1 is correct**: The NBPGR is responsible for the **collection, conservation and documentation of plant genetic resources** to preserve biodiversity and ensure food security in India.
  - It facilitates the **exchange of plant genetic resources** with other countries while ensuring compliance with biosafety and quarantine regulations.

- **Statement 2 is incorrect:** NBPGR operates under the **Indian Council of Agricultural Research (ICAR)**, which falls under the **Ministry of Agriculture and Farmers' Welfare**, not the Ministry of Environment, Forest, and Climate Change.
- **Statement 3 is correct:** NBPGR ensures the **safe storage and maintenance of germplasm in its gene bank (in New Delhi)**, which includes seeds and tissues stored under controlled conditions for long-term use.

**Thus, the correct answer is (b) 1 and 3 only.**

***101.*** *(a)* 1, 2 and 3 only

- **Statement 1 is correct:** The **high-altitude location in Ladakh** ensures **natural refrigeration**, reducing the need for artificial cooling to preserve seeds.
- **Statement 2 is correct:** The vault stores seeds of both **indigenous crops** (important for biodiversity) and **commercially valuable crops** to ensure agricultural sustainability.
- **Statement 3 is correct:** The vault is managed by the **National Bureau of Plant Genetic Resources** (NBPGR), which oversees the conservation of plant genetic resources in India.
- **Statement 4 is incorrect:** The seed vault is connected to **global seed conservation efforts**, aligning with international seed banks like the Svalbard Global Seed Vault.

**Thus, the correct answer is (a) 1, 2 and 3 only.**

## Past Learning (Answers)

| | | | | | | | | | |
|---|---|---|---|---|---|---|---|---|---|
| 1 (a) | 2 (a) | 3 (a) | 4 (d) | 5 (d) | 6 (b) | 7 (d) | 8 (d) | 9 (a) | 10 (a) |
| 11 (a) | 12 (b) | 13 (b) | 14 (c) | 15 (d) | 16 (b) | 17 (d) | | | |

CHAPTER 08

# Information and Communication (ICT) Technology

## Assessment Round

### Topic 1 : Regulatory Bodies and Legislations

**1.** With reference to the NASSCOM, consider the following statements:

1. It is a non-profit organisation that represents the IT and BPM industries in India.
2. It was founded to promote research and innovation in the Indian defense sector.
3. It provides a platform for industry stakeholders to collaborate on issues related to technology policy.

How many of the given above statements is/are correct?

(a) Only one
(b) Only two
(c) All three
(d) None

**2.** Consider the following:

1. Regulating tariffs for telecom services.
2. Monitoring and ensuring the quality of service provided by telecom operators.
3. Granting licenses to telecom companies.
4. Formulating policies for spectrum allocation.

How many of the given above is/are the functions carried out by the Telecom Regulatory Authority of India (TRAI)?

(a) Only one
(b) Only two
(c) Only three
(d) All four

**3.** With reference to the 'Telecom Regulatory Authority of India (TRAI)', consider the following statements:

1. TRAI's orders and recommendations are legally binding on the Central Government.
2. Appeals against TRAI's orders can be made to the Telecom Disputes Settlement and Appellate Tribunal (TDSAT).
3. TRAI can enforce penalties directly on telecom service providers without requiring government approval.

Which of the given above statements is/are correct?

(a) 1 and 2 only
(b) 2 only
(c) 1 and 3 only
(d) 1, 2 and 3

**4.** Which of the following best describes 'Adjusted Gross Revenue (AGR)' in the context of the telecom sector in India?

(a) The total revenue earned by telecom operators, including revenue from non-telecom sources such as deposit interests.
(b) The revenue earned from providing telecom services only, excluding income from non-core telecom activities.
(c) The revenue calculated after deducting expenses like spectrum usage charges and license fees.
(d) A regulatory measure to determine the gross profits of telecom companies for financial reporting purposes.

**5.** With reference to the 'Universal Service Obligation Fund (USOF)', consider the following statements:

1. It is managed by the Department of Telecommunications under the Ministry of Communications.
2. The USOF supports projects to promote rural broadband connectivity, including BharatNet.
3. Revenue for USOF is generated through a universal service levy charged as a percentage of the Adjusted Gross Revenue (AGR) of telecom operators.

Which of the above statements are correct?

(a) 1 and 2 only (b) 2 and 3 only
(c) 1 and 3 only (d) 1, 2 and 3

**6.** With reference to the 'National Informatics Centre (NIC)', consider the following statements:

1. NIC provides IT support to the Government of India in implementing e-governance initiatives.
2. It is responsible for developing digital infrastructure for both Central and State Governments.
3. It was established under the Ministry of Electronics and Information Technology (MeitY).

How many of the given above statements is/are correct?

(a) Only one (b) Only two
(c) All three (d) None

**7.** Where is the headquarters of the International Telecommunication Union (ITU) located?

(a) Paris, France (b) Geneva, Switzerland
(c) Vienna, Austria (d) New York, USA

**8.** With respect to the International Telecommunication Union (ITU), consider the following statements:

1. It organises the World Telecommunication Development Conference (WTDC) to address ICT development issues globally.
2. Its primary responsibility is regulating internet domain names and IP addresses worldwide.
3. ITU has member states, private sector members and academia as participants.

Which of the above statements are correct?

(a) 1 and 2 only (b) 1 and 3 only
(c) 2 and 3 only (d) 1, 2 and 3

**9.** Which of the following are key obligations for digital news and OTT platforms under the IT Rules of 2021?

1. Self-classification of content into age-based categories
2. Registration with the Ministry of Electronics and Information Technology (MeitY)
3. Implementation of parental control mechanisms
4. Setting up an internal grievance redressal mechanism

Select the correct answer using the codes given below:

(a) 1 and 3 only (b) 1, 3 and 4 only
(c) 2 and 4 only (d) 1, 2, 3 and 4

**10.** Which of the following are functions of the grievance redressal mechanism required under the IT Rules of 2021?

1. Addressing user complaints regarding content within 24 hours
2. Providing an appeals process if users are dissatisfied with grievance redressal outcomes
3. Assisting law enforcement agencies with information requests
4. Tracking content that violates user privacy

Select the correct answer using the codes given below:

(a) 1 and 4 only (b) 2 and 3 only
(c) 1, 2 and 3 only (d) 1, 2, 3 and 4

**11.** Consider the following statements:

1. India is a member of the International Telecommunication Union (ITU).
2. India has been involved in ITU's standard-setting processes and initiatives.
3. India hosts the regional headquarters of ITU for South Asia.

How many of the given above statements is/are correct?

(a) Only one (b) Only two
(c) All three (d) None

**12.** What is the Budapest Convention primarily focused on?
(a) Regulating cybersecurity policies for private companies worldwide
(b) Harmonising national laws on cybercrime and promoting international cooperation
(c) Establishing a global internet regulatory authority
(d) Creating a framework for private companies to report data breaches

**13.** Which of the following are key rights of data principals under the Digital Personal Data Protection Act, 2023?
1. Right to access personal data
2. Right to seek correction of inaccurate data
3. Right to request the deletion of personal data
4. Right to compensation for data breaches

Select the correct answer using the codes given below:
(a) 1 and 4 only (b) 1, 2 and 3 only
(c) 2 and 3 only (d) 1, 2, 3 and 4

**14.** Which of the following provisions are covered under the 'Digital Personal Data Protection Act, 2023'?
1. Data principals have the right to access and correct their personal data.
2. Processing of children's data is strictly prohibited under all circumstances.
3. Consent managers must be registered with the Data Protection Board of India.
4. A data fiduciary is required to inform the data principal about the purpose of data processing.

Select the correct answer using the codes given below:
(a) 1 and 2 only (b) 1, 3 and 4 only
(c) 2, 3 and 4 only (d) 1, 2, 3 and 4

**15.** Which of the following obligations are imposed on data fiduciaries under the Digital Personal Data Protection Act, 2023?
1. Ensure data protection by implementing security safeguards.
2. Appoint a Data Protection Officer if classified as a Significant Data Fiduciary.
3. Seek explicit consent from data principals before processing sensitive personal data.
4. Store all personal data exclusively within the territory of India.

Select the correct answer using the codes given below:
(a) 1 and 2 only (b) 1, 2 and 3 only
(c) 2, 3 and 4 only (d) 1, 2, 3 and 4

**16.** Which of the following best describes the concept of "Data Localisation"?
(a) The practice of storing and processing data outside the borders of the country of origin.
(b) The mandate to store and process certain categories of data within the borders of the country where it is generated.
(c) The global sharing of personal data across multiple jurisdictions without restrictions.
(d) The creation of decentralised data storage systems for better data management.

**17.** What categories of data are typically required to be stored within India under data localisation laws?
(a) General personal data only
(b) Sensitive personal data and critical personal data
(c) Non-personal data exclusively
(d) All categories of data, without exception

## Topic 2 : Spectrum and Telecom

**18.** Consider the following pairs of communication types and their typical frequency ranges:

| | Communication Type | Frequency Range |
|---|---|---|
| 1. | AM Radio | 535 to 1705 kHz |
| 2. | FM Radio | 88 to 108 MHz |
| 3. | Bluetooth | 2.4 to 2.485 GHz |
| 4. | Wi-Fi | 7 to 10 GHz |

How many of the given above pairs is/are correctly matched?
(a) Only one (b) Only two
(c) Only three (d) All four

**19.** Arrange the following types of electromagnetic waves in order of increasing wavelength:
1. Ultraviolet 2. X-rays
3. Radio Waves 4. Infrared

Choose the correct order from the codes below:
(a) 2 - 1 - 4 - 3 (b) 1 - 2 - 4 - 3
(c) 3 - 4 - 1 - 2 (d) 1 - 4 - 3 - 2

**20.** Consider the following uses of electromagnetic waves:
1. X-rays are used in medical imaging to view internal body structures.
2. Radio waves are used in broadcasting and communication.
3. Ultraviolet rays are used for sterilisation and disinfection.
4. Gamma rays are used in microwave ovens to heat food.

How many of the given statements is/are correct?
(a) Only one (b) Only two
(c) Only three (d) All four

**21.** Consider the following statements:
1. Spectrum auctions in India are conducted by the Ministry of Electronics and Information Technology (MeitY).
2. Bidders in spectrum auctions can pay in installments over a period specified by the government.
3. The auction allows telecom companies to acquire rights to specific frequency bands for a set number of years.

How many of the given above statements is/are correct?
(a) Only one (b) Only two
(c) All three (d) None

**22.** With respect to the role of spectrum in mobile networks, consider the following statements:
1. Lower frequency spectrum provides better coverage and penetrates buildings more effectively.
2. Higher frequency spectrum offers faster data speeds but has limited range.
3. Mid-band spectrum provides a balance between coverage and data speed, often used in 4G and 5G networks.

Which of the above statements is/are correct?
(a) Only one (b) Only two
(c) All three (d) None

**23.** Which of the following colours of light has the longest wavelength in the visible spectrum?
(a) Blue (b) Green
(c) Yellow (d) Red

**24.** With reference to the colours in the visible spectrum, consider the following statements:
1. Blue light has a shorter wavelength than green light.
2. Yellow light has a longer wavelength than red light.
3. Red light is associated with the lowest energy in the visible spectrum.

How many of the given above statements is/are correct?
(a) Only one (b) Only two
(c) All three (d) None

**25.** Consider the following applications of optical fiber technology:
1. Medical imaging, such as endoscopy
2. High-speed internet and data transmission
3. Electrical power distribution
4. Telecommunication networks

How many of the given above applications is/are correct?
(a) Only one (b) Only two
(c) Only three (d) All four

**26.** How many of the following are suitable conditions for 'Total Internal Reflection (TIR)' to occur?
1. It occurs only if the angle of refraction reaches 90 degrees.
2. It requires that the light is moving from a less dense medium to a denser medium.
3. It is more likely to occur in materials with a high refractive index.

Select the correct answer from the codes given below:
(a) Only one (b) Only two
(c) All three (d) None

**27.** Which of the following best describes the phenomenon of 'Total Internal Reflection'?
(a) The bending of light as it passes from one medium to another of different density.
(b) The complete reflection of light back into a denser medium when it strikes the interface at an angle greater than the critical angle.
(c) The dispersion of light into its constituent colours when passing through a prism.
(d) The scattering of light by small particles in the atmosphere.

**28.** Consider the following applications:
1. Binoculars for magnified vision.
2. Periscopes used in submarines.
3. Rainbows observed in the sky.
4. Mirrors used in solar panels.

How many of the above applications involve Total Internal Reflection?
(a) Only one (b) Only two
(c) Only three (d) All four

**29.** Which of the following wireless technologies are commonly used for communication in modern networks?
1. 5G
2. NFC (Near Field Communication)
3. Optical Fiber
4. LoRa (Long Range)

Select the correct answer from the codes given below:
(a) 1, 2 and 4 only (b) 1 and 3 only
(c) 2, 3 and 4 only (d) 1, 2, 3 and 4

**30.** What is Blue Snarfing primarily associated with?
(a) Unauthorised access to a Bluetooth-enabled device to retrieve data
(b) Interfering with Bluetooth signals in nearby devices
(c) Enhancing Bluetooth signal strength for remote connection
(d) Providing secure data transfer between Bluetooth devices

**31.** With reference to the advantages of Free Space Optical Communication (FSO), consider the following statements:
1. FSO allows for high-speed data transmission comparable to fiber optics.
2. FSO systems are easier and quicker to deploy than traditional wired connections.
3. FSO is highly effective in all weather conditions due to its resistance to environmental interference.

Which of the statements given above are correct?
(a) 1 and 2 only
(b) 2 and 3 only
(c) 1 and 3 only
(d) 1, 2 and 3

**32.** With reference to the differences between Wi-Fi and Li-Fi, consider the following statements:
1. Wi-Fi uses radio waves for data transmission, whereas Li-Fi uses visible light.
2. Wi-Fi can operate effectively through walls, while Li-Fi requires line-of-sight.
3. Li-Fi offers better performance in outdoor environments with direct sunlight compared to Wi-Fi.

How many of the given above statements is/are correct?
(a) Only one (b) Only two
(c) All three (d) None

**33.** With reference to Li-Fi (Light Fidelity) technology, consider the following statements:
1. Li-Fi transmits data using visible light, rather than radio waves.
2. Li-Fi is capable of providing internet connectivity at extremely high speeds.
3. Li-Fi can operate even through walls, similar to Wi-Fi.

Which of the statements given above are correct?
(a) 1 and 2 only (b) 1 and 3 only
(c) 2 and 3 only (d) 1, 2 and 3

**34.** Which of the following features of WiMAX make it suitable for rural and remote areas?

1. Wide coverage area with fewer base stations required compared to Wi-Fi.
2. High-speed internet connectivity over long distances.
3. Ability to provide reliable connectivity in all weather conditions without interference.

Select the correct answer using the codes given below:

(a) 1 and 2 only (b) 1 and 3 only
(c) 2 and 3 only (d) 1, 2 and 3

**35.** Consider the following devices:

1. Public transport card readers
2. Smartphones
3. Fitness trackers
4. Microwave ovens

How many of the given above devices can be operated using Near Field Communication (NFC) technology?

(a) Only one (b) Only two
(c) Only three (d) All four

**36.** Which of the following are specifically designed for short-range communication?

1. Wi-Fi Direct
2. Cellular LTE
3. Bluetooth Low Energy (BLE)

Select the correct answer from the codes given below:

(a) 1 and 3 only
(b) 2 and 3 only
(c) 3 only
(d) 1, 2 and 3

**37.** With reference to the 'FastTag system' in India, consider the following statements:

1. It uses Radio Frequency Identification (RFID) technology for toll collection.
2. It supports interoperability allowing seamless toll payment across all national and state highways.
3. The collected toll revenue is directly linked to the National Highways Authority of India (NHAI).

Which of the statements given above are correct?

(a) 1 and 2 only (b) 2 and 3 only
(c) 1 and 3 only (d) 1, 2 and 3

**38.** Which of the following best describes the technology behind 'White Space Wi-Fi'?

(a) A technology that uses visible light for data transmission over short distances.
(b) A wireless communication technology that utilises unused spectrum in the TV frequency bands for internet access.
(c) A system designed exclusively for providing high-speed internet to urban areas using dedicated fiber optics.
(d) A method of data transfer using microwave radiation exclusively for satellite communication.

**39.** Which of the following benefits are associated with space-based internet systems?

1. Enhanced internet access in remote and rural regions.
2. Increased data transfer rates compared to terrestrial fiber networks.
3. Resilience against natural disasters disrupting ground infrastructure.
4. Elimination of all latency issues in global communications.

Select the correct answer from the codes given below:

(a) 1, 2 and 3 only (b) 1 and 3 only
(c) 2 and 4 only (d) 1, 2, 3 and 4

**40.** Which of the following technologies or initiatives are directly associated with space-based internet services?

1. Starlink
2. OneWeb
3. Google Fiber
4. Project Kuiper

Select the correct answer from the codes given below:

(a) 1 and 2 only
(b) 1, 2 and 4 only
(c) 3 and 4 only
(d) 1, 2, 3 and 4

## Topic 3 : Mobile Technology

**41.** With reference to e-SIM technology, consider the following statements:

1. It is embedded directly into devices and eliminates the need for a physical SIM card.
2. e-SIM provides better flexibility by allowing users to switch between multiple network operators remotely.
3. It is only supported in smartphones and not in IoT devices like smartwatches.

Which of the statements given above are correct?

(a) 1 and 2 only
(b) 2 and 3 only
(c) 1 and 3 only
(d) 1, 2 and 3

**42.** With reference to LTE and VoLTE technology, consider the following statements:

1. LTE supports high-speed internet but does not inherently support voice calls.
2. VoLTE allows for voice calls to be transmitted over an LTE network.
3. VoLTE requires an active Wi-Fi connection to function.

How many of the above statements is/are correct?

(a) Only one (b) Only two
(c) All three (d) None

**43.** Consider the following pairs of cellular network generations and their primary features:

| Generation | Feature |
|---|---|
| 1. 2G | Enabled basic internet browsing and SMS services |
| 2. 3G | Provided enhanced mobile broadband for video calls and high-speed internet access |
| 3. 4G | Introduced IP-based voice calls and faster data rates |
| 4. 5G | Focused solely on voice services and text messaging |

How many of the given above pairs is/are correctly matched?

(a) Only one (b) Only two
(c) Only three (d) All four

**44.** Consider the following statements:

1. 5G networks provide high-speed internet and support low latency communication while 6G networks are expected to offer even faster speeds and ultra-low latency.
2. 5G technology primarily relies on sub-6 GHz and millimeter-wave frequencies, while 6G is anticipated to use terahertz frequencies.
3. 6G is currently available in many countries for commercial use.

Which of the statements given above are correct?

(a) 1 and 2 only (b) 1 and 3 only
(c) 2 and 3 only (d) 1, 2 and 3

## Topic 4 : Internet

**45.** Which of the following correctly describes the role of ICANN (Internet Corporation for Assigned Names and Numbers)?

(a) ICANN is responsible for the allocation of IP addresses and management of domain names globally.
(b) ICANN enforces laws related to cybercrime and online fraud across nations.
(c) ICANN governs the development of internet protocols and standards globally.
(d) ICANN manages internet content and regulates access to websites globally.

**46.** With reference to the differences between IPv4 and IPv6, consider the following statements:

1. IPv4 uses a 32-bit address format, while IPv6 uses a 128-bit address format.
2. IPv6 offers improved routing efficiency and quality of service (QoS) compared to IPv4.
3. IPv6 allows for unlimited IP addresses, whereas IPv4 has a limited address pool.

Which of the statements given above are correct?

(a) 1 and 2 only (b) 2 and 3 only
(c) 1 and 3 only (d) 1, 2 and 3

**47.** Consider the following statements with reference to the 'BharatNet project':

1. It aims to provide broadband connectivity to all gram panchayats in India.
2. BharatNet uses optical fiber cables as the primary medium for connectivity.
3. The project is being implemented entirely by the private sector.

Which of the statements given above are correct?

(a) 1 and 2 only
(b) 2 and 3 only
(c) 1 and 3 only
(d) 1, 2 and 3

**48.** Consider the following pairs regarding types of internet layers:

| Layer | Description |
|---|---|
| 1. Deep Web | Content not indexed by standard search engines, such as academic databases |
| 2. Dark Web | Part of the internet that requires specific software, like Tor, for access |
| 3. Dark Net | Legitimate websites accessible through regular search engines |

Which of the given above pairs are correctly matched?

(a) 1 and 2 only
(b) 2 and 3 only
(c) 1, 2 and 3
(d) None of the above

**49.** Consider the following pairs regarding different web generations:

| Web Version | Characteristics |
|---|---|
| 1. Web 2.0 | Dynamic content and social interaction |
| 2. Web 3.0 | Smart and connected devices |
| 3. Web 4.0 | Personalised, AI-driven experiences |
| 4. Web 5.0 | Virtual, immersive, emotion-aware internet |

Which of the given above pairs are correctly matched?

(a) 1, 2 and 4 only
(b) 1, 3 and 4 only
(c) 2 and 3 only
(d) 1, 2, 3 and 4

**50.** What is the primary focus of Web 5.0 technology?

(a) Enabling basic text and image content sharing on websites
(b) Creating a highly immersive, emotion-sensitive internet experience
(c) Developing machine-readable data and semantic understanding for the web
(d) Establishing social media platforms and user-generated content

**51.** Under the BharatNet project, which of the following benefits are provided to rural communities?

1. Improved access to online educational and healthcare services
2. Opportunities for e-commerce and digital entrepreneurship
3. Provision of free fiber optic connections to all households in rural areas

Select the correct answer using the codes below:

(a) 1 and 2 only (b) 1 and 3 only
(c) 2 and 3 only (d) 1, 2 and 3

**52.** Identify the concept described in the following hypothetical situation:

'A farmer uses a network of sensors placed in the soil to monitor moisture levels, temperature and nutrient content. The data collected by these sensors is transmitted to a central system over the internet, which automatically activates irrigation systems and suggests fertilizer usage.'

Which of the following concepts best fits the described scenario?

(a) Internet of Things (IoT)
(b) Big Data Analytics
(c) Cloud Computing
(d) Machine Learning

**53.** Consider the following statements:
1. IoT devices can operate independently of human intervention once configured.
2. IoT technology is primarily designed for use in mobile phones only.
3. IoT enables the automation of routine tasks through smart connected devices.

How many of the given above statements is/are correct about 'Internet of Things (IoT)'?
(a) Only one (b) Only two
(c) All three (d) None

**54.** Which of the following statement best defines 'Narrowband IoT (NB-IoT)' technology?
(a) A high-speed wireless standard for video streaming.
(b) A low-power, wide-area network (LPWAN) technology designed for IoT devices with limited data needs.
(c) A communication protocol focused on data security for IoT applications.
(d) A satellite-based technology to connect IoT devices globally.

**55.** Which of the following statements best describes the principle of Net Neutrality?
(a) Net Neutrality mandates that Internet Service Providers (ISPs) treat all internet traffic equally without favoring or blocking specific websites or applications.
(b) Net Neutrality allows ISPs to charge different rates for different types of content or services.
(c) Net Neutrality ensures that ISPs provide exclusive access to premium content for higher-paying customers.
(d) Net Neutrality permits ISPs to prioritise their own content over third-party services.

**56.** Which of the following correctly describes the impact of TRAI's Net Neutrality rules on consumers and businesses?
(a) Consumers benefit from a non-discriminatory internet, while businesses offering premium content can charge extra for faster access.
(b) Consumers can access all internet content equally, and businesses are prohibited from paying ISPs for faster delivery of their content.
(c) Consumers must pay ISPs additional fees to access specific online services, while businesses can pay ISPs to ensure their content reaches users faster.
(d) Consumers can only access content from platforms approved by ISPs, while businesses must adhere to ISP guidelines for content delivery.

## Topic 5 : Computing Technology

**57.** Arrange the following units of computer data storage in ascending order:
1. Terabyte
2. Petabyte
3. Yottabyte
4. Zettabyte

Choose the correct order from the options below:
(a) Terabyte, Petabyte, Zettabyte, Yottabyte
(b) Yottabyte, Zettabyte, Petabyte, Terabyte
(c) Terabyte, Zettabyte, Petabyte, Yottabyte
(d) Petabyte, Terabyte, Yottabyte, Zettabyte

**58.** What is a Trojan Horse in the context of computer security?
(a) A type of malware that replicates itself and spreads across multiple computers
(b) A malicious software disguised as legitimate software to deceive users
(c) A software that only affects hardware components of a computer
(d) A tool that exclusively targets mobile operating systems

**59.** Consider the following pairs regarding types of cybersecurity threats:

| Type | Description |
|---|---|
| 1. Spyware | Malicious software that collects information from a device without the user's knowledge |
| 2. Keylogger | Software designed to prevent unauthorised access by encrypting keyboard inputs |
| 3. Phishing | A method of tricking users into revealing sensitive information through fake websites |
| 4. Malware | Any software intentionally designed to cause harm to a device or network |

Which of the given above pairs are correctly matched?
(a) 1, 2 and 4 only (b) 1, 3 and 4 only
(c) 2 and 3 only (d) 1, 2, 3 and 4

**60.** What is the primary purpose of 'sandboxing' in computer security?
(a) To restrict potentially harmful programs from affecting the rest of the system
(b) To enable the replication of malware across multiple systems
(c) To enhance the network speed by removing unused files
(d) To permanently delete suspicious files without examination

**61.** With reference to the 'Deepfake Technology', consider the following statements:
1. This technology uses artificial intelligence to manipulate audio, video or images to create realistic but fake content.
2. Deepfakes are commonly used in cybersecurity to enhance data protection by creating realistic avatars.

Which of the statement(s) given above is/are correct?
(a) 1 only (b) 2 only
(c) Both 1 and 2 (d) Neither 1 nor 2

**62.** Which of the following best describes the objective of the 'National Cybersecurity Policy, 2013'?
(a) To create a framework for monitoring internet usage of citizens for national security purposes.
(b) To secure cyberspace by protecting critical information infrastructure and promoting a safe digital environment.
(c) To restrict the use of social media platforms for sharing sensitive information.
(d) To mandate private companies to store all user data within the country for enhanced surveillance.

**63.** Which of the following best describes the primary purpose of Cyber Swachhta Kendra (Botnet Cleaning and Malware Analysis Centre) in India?
(a) To monitor all online activities of Indian citizens for national security purposes.
(b) To detect and clean infected systems of individuals and organisations, ensuring cybersecurity.
(c) To develop offensive cybersecurity measures to counter global cyber threats.
(d) To regulate internet access across the country by blocking malware-prone websites.

**64.** Which of the following best describes the goal of the 'Cyber Swachhta Bharat' initiative?
(a) To create awareness about cyber hygiene and provide tools to secure digital devices against malware.
(b) To enforce strict penalties for organisations that fail to implement cybersecurity protocols.
(c) To establish a national database of all internet users for tracking online activity.
(d) To develop indigenous cybersecurity software for export to other countries.

**65.** Which of the following supercomputers are developed in India?
1. PARAM 8000 2. Pratyush
3. SahasraT 4. Mihir

Select the correct answer from the codes given below:
(a) 1 and 4 only (b) 1, 2 and 3 only
(c) 2, 3 and 4 only (d) 1, 2, 3 and 4

**66.** Consider the following applications:
1. Weather forecasting
2. Genome sequencing
3. Video streaming services
4. Space exploration

How many of the above significantly on supercomputers?
(a) Only one (b) Only two
(c) Only three (d) All four

**67.** With reference to 'Cloud Computing', consider the following statements:
1. Cloud computing allows users to access computing resources remotely over the internet.
2. It eliminates the need for local data storage and IT infrastructure.
3. It is only suitable for small-scale applications and not for large enterprises.

How many of the statements given above is/are correct?
(a) Only one (b) Only two
(c) All three (d) None

**68.** Consider the following pairs regarding cloud service models:

| Service Model | Description |
|---|---|
| 1. Infrastructure as a Service (IaaS) | Provides virtualised computing resources over the internet, including storage, servers and networking |
| 2. Platform as a Service (PaaS) | Offers a platform allowing customers to develop, run and manage applications without infrastructure concerns |
| 3. Software as a Service (SaaS) | Allows users to access software applications on a subscription basis via the internet |

Which of the above pairs are correctly matched?
(a) 1 and 2 only
(b) 1 and 3 only
(c) 2 and 3 only
(d) 1, 2 and 3

**69.** What is the primary purpose of 'Edge Computing' in modern communication networks?
(a) To centralise data processing to a single remote data center.
(b) To process data closer to the data source, reducing latency and bandwidth use.
(c) To increase the range of cellular networks in rural areas.
(d) To replace cloud computing for all data processing tasks.

**70.** With reference to Edge Computing, consider the following statements:
1. It reduces data transmission costs by processing data locally.
2. It eliminates the need for cloud computing in all applications.
3. It is beneficial for applications that require real-time data processing, like autonomous vehicles and IoT devices.

How many of the given above statements is/are correct?
(a) Only one
(b) Only two
(c) All three
(d) None

**71.** Consider the following statements about 'Quantum Communication technology':

**Statement 1:** Quantum entanglement is used in Quantum Communication to create instantaneous data transfer between two points, regardless of distance.

**Statement 2:** Quantum Key Distribution (QKD) provides a secure way to share encryption keys by detecting any eavesdropping attempts.

In the context of the above statements, which of the following is correct?
(a) Both statements are correct, and statement 2 is the correct explanation of statement 1.
(b) Both statements are correct but statement 2 is not the correct explanation of statement 1.
(c) Only statement 1 is correct.
(d) Only statement 2 is correct.

**72.** What is 'Quantum Entanglement' in the context of quantum physics?
(a) A phenomenon where two particles interact and then move independently without any connection.
(b) A process where particles become connected and the state of one instantaneously influences the state of the other, regardless of distance.
(c) A technique used in classical physics to understand atomic structure.
(d) A form of interference where two particles collide and scatter in opposite directions.

**73.** Consider the following statements about 'Quantum Superposition':
1. It allows a quantum particle to exist in multiple states at once.
2. It is exclusive to electrons and does not apply to other particles.
3. Observing a quantum particle collapses its superposition into a single state.

How many of the given above statements is/are correct?
(a) Only one
(b) Only two
(c) All three
(d) None

## Topic 6 : Electronics and IT

**74.** Consider the following human characteristics:
1. Fingerprints
2. Voice patterns
3. Skin tone
4. Iris patterns

How many of the given above is/are commonly used for 'Biometric Recognition'?
(a) Only one
(b) Only two
(c) Only three
(d) All four

**75.** Which of the following types of information can be gathered from wearable devices?
1. Heart rate data
2. Sleep patterns
3. Blood oxygen levels
4. Step count

Select the correct answer using the codes given below:
(a) 1, 2 and 3 only
(b) 2, 3 and 4 only
(c) 1, 2 and 4 only
(d) 1, 2, 3 and 4

**76.** Which of the following statements about End-to-End Encryption (E2EE) is/are correct?
1. E2EE protects data from being intercepted during transmission.
2. E2EE allows service providers to access the content of encrypted messages for troubleshooting.
3. E2EE ensures that encryption keys are stored only on user devices.

Select the correct answer using the codes given below:
(a) 1 and 2 only (b) 1 and 3 only
(c) 2 and 3 only (d) 1, 2 and 3

**77.** Which of the following statements are correct about the applications of 3D printing?
1. 3D printing is used in the automotive industry to produce custom car parts and prototypes.
2. 3D printing is limited to plastic materials and cannot be applied to metals or ceramics.
3. The education sector uses 3D printing to create teaching aids and prototypes for student projects.

Select the correct answer from the codes given below:
(a) 1 and 2 only (b) 1 and 3 only
(c) 2 and 3 only (d) 1, 2 and 3

# OMR SHEET

**Assessment Round**

| | | | | | | | |
|---|---|---|---|---|---|---|---|
| 1 | a b c d | 31 | a b c d | 61 | a b c d | 91 | a b c d |
| 2 | a b c d | 32 | a b c d | 62 | a b c d | 92 | a b c d |
| 3 | a b c d | 33 | a b c d | 63 | a b c d | 93 | a b c d |
| 4 | a b c d | 34 | a b c d | 64 | a b c d | 94 | a b c d |
| 5 | a b c d | 35 | a b c d | 65 | a b c d | 95 | a b c d |
| 6 | a b c d | 36 | a b c d | 66 | a b c d | 96 | a b c d |
| 7 | a b c d | 37 | a b c d | 67 | a b c d | 97 | a b c d |
| 8 | a b c d | 38 | a b c d | 68 | a b c d | 98 | a b c d |
| 9 | a b c d | 39 | a b c d | 69 | a b c d | 99 | a b c d |
| 10 | a b c d | 40 | a b c d | 70 | a b c d | 100 | a b c d |
| 11 | a b c d | 41 | a b c d | 71 | a b c d | 101 | a b c d |
| 12 | a b c d | 42 | a b c d | 72 | a b c d | 102 | a b c d |
| 13 | a b c d | 43 | a b c d | 73 | a b c d | 103 | a b c d |
| 14 | a b c d | 44 | a b c d | 74 | a b c d | 104 | a b c d |
| 15 | a b c d | 45 | a b c d | 75 | a b c d | 105 | a b c d |
| 16 | a b c d | 46 | a b c d | 76 | a b c d | 106 | a b c d |
| 17 | a b c d | 47 | a b c d | 77 | a b c d | 107 | a b c d |
| 18 | a b c d | 48 | a b c d | 78 | a b c d | 108 | a b c d |
| 19 | a b c d | 49 | a b c d | 79 | a b c d | 109 | a b c d |
| 20 | a b c d | 50 | a b c d | 80 | a b c d | 110 | a b c d |
| 21 | a b c d | 51 | a b c d | 81 | a b c d | 111 | a b c d |
| 22 | a b c d | 52 | a b c d | 82 | a b c d | 112 | a b c d |
| 23 | a b c d | 53 | a b c d | 83 | a b c d | 113 | a b c d |
| 24 | a b c d | 54 | a b c d | 84 | a b c d | 114 | a b c d |
| 25 | a b c d | 55 | a b c d | 85 | a b c d | 115 | a b c d |
| 26 | a b c d | 56 | a b c d | 86 | a b c d | 116 | a b c d |
| 27 | a b c d | 57 | a b c d | 87 | a b c d | 117 | a b c d |
| 28 | a b c d | 58 | a b c d | 88 | a b c d | 118 | a b c d |
| 29 | a b c d | 59 | a b c d | 89 | a b c d | 119 | a b c d |
| 30 | a b c d | 60 | a b c d | 90 | a b c d | 120 | a b c d |

## Calculate Your Score

| | |
|---|---|
| **Correct (✓)** | |
| **Incorrect (✓)** | |
| **Unattempted** | |
| **Total Score** | |
| **Accuracy (%)** | |

## Reasons for Incorrect Answers?

| | |
|---|---|
| 1. Lack of Knowledge/Existing Source Insufficient | |
| 2. Lack of Multiple Revision | |
| 3. Common Sense Mistakes | |

**Note :**

1. Calculate total score as correct answers carry 2 marks each 1/3rd marks will deducted for **Incorrect** Answers.
2. Calculate Accuracy (%) by dividing the number of correct answers to the total number of attempted questions.

## Past Learning

**1.** Consider the following communication technologies. **(2022)**

1. Closed-Circuit Television
2. Radio Frequency Identification
3. Wireless Local Area Network

Which of the above are considered Short-Range devices/ technologies?

(a) 1 and 2
(b) 2 and 3
(c) 1 and 3
(d) 1, 2 and 3

**2.** With reference to 'software as a Service (SaaS)', consider the following statements. **(2022)**

1. SaaS buyers can customise the user interface and can change data fields.
2. SaaS users can access their data through their mobile devices.
3. Outlook, Hotmail and Yahoo! Mail are forms of SaaS.

Which of the statements given above are correct?

(a) 1 and 2
(b) 2 and 3
(c) 1 and 3
(d) 1, 2 and 3

**3.** Which one of the following is the context in which the term 'Qubit' is mentioned? **(2022)**

(a) Cloud Services
(b) Quantum Computing
(c) Visible Light Communication Technologies
(d) Wireless Communication Technologies

**4.** In India, under cyber insurance for individuals, which of the following benefits are generally covered, in addition to payment for the loss of funds and other benefits? **(2020)**

1. Cost of restoration of the computer system in case of malware disrupting access to one's computer
2. Cost of a new computer if some miscreant will fully damage it, if proved so
3. Cost of hiring a specialied consultant to minimise the loss in case of cyber extortion
4. Cost of defence in the Court of Law if any third-party files a suit

Select the correct answer using the codes given below:

(a) 1, 2 and 4 only
(b) 1, 3 and 4 only
(c) 2 and 3 only
(d) 1, 2, 3 and 4

**5.** With reference to communication technologies, what is/are the difference/ differences between LTE (Long-Term Evolution) and VoLTE (Voice over Long-Term Evolution)? **(2019)**

1. LTE is commonly marketed as 3G and VoLTE is commonly marketed as advanced 3G.
2. LTE is data-only technology and VoLTE is voice-only technology.

Select the correct answer by using the codes given below.

(a) Only 1
(b) Only 2
(c) Both 1 and 2
(d) Neither 1 nor 2

**6.** In the context of wearable technology, which of the following tasks is/are accomplished by wearable devices? **(2019)**

1. Location/identification of a person
2. Sleep monitoring of a person
3. Assisting the hearing-impaired person

Select the correct answer by using the codes given below.

(a) Only 1
(b) 2 and 3
(c) Only 3
(d) 1, 2 and 3

**7.** Consider the following statements: **(2019)**
A digital signature is
1. an electronic record that identifies the certifying authority issuing it.
2. used to serve as a proof of identity of an individual to access information or server on Internet.
3. an electronic method of signing an electronic document and ensuring that the original content is unchanged.

Which of the statements given above is/are correct?
(a) 1 only (b) 2 and 3
(c) 3 only (d) 1, 2 and 3

**8.** Which of the following adopted a law on data protection and privacy for its citizens known as 'General Data Protection Regulation' in April 2016 and started implementation of it from 25th May, 2018? **(2019)**
(a) Australia
(b) Canada
(c) The European Union
(d) The United States of America

**9.** The terms WannaCry, Petya and Eternal Blue sometimes mentioned in the news recently are related to **(2018)**
(a) exoplanets (b) cryptocurrency
(c) cyber-attacks (d) mini satellites

**10.** When the alarm of your smartphone rings in the morning, you wake up and tap it to stop the alarm which causes your geyser to be switched on automatically. The smart mirror in your bathroom shows the day's weather and also indicates the level of water in your overhead tank. After you take some groceries from your refrigerator for making breakfast, it recognises the shortage of stock in it and places an order for the supply of fresh grocery items. When you step out of your house and lock the door, all lights, fans, geysers and AC machines get switched off automatically. On your way 482 IAS (Pre) Chapterwise Topic wise Solved Papers to office, your car warns you about traffic congestion ahead and suggests an alternative route, and if you are late for a meeting, it sends a message to your office accordingly. In the context of emerging communication technologies, which one of the following terms best applies to the above scenario? **(2018)**
(a) Border Gateway Protocol
(b) Internet of Things
(c) Internet Protocol
(d) Visual Private Network

**11.** '3D printing' has applications in which of the following? **(2018)**
1. Preparation of confectionery items
2. Manufacture of bionic ears
3. Automotive industry
4. Reconstructive surgeries
5. Data processing technologies

Select the correct answer using the codes given below:
(a) 1, 3 and 4 only (b) 2, 3 and 5 only
(c) 1 and 4 only (d) 1, 2, 3, 4 and 5

**12.** In India, it is legally mandatory for which of the following to report on cyber security incidents? **(2017)**
1. Service providers
2. Data centres
3. Body corporate

Select the correct answer using the codes given below.
(a) 1 only (b) 1 and 2
(c) 3 only (d) 1, 2 and 3

**13.** With reference to 'Near Field Communication (NFC) Technology', which of the following statements is/are correct? **(2015)**
1. It is a contactless communication technology that uses electromagnetic radio fields.
2. NFC is designed for use by devices which can be at a distance of even a metre from each other.
3. NFC can use encryption when sending sensitive information.

Select the correct answer using the codes given below.
(a) 1 and 2 (b) Only 3
(c) 1 and 3 (d) 1, 2 and 3

**14.** In addition to fingerprint scanning, which of the following can be used in the biometric identification of a person? **(2014)**

1. Iris scanning
2. Retinal scanning
3. Voice recognition

Select the correct answer using the codes given below:

(a) 1 only
(b) 2 and 3 only
(c) 1 and 3 only
(d) 1, 2 and 3

**15.** What is 'Virtual Private Network'? **(2011)**

(a) It is a private computer network of an organisation where the remote users can transmit encrypted information through the server of the organisation.
(b) It is a computer network across a public internet that provides users access their organisation's network while maintaining the security of the information transmitted.
(c) It is a computer network in which users can access a shared pool of computing resources through a service provider.
(d) None of the statements (a), (b) and (c) given above is a correct description of 'Virtual Private Network'.

**16.** What is the difference between Bluetooth and Wi-Fi devices? **(2011)**

(a) Bluetooth uses 2.4 GHz radio frequency band whereas Wi-Fi can use 2.4 GHz or 5 GHz frequency band.
(b) Bluetooth is used for Wireless Local Area Networks (WLAN) only, whereas Wi-Fi is used for Wireless Wide Area Networks (WWAN) only.
(c) When information is transmitted between two devices using Bluetooth technology, the devices have to be in the line of sight of each other, but when Wi-Fi technology is used the devices need not be in the line of sight of each other.
(d) The statements (a) and (b) given above are correct in this context.

**17.** Consider the following. **(2010)**

1. Bluetooth device
2. Cordless phone
3. Microwave oven
4. Wi-Fi device

Which of the above can operate between 2.4 and 2.5 GHz range of radio frequency band?

(a) 1 and 2
(b) 3 and 4
(c) 1, 2 and 4
(d) 1, 2, 3 and 4

# Detailed Solutions

## Assessment Round

**1.** *(b)* Only two

- **Statement 1 is correct:** NASSCOM **(National Association of Software and Service Companies)** is indeed a **non-profit organisation** that represents India's IT and Business Process Management (BPM) sectors. It plays a significant role in advocating for the interests of these industries in India and internationally.
- **Statement 2 is incorrect:** NASSCOM was **not founded to promote research and innovation in the defense sector.** Its primary focus is on the IT and BPM sectors, aiming to foster growth and innovation within India's technology industry.
- **Statement 3 is correct:** NASSCOM provides a platform for various **industry stakeholders** to collaborate on issues related to technology policy, regulatory matters and innovation. This collaboration supports the creation of a favourable business environment and drives technological advancement in India.

**Thus, two statements are correct, making the correct answer (b) Only two.**

**2.** *(b)* Only two

- **Statement 1 is correct:** One of the key roles of TRAI is to **regulate tariffs** for telecom services, ensuring fair pricing for consumers while enabling healthy competition among service providers.
- **Statement 2 is correct:** TRAI is responsible for **monitoring and maintaining the quality of service** provided by telecom operators. It sets quality benchmarks to ensure consumers receive reliable telecom services, such as minimum call drops and internet speeds.
- **Statement 3 is incorrect:** TRAI does not have the authority to **grant licenses** to telecom companies. The licensing authority rests with the Department of Telecommunications (DoT) under the Ministry of Communications, which issues licenses for telecom operations.
- **Statement 4 is incorrect:** Spectrum allocation policy is under the purview of the **Department of Telecommunications** (DoT), not TRAI. TRAI, however, does provide recommendations on spectrum pricing and allocation policy to the government.

**Thus, only two functions are correct, making the answer (b) Only two.**

**3.** *(b)* 2 only

- **Statement 1 is incorrect:** TRAI is the regulatory body for telecommunications, broadcasting and cable services in India. It ensures fair competition, consumer protection and transparency in the sector.
  - **TRAI's recommendations are advisory in nature and not legally binding** on the central government. However, the government often considers them while formulating policies.
- **Statement 2 is correct:** Any person aggrieved by an order of TRAI can appeal to the Telecom Disputes Settlement and Appellate Tribunal (TDSAT), which has jurisdiction over disputes between service providers, consumers and TRAI.
- **Statement 3 is incorrect:** While TRAI can recommend penalties, its enforcement powers are limited and government approval is often required for imposing significant penalties.

**Thus, the correct answer is (b) 2 only.**

**4.** *(b)* The revenue earned from providing telecom services only, excluding certain income from non-core telecom activities.

- AGR is the **usage and licensing** fee that telecom operators are charged by the Department of Telecommunications (DoT).
- It forms the basis for calculating telecom companies' dues to the government, including the **license fee** and **Spectrum Usage Charges** (SUC).

- The AGR is divided into:
  - **Spectrum Usage Charges (SUC):** These are pegged at 3-5% of AGR, depending on the telecom company's spectrum holdings.
  - **License Fees:** Telecom operators are required to pay **8%** of their AGR as a license fee to the government
- **Supreme Court Ruling (2019):** Setting aside the TDSAT decision, the SC upheld the DoT's definition of AGR on 24th October, 2019, declaring that AGR must include all revenue sources, including non-telecom activities like interest and capital gains.
- **DoT introduced the concept of the Applicable Gross Revenue (ApGR) in 2021 arrived at by removing all the non-telecom revenues earned by telcos from their gross revenue. It has removed several non-telecom income items, such as those from property rents, dividends and interests from the calculation of Adjusted Gross Revenue (AGR).**
  - Gains from forex fluctuations, insurance claims, capital gains on account of sale of fixed assets and securities, receipts from Universal Service Obligation Fund, bad debts recovered, excess provisions written back, revenue from activities under the I&B licence and revenue from operations other than telecom activities will **now be excluded from gross revenue to arrive at the ApGR.**
- **AGR would then be arrived at from the ApGR, after further removing some more non-telecom service related items.** Items to be removed include 'roaming revenue passed onto other eligible/entitled telecommunication services providers'.

**Thus, option (b) is the correct answer.**

**5.** *(d)* 1, 2 and 3

- **Statement 1 is correct:** The Universal Service Obligation Fund (USOF) is managed by the Department of Telecommunications (DoT) under the Ministry of Communications. It was established to ensure that underserved areas, including rural and remote regions, have access to affordable and reliable telecommunication services.
- **Statement 2 is correct:** The USOF supports several projects aimed at improving rural broadband connectivity, including **BharatNet**, which is one of the largest initiatives to connect villages and rural areas through high-speed optical fibre networks. This ensures the digital inclusion of remote communities.
- **Statement 3 is correct:** Revenue for the USOF is generated through a **Universal Service Levy (USL)**, which is charged as a percentage (currently 5%) of the Adjusted Gross Revenue (AGR) of telecom service providers. This levy is used to finance telecom infrastructure and connectivity projects in areas where market-driven services are not viable.

**Thus, the correct answer is (d) 1, 2 and 3.**

**6.** *(c)* All three

- **Statement 1 is correct: The National Informatics Centre (NIC)** plays a crucial role in providing **IT support to the Government of India** for implementing e-governance initiatives. It has been instrumental in creating and managing many digital platforms used by government departments to provide services to citizens efficiently.
- **Statement 2 is correct:** NIC is responsible for developing **digital infrastructure** that supports both central and state governments. This includes the development and maintenance of websites, applications, and data centers used by various government agencies across India.
- **Statement 3 is correct:** NIC was established under the **Ministry of Electronics and Information Technology (MeitY)** in 1976. Since then, it has been the technology backbone of the Indian government, providing secure, reliable and scalable digital solutions for governance.

**Thus, all three statements are correct, making the answer (c) All three.**

**7.** *(b)* Geneva, Switzerland

- **ITU, headquartered in Geneva, Switzerland** is an **international organisation within the United Nations System** where governments and the private sector coordinate global telecom networks and services. The ITU is the leading publisher of telecommunication technology, regulatory and standards information.

- It was established in **1865** and is one of the oldest international organisations, initially formed to standardise and regulate telecommunication.
- It plays a pivotal role in coordinating the global use of the radio spectrum, managing satellite orbits and developing international standards for telecommunications and information technology.

**Thus, option (b) is the correct answer.**

**8.** *(b)* 1 and 3 only

- **Statement 1 is correct:** The ITU organises the World Telecommunication Development Conference (WTDC), which focuses on the promotion of equitable and universal access to information and communication technologies (ICTs) worldwide. This initiative aims to address challenges like digital inclusion and sustainable development.
- **Statement 2 is incorrect:** The regulation of internet domain names and IP addresses is not the responsibility of ITU. **This task is managed by the Internet Corporation for Assigned Names and Numbers (ICANN).** ITU's focus is on telecommunications and ICT infrastructure.
- **Statement 3 is correct:** ITU has a **diverse membership structure, which includes member states, private sector entities and academic institutions.** This ensures a multi-stakeholder approach in its policymaking and standard-setting activities.

**Thus, the correct answer is (b) 1 and 3 only.**

**9.** *(b)* **1, 3 and 4 only**

- **Statement 1 is correct:** OTT (Over-the-Top) platforms are required to **self-classify content** based on age categories, including 'U' (Universal), 'U/A 7+', 'U/A 13+', 'U/A 16+', and 'A' (Adult). This classification system helps users identify appropriate content for different age groups.
- **Statement 2 is incorrect:** The IT Rules 2021 do not require **registration with MeitY.** However, digital news platforms are expected to adhere to a code of ethics and provide information to the government when requested.
- **Statement 3 is correct:** OTT platforms are required to have **parental control mechanisms** for content classified under specific age groups, such as 'U/A 13+' and above, to restrict access for younger audiences.
- **Statement 4 is correct:** The rules mandate that digital news and OTT platforms establish an **internal grievance redressal mechanism.** They must appoint a grievance officer to handle complaints related to content and this officer should resolve issues within a specific timeframe.

**Thus, statements 1, 3 and 4 are correct, making the answer (b) 1, 3 and 4 only.**

**10.** *(c)* 1, 2 and 3 only

- **Statement 1 is correct:** The grievance redressal mechanism is designed to **address user complaints promptly.** Social media platforms are required to acknowledge complaints within 24 hours and resolve them within 15 days, depending on the severity of the issue.
- **Statement 2 is correct:** Under the IT Rules 2021, users have the right to **appeal decisions made by the grievance officer** if they feel their complaint has not been adequately addressed. This allows for a secondary review process.
- **Statement 3 is correct:** The grievance redressal mechanism includes provisions to **assist law enforcement agencies** by providing data when required for legal investigations or public safety.
- **Statement 4 is incorrect:** While the IT Rules address user privacy, the grievance mechanism is primarily focused on resolving content complaints, not on actively tracking content related to user privacy violations. Privacy issues are covered under separate guidelines.

**Thus, statements 1, 2 and 3 are correct, making the answer (c) 1, 2 and 3 only.**

**11.** *(c)* All three

- **Statement 1 is correct: India is a member of the ITU** and actively participates in its conferences, discussions and initiatives, contributing to global standards and policies on telecommunications and ICT.
- **Statement 2 is correct:** India has played an active role in **ITU's standard-setting processes.** It participates in ITU conferences and contributes to initiatives aimed at addressing global telecom challenges, such as improving rural connectivity and cybersecurity.
- **Statement 3 is correct:** India host the regional headquarters of the ITU for South Asia. This regional office and innovation centre opened in New Delhi on 22nd March, 2023. It aims to strengthen technology cooperation and boost regional telecommunications development in the South Asian region.

**Thus, all three statements are correct, making the answer (c) All three.**

**12.** *(b)* Harmonising national laws on cybercrime and promoting international cooperation.

- The **Budapest Convention on Cybercrime,** also known as the **Council of Europe Convention on Cybercrime,** was signed in **2001** and is the first international treaty aimed at **harmonising national laws on cybercrime, improving investigative techniques and enhancing international cooperation.**
- This Convention addresses cybercrime issues such as illegal access, data interference, and online fraud, among others.
- The Budapest Convention provides a legal framework that encourages member countries to adopt consistent cybercrime laws, allowing them to work together more effectively when investigating and prosecuting cybercriminals who operate across borders.
- It facilitates mutual legal assistance between countries, which is essential in dealing with cybercrime in a globally connected world.
- **India is not a signatory to the Budapest Convention,** citing concerns about data-sharing provisions impacting its sovereignty.

**Thus, option (b) is the correct answer.**

**13.** *(b)* 1, 2 and 3 only

- **Statement 1 is correct:** The Digital Personal Data Protection Act 2023 grants data principals (individuals to whom the data belongs) the **right to access their personal data** held by data fiduciaries (organisations collecting and processing the data).
- **Statement 2 is correct:** Data principals also have the **right to seek correction** of inaccurate or incomplete personal data, ensuring that the data held about them is accurate and up-to-date.
- **Statement 3 is correct:** Data principals can request the **deletion of personal data** under certain conditions, allowing individuals more control over their personal information.
- **Statement 4 is incorrect:** The Act does not explicitly provide a **right to compensation** for data breaches; however, it outlines penalties for data fiduciaries in case of non-compliance or breach of data security.

**Thus, statements 1, 2 and 3 are correct, making the answer (b) 1, 2 and 3 only.**

**14.** *(b)* 1, 3 and 4 only

- **Statement 1 is correct:** The Act provides data principals (individuals whose data is being collected) the right to access and correct their personal data, ensuring greater control over their information.
- **Statement 2 is incorrect:** The processing of children's data is not completely prohibited but is subject to specific safeguards to ensure it is not harmful to their rights and well-being.
- **Statement 3 is correct:** Consent managers, entities facilitating the data principal's consent, must register with the Data Protection Board of India to operate legally.

- **Statement 4 is correct:** Data fiduciaries are mandated to inform data principals about the purpose of data processing, ensuring transparency and accountability in handling personal data.

**Thus, the correct answer is (b) 1, 3 and 4 only.**

**15.** *(b)* 1, 2 and 3 only

- **Statement 1 is correct:** Data fiduciaries are required to implement robust security measures to ensure the protection of personal data and prevent unauthorised access or breaches.
- **Statement 2 is correct:** Significant Data Fiduciaries, as identified based on factors like the volume of data processed and its sensitivity, must appoint a Data Protection Officer to oversee compliance with the Act.
- **Statement 3 is correct:** Explicit consent from the data principal is mandatory for processing sensitive personal data, such as financial or health information.
- **Statement 4 is incorrect:** The Digital Personal Data Protection Act, 2023, **provides for the transfer of personal data outside India only to countries designated by the Indian government.** These countries must meet the prescribed adequacy standards to ensure that the data enjoys the same level of protection as in India. This regulation strikes a balance between data localisation and cross-border data sharing.

**Thus, the correct answer is (b) 1, 2 and 3 only.**

**16.** *(b)* The mandate to store and process certain categories of data within the borders of the country where it is generated.

Data localisation refers to the legal requirement for businesses and entities to store and process specific categories of data within the territorial boundaries of the country where it is generated. This regulation is aimed at ensuring national security, protecting citizens' privacy, and enhancing law enforcement access.

**Thus, option (b) is the correct answer.**

**17.** *(b)* Sensitive personal data and critical personal data

Data localisation laws in India, including regulations under the Reserve Bank of India (RBI) and sectoral guidelines, require sensitive personal data (such as health or financial data) and critical personal data to be stored and processed within the country. This helps safeguard national security and protect individual privacy.

**Thus, option (b) is the correct answer.**

**18.** *(c)* Only three

- **Pair 1 is correct: AM Radio operates in the 535 to 1705 kHz frequency range,** which is typically used for amplitude modulation broadcasting, providing longer-range signals with lower fidelity than FM.
- **Pair 2 is correct: FM Radio operates within 88 to 108 MHz, allowing for frequency modulation,** which provides higher-quality audio signals but with a more limited range compared to AM.
- **Pair 3 is correct: Bluetooth operates in the 2.4 to 2.485 GHz range,** which is within the Industrial, Scientific and Medical (ISM) band, allowing for short-range wireless communication between devices.
- **Pair 4 is incorrect: Wi-Fi operates in 2.4 GHz and 5 GHz bands,** not 7 to 10 GHz. The 2.4 GHz band offers wider coverage but is more prone to interference, while the 5 GHz band provides faster speeds over shorter distances.

**Thus, three pairs are correct, making the answer (c) Only three.**

**19.** *(a)* 2 - 1 - 4 - 3

To arrange electromagnetic waves in **increasing order of wavelength,** we start with waves that have the **shortest wavelength** and progress to those with the **longest wavelength:**

- **X-rays** have very short wavelengths, typically shorter than ultraviolet waves.
- **Ultraviolet** waves have a shorter wavelength than visible light but are longer than X-rays.
- **Infrared** waves are longer than ultraviolet but shorter than radio waves.
- **Radio Waves** have the longest wavelength in the electromagnetic spectrum.

**Therefore, the order of increasing wavelength is X-rays < Ultraviolet < Infrared < Radio Waves, making the answer** (a) **2 - 1 - 4 - 3.**

**20.** *(c)* Only three

- **Statement 1 is correct: X-rays** have high energy and the ability to penetrate soft tissues, making them useful for **medical imaging** to view bones and other internal structures.
- **Statement 2 is correct: Radio waves** have low frequencies and long wavelengths, making them ideal for **broadcasting and communication**, including radio, television, and mobile networks.
- **Statement 3 is correct: Ultraviolet (UV) rays** have sufficient energy to **sterilise and disinfect** surfaces by killing bacteria and viruses. They are often used in water purification systems and sterilisation equipment.
- **Statement 4 is incorrect: Gamma rays** are not used in microwave ovens. Microwave ovens operate using microwaves, which are specifically chosen for their ability to excite water molecules and generate heat efficiently. Gamma rays are much higher in energy and are not suitable for cooking.

**Thus, three statements are correct, making the answer** (c) **Only three.**

**21.** *(b)* Only two

- **Statement 1 is incorrect:** In India, spectrum auctions are conducted by the **Department of Telecommunications (DoT)**, which operates under the Ministry of Communications, not the Ministry of Electronics and Information Technology (MeitY).
- **Statement 2 is correct:** The Government of India allows successful bidders to pay for spectrum in **installments** over a specified period, easing the financial burden on telecom companies and encouraging more participation in the auction process.
- **Statement 3 is correct:** Through spectrum auctions, telecom companies acquire rights to **specific frequency bands** for a **defined period**, typically 20 years. This period gives companies the stability to plan their services and infrastructure investments.

**Thus, two statements are correct, making the answer (b) Only two.**

**22.** *(c)* All three

- **Statement 1 is correct:** Lower frequencies have greater coverage and penetrate buildings effectively, which is beneficial in areas with many obstacles.
- **Statement 2 is correct:** Higher frequencies, such as millimeter waves, support high data rates but have a limited range and struggle with obstacles.
- **Statement 3 is correct:** Mid-band frequencies are often used in 4G and 5G networks because they offer a compromise between coverage and data speed, making them versatile.

**Therefore, all three statements are correct, making the answer (c) All three.**

**23.** *(d)* Red

The **visible spectrum** is the portion of the electromagnetic spectrum that is visible to the human eye, typically ranging from wavelengths of approximately **400 nm (violet) to 700 nm (red).** Different colors correspond to different wavelengths within this range:

- **Violet** has the shortest wavelength (around 400 nm) and is at the high-energy end of the visible spectrum.
- **Blue** and **Green** have wavelengths in the middle range of the spectrum (roughly 450-570 nm).
- **Yellow** falls between green and red, with wavelengths around 570-590 nm.
- **Red** has the **longest wavelength** in the visible spectrum, typically around **620-700 nm.**

The **longer the wavelength, the lower the frequency** and energy of the light. Thus, red light, having the longest wavelength in the visible spectrum, is associated with lower energy than colors like blue and violet, which have shorter wavelengths and higher energy. Red's longer wavelength is also why it is less prone to scattering and can be seen from a greater distance, which is why it's used in stop signs and other signaling.

**Therefore, the correct answer is (d) Red.**

**24.** *(b)* Only two

- **Statement 1 is correct: Blue light** has a **shorter wavelength** than **green light**, and it falls closer to the violet end of the spectrum (around 450 nm).
- **Statement 2 is incorrect: Yellow light** actually has a **shorter wavelength** than **red light**. Yellow is around 570-590 nm, while red is 620-700 nm.
- **Statement 3 is correct: Red light** is indeed associated with the **lowest energy** in the visible spectrum, as it has the longest wavelength and lowest frequency among visible colors.

**Thus, only two statements are correct, making the answer (b) Only two.**

**25.** *(c)* Only two

- **Medical Imaging:** Optical fibers are widely used in **medical imaging** tools like **endoscopy**, where flexible fibers transmit light and images within the human body for diagnosis.
- **High-Speed Internet:** Optical fibers provide the infrastructure for **high-speed internet and data transmission** due to their ability to transmit large amounts of data with minimal signal loss.
- **Electrical Power Distribution:** Optical fibers are not used for **electrical power distribution** as they transmit data through light, not electrical currents.
- **Telecommunication Networks:** Optical fibers are integral to **telecommunication networks** because of their high bandwidth and long-distance data transmission capabilities.

**Thus, three applications are correct, making the answer (c) Only three.**

**26.** *(a)* Only one

- **Statement 1 is correct:** Total internal reflection occurs when the angle of refraction reaches **90 degrees**. At this point, the refracted ray travels along the boundary between the two media, and any angle of incidence greater than this critical angle will result in total internal reflection.
- **Statement 2 is incorrect:** Total internal reflection requires light to travel from a **denser medium to a less dense medium** (e.g., from water to air), not the other way around.
- **Statement 3 is incorrect:** Total internal reflection depends on the angle of incidence and the refractive indices of the two media, not necessarily a high refractive index in a single material. However, materials with high refractive indices (like diamond) tend to exhibit TIR at lower critical angles, making TIR more noticeable in these materials.

**Thus, only one statement is correct, making the answer (a) Only one.**

**27.** *(b)* The complete reflection of light back into a denser medium when it strikes the interface at an angle greater than the critical angle.

Total Internal Reflection occurs when light traveling from a **denser medium to a rarer medium strikes the interface at an angle greater than the critical angle.** In this scenario, instead of refracting into the second medium, the light is completely reflected back into the denser medium. **This phenomenon is commonly observed in optical fibers and diamond cutting.**

**Thus, option (b) is the correct answer.**

**28.** *(b)* Only two

- **Statement 1 is correct:** Binoculars use Total Internal Reflection in prisms to reduce the size of the device while enhancing image clarity.
- **Statement 2 is correct:** Periscopes used in submarines utilise Total Internal Reflection for bending light at right angles, allowing users to see objects above the surface.
- **Statement 3 is incorrect:** Rainbows are caused by refraction, dispersion and reflection of light in water droplets, not Total Internal Reflection.

- **Statement 4 is incorrect:** Mirrors in solar panels do not involve Total Internal Reflection; they rely on standard reflection principles.

**Thus, the correct answer is (b) Only two.**

***29.*** *(a)* 1, 2 and 4 only

- **Statement 1 is correct:** 5G is the fifth-generation wireless technology for broadband cellular networks, offering high-speed internet and low latency.
- **Statement 2 is correct:** NFC is a wireless communication technology used for short-range communication, such as mobile payments and access cards.
- **Statement 3 is incorrect: Optical Fiber is a wired communication medium** that transmits data using light, not a wireless technology.
- **Statement 4 is correct: LoRa is a wireless communication technology** designed for long-range, low-power IoT applications, such as smart agriculture and industrial monitoring.

**Thus, option (a) is the correct answer.**

***30.*** *(a)* Unauthorised access to a Bluetooth-enabled device to retrieve data

**Blue Snarfing** is a form of **Bluetooth attack** where an unauthorised person accesses a Bluetooth-enabled device, such as a smartphone or laptop, to retrieve sensitive data like contacts, messages, or files. This is done without the device owner's knowledge or consent, often exploiting security weaknesses in the device's Bluetooth connection. Blue Snarfing can lead to significant privacy breaches and is considered a serious security threat.

**Thus, the correct answer is (a).**

***31.*** *(a)* 1 and 2 only

- **Statement 1 is correct:** FSO provides **high-speed data transmission** rates that can be comparable to those of fiber-optic networks, making it suitable for applications where high bandwidth is required.
- **Statement 2 is correct: FSO systems** are typically faster and more convenient to deploy than traditional wired systems, as they do not require digging trenches or laying cables. This makes FSO a cost-effective and flexible solution for establishing temporary or rapidly deployed communication links.
- **Statement 3 is incorrect: FSO technology is vulnerable to environmental factors like fog, rain and snow,** which can interfere with the transmission of light signals. Adverse weather conditions can significantly reduce signal quality and cause data transmission interruptions.

**Thus, statements 1 and 2 are correct, making the answer (a) 1 and 2 only.**

***32.*** *(b)* Only two

- **Statement 1 is correct: Wi-Fi** uses **radio waves** for transmitting data wirelessly, while Li-Fi relies on visible light, typically from LEDs, for data transmission.
- **Statement 2 is correct:** Wi-Fi signals can pass through walls, providing connectivity in multiple rooms. In contrast, **Li-Fi requires line-of-sight** as visible light cannot penetrate solid objects like walls.
- **Statement 3 is incorrect: Li-Fi does not perform well in outdoor environments with direct sunlight,** as ambient light can interfere with data signals. Wi-Fi, on the other hand, is not affected by sunlight as it uses radio waves.

**Thus, two statements are correct, making the answer (b) Only two.**

***33.*** *(a)* 1 and 2 only

- **Statement 1 is correct: Li-Fi (Light Fidelity)** technology uses **visible light** to transmit data. Light-emitting diodes (LEDs) are commonly used in Li-Fi setups to send data by modulating the light intensity, which is then detected by a receiver.
- **Statement 2 is correct: Li-Fi is capable of extremely high data transmission speeds,** potentially surpassing traditional Wi-Fi speeds. This is because visible light has a broader spectrum than radio waves, enabling faster data transmission.
- **Statement 3 is incorrect:** Unlike Wi-Fi, **Li-Fi cannot operate through walls.** Since it relies on visible light, which cannot penetrate solid objects, Li-Fi's range is limited to

line-of-sight areas where the light can directly reach the receiver.

**Thus, statements 1 and 2 are correct, making the answer (a) 1 and 2 only.**

***34.*** *(a)* 1 and 2 only

- **Statement 1 is correct: WiMAX** has a **wide coverage area** and can provide internet access over long distances, requiring fewer base stations than Wi-Fi. This makes it cost-effective and practical for deployment in sparsely populated rural areas.
- **Statement 2 is correct: WiMAX** offers **high-speed internet connectivity over long distances**, making it ideal for rural and remote locations where traditional wired broadband infrastructure may not be feasible.
- **Statement 3 is incorrect:** While WiMAX can be reliable, it can still experience **interference from environmental factors** such as heavy rain or obstacles. These factors can impact signal quality, especially over long distances.

**Thus, statements 1 and 2 are correct, making the answer (a) 1 and 2 only.**

***35.*** *(c)* Only three

- **Option 1 is correct:** Public transport card readers use NFC to validate fare payments through contactless smart cards..
- **Option 2 is correct:** Smartphones commonly support NFC for functions such as mobile payments, data sharing and access control.
- **Option 3 is correct:** Fitness trackers often use NFC for syncing data with smartphones or enabling payments.
- **Option 4 is incorrect:** Microwave ovens are not NFC-enabled as they rely on traditional electronic controls rather than wireless communication.

**Thus, option (c) is the correct answer.**

***36.*** *(a)* 1 and 3 only.

- **Option 1 (Wi-Fi Direct)** enables device-to-device communication over short distances without the need for a router, making it suitable for tasks like file sharing.
- **Option 2 (Cellular LTE)** is a long-range communication technology used in cellular networks, supporting communication over distances far beyond typical short-range technologies.
- **Option 3 (Bluetooth Low Energy)** is designed for short-range communication with low power consumption, commonly used in wearables and IoT devices.

**Thus, the correct answer is (a) 1 and 3 only.**

***37.*** *(d)* 1, 2 and 3

- **Statement 1 is correct:** FastTag utilises **Radio Frequency Identification (RFID)** technology to enable automatic toll collection. This allows vehicles to pass through toll plazas without stopping, as the toll is deducted directly from the linked account. This technology ensures convenience and reduces congestion at toll booths.
- **Statement 2 is correct:** FastTag supports **interoperability**, meaning it can be used across all **national highways** and several **state highways**. This allows seamless toll payment regardless of the highway being used, thus facilitating uninterrupted travel for users.
- **Statement 3 is correct:** The toll revenue collected through the FastTag system is directly linked to the **National Highways Authority of India (NHAI)**, which is responsible for managing and maintaining the infrastructure of national highways.

**Thus, the correct answer is (d) 1, 2 and 3.**

***38.*** *(b)* A wireless communication technology that utilises unused spectrum in the TV frequency bands for internet access.

- **White Space Wi-Fi** refers to the use of **unused spectrum** in the TV broadcasting frequency bands (usually between **50 MHz and 700 MHz**) for wireless internet communication.
- This technology enables **long-range and low-cost internet connectivity**, particularly in **rural or remote areas** where traditional internet infrastructure is not feasible.
- By utilising TV white spaces, this technology minimises interference and provides a robust connection for underserved regions.

**Thus, option (b) is the correct answer.**

**39.** *(b)* 1 and 3 only

- **Statement 1 is correct:** Space-based internet systems, such as those provided by Starlink and OneWeb, significantly enhance **internet access in remote and rural regions** where terrestrial infrastructure like fiber-optic cables or cellular towers is not feasible or economically viable. This has been a key driver behind deploying satellite constellations.
- **Statement 2 is incorrect:** While space-based systems can offer high data speeds, they do not consistently outperform **terrestrial fiber networks** in terms of data transfer rates, especially in densely populated or urban regions with robust terrestrial infrastructure.
- **Statement 3 is correct:** Space-based internet is inherently **resilient against natural disasters** such as earthquakes, floods, or hurricanes that could damage ground-based networks. This makes it particularly advantageous for disaster-prone areas.
- **Statement 4 is incorrect:** Space-based internet systems, particularly those relying on satellites in Medium Earth Orbit (MEO) or Geostationary Earth Orbit (GEO), cannot completely eliminate **latency issues** due to the physical distances signals must travel. However, Low Earth Orbit (LEO) systems, such as Starlink, reduce latency significantly compared to traditional satellite systems but still do not achieve zero latency.

**Thus, statements 1 and 3 are correct, making option (b) the right answer.**

**40.** *(b)* 1, 2 and 4 only

- **Starlink:** A satellite internet constellation project by SpaceX aimed at providing high-speed internet globally, especially in remote areas.
- **OneWeb:** A UK-based initiative to build a global satellite network for internet connectivity.
- **Google Fiber:** It is a terrestrial fiber-optic internet service, not space-based.
- **Project Kuiper:** Amazon's venture into building a satellite constellation to deliver broadband internet worldwide.

**Thus, the correct answer is (b) 1, 2 and 4 only.**

**41.** *(a)* 1 and 2 only

- **Statement 1 is correct:** e-SIM is directly embedded into the device during manufacturing. It does not require a physical SIM card, making it more convenient and compact for modern devices.
- **Statement 2 is correct:** e-SIM allows users to switch between different network operators remotely through software updates, making it highly flexible and user-friendly.
- **Statement 3 is incorrect:** e-SIM is not limited to smartphones; it is also widely used in IoT devices like smartwatches, tablets, and connected cars.

**Thus, the correct answer is (a) 1 and 2 only.**

**42.** *(b)* Only two

- **Statement 1 is correct: LTE (Long-Term Evolution)** is primarily a data transmission technology that supports high-speed internet. **By itself, LTE does not inherently support voice calls**; it was designed **mainly for data services.**
- **Statement 2 is correct: VoLTE (Voice over LTE)** allows voice calls to be transmitted over an LTE network by using IP-based voice protocols. This enables **high-quality voice calls on the LTE network without switching to a separate network for voice.**
- **Statement 3 is incorrect: VoLTE does not require a Wi-Fi connection.** VoLTE works over the LTE network, not Wi-Fi, allowing users to make voice calls using the cellular LTE infrastructure without additional Wi-Fi requirements.

**Thus, two statements are correct, making the answer (b) Only two.**

**43.** *(c)* Only three

- **Pair 1 is correct:** 2G introduced basic mobile internet browsing, SMS services, and voice calls, marking the transition from analog to digital cellular networks.
- **Pair 2 is correct:** 3G significantly enhanced mobile internet speeds and enabled video calls, supporting applications like high-speed internet browsing.

- **Pair 3 is correct:** 4G brought higher data rates and supported IP-based services, including VoLTE for voice calls, improving both voice and data quality.
- **Pair 4 is incorrect:** 5G does not focus solely on voice and text; it is designed to support ultra-fast data rates, low latency, and a massive number of connected devices, enabling technologies like IoT and real-time applications.

**Thus, only three pairs are correctly matched.**

**44.** *(a)* 1 and 2 only

- **Statement 1 is correct: 5G networks** deliver high-speed internet with low latency, suitable for applications like real-time gaming and autonomous driving. **6G networks,** currently under research, are expected to achieve even higher speeds and **ultra-low latency,** enabling advanced applications in areas like immersive virtual reality and real-time remote surgery.
- **Statement 2 is correct:** 5G technology uses frequencies in the **sub-6 GHz and millimeter-wave bands** (24 GHz and above). **6G networks** are anticipated to operate in the **terahertz (THz) spectrum,** enabling much higher data rates and connectivity speeds.
- **Statement 3 is incorrect: 6G is still in the research and development phase** and is not yet available for commercial use. It is expected to be rolled out around 2030, after further development and standardisation.

**Thus, statements 1 and 2 are correct, making the answer (a) 1 and 2 only.**

**45.** *(a)* ICANN is responsible for the allocation of IP addresses and management of domain names globally.

- **Option (a) is correct:** ICANN oversees the global coordination of the internet's unique identifiers, including domain names and IP addresses, ensuring the stable and secure operation of the Domain Name System (DNS).
- **Option (b) is incorrect:** ICANN does not enforce cybercrime laws or regulate online fraud. These functions fall under the jurisdiction of national governments and international law enforcement agencies.
- **Option (c) is incorrect:** ICANN does not directly govern the development of internet protocols; this is the responsibility of organisations like the Internet Engineering Task Force (IETF).
- **Option (d) is incorrect:** ICANN does not regulate internet content or access to websites; it focuses solely on technical and operational aspects of the internet infrastructure.

**Thus, the correct answer is (a).**

**46.** *(a)* 1 and 2 only

- **Statement 1 is correct:** IPv4 uses a 32-bit address format, allowing approximately 4.3 billion unique addresses. IPv6, with its 128-bit address format, supports a vastly larger address space.
- **Statement 2 is correct:** IPv6 offers better routing efficiency due to simplified headers and enhanced Quality of Service (QoS) features, making it suitable for modern internet requirements.
- **Statement 3 is incorrect:** IPv6 provides a virtually unlimited address pool but not 'unlimited.' While it significantly expands the address capacity compared to IPv4, it still operates within finite bounds.

**Thus, the correct answer is (a) 1 and 2 only.**

**47.** *(a)* 1 and 2 only

- **Statement 1 is correct:** BharatNet is a flagship project of the Government of India to provide high-speed broadband connectivity to all gram panchayats, bridging the digital divide in rural areas.
- **Statement 2 is correct:** BharatNet primarily relies on optical fiber cables to ensure high-speed and reliable internet connectivity across the country.
- **Statement 3 is incorrect:** The project is implemented by a combination of public and private sector entities, with significant involvement of government agencies like Bharat Broadband Network Limited (BBNL).

**Thus, the correct answer is (a) 1 and 2 only.**

**48.** *(a)* 1 and 2 only

- **Pair 1 is correct:** The **Deep Web** includes all content on the internet that is **not indexed by** traditional search engines, meaning it **cannot be accessed through a simple Google search.** This includes academic databases, medical records, private websites and subscription-based content that requires login credentials.

- **Pair 2 is correct:** The **Dark Web** is a part of the Deep Web but requires **specific software, like Tor or I2P,** to access. It **contains anonymous websites that are hidden from the public,** often hosting forums, marketplaces, and sites that prioritise privacy or, in some cases, illegal content.
- **Pair 3 is incorrect: Dark Net** refers to a network overlay that is **only accessible through specific software like Tor, not through regular search engines.** It is often associated with hidden services that prioritise user anonymity and privacy. It is distinct from the regular internet, where legitimate sites are indexed and accessible via search engines.

**Thus, pairs 1 and 2 are correctly matched, making the answer (a) 1 and 2 only.**

***49.*** *(b)* 1, 3 and 4 only

- **Pair 1 is correct: Web 2.0** is characterised by **dynamic content and social interaction,** enabling users to create and interact with content in real-time, particularly on social media platforms and collaborative sites.
- **Pair 2 is incorrect: Smart and connected devices** are more aligned with **Web 4.0,** which integrates the Internet of Things (IoT), allowing interconnected devices to communicate and share data seamlessly.
- **Pair 3 is correct: Web 4.0** is driven by **personalised, AI-driven experiences** that adapt to individual preferences and make use of smart technologies and predictive analytics to provide more customised interactions.
- **Pair 4 is correct:** Web 5.0 envisions a **virtual, immersive and emotion-aware internet,** where advancements in technology make it possible for the web to respond to users' emotional states and provide fully immersive experiences.

**Thus, the correct answer is (b) 1, 3 and 4 only.**

***50.*** *(b)* Creating a highly immersive, emotion-sensitive internet experience

**Web 5.0** is anticipated to be a groundbreaking evolution of the internet, focusing on creating an **emotion-sensitive and immersive online experience.** Unlike previous web generations, Web 5.0 aims to go beyond traditional interactions by incorporating **advanced AI, Augmented Reality (AR), Virtual Reality (VR), and sensory technologies.** These technologies will allow the web to respond to users' emotions, behaviours and sensory inputs, making online experiences more personalised and interactive.

**Thus, option (b) is the correct answer.**

***51.*** *(a)* 1 and 2 only

- **Statement 1 is correct: BharatNet facilitates access to online educational resources and healthcare services** by providing high-speed internet in rural areas, enabling remote learning, telemedicine and other essential services for rural communities.
- **Statement 2 is correct:** BharatNet's connectivity helps rural communities participate in **e-commerce and digital entrepreneurship,** providing new economic opportunities and reducing geographic limitations by connecting rural areas to larger markets.
- **Statement 3 is incorrect:** BharatNet does not provide free fiber optic connections to individual households. Instead, it focuses on connecting gram panchayats and local community centers, which can then extend connectivity to residents through Wi-Fi or other distribution methods, often with associated costs.

**Thus, the correct answer is (a) 1 and 2 only.**

***52.*** *(a)* Internet of Things (IoT)

- **Option (a) is correct:** The scenario describes IoT, where sensors collect data from the physical environment (soil) and transmit it over the internet to automate actions like irrigation, demonstrating the essence of IoT technology in agriculture.

- **Option (b) is incorrect:** While Big Data Analytics could be applied to analyse collected data, it is not the technology facilitating the connection and automation of sensors and devices.
- **Option (c) is incorrect:** Cloud Computing may provide a platform for data storage or processing, but it is not the primary concept enabling sensor-based automation.
- **Option (d) is incorrect:** Machine Learning could analyse data patterns to improve decision-making but is not directly responsible for the device interconnectivity described in the scenario.

**Thus, the correct answer is (a) Internet of Things (IoT).**

**53.** *(b)* Only two

- **Statement 1 is correct: IoT devices can operate independently** once set up. They communicate autonomously with each other, often using sensors and real-time data processing to perform tasks without needing constant human input.
- **Statement 2 is incorrect:** IoT is not limited to mobile phones; it encompasses a wide range of devices like **wearables, home appliances, industrial equipment, medical devices** and even vehicles. IoT networks include any internet-connected device capable of collecting and sharing data.
- **Statement 3 is correct: IoT enables automation** by connecting smart devices, allowing for the automated performance of routine tasks. For instance, a smart thermostat can automatically adjust the temperature based on user preferences and real-time conditions, improving efficiency and convenience.

**Thus, two statements are correct, making the answer (b) Only two.**

**54.** *(b)* A low-power, wide-area network (LPWAN) technology designed for IoT devices with limited data needs.

**Narrowband IoT (NB-IoT)** is designed for IoT devices that transmit small amounts of data at low power over long distances. This LPWAN technology is ideal for use cases such as smart metering, agriculture and logistics, where only intermittent, low-data transmissions are needed.

**Thus, option (b) is the correct answer.**

**55.** *(a)* Net Neutrality mandates that internet service providers (ISPs) treat all internet traffic equally without favouring or blocking specific websites or applications.

**Net neutrality** is a principle that ensures **all internet data is treated equally**, regardless of its content, source or destination. Under net neutrality, **Internet Service Providers (ISPs) cannot block, slow down, or prioritise specific content or websites** over others. This principle aims to maintain an open and fair internet, where users have **equal access to all content** without interference from ISPs.

**Thus, option (a) is the correct answer.**

**56.** *(b)* Consumers can access all internet content equally, and businesses are prohibited from paying ISPs for faster delivery of their content.

- **Option (b) is correct:** TRAI's Net Neutrality rules ensure that consumers have equal access to all internet content without discrimination and businesses are prohibited from engaging in paid prioritisation to gain an unfair advantage.
- **Option (a) is incorrect:** Businesses are not allowed to pay for faster access; this would violate Net Neutrality principles.
- **Option (c) is incorrect:** Consumers are not required to pay additional fees for specific services; the rules aim to provide an open internet to everyone.
- **Option (d) is incorrect:** ISPs cannot restrict user access to specific platforms or enforce such guidelines on businesses under TRAI's Net Neutrality framework.

**Thus, the correct answer is (b).**

**57.** *(a)* Terabyte, Petabyte, Zettabyte, Yottabyte

The correct ascending order of data storage units is based on their sizes. Starting from the smallest to the largest:

- **Terabyte (TB):** Equal to 1012 bytes.
- **Petabyte (PB):** Equal to 1015 bytes.
- **Zettabyte (ZB):** Equal to 1021 bytes.
- **Yottabyte (YB):** Equal to 1024 bytes.

**Thus, option (a) is the correct answer.**

**58.** *(b)* A malicious software disguised as legitimate software to deceive users

A **Trojan Horse** in computer security is a **type of malware** that is **disguised as legitimate software** to deceive users into installing it on their systems. Unlike viruses or worms, Trojans do not replicate themselves. Instead, they rely on users to unknowingly install them, often by disguising themselves as trustworthy applications or files. Once installed, a Trojan can perform malicious activities like stealing data, creating backdoors, or giving remote control of the computer to attackers.

**Thus, option (b) is the correct answer.**

**59.** *(b)* 1, 3 and 4 only

- **Pair 1 is correct: Spyware** is malicious software that operates in the background to collect information about a user's activity, such as browsing habits, passwords and other sensitive information, without the user's knowledge.
- **Pair 2 is incorrect:** A **keylogger** is a type of spyware that records keystrokes made on a device, rather than encrypting them. This can be used to capture sensitive data like passwords and credit card numbers.
- **Pair 3 is correct: Phishing** is a social engineering technique where attackers create **fake websites or emails** that appear legitimate, tricking users into revealing sensitive information such as passwords or financial details.
- **Pair 4 is correct: Malware** is a broad term that encompasses any **malicious software** designed to harm, exploit, or otherwise compromise a device, system, or network. It includes viruses, spyware, ransomware and more.

**Thus, pairs 1, 3 and 4 are correctly matched, making the answer (b) 1, 3 and 4 only.**

**60.** *(a)* To restrict potentially harmful programs from affecting the rest of the system

**Sandboxing** is a security practice that involves running programs or files in a **controlled, isolated environment** to restrict their access to the main system. This isolation allows security professionals to **test and analyse potentially harmful software** without risking the integrity or security of the main operating system. Sandboxing is especially useful for examining unknown or suspicious files, as it can contain any malicious actions within the sandbox environment.

**Thus, option (a) is the correct answer.**

**61.** *(a)* 1 only

- **Statement 1 is correct: Deepfake technology** uses **Artificial Intelligence (AI)**, particularly **machine learning and neural networks,** to manipulate or generate realistic images, videos and audio that appear authentic but are, in fact, fake. Techniques like Generative Adversarial Networks (GANs) are often used to achieve this.
- **Statement 2 is incorrect:** Deepfakes are generally not used in cybersecurity to enhance data protection. Instead, they are primarily used in entertainment, media, and, unfortunately, in some cases, for malicious purposes like misinformation, identity theft, and online harassment.
- The **ethical concerns** surrounding deepfakes are significant, as they can be easily misused for **spreading misinformation**, creating fake news, or harassing individuals by placing them in fabricated videos. This misuse poses serious risks to privacy, reputation and trust in media.

**Thus, statement 1 is correct, making the correct answer (a) 1 only.**

**62.** *(b)* To secure cyberspace by protecting critical information infrastructure and promoting a safe digital environment.

- **Option (b) is correct:** The National Cybersecurity Policy, 2013, aims to protect the nation's critical information infrastructure, secure cyberspace from threats, and promote the adoption of robust cybersecurity practices to ensure a safe digital environment for all stakeholders.
- **Option (a) is incorrect:** The policy does not focus on monitoring internet usage of citizens but emphasises the protection of digital assets.
- **Option (c) is incorrect:** While sharing sensitive information responsibly is important, the policy does not specifically target social media platforms.

- **Option (d) is incorrect:** The policy encourages secure data practices but does not mandate localised data storage for surveillance.

**Thus, the correct answer is (b).**

**63.** *(b)* To detect and clean infected systems of individuals and organisations, ensuring cybersecurity.

- **Option (b) is correct:** Cyber Swachhta Kendra is a government initiative aimed at identifying and removing malware and botnets from infected devices, promoting cybersecurity for individuals and organisations.
- **Option (a) is incorrect:** The center does not monitor online activities but focuses on system cleaning and awareness.
- **Option (c) is incorrect:** Its objective is defensive in nature, focusing on detection and mitigation of threats rather than developing offensive measures.
- **Option (d) is incorrect:** It does not regulate internet access but provides tools and guidelines for preventing malware infections.

**Thus, the correct answer is (b).**

**64.** *(a)* To create awareness about cyber hygiene and provide tools to secure digital devices against malware.

- **Option (a) is correct:** The Cyber Swachhta Bharat initiative focuses on promoting cybersecurity awareness among citizens and organisations while offering tools like antivirus software to protect devices from malware.
- **Option (b) is incorrect:** The initiative emphasises education and prevention, not enforcement or penalties.
- **Option (c) is incorrect:** It does not involve tracking internet users or maintaining a centralised database.
- **Option (d) is incorrect:** While it supports cybersecurity measures, the initiative does not focus on developing software for export.

**Thus, the correct answer is (a).**

**65.** *(d)* 1, 2, 3 and 4

- **PARAM 8000:** Developed by the **Centre for Development of Advanced Computing** (C-DAC) in 1991, PARAM 8000 was India's first supercomputer. It marked a significant achievement, demonstrating India's capability in advanced computing.
- **Pratyush:** Pratyush is a High-Performance Computing (HPC) system installed at the **Indian Institute of Tropical Meteorology** (IITM), Pune. It is used for weather forecasting, climate research and atmospheric studies, and it is among the fastest supercomputers in India.
- **SahasraT:** Developed and hosted at the **Indian Institute of Science** (IISc), Bengaluru, SahasraT is one of the leading supercomputers in India, supporting research in science and engineering.
- **Mihir:** Mihir is a powerful supercomputer located at the **National Centre for Medium Range Weather Forecasting** (NCMRWF) in Noida. Like Pratyush, it is used for climate research and weather forecasting.

**Thus, the correct answer is (d) 1, 2, 3 and 4.**

**66.** *(c)* Only three

- **Option 1 is correct:** Weather forecasting involves processing vast amounts of meteorological data, which requires the computational power of supercomputers for accurate predictions.
- **Option 2 is correct:** Genome sequencing involves analysing large datasets of genetic material, a task supercomputers excel at due to their speed and capacity.
- **Option 3 is incorrect:** Video streaming services primarily rely on cloud computing and data centres, not supercomputers.
- **Option 4 is correct:** Space exploration, including simulations of spacecraft and cosmic phenomena, relies on the advanced computational abilities of supercomputers.

**Thus, the correct answer is (c) Only three.**

**67.** *(b)* Only two

- **Statement 1 is correct: Cloud computing** enables users to **access computing resources** like servers, storage and databases remotely over the internet, which allows users to scale their resources based on demand.

- **Statement 2 is correct:** Cloud computing reduces or eliminates the need for **local data storage** and IT infrastructure by providing resources that can be accessed from anywhere with an internet connection. This is especially beneficial for businesses looking to save on hardware and maintenance costs.
- **Statement 3 is incorrect:** Cloud computing is not limited to small-scale applications; it is widely used by **large enterprises** to run complex and large-scale applications, including data analysis, machine learning, and Enterprise Resource Planning (ERP) systems.

**Thus, two statements are correct, making the answer (b) Only two.**

***68.*** *(d)* 1, 2 and 3

- **Pair 1 is correct: Infrastructure as a Service (IaaS)** provides **virtualised computing resources** over the internet, including virtual machines, storage and networking. Users can manage operating systems, storage, and deployed applications but do not manage the underlying physical infrastructure.
- **Pair 2 is correct: Platform as a Service (PaaS)** offers a **platform** that allows users to **develop, run and manage applications** without worrying about the underlying infrastructure. It provides a development environment, databases and other services to streamline the software development process.
- **Pair 3 is correct: Software as a Service (SaaS)** enables users to **access software applications** on a subscription basis via the internet. Users access applications directly through a web browser, without needing to install or maintain the software on their local machines.

**All pairs are correctly matched, making the answer (d) 1, 2 and 3.**

***69.*** *(b)* To process data closer to the data source, reducing latency and bandwidth use.

**Edge Computing** processes data closer to where it's generated, reducing the need to send large amounts of data back to centralised servers. This reduces latency, conserves bandwidth and improves performance for real-time applications such as **IoT devices,** autonomous vehicles, and smart manufacturing.

**Thus, option (b) is the correct answer.**

***70.*** *(b)* Only two

- **Statement 1 is correct:** By processing data locally, Edge Computing reduces the need to send large amounts of data to central servers, lowering transmission costs.
- **Statement 2 is incorrect:** Edge Computing does not replace cloud computing entirely; it complements it by handling immediate processing locally, while cloud computing can still manage larger data storage and non-time-sensitive tasks.
- **Statement 3 is correct:** Edge Computing is particularly useful for real-time applications like autonomous vehicles and IoT, where fast data processing is essential.

**Thus, the correct answer is (b) Only two.**

***71.*** *(d)* Only statement 2 is correct.

- **Statement 1 is incorrect: Quantum entanglement**, a phenomenon in quantum mechanics, creates a link between two particles such that the state of one particle instantaneously influences the state of the other, regardless of distance. However, this **does not allow for instantaneous data transfer** in the traditional sense. Instead, entanglement is used to establish secure communication channels in Quantum Communication, but any actual data transfer still requires classical communication methods, which are limited by the speed of light.
- **Statement 2 is correct:** Quantum Key Distribution (QKD) allows for secure sharing of encryption keys, where any eavesdropping attempt would be detected by changes in the quantum states.

**Thus, only statement 2 is correct so, the correct answer is (d).**

**72.** *(b)* A process where particles become connected, and the state of one instantaneously influences the state of the other, regardless of distance

**Quantum entanglement** is a phenomenon in quantum physics where two or more particles become linked in such a way that the **state of one particle instantly influences the state of the other(s)**, no matter how far apart they are. This behaviour defines classical understanding, as changes in the entangled particles are immediate and seem to violate the limitations of the speed of light.

**Thus, option (b) is the correct answer.**

**73.** *(b)* Only two

- **Statement 1 is correct: Quantum superposition** is a principle in quantum mechanics where a **particle can exist in multiple states simultaneously.** For example, an electron can be in multiple positions or have multiple energy levels at once until it is observed.
- **Statement 2 is incorrect:** Quantum superposition is not exclusive to electrons; it applies to all **quantum particles**, including photons, protons and larger particles under certain conditions. The principle of superposition is fundamental in quantum mechanics, applying broadly to all quantum entities.
- **Statement 3 is correct:** When a quantum particle in superposition is **observed or measured,** its wave function collapses, and the particle settles into a **single state.** This phenomenon is part of what's known as the 'measurement problem' in quantum mechanics, highlighting the effect of observation on quantum states.

**Thus, two statements are correct, making the answer (b) Only two.**

**74.** *(c)* Only three

- **Characteristic 1 is correct:** Fingerprints are widely used for biometric recognition due to their uniqueness and ease of capture.
- **Characteristic 2 is correct:** Voice patterns are used in voice recognition systems for identifying individuals based on unique vocal features.
- **Characteristic 3 is incorrect:** Skin tone is not a reliable or commonly used characteristic for biometric recognition as it lacks sufficient individuality.
- **Characteristic 4 is correct:** Iris patterns are unique and highly reliable, making them a popular choice for biometric systems.

**Thus, the correct answer is (c) Only three.**

**75.** *(d)* 1, 2, 3 and 4

- **Option 1 is correct:** Wearable devices like **fitness trackers and smartwatches are equipped with heart rate sensors that measure heartbeats per minute in real time,** providing valuable insights into cardiovascular health.
- **Option 2 is correct:** Wearables can track sleep patterns by analysing motion and heart rate data, providing insights into sleep stages such as deep sleep, light sleep and REM cycles.
- **Option 3 is correct:** Advanced wearables include SpO2 sensors to monitor blood oxygen levels, an important indicator of respiratory and circulatory health.
- **Option 4 is correct:** Step counting is a standard feature in most wearables, using accelerometers to track the number of steps taken daily, contributing to fitness goals.

**Thus, the correct answer is (d) 1, 2, 3 and 4.**

**76.** *(b)* 1 and 3 only

- **Statement 1 is correct:** End-to-End Encryption protects data from interception by encrypting it during transmission, ensuring only the intended recipient can decrypt it.
- **Statement 2 is incorrect:** Service providers cannot access the content of encrypted messages in E2EE, as the encryption keys are not shared with them.
- **Statement 3 is correct:** In E2EE, encryption keys are stored on user devices, ensuring that only the sender and receiver can access the keys to decrypt the communication.

**Thus, the correct answer is (b) 1 and 3 only.**

**77.** *(b)* 1 and 3 only

- **Statement 1 is correct:** In the **automotive industry**, 3D printing is used to create **custom parts and prototypes**, allowing manufacturers to test designs before mass production. This reduces costs and speeds up the design process. Car manufacturers also use 3D printing for parts like brackets, grills and trim pieces.
- **Statement 2 is incorrect:** While 3D printing initially started with plastics, it has expanded to include a wide range of materials, including **metals**, **ceramics** and even **biocompatible materials** for medical applications. Metal 3D printing, in particular, is essential for aerospace and automotive industries.
- **Statement 3 is correct:** In **education**, 3D printing is used as a hands-on tool to **create models and prototypes** that help students understand complex concepts in subjects like engineering, biology, and design. Schools and universities use 3D printing to make teaching aids, such as anatomical models and architectural prototypes.

**Thus, the correct answer is (b) 1 and 3 only.**

## Past Learning (Answers)

| | | | | | | | | | |
|---|---|---|---|---|---|---|---|---|---|
| **1** (d) | **2** (d) | **3** (b) | **4** (b) | **5** (d) | **6** (d) | **7** (c) | **8** (c) | **9** (c) | **10** (b) |
| **11** (d) | **12** (d) | **13** (c) | **14** (d) | **15** (b) | **16** (a) | **17** (d) | | | |

# CHAPTER 09 Emerging Technologies

## Assessment Round

### Topic 1 : Artificial Intelligence

*1.* With reference to Artificial Intelligence, consider the following statements:

1. Artificial Intelligence aims to create machines that can mimic human cognitive functions.
2. AI is incapable of processing and analysing natural human languages.
3. AI systems do not require any form of human supervision to function.

How many of the above statements is/are correct?

(a) Only one
(b) Only two
(c) All three
(d) None

*2.* Which of the following best describes 'Natural Language Processing' (NLP)?

(a) A field of AI focused on enabling machines to interpret and generate human language.
(b) A subset of AI used exclusively in voice recognition technology.
(c) A programming language specifically designed for AI applications.
(d) A hardware component used in deep learning systems.

*3.* Consider the following pairs of terms and their descriptions:

| | Term | Description |
|---|---|---|
| 1. | Artificial Intelligence | A field that focuses solely on building humanoid robots |
| 2. | Machine Learning | A subset of AI that enables systems to learn and improve from data |
| 3. | Artificial Neural Network | A computational model inspired by the human brain's network of neurons |
| 4. | Deep Learning | A specialised area of Machine Learning involving neural networks with multiple layers |

How many of the above pairs is/are correctly matched?

(a) Only one (b) Only two
(c) Only three (d) All four

*4.* Which of the following best explains the purpose of 'Computer Vision' in AI?

(a) To improve the speed of data processing in AI systems.
(b) To allow machines to identify, analyse and interpret visual data from the world.
(c) To optimise memory usage in AI applications.
(d) To enable AI systems to store large volumes of data.

***5.*** Which of the following applications reflect the present capabilities of AI in effectively performing basic tasks?

1. Automated customer support through chatbots.
2. Autonomous creative writing without human input.
3. Real-time language translation.
4. Understanding and responding to human emotions accurately.
5. Image recognition for medical diagnostics.

Select the correct options:

(a) 1, 3 and 5 only (b) 2, 4 and 5 only
(c) 1, 2 and 4 only (d) 1, 3 and 4 only

***6.*** Consider the following sectors:

1. Agriculture
2. Healthcare
3. Entertainment
4. Transportation

How many of the given above sectors is/are currently leveraging AI for advancements and innovations?

(a) Only one
(b) Only two
(c) Only three
(d) All four

***7.*** Consider the various types of Artificial Intelligence matched with the examples of their applications:

| Type of AI | Example Application |
|---|---|
| 1. Reactive AI | Chess-playing systems like IBM's Deep Blue |
| 2. Limited Memory AI | Autonomous vehicles that analyse past and real-time data |
| 3. Theory of Mind AI | Chatbots that understand and respond to human emotions |
| 4. Self-aware AI | Advanced AI systems that have their own consciousness and self-perception |

How many of the given above pairs is/are correctly matched?

(a) Only one pair (b) Only two pairs
(c) Only three pairs (d) All four pairs

***8.*** With reference to the 'Centre for Artificial Intelligence and Robotics (CAIR)', consider the following statements:

1. It is a research unit under the Ministry of Electronics and Information Technology.
2. Its primary objective is to develop AI and robotics technologies solely for civilian applications.

Which of the above statements is/are correct?

(a) 1 only (b) 2 only
(c) Both 1 and 2 (d) Neither 1 nor 2

***9.*** With reference to the 'India's National Strategy on Artificial Intelligence', consider the following statements:

1. The strategy aims to position India as a global leader in Artificial Intelligence by focusing on inclusive AI growth.
2. National Strategy on AI was developed by NITI Aayog.
3. One of the key pillars of the strategy is to establish a regulatory framework to strictly control AI development and usage.

How many of the given above statements is/are correct?

(a) Only one (b) Only two
(c) All three (d) None

***10.*** Which committee was formed by the Indian government to study and recommend frameworks for Artificial Intelligence and cybersecurity?

(a) Natarajan Committee
(b) V. Kamakoti Committee
(c) Srikrishna Committee
(d) Justice Verma Committee

***11.*** Consider the following:

1. Text generation
2. Image synthesis
3. Data encryption
4. Speech synthesis
5. Database management

How many of the given above is/are valid applications of Generative AI?

(a) Only two (b) Only three
(c) Only four (d) All five

**12.** With reference to the 'Global Partnership on Artificial Intelligence (GPAI)', consider the following statements:
1. It is a multi-stakeholder initiative launched to ensure the responsible use of AI globally.
2. India joined GPAI as a founding member in 2020.
3. It works under the direct governance of the United Nations to regulate AI policies.

Which of the given above statements are correct?
(a) 1 and 2 only (b) 2 and 3 only
(c) 1 and 3 only (d) 1, 2 and 3

**13.** Consider the following AI initiatives in India matched with its description:

| AI Initiative | Description |
|---|---|
| 1. Responsible AI for Youth | Framework to establish a common AI infrastructure for various applictions. |
| 2. AIRAWAT | Government program to train students in AI fundamentals and problem-solving skills. |
| 3. National AI Portal | Dedicated platform for sharing AI-related resources, news, and research in India. |

How many of the above pairs is/are correctly matcehd.
(a) Only one pair (b) Only two pairs
(c) Only three pairs (d) None

## Topic 2 : Extended Reality (XR) Technology

**14.** With reference to the 'Extended Reality (XR)' technologies, consider the following statements:
1. Virtual Reality (VR) requires a head-mounted display to fully immerse the user in a digital environment.
2. Augmented Reality (AR) can only function outdoors and requires GPS.
3. Mixed Reality (MR) can use standard smartphones for full interactivity between physical and digital elements.

How many of the given above statements is/are correct?
(a) Only one (b) Only two
(c) All three (d) None

**15.** Consider the following statements:
1. Snapchat's AR filters allow users to overlay digital effects on real-time videos.
2. Google Earth VR enables users to explore real-world locations in an immersive virtual environment.
3. Microsoft HoloLens is used in industrial training and design, combining real and virtual elements.

How many of the above statements is/are correct?
(a) Only one (b) Only two
(c) All three (d) None

**16.** Consider the following hypothetical scenario:
'Imagine a digital conference hosted in a 3D virtual world where users create avatars to represent themselves. Attendees can explore digital exhibits, participate in workshops, and network with others in real time. Payments for workshops are made using blockchain-based tokens and users can buy virtual goods like digital outfits for their avatars.'
Which concept best explains the technology enabling this experience?
(a) Internet of Things (IoT)
(b) Virtual Reality (VR)
(c) Metaverse
(d) Cloud Computing

**17.** Consider the following scenario:
'A museum introduces an app where visitors point their smartphones at artifacts to view detailed 3D reconstructions, animations explaining their historical significance and interactive elements like virtual models of ancient tools.'
Which technology is powering this experience?
(a) Digital Twin
(b) Augmented Reality
(c) Internet of Things
(d) Blockchain

## Topic 3 : Blockchain Technology

**18.** Which of the following best describes the function of blockchain technology?

(a) A central database that records data for easy modification.

(b) A decentralised ledger that securely records transactions across multiple nodes.

(c) A social media tool designed for sharing and tracking content.

(d) A protocol used only for cryptocurrencies and online payments.

**19.** Which of the following are key components in the structure and design of Blockchain technology?

1. Blocks that contain transaction data and a unique hash of the previous block.
2. Nodes that represent individual computers participating in the network.
3. Immutability which prevents alteration of recorded transactions once they are added to the blockchain.
4. Consensus mechanisms that validate transactions and agree on the blockchain's state.

Select the correct answer from the codes given below:

(a) 1, 2 and 4 only (b) 1, 3 and 4 only
(c) 2 and 3 only (d) 1, 2, 3 and 4

**20.** Which of the following best describes the process of mining in Blockchain technology?

(a) A process where transactions are grouped and validated to create new blocks.

(b) A method for determining consensus without needing any computational power.

(c) A system for encrypting data to prevent unauthorised access.

(d) A technique used to remove outdated data from the blockchain ledger.

**21.** Consider the following statements about the features of 'Blockchain Technology':

1. Blockchain technology provides transparency by allowing all participants to view and verify transactions.
2. Once a transaction is recorded on the blockchain, it can be easily edited or removed.
3. Each record in a blockchain is linked to the previous record, forming a secure chain of blocks.

How many of the given above statements is/are correct?

(a) Only one (b) Only two
(c) All three (d) None

**22.** Which of the following correctly describes the difference between Proof of Stake (PoS) and Proof of Work (PoW)?

(a) PoS relies on computational power, while PoW is based on coin ownership for validating transactions.

(b) PoS selects validators based on stake ownership, whereas PoW uses miners competing to solve complex mathematical problems.

(c) PoW is energy-efficient, while PoS requires substantial energy consumption.

(d) Both PoS and PoW involve staking coins for transaction validation.

**23.** Which of the following best describes a consortium blockchain?

(a) A completely open network where anyone can validate transactions.

(b) A blockchain where multiple organisations jointly govern the network, ensuring partial decentralisation.

(c) A blockchain that is controlled solely by a single private entity for its internal processes.

(d) A blockchain where users need government-issued IDs for participation.

**24.** Consider the following characteristics:

1. Governance is managed by a specific entity.
2. Transactions are visible to all participants in the network.
3. Access is restricted to authorised participants.
4. Data confidentiality is a priority, with only selected participants having access.

How many of the given above characteristics apply to 'Private and Permissioned' blockchains?

(a) Only one
(b) Only two
(c) Only three
(d) All four

**25.** With reference to the cryptocurrencies, consider the following statements:

1. Cryptocurrencies operate on a decentralised system known as blockchain, which records all transactions on multiple computers.
2. Transactions in cryptocurrencies are anonymous and cannot be traced back to any individual.
3. Cryptocurrencies are regulated by central banks worldwide to ensure stability and prevent fraud.

Which of the statements given above is/are correct?

(a) 1 only (b) 1 and 2 only
(c) 2 and 3 only (d) All three

**26.** Consider the following statements about 'Non-Fungible Tokens (NFTs)':

1. NFTs are used to represent unique ownership of digital items, like virtual real estate in online games.
2. These can be exchanged on a one-to-one basis, similar to cryptocurrencies like Bitcoin.
3. These can be traded or transferred across different blockchain networks without any compatibility issues.

Which of the statements above is/are correct?

(a) Only one
(b) Only two
(c) All three
(d) None

**27.** Consider the following statements with respect to the concept of 'Non-Fungibility':

**Statement I:** Non-fungible assets have unique characteristics that distinguish them from other assets, preventing them from being exchanged on an equal basis.

**Statement II:** Real estate is the example of non-fungible assets, as property is distinct in value and attributes.

In the context of given above statements, which of the following is correct?

(a) Both statements are correct, and statement II is the correct explanation of statement I.
(b) Both statements are correct, but statement II is not the correct explanation of statement I.
(c) Only statement I is correct.
(d) Only statement II is correct.

**28.** Which of the following best describes the primary purpose of 'PRESIDIO Principles' in the context of digital ethics and responsibility?

(a) To establish ethical guidelines for responsible data usage and digital interactions, encouraging transparency and user-centricity in digital governance
(b) To enforce strict regulatory measures on digital content and limit users' online freedom
(c) To provide specific technical guidelines on cybersecurity infrastructure for companies
(d) To focus solely on data monetization strategies for tech companies

**29.** Consider the following statements with reference to the regulation of cryptocurrency in India:

1. These are recognised as legal tender by the Reserve Bank of India (RBI).
2. The trading of cryptocurrencies is subject to taxation under the Income Tax Act.
3. Securities and Exchange Board of India (SEBI) currently regulates cryptocurrency trading in India.

How many of the statements given above is/are correct?

(a) Only one
(b) Only two
(c) All three
(d) None

**30.** Which of the following accurately describes the purpose of India's 'National Blockchain Framework (NBF)'?

(a) A government initiative to regulate cryptocurrencies in India and ensure their compliance with national laws.
(b) A framework aimed at standardising blockchain adoption across sectors such as land records, health and education.
(c) A framework designed exclusively to manage cross-border digital transactions.
(d) An initiative for creating private blockchain networks exclusively for government entities.

## Topic 4 : Nanotechnology

**31.** In the context of material science, which one of the following best describes Nanotechnology?
(a) Development of large-scale industrial machines for efficient material processing
(b) Control and manipulation of matter at the nanoscale to create materials with unique properties
(c) Exclusive use of biological materials for healthcare applications
(d) Engineering of lightweight materials only for aerospace applications

**32.** Which one of the following best defines the function of a 'Scanning Tunneling Microscope (STM')?
(a) Detects atomic-level surface features of conductive materials by measuring tunneling currents.
(b) Uses high-energy beams to determine the chemical makeup of samples.
(c) Examines cell structures in biological samples.
(d) Produces images through the reflection of laser light.

**33.** In which of the following fields is nanotechnology widely used to improve existing technology?
1. Water purification and filtration
2. Food packaging and preservation
3. High-speed computing and data storage

Select the correct answer from the codes given below:
(a) 1 and 2 only
(b) 2 and 3 only
(c) 1 and 3 only
(d) 1, 2 and 3

**34.** Consider the following:
1. Drug delivery systems
2. Gene therapy
3. Catalysis in industrial reactions
4. Targeted cancer treatment
5. Solar cell development

How many of the given above are common applications of 'Organic Nanoparticles'?
(a) Only two
(b) Only three
(c) Only four
(d) All five

**35.** Who is credited with coining the term 'nanotechnology'?
(a) Richard Feynman
(b) Norio Taniguchi
(c) Eric Drexler
(d) Sumio Iijima

**36.** With reference to Top-Down and Bottom-Up approaches in nanotechnology, consider the following statements:
1. Top-Down methods generally involve techniques like lithography and milling.
2. Bottom-Up methods are primarily focused on breaking down larger structures into nanoscale components.
3. Top-Down methods are less precise at the atomic level compared to Bottom-Up methods.

How many of the given above statements is/are correct?
(a) Only one (b) Only two
(c) All three (d) None

**37.** Consider the following statements:
1. Aluminium nanoparticles are widely used in rocket fuel.
2. Gold nanoparticles have significant applications in medical diagnostics and targeted drug delivery systems.
3. Silver nanoparticles are utilised primarily for their anti-bacterial properties.
4. Carbon nanotubes exhibit exceptional mechanical strength and electrical conductivity.

Which of the given above statements are correct?
(a) 1 and 4 only
(b) 1, 2 and 3 only
(c) 2, 3 and 4 only
(d) 1, 2, 3 and 4

**38.** Consider the following pairs of carbon allotropes and their primary applications:

| Carbon Allotrope | Primary Application |
|---|---|
| 1. Graphene | High-strength, lightweight composites |
| 2. Fullerene ($C_{60}$) | Drug delivery systems due to its hollow structure |
| 3. Graphite | Conductive material for electronics and batteries |
| 4. Carbon Nanotubes | Enhanced fuel efficiency as additives |

How many of the given above pairs is/are correctly matched?
(a) Only one pair (b) Only two pairs
(c) Only three pairs (d) All four pairs

**39.** Consider the following statements about 'Graphene':
1. It is known for its exceptional electrical conductivity and mechanical strength.
2. It is primarily used as a fuel additive to improve combustion efficiency.
3. Graphene is widely used in medical implants because it is biodegradable.

How many of the given above statements is/are incorrect?
(a) Only one
(b) Only two
(c) All three
(d) None

**40.** With reference to the 'Carbon Nanotubes (CNTs)', consider the following statements:
1. These are cylindrical structures composed entirely of carbon atoms.
2. They are excellent conductors of both electricity and heat.
3. Carbon nanotubes are widely used as fuel additives to increase combustion efficiency.

How many of the given above statements is/are correct?
(a) Only one
(b) Only two
(c) All three
(d) None

**41.** Which of the following statements are correct about 'Buckminsterfullerene (C)'?
1. It has a spherical structure with carbon atoms arranged in a pattern similar to a soccer ball.
2. It is highly reactive in comparison to other carbon allotropes like graphite and diamond.
3. It is known for its superconducting properties at room temperature.
4. It is insoluble in organic solvents such as benzene and toluene.

Select the correct answer from the codes given below:
(a) 1 and 2 only
(b) 1, 2 and 3 only
(c) 2 and 4 only
(d) 1, 2 and 4 only

**42.** Which of the following are common applications or properties of Fullerene?
1. Used in drug delivery systems due to its hollow structure.
2. Acts as a superconductor at specific temperatures.
3. Serves as a lubricant because of its spherical shape.
4. Exclusively used as a fuel additive.

Select the correct answer from the codes given below:
(a) Only one (b) Only two
(c) Only three (d) All four

**43.** In the context of Quantum Dot technology, which one of the following statements best captures its essence?
(a) Quantum Dots are primarily developed to enhance the thermal stability of electronic circuits in high temperatures.
(b) Quantum Dots act as energy storage devices, similar to batteries, due to their high charge retention capabilities.
(c) Quantum Dots are used to emit specific wavelengths of light, improving display colour precision in screens.
(d) Quantum Dots provide electromagnetic shielding in advanced materials used in aerospace.

**44.** In how many of the following fields are quantum dots commonly applied due to their unique optical and electronic properties?
1. Medical imaging
2. Solar cells
3. Conventional incandescent lighting
4. Quantum computing

Select the correct answer using the codes given below:
(a) Only one
(b) Only two
(c) Only three
(d) All four

**45.** Which of the following best describes 'Wet Nanotechnology'?
(a) Nanotechnology that operates solely in dry, vacuum conditions
(b) Nanotechnology involving the manipulation and synthesis of nanoparticles in a liquid environment
(c) Nanotechnology used exclusively in electronics manufacturing
(d) A form of nanotechnology that uses only organic materials

**46.** Match each nanotechnology tool with its description in healthcare applications:

| Nanotechnology Tool | Description |
|---|---|
| 1. Nanochips | Miniaturised diagnostic chips capable of detecting pathogens at the molecular level |
| 2. Nanosponge | Tiny particles designed to absorb and neutralise bacterial toxins in the body |
| 3. Nanoflare | Probes that bind to target mRNA within cells to monitor gene expression changes |
| 4. Nanopores | Structures used to filter specific molecules, aiding in gene sequencing and disease detection |

How many of the given above pairs is/are correctly matched?
(a) Only one pair
(b) Only two pairs
(c) Only three pairs
(d) All four pairs

**47.** Consider the following:
1. Targeted drug delivery in medical treatments
2. Environmental cleanup through pollutant detection and neutralisation
3. Energy storage in high-capacity batteries
4. Minimally invasive surgeries
5. Precision manufacturing at the nanoscale

How many of the given above are common applications of Nano-Robots?
(a) Only two (b) Only three
(c) Only four (d) All five

**48.** Which of the following best describes 'Ecophagy', also known as the 'Grey Goo' scenario?
(a) A process enhancing ecosystems with biodegradable nanotech.
(b) A scenario where self-replicating nanobots consume all biomass.
(c) A method using biological nanobots to recycle organic matter.
(d) An application of nanotechnology in food preservation.

**49.** With reference to the 'Liquid Nano Urea', consider the following statements:
1. It is an innovative nitrogen-based fertilizer that aims to reduce the excessive usage of conventional urea.
2. It is produced by breaking down urea into nanoscale particles, enhancing nutrient efficiency and uptake by plants.
3. It is primarily targeted at replacing chemical fertilizers with organic nutrients.

Which of the given above statements is/are correct?
(a) 1 and 2 only
(b) 2 and 3 only
(c) 1 only
(d) 1, 2 and 3

**50.** Identify the Indian scientist widely regarded as the 'Father of Indian Nanotechnology' for his pioneering contributions to nanoscience and materials research.
(a) Dr. Vikram Sarabhai
(b) Dr. Homi J. Bhabha
(c) Dr. A.P.J. Abdul Kalam
(d) Dr. C.N.R. Rao

## Topic 5 : Robotics

**51.** Consider the following pairs related to Isaac Asimov's Three Laws of Robotics:

| Law of Robotics | Description |
|---|---|
| 1. First Law | A robot may not harm a human being, or through inaction, allow harm to come to a human. |
| 2. Second Law | A robot must obey the orders given by humans, even if these orders conflict with the First Law. |
| 3. Third Law | A robot must protect its own existence as long as it does not interfere with the First or Second Law. |

How many of the given above pairs is/are correctly matched?
(a) Only one pair (b) Only two pairs
(c) All three pairs (d) None

**52.** Robots have a wide range of applications across various fields. Which of the following are primary applications of robotics?
1. Autonomous surgery in healthcare
2. Precision farming in agriculture
3. Underwater exploration
4. Mass production in manufacturing

Select the correct answer from the codes given below:
(a) 1 and 2 only (b) 2, 3 and 4 only
(c) 1, 3 and 4 only (d) 1, 2, 3 and 4

**53.** With reference to the 'Robotic Process Automation (RPA)', consider the following statements:
1. RPA automates repetitive tasks by mimicking human actions on a computer.
2. RPA requires extensive changes to existing IT infrastructure to be implemented.
3. RPA relies on artificial intelligence and machine learning to make complex decisions

How many of the given above statements is/are correct?
(a) Only one (b) Only two
(c) All three (d) None

**54.** With reference to the humanoid robots, consider the following statements:
1. These are designed to resemble human form and motion.
2. These robots can perform complex tasks that require human-like cognition and problem-solving.
3. They are equipped to perform human-like reasoning and decision-making autonomously.

How many of the given above statements is/are correct?
(a) Only one (b) Only two
(c) All three (d) None

**55.** Which of the following is India's first 3-D printed humanoid robot?
(a) Manav (b) Shalu
(c) Vyommitra (d) Rashmi

**56.** Consider the following statements with respect to India's robotics projects:
1. DAKSHA is an automated mobile platform with stair-climbing capabilities, designed to handle Improvised Explosive Devices (IEDs).
2. Vyommitra is a spacefaring humanoid robot developed by ISRO to assist in the Gaganyaan mission.
3. Manav is India's first 3D-printed humanoid robot, equipped with vision and sound processing abilities, enabling it to respond to human commands.

How many of the given above statements is/are correct?
(a) Only one (b) Only two
(c) All three (d) None

**57.** Which of the following best describes the 'e-Yantra programme'?
(a) A project focused solely on creating robotic prototypes for defence applications.
(b) A robotics outreach initiative funded by the Ministry of Education to nurture young engineering talent.
(c) An initiative aimed at setting up robotics labs in educational institutions across India.
(d) A government programme that provides scholarships for students to pursue studies abroad in robotics.

## Topic 6 : Light Technology

**58.** With regard to the properties of light, consider the following statements:
1. Light travels faster in a vacuum than in any other medium.
2. Light can exhibit properties of both waves and particles.
3. Light always moves in straight lines without bending or refracting.

How many of the given above statements is/are correct?
(a) Only one (b) Only two
(c) All three (d) None

**59.** Consider the following pairs related to the properties of light:

| Property | Description |
|---|---|
| 1. Reflection | Light bounces off a surface |
| 2. Refraction | Light changes speed when it enters a new medium |
| 3. Dispersion | Light spreads out into different colours or wavelengths |
| 4. Polarisation | Light intensity increases as it passes through a lens |

How many of the given above pairs is/are correctly matched?
(a) Only one pair (b) Only two pairs
(c) Only three pairs (d) All four pairs

**60.** Consider the following examples:
1. Light Emitting Diodes (LEDs)
2. Lasers
3. Fiber Optic Cables
4. Cathode Ray Tubes (CRTs)

How many of the given above devices is/are based on 'Photonics Technology'?
(a) Only one (b) Only two
(c) Only three (d) All four

**61.** Which of the following best describes the field of 'Optoelectronics'?
(a) The study of electrical systems without any interaction with light.
(b) The development and application of electronic devices that source, detect and control light.
(c) The exclusive study of fibre optics in telecommunications.
(d) A branch of electronics that focuses only on solar panel technology.

**62.** With reference to OLED (Organic Light Emitting Diode) displays, consider the following statements:
1. OLED displays provide deeper blacks by turning off individual pixels entirely.
2. It is more energy-efficient than LCD technology when displaying dark images.
3. These are known for having a longer lifespan than traditional LED displays.

How many of the given above statements are correct?
(a) Only one (b) Only two
(c) All three (d) None

**63.** With reference to the challenges associated with LED technology, consider the following statements:
1. LEDs have a higher upfront cost compared to traditional lighting options.
2. LED performance can be impacted by extreme temperatures, affecting lifespan and efficiency.
3. LEDs emit minimal blue light, making them safe for prolonged exposure in screens and displays.

How many of the given above statements is/are correct?
(a) Only one (b) Only two
(c) All three (d) None

**64.** Consider the following pairs related to applications of light technology:

| Technology | Application |
|---|---|
| 1. Li-Fi | Wireless internet connectivity using light |
| 2. Laser Technology | Precision cutting in manufacturing |
| 3. Photovoltaic Cells | Data transmission at high speeds |
| 4. LED Lighting | Energy-efficient lighting for homes and offices |

How many of the given above pairs is/are correctly matched?
(a) Only one pair
(b) Only two pairs
(c) Only three pairs
(d) All four pairs

**65.** With reference to the LED (Light Emitting Diode) technology, consider the following statements:
1. LEDs consume less power and have a longer lifespan compared to incandescent bulbs.
2. LEDs operate by heating up a filament to emit light.
3. LEDs are capable of providing various colors of light without using filters.

Which of the statements given above is/are correct?
(a) 1 and 2 only (b) 1 and 3 only
(c) 2 and 3 only (d) 1, 2 and 3

**66.** Which of the following features of Li-Fi make it suitable for secure data transmission?
1. Limited to short-range, line-of-sight communication
2. Ability to transmit data over visible light without RF interference
3. High data transmission speed comparable to fiber optics

Select the correct answer from the codes given below:
(a) 1 and 2 only (b) 1 and 3 only
(c) 2 and 3 only (d) 1, 2 and 3

**67.** Consider the following statements with respect to the differences between Li-Fi and Wi-Fi technologies:
1. Li-Fi uses visible light for data transmission, whereas Wi-Fi uses radio waves.
2. Li-Fi is generally faster than Wi-Fi due to a higher data transfer rate potential.
3. Li-Fi can be used effectively for outdoor long-distance communication.

How many of the given above statements is/are correct?
(a) Only one
(b) Only two
(c) All three
(d) None

**68.** What was the primary objective of 'Project Loon' by Alphabet Inc.?
(a) To provide high-speed internet to remote and rural areas using balloons in the stratosphere.
(b) To develop autonomous drones for medical supply delivery.
(c) To use satellite-based systems for global internet coverage.
(d) To create a network of ground-based internet towers in underserved regions.

**69.** Which of the following statements are correct about the 'Liquid Crystal Displays (LCDs)'?
1. LCDs use liquid crystals to block or allow light to pass through them.
2. Backlight is essential in LCDs to produce visible images.
3. LCDs do not consume any power when displaying a static image.
4. Polarising filters are used in LCDs to control the light that reaches the screen.

Select the correct answer using the codes given below:
(a) 1 and 3 only
(b) 2, 3 and 4 only
(c) 1, 2 and 4 only
(d) 1, 2, 3 and 4

**70.** Which of the following statements correctly differentiates between LED (Light Emitting Diode) displays and LCD (Liquid Crystal Display) displays?

1. LEDs use an array of light-emitting diodes as the light source, while LCDs use a fluorescent backlight.
2. LCDs offer better contrast ratios than LED displays.
3. LED displays can be thinner and lighter than traditional LCDs.
4. LCDs are more energy-efficient than LED displays.

Select the correct answer using the codes given below:

(a) 1 and 3 only
(b) 2, 3 and 4 only
(c) 1, 3 and 4 only
(d) 1, 2 and 4 only

**71.** In the context of AMOLED technology, consider the following statements:

1. AMOLED displays are more energy-efficient for darker images as individual pixels can turn off completely.
2. They provide better viewing angles than traditional LCD screens.
3. AMOLED screens require a constant backlight to maintain brightness.

How many of the above statements is/are correct?

(a) Only one
(b) Only two
(c) All three
(d) None

**72.** Which of the following best describes the phenomenon of 'Dispersion'?

(a) The bending of light as it passes from one medium to another.
(b) The splitting of white light into its component colours when it passes through a prism.
(c) The reflection of light waves from a smooth surface.
(d) The scattering of light by particles in the atmosphere.

**73.** Consider the following events that occur in everyday life:

1. Formation of a rainbow after rain
2. The splitting of light in a prism
3. The twinkling of stars
4. colours seen in soap bubbles

How many of the given above is/are correct examples of 'Dispersion'?

(a) Only one
(b) Only two
(c) Only three
(d) All four

## Topic 7 : Laser Technology

**74.** Consider the following statements:

1. Coherence refers to the property of light waves being in phase with each other, which enhances the beam's focus and directionality.
2. Monochromaticity means that the light consists of multiple wavelengths, creating a broad spectrum of colours.
3. Laser light is both coherent and monochromatic, making it ideal for precise applications in industries and research.

How many of the above statements are correct?

(a) Only one
(b) Only two
(c) All three
(d) None

**75.** Consider the following characteristics:

1. Monochromatic (single wavelength)
2. Coherent (light waves are in phase)
3. Highly divergent (spreads out widely)
4. Directional (focused beam with minimal spread)
5. Produced by nuclear fusion reactions

How many of the given above are correct characteristics of laser light?

(a) Only two
(b) Only three
(c) Only four
(d) All five

**76.** How many of the following are key advantages of using laser technology for deep space communications?

1. Higher data transmission speeds
2. Greater energy efficiency for long-distance transmission
3. Complete immunity to interference from other space-based communication systems
4. Compact and lightweight communication equipment

Select the correct answer using the codes given below:

(a) Only two
(b) Only three
(c) All four
(d) None

**77.** Consider the following statements with respect to the concept of an 'Anti-Laser':

1. It is a device that absorbs light rather than emitting it.
2. The anti-laser works by trapping and absorbing incoming photons, converting them to thermal energy.
3. Unlike lasers, anti-lasers are widely used in fibre-optic communication systems to amplify light signals.

How many of the given above statements are correct?

(a) Only one
(b) Only two
(c) All three
(d) None

**78.** Consider the following characteristics:

1. Compact size and low power consumption
2. Tunable wavelength across a broad spectrum
3. Widely used in telecommunications and consumer electronics
4. Suitable for medical applications requiring a specific wavelength range

How many of the given above characteristics is/are generally associated with 'Semi-conductor Lasers'?

(a) Only one (b) Only two
(c) Only three (d) All four

**79.** Which of the following applications are commonly associated with laser technology?

1. Eye surgery and vision correction
2. High-speed internet through fiber optic communication
3. Surface engraving and cutting in manufacturing
4. Powering consumer LED displays

Select the correct answer from the codes given below:

(a) 1, 2 and 3 only
(b) 1 and 4 only
(c) 2, 3 and 4 only
(d) 1, 2, 3 and 4

**80.** Which of the following best describes 'Raman Spectroscopy'?

(a) A technique that measures the absorption of light to determine its chemical composition.
(b) A method that analyses the scattering of monochromatic light to information about molecular vibrations.
(c) A process that measures the reflection of light to identify surface characteristics.
(d) A technique that detects the refraction of light in transparent samples.

**81.** How many of the following are common applications of Raman Spectroscopy?

1. Identification of chemical compounds in pharmaceuticals
2. Analysis of molecular structure in biological samples
3. Monitoring of environmental pollutants
4. Imaging of internal organs in medical diagnostics

Select the correct answer from the codes given below:

(a) Only one
(b) Only two
(c) Only three
(d) All four

**82.** Consider the following statements:

1. Infrared (IR) spectroscopy is primarily used to identify the functional groups in organic compounds.
2. Nuclear Magnetic Resonance (NMR) spectroscopy provides detailed information about the carbon-hydrogen framework of molecules.
3. Ultraviolet-visible (UV-Vis) spectroscopy is commonly used to analyse the molecular structure of DNA.

How many of the given above statements is/are correct?

(a) Only one (b) Only two
(c) All three (d) None

**83.** With reference to LiDAR (Light Detection and Ranging) technology, consider the following statements:

1. LiDAR relies on radio waves to detect distances and create images.
2. This technology is effective in mapping underwater terrain.
3. LiDAR is commonly used in environmental studies, including mapping forests and measuring terrain elevations.

How many of the given above statements is/are correct?

(a) Only one
(b) Only two
(c) All three
(d) None

**84.** Which of the following are applications of LiDAR technology in environmental monitoring and conservation?

1. Mapping forest canopy height and density.
2. Detecting underwater archaeological sites.
3. Monitoring glacier movement and changes in snow cover.

Select the correct answer from the codes given below:

(a) 1 and 2 only
(b) 1 and 3 only
(c) 2 and 3 only
(d) 1, 2 and 3

# OMR SHEET

**Assessment Round**

| | | | | | | | | | | | | | | | | | | | |
|---|---|---|---|---|---|---|---|---|---|---|---|---|---|---|---|---|---|---|---|
| 1 | a | b | c | d | 31 | a | b | c | d | 61 | a | b | c | d | 91 | a | b | c | d |
| 2 | a | b | c | d | 32 | a | b | c | d | 62 | a | b | c | d | 92 | a | b | c | d |
| 3 | a | b | c | d | 33 | a | b | c | d | 63 | a | b | c | d | 93 | a | b | c | d |
| 4 | a | b | c | d | 34 | a | b | c | d | 64 | a | b | c | d | 94 | a | b | c | d |
| 5 | a | b | c | d | 35 | a | b | c | d | 65 | a | b | c | d | 95 | a | b | c | d |
| 6 | a | b | c | d | 36 | a | b | c | d | 66 | a | b | c | d | 96 | a | b | c | d |
| 7 | a | b | c | d | 37 | a | b | c | d | 67 | a | b | c | d | 97 | a | b | c | d |
| 8 | a | b | c | d | 38 | a | b | c | d | 68 | a | b | c | d | 98 | a | b | c | d |
| 9 | a | b | c | d | 39 | a | b | c | d | 69 | a | b | c | d | 99 | a | b | c | d |
| 10 | a | b | c | d | 40 | a | b | c | d | 70 | a | b | c | d | 100 | a | b | c | d |
| 11 | a | b | c | d | 41 | a | b | c | d | 71 | a | b | c | d | 101 | a | b | c | d |
| 12 | a | b | c | d | 42 | a | b | c | d | 72 | a | b | c | d | 102 | a | b | c | d |
| 13 | a | b | c | d | 43 | a | b | c | d | 73 | a | b | c | d | 103 | a | b | c | d |
| 14 | a | b | c | d | 44 | a | b | c | d | 74 | a | b | c | d | 104 | a | b | c | d |
| 15 | a | b | c | d | 45 | a | b | c | d | 75 | a | b | c | d | 105 | a | b | c | d |
| 16 | a | b | c | d | 46 | a | b | c | d | 76 | a | b | c | d | 106 | a | b | c | d |
| 17 | a | b | c | d | 47 | a | b | c | d | 77 | a | b | c | d | 107 | a | b | c | d |
| 18 | a | b | c | d | 48 | a | b | c | d | 78 | a | b | c | d | 108 | a | b | c | d |
| 19 | a | b | c | d | 49 | a | b | c | d | 79 | a | b | c | d | 109 | a | b | c | d |
| 20 | a | b | c | d | 50 | a | b | c | d | 80 | a | b | c | d | 110 | a | b | c | d |
| 21 | a | b | c | d | 51 | a | b | c | d | 81 | a | b | c | d | 111 | a | b | c | d |
| 22 | a | b | c | d | 52 | a | b | c | d | 82 | a | b | c | d | 112 | a | b | c | d |
| 23 | a | b | c | d | 53 | a | b | c | d | 83 | a | b | c | d | 113 | a | b | c | d |
| 24 | a | b | c | d | 54 | a | b | c | d | 84 | a | b | c | d | 114 | a | b | c | d |
| 25 | a | b | c | d | 55 | a | b | c | d | 85 | a | b | c | d | 115 | a | b | c | d |
| 26 | a | b | c | d | 56 | a | b | c | d | 86 | a | b | c | d | 116 | a | b | c | d |
| 27 | a | b | c | d | 57 | a | b | c | d | 87 | a | b | c | d | 117 | a | b | c | d |
| 28 | a | b | c | d | 58 | a | b | c | d | 88 | a | b | c | d | 118 | a | b | c | d |
| 29 | a | b | c | d | 59 | a | b | c | d | 89 | a | b | c | d | 119 | a | b | c | d |
| 30 | a | b | c | d | 60 | a | b | c | d | 90 | a | b | c | d | 120 | a | b | c | d |

## Calculate Your Score

| | |
|---|---|
| **Correct (✓)** | |
| **Incorrect (✓)** | |
| **Unattempted** | |
| **Total Score** | |
| **Accuracy (%)** | |

## Reasons for Incorrect Answers?

| | |
|---|---|
| 1. Lack of Knowledge/Existing Source Insufficient | |
| 2. Lack of Multiple Revision | |
| 3. Common Sense Mistakes | |

**Note :**

1. Calculate total score as correct answers carry 2 marks each 1/3rd marks will deducted for **Incorrect** Answers.
2. Calculate Accuracy (%) by dividing the number of correct answers to the total number of attempted questions.

## Past Learning

**1.** Which one of the following words/phrases is most appropriately used to denote 'an interoperable network of 3D virtual worlds that can be accessed simultaneously by millions of users, who can exert property rights over virtual items'? **(2024)**

(a) Big data analytics (b) Cryptography
(c) Metaverse (d) Virtual matrix

**2.** In which of the following are hydrogelsused? **(2024)**

1. Controlled drug delivery in patients
2. Mobile air-conditioning systems
3. Preparation of industrial lubricants

Select the correct answer using the codes given below:

(a) 1 only (b) 1 and 2 only
(c) 2 and 3 only (d) 1, 2 and 3

**3.** Consider the following statements: **(2023)**

1. Carbon fibres are used in the manufacture of components used in automobiles and aircrafts.
2. Carbon fibres once used cannot be recycled.

Which of the statements given above is/are correct?

(a) 1 only (b) 2 only
(c) Both 1 and 2 (d) Neither 1 nor 2

**4.** Consider the following actions: **(2023)**

1. Detection of car crash/collision which results in the deployment of airbags almost instantaneously
2. Detection of accidental free fall of a laptop towards the ground which results in the immediate turning off of the hard drive
3. Detection of the tilt of the smartphone which results in the rotation of display between portrait and landscape mode

In how many of the above actions is/are the function of accelerometer required?

(a) Only one
(b) Only two
(c) All three
(d) None

**5.** Consider the following statements: **(2022)**

1. Other than those made by humans, nanoparticles do not exist in nature.
2. Nanoparticles of some metallic oxides are used in the manufacture of some cosmetics.
3. Nanoparticles of some commercial products which enter the environment are unsafe for humans.

Which of the statements given above is/are correct?

(a) 1 only
(b) 3 only
(c) 1 and 2 only
(d) 2 and 3 only

**6.** With reference to Web 3.0, consider the following statements. **(2022)**

1. Web 3.0 technology enables people to control their own data.
2. In Web 3.0 world, there can be blockchain based social networks.
3. Web 3.0 is operated by users collectively rather than a corporation.

Which of the statements given above are correct?

(a) 1 and 2 (b) 2 and 3
(c) 1 and 3 (d) 1, 2 and 3

**7.** Consider the following: **(2022)**

1. Aarogya Setu 2. CoWIN
3. DigiLocker 4. DIKSHA

Which of the above are built on top of open-source digital platforms?

(a) 1 and 2 (b) 2, 3 and 4
(c) 1, 3 and 4 (d) 1, 2, 3 and 4

**8.** With reference to Non-Fungible Tokens (NFTs), consider the following statements: **(2022)**

1. They enable the digital representation of physical assets.
2. They are unique cryptographic tokens that exist on a blockchain.
3. They can be traded or exchanged at equivalency and therefore can be used as a medium of commercial transactions.

Which of the statements given above are correct?

(a) 1 and 2 only (b) 2 and 3 only
(c) 1 and 3 only (d) 1, 2 and 3

**9.** With reference to street-lighting, how do sodium lamps differ from LED lamps? **(2021)**

1. Sodium lamps produce light in 360 degrees but it is not so in the case of LED lamps.
2. As street-lights, sodium lamps have longer life span than LED lamps.
3. The spectrum of visible light from sodium lamps is almost monochromatic while LED lamps offer significant colour advantages in street-lighting.

Select the correct answer using the codes given below:

(a) 3 only (b) 2 only
(c) 1 and 3 only (d) 1, 2 and 3

**10.** With reference to Visible Light Communication (VL technology), which of the following statements are correct? **(2020)**

1. VLC uses electromagnetic spectrum wavelengths 375 to 780 nm.
2. VLC is known as long-range optical wireless communication.
3. VLC can transmit large amounts of data faster than Bluetooth.
4. VLC has no electromagnetic interference.

Select the correct answer using the code given below:

(a) 1, 2 and 3 only (b) 1, 2 and 4 only
(c) 1, 3 and 4 only (d) 2, 3 and 4 only

**11.** With reference to carbon nanotubes, consider the following statements: **(2020)**

1. They can be used as carriers of drugs and antigens in the human body.
2. They can be made into artificial blood capillaries for an injured part of the human body.
3. They can be used in biochemical sensors.
4. Carbon nanotubes are biodegradable.

Which of the statements given above are correct?

(a) 1 and 2 only
(b) 2, 3 and 4 only
(c) 1, 3 and 4 only
(d) 1, 2, 3 and 4

**12.** Consider the following activities: **(2020)**

1. Spraying pesticides on a crop field
2. Inspecting the craters of active volcanoes
3. Collecting breath samples from spouting whales for DNA analysis

At the present level of technology, which of the above activities can be successfully carried out by using drones?

(a) 1 and 2 only
(b) 2 and 3 only
(c) 1 and 3 only
(d) 1, 2 and 3

**13.** With the present state of development, Artificial Intelligence can effectively do which of the following? **(2020)**

1. Bring down electricity consumption in industrial units
2. Create meaningful short stories and songs
3. Disease diagnosis
4. Text-to-Speech Conversion
5. Wireless transmission of electrical energy

Select the correct answer using the codes given below.

(a) 1, 2, 3 and 5
(b) 1, 3 and 4
(c) 2, 4 and 5
(d) 1, 2, 3, 4 and 5

**14.** With reference to 'Blockchain Technology', consider the following statements: **(2020)**

1. It is a public ledger that everyone can inspect, but which no single user controls.
2. The structure and design of blockchain is such that all the data in it are about cryptocurrency only.
3. Applications that depend on basic features of blockchain can be developed without anybody's permission.

Which of the statements given above is/are correct?

(a) 1 only (b) 1 and 2 only
(c) 2 only (d) 1 and 3 only

**15.** In the context of digital technologies for entertainment, consider the following statements. **(2019)**

1. In Augmented Reality (AR), a simulated environment is created and the physical world is completely shut out.
2. In Virtual Reality (VR), images generated from a computer are projected onto real life objects or surroundings.
3. AR allows individuals to be present in the world and improves the experience using the camera of smartphone or PC.
4. VR closes the world and transposes an individual, providing complete immersion experience.

Which of the statements given above is/are correct?

(a) 1 and 2 (b) 3 and 4
(c) 1, 2 and 3 (d) 4 only

**16.** Consider the following pairs. **(2018)**

| Terms sometimes seen in news | Contexts/Topics |
|---|---|
| 1. Belle II | Artificial Intelligence experiment |
| 2. Blockchain Technology | Digital/Cryptocurrency |
| 3. CRISPR-Cas 9 | Particle Physics |

Which of the above pairs is/are correctly matched?

(a) 1 and 3 (b) 2 only
(c) 2 and 3 (d) 1, 2 and 3

**17.** The identity platform Aadhaar provides open Application Programming Interfaces (APIs). What does it imply? **(2018)**

1. It can be integrated into an electronic device.
2. Online authentication using iris is possible.

Which of the statements given above is/are correct?

(a) Only 1 (b) Only 2
(c) Both 1 and 2 (d) Neither 1 nor 2

**18.** Organic Light Emitting Diodes (OLEDs) are used to create digital display in many devices. What is the advantage of OLED displays over Liquid Crystal displays? **(2017)**

1. OLED displays can be fabricated on flexible plastic substrates.
2. Roll-up displays embedded in clothing can be made using OLEDs.
3. Transparent displays are possible using OLEDs.

Select the correct answer using the codes given below:

(a) 1 and 3 only (b) 2 only
(c) 1, 2 and 3 (d) None of these

**19.** With reference to 'LiFi', recently in the news, which of the following statements is/are correct? **(2016)**

1. It uses light as the medium for high-speed data transmission.
2. It is a wireless technology and is several times faster than 'WiFi'.

Select the correct answer using the codes given below:

(a) 1 only (b) 2 only
(c) Both 1 and 2 (d) Neither 1 nor 2

**20.** With reference to the use of nanotechnology in the health sector, which of the following statements is/are correct? **(2015)**

1. Targeted drug delivery is made possible by nanotechnology.
2. Nanotechnology can largely contribute to gene therapy.

Select the correct answer using the codes given below:

(a) 1 only (b) 2 only
(c) Both 1 and 2 (d) Neither 1 nor 2

# Detailed Solutions

## Assessment Round

1. *(a)* Only one
   - **Statement 1 is correct:** Artificial Intelligence involves creating machines that can perform tasks associated with human cognitive functions, such as decision-making and language understanding.
   - **Statement 2 is incorrect:** AI can process and analyse human languages through Natural Language Processing (NLP), which is widely used in chatbots, translation tools and voice assistants.
   - **Statement 3 is incorrect:** While some AI systems are designed to function **autonomously, but many AI systems still require human supervision** to some extent especially for tasks that involve complex decision-making, ethical considerations or scenarios where AI needs guidance to improve its accuracy and relevance.

   **Therefore, the correct answer is (a) Only one.**

2. *(a)* A field of AI focused on enabling machines to interpret and generate human language.
   - **Option (a) is correct:** Natural Language Processing (NLP) is a branch of artificial intelligence that enables machines to process, interpret and generate human language in a meaningful way. It involves tasks like language translation, sentiment analysis, speech recognition and text summarisation.
   - **Option (b) is incorrect:** NLP is not limited to voice recognition; it also applies to text-based applications like chatbots, search engines and document classification.
   - **Option (c) is incorrect:** NLP is not a programming language but a multidisciplinary field combining linguistics, computer science and machine learning.
   - **Option (d) is incorrect:** NLP is a software-based field, not a hardware component used in AI systems.

   **Thus, the best description of NLP is option (a).**

3. *(c)* Only three
   - **Pair 1 is incorrect:** Artificial Intelligence is a broad field encompassing various techniques, not limited to building humanoid robots. It includes areas like Machine Learning, Computer Vision and Natural Language Processing.
   - **Pair 2 is correct:** Machine Learning is indeed a subset of AI that allows systems to learn from data and improve over time.
   - **Pair 3 is correct:** Artificial Neural Networks are computational models inspired by the structure and function of the human brain's neurons, used in various Machine Learning applications.
   - **Pair 4 is correct:** Deep Learning is a branch of Machine Learning that uses neural networks with multiple layers (deep networks) to process complex data and improve accuracy.

   **Thus, the correct answer is (c) Only three.**

4. *(b)* To allow machines to identify, analyse and interpret visual data from the world.

   Computer Vision in AI aims to provide machines with the ability to 'see' and interpret visual information, similar to human vision. This enables applications such as object detection, image classification and scene understanding in various fields, including healthcare, surveillance and autonomous driving.

   **Thus, option (b) is the correct answer.**

5. *(a)* 1, 3 and 5 only
   - **Statement 1 is correct:** Automated customer support through chatbots is a well-established AI application. AI systems like ChatGPT or other customer support bots use Natural Language Processing (NLP) to understand and respond to user queries effectively. For instance, companies like Amazon and banks deploy chatbots for 24/7 customer assistance.

- **Statement 2 is incorrect:** While AI tools like GPT can assist in creative writing, complete autonomous creative writing without any human input remains limited. AI lacks nuanced understanding and creativity to produce universally accepted literature or stories.
- **Statement 3 is correct**: Real-time language translation is a successful AI application. Tools like Google Translate and Microsoft Translator use AI for effective real-time translations across numerous languages, enabling seamless global communication.
- **Statement 4 is incorrect**: Understanding and accurately responding to human emotions is a developing area in AI. While sentiment analysis tools can identify emotions in text, accurately interpreting complex human emotions and responding empathetically is beyond current AI capabilities.
- **Statement 5 is correct**: Image recognition for medical diagnostics is an advanced AI application. For example, AI-powered tools like IBM Watson or Zebra Medical Vision assist doctors in detecting anomalies in X-rays, MRIs or CT scans, aiding faster and more accurate diagnoses.

**Thus, the correct answer is (a) 1, 3 and 5 only.**

**6.** *(d)* All four

- **Agriculture:** AI is used for precision farming, crop monitoring, pest detection, and yield prediction. **Ex: AI-powered drones** can provide real-time insights into soil conditions and plant health.
- **Healthcare:** AI applications include diagnostic tools, robotic surgeries and personalised medicine. AI systems like **IBM Watson assist in analysing medical data.**
- **Entertainment:** Streaming services like **Netflix** use AI for personalised recommendations and video game developers employ AI for creating immersive experiences.
- **Transportation:** AI powers autonomous vehicles, traffic management systems, and predictive maintenance in logistics and aviation industries.

**Thus, option (d) is the correct answer.**

**7.** *(c)* Only three pairs

- **Pair 1 is correct:** Reactive AI, such as IBM's Deep Blue, operates without memory or past experience, focusing solely on analysing the present scenario.
- **Pair 2 is correct:** Limited Memory AI is used in autonomous vehicles, which analyse historical and real-time data to make driving decisions.
- **Pair 3 is correct:** Theory of Mind AI aims to understand human emotions and mental states but current chatbots do not yet fully comprehend or respond to human emotions.
- **Pair 4 is incorrect:** Self-aware AI, which would imply a conscious system with self-perception, does not exist at present and remains a theoretical concept.

**Thus, option (c) is the correct answer.**

**8.** *(d)* Neither 1 nor 2

- **Statement 1 is incorrect:** CAIR is not under the Ministry of Electronics and Information Technology; **it operates under the Defence Research and Development Organisation (DRDO) (Ministry of Defence).**
- **Statement 2 is incorrect:** While CAIR develops technologies that could potentially have civilian uses, **its primary focus is on defence applications** to support India's security needs.
- CAIR focuses on research in areas such as Artificial Intelligence, Robotics, Command and Control, and Communication Security.

**Thus, option (d) is the correct answer.**

**9.** *(b)* Only two

- **Statement 1 is correct:** India's National Strategy on AI, led by NITI Aayog, aims to position India as a global hub for AI, emphasising inclusive growth across sectors.
- **Statement 2 is correct:** NITI Aayog developed this strategy with a focus on applying AI in key sectors like healthcare, agriculture, education, and transportation to foster economic growth and social impact.
- **Statement 3 is incorrect:** The strategy does not primarily focus on establishing a strict regulatory framework but rather promotes a

balanced approach to AI development, encouraging innovation while addressing ethical and privacy concerns.

**Thus, the correct answer is (b) Only two.**

***10.*** (b) V. Kamakoti Committee

- The **V. Kamakoti Committee** was formed to focus on Artificial Intelligence and cybersecurity concerns, providing recommendations on policy frameworks and strategic measures to harness AI safely and effectively in India. The committee's work contributes to ensuring that AI development aligns with national security and ethical guidelines.
- **Natarajan Committee:** Focused on defence and security policies, not specifically on AI or cybersecurity.
- **Srikrishna Committee:** Formed to draft a data protection law for India, crucial for managing AI-related data privacy.
- **Justice Verma Committee:** Established to recommend changes to criminal law for women's safety, unrelated to AI or cybersecurity.

**Thus, the correct answer is (b) V. Kamakoti Committee.**

***11.*** *(b)* Only three

**Generative AI** refers to a type of artificial intelligence that is capable of creating new content by learning from existing data. Unlike traditional AI, which typically analyses data or performs tasks based on predefined rules, generative AI can produce original outputs such as text, images, music or even synthetic data.

- **Option 1 is correct: Text generation** is a key application of Generative AI, used in content creation, chatbots and automated writing tools.
- **Option 2 is correct: Image synthesis** is another application, where Generative AI models can create realistic images or art.
- **Option 3 is incorrect: Data encryption** is not an application of Generative AI; it's a security measure to protect information.
- **Option 4 is correct: Speech synthesis** is a valid use, enabling AI to generate human-like voice outputs.
- **Option 5 is incorrect: Database management** is unrelated to Generative AI, as it focuses on organising and querying structured data.

**Thus, option (b) is the correct answer.**

***12.*** *(a)* 1 and 2 only

- **Statement 1 is correct:** The Global Partnership on Artificial Intelligence (GPAI) is a **collaborative initiative involving governments, academia and industry stakeholders.** It aims to ensure the responsible development and deployment of AI, focusing on its ethical, social, and economic implications.
- **Statement 2 is correct: India joined GPAI as a founding member in June 2020,** signifying its commitment to advancing responsible AI development and governance.
- **Statement 3 is incorrect: GPAI does not operate under the United Nations.** Instead, it functions as an independent initiative supported by its member nations.

**Thus, the correct answer is (a) 1 and 2 only.**

***13.*** *(d)* Only one pair

- **Pairs 1 is incorrect: Responsible AI for Youth-** This programme, run by the Government of India, aims to empower school students with AI problem-solving skills.
- **Pairs 2 is incorrect: AIRAWAT** - A platform aimed at creating common AI infrastructure for research and applications, supporting India's AI ambitions.
- **Pairs 3 is correct: National AI Portal** - Functions as a resource-sharing platform for AI-related developments and news in India.

**Thus, the correct answer is (d) Only one pair.**

***14.*** *(a)* Only one

- **Statement 1 is correct:** VR typically requires a head-mounted display to immerse users completely in a virtual environment.

- **Statement 2 is incorrect:** AR can function indoors and outdoors; it does not require GPS for all applications (e.g., indoor navigation and real-time information overlay).
- **Statement 3 is incorrect:** MR generally requires more advanced hardware, such as the Microsoft HoloLens, to enable interactive blending of real and virtual elements, which is beyond the capabilities of standard smartphones.

**Thus, the correct answer is (a) Only one.**

**15.** *(c)* All three

- **Statement 1 is correct:** Snapchat's AR filters allow users to apply real-time digital effects to photos and videos using Augmented Reality.
- **Statement 2 is correct:** Google Earth VR uses Virtual Reality to let users explore locations around the globe in an immersive way.
- **Statement 3 is correct:** Microsoft HoloLens is a Mixed Reality (MR) device, enabling industries to use it for tasks like training and design by blending virtual elements with the real world.

**Thus, the correct answer is (c) All three.**

**16.** *(c)* Metaverse

- The conference described is held in a 3D virtual world, characteristic of the Metaverse.
- Blockchain tokens for payments and customisable avatars are essential features of the Metaverse.
- Real-time interaction within the virtual space aligns perfectly with Metaverse characteristics.

**Thus, the correct answer is (c) Metaverse.**

**17.** *(b)* Augmented Reality

- The museum app enhances the visitor's experience by integrating virtual elements with real-world artifacts.
- AR allows real-time interaction and visualization of 3D digital objects over physical environments.

**Thus, the correct answer is (b) Augmented Reality.**

**18.** *(b)* A decentralised ledger that securely records transactions across multiple nodes.

Blockchain is a **decentralised digital ledger** that records transactions in a secure, transparent and tamper-resistant way across a distributed network of nodes. This structure makes it suitable for a variety of applications beyond just cryptocurrencies.

**Thus, option (b) is the correct answer.**

**19.** *(d)* 1, 2, 3 and 4

- **Statement 1 is correct:** Blocks are fundamental units in Blockchain, storing transaction data and a hash that links each block to the previous one, forming a secure chain.
- **Statement 2 is correct:** Nodes are individual computers or devices that participate in the Blockchain network, maintaining and validating the ledger.
- **Statement 3 is correct:** Immutability ensures that once transactions are recorded, they cannot be modified, preventing tampering and ensuring a reliable record.
- **Statement 4 is correct:** Consensus mechanisms, such as Proof of Work or Proof of Stake, are crucial for validating transactions and ensuring the accuracy of the blockchain's state.

**Therefore, the correct options is (d) 1, 2, 3 and 4.**

**20.** *(a)* A process where transactions are grouped and validated to create new blocks.

**Mining in Blockchain** involves validating and grouping transactions to create new blocks, which are then added to the blockchain. This process often requires computational power to solve complex cryptographic puzzles, especially in Proof of Work systems. Mining is essential for maintaining the security and integrity of decentralised networks like Bitcoin.

**Thus, option (a) is the correct answer.**

**21.** *(b)* Only two

- **Statement 1 is correct:** Blockchain allows all participants in the network to view and verify transactions, enhancing transparency. For example, in a public blockchain like Bitcoin, all transactions are visible to anyone in the network, building trust among users.

- **Statement 2 is incorrect:** Blockchain's immutability feature ensures that once a transaction is recorded, it cannot be altered or removed. This makes blockchain highly secure and resistant to tampering.
- **Statement 3 is correct:** Each block in the blockchain is linked to the previous one through cryptographic hashing, forming a secure chain of blocks. This link between blocks strengthens data integrity and prevents unauthorised changes.

**Therefore, the correct answer is (b) Only two.**

**22.** *(b)* PoS selects validators based on stake ownership, whereas PoW uses miners competing to solve complex mathematical problems.

- **Proof of Work (PoW) requires miners** to solve complex mathematical problems, consuming significant computational resources to validate transactions.
- **Proof of Stake (PoS) selects validators** based on the amount of cryptocurrency they 'stake,' rather than requiring extensive computational work.
- Only Proof of Work requires high computational power for validation, while Proof of Stake is generally more energy-efficient and does not demand extensive computing power.

**Thus, option (b) is the correct answer.**

**23.** *(b)* A blockchain where multiple organisations jointly govern the network, ensuring partial decentralisation.

**A consortium blockchain** is a type of permissioned blockchain that is governed by multiple organisations collaboratively. This ensures partial decentralisation as control is not limited to a single entity.

**Thus, option (b) is the correct answer.**

**24.** *(c)* Only three

- **Statement 1 is correct:** Governance in private and permissioned blockchains is usually managed by a single organisation.
- **Statement 2 is incorrect:** Unlike public blockchains, transactions in private or permissioned blockchains are not visible to all participants; access is limited to authorised entities.
- **Statement 3 is correct:** Private and permissioned blockchains restrict access to authorised participants for enhanced security and control.
- **Statement 4 is correct:** Data confidentiality is a key feature in these blockchains, ensuring limited visibility to authorised members only.

**Thus, the correct answer is (c) Only three.**

**25.** *(a)* 1 only

- **Statement 1 is correct:** Cryptocurrencies rely on a decentralised system called blockchain technology, which records all transactions across a network of computers (nodes). **This decentralised nature eliminates the need for intermediaries, such as banks,** and makes the transaction history public and transparent.
- **Statement 2 is incorrect:** While cryptocurrencies offer a degree of anonymity, transactions are not completely untraceable. Each transaction is recorded on the blockchain, creating a digital footprint. Users' identities can sometimes be traced through wallet addresses, especially when exchanges require identity verification.
- **Statement 3 is incorrect:** Cryptocurrencies are not uniformly regulated by central banks. **Many countries do not have clear regulations for cryptocurrencies and some countries restrict or even ban their use.** Unlike traditional currency, cryptocurrencies are generally not backed by a central authority, which can make them volatile and susceptible to fraud.

**Thus, the correct answer is (a) 1 only.**

**26.** *(a)* Only one

- **Statement 1 is correct:** NFTs are often used to represent ownership of unique digital assets, such as virtual real estate or rare items in online games, created using blockchain technology. Each NFT has unique metadata and identifiers that make it distinguishable from other tokens.
- **Statement 2 is incorrect:** Unlike cryptocurrencies, NFTs are non-fungible and cannot be exchanged on a one-to-one basis because each NFT has a unique value and identity.

- **Statement 3 is incorrect:** NFTs are often created on specific blockchain networks (like Ethereum or Solana), and they may not be easily transferable across different blockchains unless compatible or interoperable solutions are in place.

**Thus, the correct answer is (a) Only one.**

**27.** *(a)* Both Statements are correct and Statement II is the correct explanation of Statement I.

- **Statement I is correct:** Non-fungible assets are unique and cannot be exchanged on a one-to-one basis with others because they hold distinct value and features.
- **Statement II is correct and explains Statement I :** Real estate is the example of non-fungible assets. As real estate has unique characteristics (location, size, condition), just as each NFT is uniquely identifiable and holds a different value.

**Thus, option (a) is the correct answer.**

**28.** *(a)* To establish ethical guidelines for responsible data usage and digital interactions, encouraging transparency and user-centricity in digital governance

**The PRESIDIO Principles,** formally titled 'Presidio Principles : Foundational Values for a Decentralised Future,' aim to guide ethical digital practices, focusing on **user-centricity, privacy, and transparency**. These principles advocate responsible handling of data and interactions to build user trust in digital systems, emphasising values such as **accountability and fairness** in digital governance. They do not mandate strict regulations, nor do they provide technical cybersecurity guidelines.

**Thus, option (a) is the correct answer.**

**29.** *(a)* Only one

- **Statement 1 is incorrect : Cryptocurrencies are not recognised as legal tender by the Reserve Bank of India (RBI).** The RBI has made it clear that the only recognised legal tender in India is the Indian Rupee (INR). Cryptocurrencies such as Bitcoin, Ethereum, and others are not accepted as official currency for transactions and do not have the status of legal tender in India.
- **Statement 2 is correct: The trading of cryptocurrencies is subject to taxation under the Income Tax Act in India.** Profits made from cryptocurrency transactions are considered capital gains and individuals are required to report them under the applicable tax regime. Depending on the holding period, they may be classified as short-term or long-term capital gains, and taxed accordingly. This taxation ensures that cryptocurrency earnings are treated similarly to other investment gains.
- **Statement 3 is incorrect: The Securities and Exchange Board of India (SEBI) does not currently regulate cryptocurrency trading.** While SEBI oversees securities and the stock market in India, cryptocurrencies do not fall under its jurisdiction as they are not officially classified as securities. As of now, India does not have a specific regulatory framework for cryptocurrencies, although discussions around potential regulations are ongoing.

**Therefore, the correct answer is (a) Only one.**

**30.** *(b)* A framework aimed at standardising blockchain adoption across sectors such as land records, health and education.

The **National Blockchain Framework** is a comprehensive initiative by the Indian government to facilitate the adoption of blockchain technology in diverse domains.

- It focuses on **standardisation**, enabling blockchain solutions in areas like **land records, healthcare and education.**
- It is **not limited** to cryptocurrency regulation or private blockchain networks.
- The framework emphasises **efficiency and transparency**, leveraging blockchain for **interoperability** and scalability across public and private systems.

**Thus, option (b) is the correct answer.**

**31.** *(b)* Control and manipulation of matter at the nanoscale to create materials with unique properties.

- Nanotechnology involves the **manipulation and control of matter at the nanoscale, typically below 100 nanometres, to produce materials with unique and enhanced properties.**

- At this scale, materials can exhibit distinct characteristics - such as increased strength, enhanced chemical reactivity, or improved electrical conductivity - that they may not display in their bulk form.
- This versatility allows nanotechnology to be applied across multiple fields, including medicine (for targeted drug delivery), electronics (for creating smaller, faster components), and energy (for improving solar cells and batteries).

**Thus, option (b) is the correct answer.**

**32.** *(a)* Detects atomic-level surface features of conductive materials by measuring tunneling currents.

- The **Scanning Tunneling Microscope (STM)** operates by detecting tunneling currents between a sharp probe and the sample surface, which allows it to image surfaces with atomic precision.
- The STM is particularly useful for conductive materials because the tunneling current depends on the electrical properties of the surface.
- For example, STM has been widely used to study the surface atoms of metals like copper, as well as for imaging complex structures in nanotechnology and materials science, providing insights into the atomic arrangement on conductive surfaces.

**Thus, option (a) is the correct answer.**

**33.** *(d)* All three

- **Statement 1 is correct**: Nanotechnology has significantly advanced water purification and filtration. **Nanomaterials like carbon nanotubes and nano-filters are used to remove impurities, heavy metals, and pathogens from water.** Their high surface area and functional properties make them effective in desalination and filtration systems.
- **Statement 2 is correct**: In the food industry, nanotechnology enhances food packaging and preservation. **Nano-sensors are used to monitor food freshness**, while nano-coatings help extend shelf life by preventing microbial growth and maintaining the integrity of the packaging.
- **Statement 3 is correct**: Nanotechnology has revolutionised high-speed computing and data storage. **Nanoscale materials are used in advanced transistors and memory devices**, leading to faster processors and more efficient data storage solutions. For instance, spintronics and quantum dots have applications in enhancing computing power and data storage.

**Thus, the correct answer is (d) 1, 2 and 3.**

**34.** *(c)* Only four

**Organic nanoparticles** are nanoscale particles primarily composed of organic compounds such as lipids, polymers, and proteins. Unlike inorganic nanoparticles, which are based on metals or metal oxides, organic nanoparticles are carbon-based, making them biocompatible and often biodegradable. This unique composition allows them to interact safely within biological systems, which is especially advantageous in medical applications.

- **Drug delivery systems**: Organic nanoparticles, such as liposomes, are widely used in drug delivery due to their biocompatibility and ability to deliver drugs directly to target sites.
- **Gene therapy**: Organic nanoparticles can be engineered to carry genetic material into cells, making them valuable in gene therapy.
- **Catalysis in industrial reactions**: Catalysis is generally dominated by **inorganic nanoparticles**, not organic ones.
- **Targeted cancer treatment**: Organic nanoparticles are often used in cancer treatment, delivering drugs directly to cancerous cells, reducing side effects.
- **Solar cell development**: Organic nanoparticles, such as organic photovoltaics, are used in solar cell development for efficient energy absorption.

**Thus, the correct answer is (c) Only four.**

**35.** *(b)* Norio Taniguchi

**The term 'nanotechnology'** was first coined by **Norio Taniguchi**, a professor at Tokyo University of Science, in **1974**. Taniguchi used the term to describe the precision machining and materials processing on the nanoscale, specifically focusing on dimensions of less than a micrometer. He envisioned the manipulation of materials at the atomic or molecular scale, which laid the foundation for modern nanotechnology.

Though **Richard Feynman** is often associated with the field due to his famous lecture, 'There's Plenty of Room at the Bottom,' where he discussed the possibility of manipulating atoms and molecules, he did not coin the term itself. **Eric Drexler** later popularised the concept of nanotechnology in the 1980s with his work on molecular manufacturing, but the original term traces back to Norio Taniguchi.

Therefore, the correct answer is **(b) Norio Taniguchi.**

**36.** *(b)* Only two

- **Statement 1 is correct:** Top-Down methods include techniques like lithography, milling, and etching to reduce larger materials to the nanoscale.
- **Statement 2 is incorrect:** Bottom-Up methods focus on building nanoscale structures from individual atoms or molecules, not breaking down larger structures.
- **Statement 3 is correct:** Top-Down methods can lack precision at the atomic level due to limitations in breaking down bulk materials, whereas Bottom-Up methods offer greater precision.

**Therefore, the correct answer is (b) Only two.**

**37.** *(d)* 1, 2, 3 and 4

- **Statement 1 is correct:** Aluminium nanoparticles are indeed used in rocket fuel and other pyrotechnic applications. Due to their high surface area-to-volume ratio, these nanoparticles oxidise rapidly, releasing a significant amount of energy, which enhances the fuel's performance in propulsion systems.
- **Statement 2 is correct:** Gold nanoparticles have unique properties at the nanoscale, particularly in medical applications. Their ability to be easily modified makes them ideal for **diagnostics and drug delivery**, as they can bind to specific molecules and target cells within the body, minimising side effects in treatments like cancer therapy.
- **Statement 3 is correct:** Silver nanoparticles are well-known for their **anti-microbial properties**, which are effective against bacteria and some viruses. As a result, they are extensively used in **medical equipment, wound dressings, and textiles** to prevent bacterial growth, making them beneficial in healthcare and consumer products.
- **Statement 4 is correct:** Carbon nanotubes (CNTs) possess remarkable **strength, flexibility and electrical conductivity.** These properties make them highly useful in **electronics, structural reinforcement materials and nanocomposite manufacturing.** CNTs are also used in energy storage devices like batteries and capacitors due to their conductivity.

**Therefore, the correct answer is (d) 1, 2, 3 and 4.**

**38.** *(c)* Only three pairs

- **Pair 1 is correct:** Graphene is widely used in high-strength, lightweight composites due to its exceptional strength and flexibility.
- **Pair 2 is correct:** Fullerene ($C_{60}$), with its hollow cage structure, is utilised in drug delivery for targeted therapies.
- **Pair 3 is correct:** Graphite's conductive properties make it valuable in batteries and electronics.
- **Pair 4 is incorrect:** Carbon nanotubes are not primarily used as fuel additives; they are more commonly applied in nanotechnology, electronics and materials science for their strength and conductivity.

**Therefore, the correct answer is (c) Only three pairs.**

**39.** *(b)* Only two

**Graphene** is a single layer **of carbon atoms arranged in a two-dimensional hexagonal lattice.** Known for being the thinnest yet one of the strongest materials discovered, graphene has exceptional properties, including high electrical and thermal conductivity, mechanical strength, and flexibility. These characteristics make it a revolutionary material with diverse applications, from electronics and energy storage to composite materials and medical devices.

- **Statement 1 is correct:** Graphene is celebrated for its high electrical conductivity, mechanical strength and flexibility, making it useful in various applications.
- Graphene is one of the strongest materials known, with a **tensile strength approximately 100 times greater than steel of the same thickness**. This remarkable strength makes it useful in applications that require durability and flexibility
- **Statement 2 is incorrect:** Graphene is **not primarily used as a fuel additive**. Instead, it is utilised in fields like electronics, composites, and energy storage due to its exceptional properties.
- **Statement 3 is incorrect:** While **graphene has many applications, it is not biodegradable**, which limits its use in medical implants that require biocompatibility and degradation within the body.

**Therefore, the correct answer is (b) Only two.**

***40.*** *(b)* Only two

**Carbon Nanotubes (CNTs) are cylindrical molecules composed entirely of carbon atoms, arranged in a hexagonal lattice structure.** CNTs are a unique form of carbon allotrope that exhibit remarkable physical and chemical properties. Due to their nanoscale dimensions, CNTs possess extraordinary mechanical strength, being several times stronger than steel by weight, and electrical conductivity, making them highly efficient conductors or semiconductors depending on their structure.

- **Statement 1 is correct:** Carbon nanotubes are indeed cylindrical structures made entirely of carbon atoms, arranged in a hexagonal lattice.
- **Statement 2 is correct:** Carbon nanotubes are **excellent conductors of both electricity and heat.** Their electrical conductivity can be attributed to their unique structure, and they have a thermal conductivity much higher than that of metals like copper.
- **Statement 3 is incorrect:** Carbon nanotubes are not commonly used as fuel additives; their applications are mainly in electronics, materials science and nanotechnology due to their unique properties.

**Therefore, the correct answer is (b) Only two.**

***41.*** *(a)* 1 and 2 only

- **Statement 1 is correct:** Buckminsterfullerene, or $C_{60}$, has a **unique spherical shape where 60 carbon atoms are arranged in a structure that resembles a soccer ball, with alternating pentagonal and hexagonal rings.** This distinctive structure is what gives Buckminsterfullerene its stability and is characteristic of its molecular geometry.
- **Statement 2 is correct:** Compared to other carbon allotropes, **$C_{60}$ is relatively reactive due to its high electron affinity.** This reactivity makes it useful in various chemical modifications and applications in materials science.
- **Statement 3 is incorrect:** While $C_{60}$ has shown superconducting properties when doped with certain elements (such as alkali metals), **it does not exhibit superconductivity at room temperature.** It generally needs very low temperatures to achieve superconductivity.
- **Statement 4 is incorrect:** Unlike graphite, **$C_{60}$ is actually soluble in some organic solvents like benzene and toluene,** which is an unusual property for carbon-based materials. This solubility is due to its molecular structure and size.

**Therefore, the correct answer is (a) 1 and 2 only.**

***42.*** (c) Only three

**Fullerenes** are a unique class of carbon-based molecules known for their distinct hollow, cage-like structures. The most famous example is $C_{60}$, also called 'Buckminsterfullerene,' which resembles a soccer ball with a spherical arrangement of 60 carbon atoms. Discovered in 1985, fullerenes have since gained significant interest due to their exceptional physical and chemical properties, including high stability, electrical conductivity, and ability to act as antioxidants.

- **Drug delivery systems:** Fullerenes can be used in drug delivery due to their hollow, cage-like structure, which allows them to carry drug molecules.

- **Superconductivity:** Certain types of fullerenes exhibit superconducting properties when modified or combined with other materials, especially at specific temperatures.
- **Lubricant:** Due to their spherical shape, fullerenes can act as lubricants, reducing friction between surfaces.
- **Fuel additive:** This is less common for fullerenes; they are not primarily used as fuel additives.

**Therefore, the correct answer is (c) Only three.**

**43.** *(c)* Quantum Dots are used to emit specific wavelengths of light, improving display colour precision in screens.

- Quantum Dots are **semi-conductor nanoparticles** that emit specific colours of light when excited by energy. This unique property is utilised in display technology, where **Quantum Dots enhance colour accuracy and brightness, such as in QLED screens.**
- The other options describe properties and applications unrelated to Quantum Dots. Quantum Dots are not primarily designed for thermal stability in circuits, energy storage, or electromagnetic shielding.

**Thus, option (c) is the correct answer.**

**44.** *(c)* Only three

- **Option 1 is correct:** Quantum dots are **widely used in medical imaging because of their ability to emit different colours at specific wavelengths when exposed to UV light**. This property enables high-contrast imaging and tagging of biomolecules in biological research.
- **Option 2 is correct:** Quantum dots are **used in solar cells to enhance light absorption and improve the efficiency of solar energy conversion,** making them valuable in renewable energy applications.
- **Option 3 is incorrect:** Quantum dots are **not typically used in conventional incandescent lighting;** instead, they are applied in advanced display technologies like QLEDs, where they improve brightness, color accuracy, and energy efficiency.
- **Option 4 is correct:** In quantum computing, **quantum dots serve as qubits (quantum bits),** essential for processing and storing information in quantum computers, due to their quantum properties.

**Thus, the correct answer is (c) Only three.**

**45.** *(b)* Nanotechnology involving the manipulation and synthesis of nanoparticles in a liquid environment.

Wet nanotechnology is specifically concerned with **working in a liquid medium, which allows precise control over nanoparticle formation and manipulation.** This method is widely applied in biomedical fields, such as drug delivery systems, where nanoparticles created in a liquid can be designed to interact accurately with biological systems.

**Unlike dry nanotechnology, which operates in a vacuum or dry conditions, wet nanotechnology leverages liquid solutions to support controlled chemical reactions and particle stability.**

**Thus, option (b) is the correct answer.**

**46.** *(d)* All four pairs

- **Pair 1: Nanochips are used in diagnostics** due to their ability to detect pathogens and biomarkers at a very fine molecular scale, allowing for early and precise disease identification.
- **Pair 2: Nanosponge particles** are designed to **capture and neutralise bacterial toxins,** which can circulate within the bloodstream, helping treat conditions like sepsis by reducing toxic load in the body.
- **Pair 3: Nanoflares function by targeting mRNA,** making them useful in observing real-time cellular activity. This aids in early disease detection by identifying specific gene expression changes within live cells.
- **Pair 4: Nanopores are widely used in genetic research** for their ability to analyse single molecules, making them suitable for rapid DNA sequencing and other genetic diagnostics.

**Thus, the correct answer is (d) All four pairs.**

**47.** *(c)* Only four

**Nano-Robots (Nanobots)** are tiny, microscopic robots designed to perform specific tasks at the nanoscale, typically in the range of 1 to 100 nanometres. These robots are developed to work with extreme precision, often manipulating atoms and molecules to achieve desired results in fields like medicine, environmental science, and materials engineering.

- **Targeted drug delivery:** Nanobots can be used to deliver drugs directly to specific sites in the body, increasing treatment accuracy and minimising side effects.
- **Environmental cleanup:** Nanobots are used to detect and neutralise pollutants, offering potential solutions for environmental remediation.
- **Minimally invasive surgeries:** Surgical nanobots are developed for precise operations within the body, allowing for minimally invasive procedures.
- **Precision manufacturing:** Nanobots are used in nanoscale manufacturing processes to build and manipulate materials at the atomic or molecular level.
- **Energy storage:** This is **not a typical application of nanobots**; energy storage generally involves different nanotechnology applications, such as nanomaterials rather than autonomous nanobots.

**Thus, the correct answer is (c) Only four.**

**48.** *(b)* A scenario where self-replicating nanobots consume all biomass.

**Ecophagy**, or the 'Grey Goo' scenario, is a hypothetical risk in nanotechnology where self-replicating nanobots could consume all organic matter uncontrollably. This term, introduced by researcher Eric Drexler, highlights potential dangers if such nanobots were to malfunction or lack safeguards. In this scenario, the nanobots would replicate exponentially, consuming biomass and converting it into more nanobots, which could theoretically lead to environmental collapse.

**Thus, option (b) is the correct answer.**

**49.** *(a)* 1 and 2 only

- **Statement 1 is correct:** Liquid Nano Urea is indeed an **advanced fertilizer designed to reduce the reliance on conventional urea.** By delivering nitrogen in nanoscale form, it aims to **increase nitrogen-use efficiency in crops,** thus reducing the amount of nitrogen fertilizer needed and minimising environmental impact.
- **Statement 2 is correct:** The production process of Liquid Nano Urea involves reducing urea particles to a nanoscale level, which enhances nutrient absorption by plants. This allows for **more efficient delivery of nitrogen, as the nanosised particles can penetrate plant cells more effectively.**
- **Statement 3 is incorrect:** Liquid Nano Urea **is not classified as an organic fertilizer; it is a synthetic nitrogen fertilizer in nano form.** It is intended to complement conventional fertilisers, not to replace them with organic alternatives.

**Thus, the correct answer is (a) 1 and 2 only.**

**50.** *(d)* **Dr. C.N.R. Rao**

**Dr. Chintamani Nagesa Ramachandra Rao (C.N.R. Rao)** is recognised as the 'Father of Indian Nanotechnology' due to his groundbreaking research and contributions to nanoscience and materials science in India. His work has significantly advanced the understanding and development of nanotechnology in the country.

**Thus, option (d) is the correct answer.**

**51.** *(b)* Only two pairs

- **Pair 1 is correct:** The First Law states that a robot must not harm a human or allow harm through inaction.
- **Pair 2 is incorrect:** The Second Law requires a robot to obey human orders, provided these do not conflict with the First Law.
- **Pair 3 is correct:** The Third Law requires a robot to protect its own existence as long as it does not interfere with the First or Second Law.

**Thus, the correct answer is (b) Only two pairs.**

**52.** *(d)* 1, 2, 3 and 4

- **Statement 1 is correct:** Robotics has significant applications in **autonomous surgery. Surgical robots, such as the Da Vinci robot,** assist surgeons with precision in minimally invasive procedures, enhancing accuracy, reducing recovery time, and minimising complications.
- **Statement 2 is correct: Precision farming** uses **robotic systems to increase agricultural productivity** by automating tasks like planting, watering and harvesting, while also minimising resource usage, thereby improving efficiency in agriculture.
- **Statement 3 is correct:** Robotics plays a crucial role in **underwater exploration.** Robotic submarines, remotely operated vehicles (ROVs) and autonomous underwater vehicles (AUVs) are used for mapping ocean floors, studying marine ecosystems, and conducting research in hostile underwater environments.
- **Statement 4 is correct:** In **mass production,** especially in industries such as automotive and electronics, robotics ensures fast, efficient and consistent assembly, reducing human error and increasing productivity in manufacturing processes.

**Thus, the correct answer is (d) 1, 2, 3 and 4.**

**53.** *(a)* Only one

- **Statement 1 is correct:** RPA is primarily designed to automate repetitive, rule-based tasks that follow predefined workflows, such as data entry and processing invoices.
- **Statement 2 is incorrect:** One advantage of RPA is that it can often be implemented without extensive changes to existing IT systems.
- **Statement 3 is incorrect:** RPA does not inherently rely on artificial intelligence or machine learning for its operations. It works on rule-based automation, focusing on structured tasks without the complexity of AI decision-making.

**Thus, the correct answer is (a) Only one.**

**54.** *(a)* Only one

- **Statement 1 is correct:** Humanoid robots are indeed designed to mimic the human form and some human-like movements.
- **Statement 2 is incorrect:** While humanoid robots can perform certain tasks, most do not yet possess advanced human-like cognition and problem-solving.
- **Statement 3 is incorrect:** While some humanoid robots can make limited decisions, they generally lack the complex reasoning capabilities of humans.

**Thus, the correct answer is (a) Only one.**

**55.** *(a)* Manav

- **Option (a) is correct: Manav** is indeed India's first 3-D printed humanoid robot. Developed by A-SET Training and Research Institute in Delhi, Manav is designed to perform human-like actions such as walking, dancing, and even push-ups. It was created as an educational and research tool to promote advancements in robotics, and artificial intelligence in India.
- **Option (b) is incorrect: Shalu** is a humanoid robot developed by a teacher in India using inexpensive materials. While Shalu can speak multiple languages and serve as a teaching assistant, it is not 3-D printed.
- **Option (c) is incorrect: Vyommitra** is a half-humanoid robot developed by ISRO for its upcoming Gaganyaan mission, designed to perform limited human-like actions in space. However, Vyommitra is not a fully humanoid robot and was not created using 3-D printing technology.
- **Option (d) is incorrect: Rashmi** is India's first lip-syncing humanoid robot capable of mimicking emotions and speaking multiple Indian languages. However, Rashmi was not created using 3-D printing technology.

**Thus, option (a) is the correct answer.**

**56.** *(c)* All three

- **Statement 1 is correct:** DAKSHA is a mobile platform with stair-climbing abilities, designed for IED handling and multi-purpose payloads.

- **Statement 2 is correct:** Vyommitra is being developed by ISRO as a humanoid robot to operate onboard Gaganyaan and assist with various tasks in space.
- **Statement 3 is correct:** Manav is India's first 3D-printed humanoid robot with capabilities to process vision and sound, allowing it to walk, talk and perform actions in response to human commands.

**Thus, the correct answer is (c) All three.**

**57.** *(b)* A robotics outreach initiative funded by the Ministry of Education to nurture young engineering talent.

- The **e-Yantra Programme**, funded by India's Ministry of Education, is designed to foster interest and skill in robotics among young engineering students.
- It includes activities such as setting up robotics labs, hosting competitions, and offering hands-on training, aiming to build a strong foundation in robotics and automation.
- e-Yantra's primary focus is on outreach and talent development in robotics for a broad range of applications, not restricted to defence or foreign education.

**Thus, option (b) is the correct answer.**

**58.** *(b)* Only two

- **Statement 1 is correct:** Light travels fastest in a vacuum, where it encounters no resistance. When it passes through other media, such as air, water, or glass, it slows down due to interactions with particles in these materials.
- **Statement 2 is correct:** Light exhibits wave-particle duality, meaning it behaves as both a wave and a particle. This is evident in phenomena like interference and diffraction (wave properties) and the photoelectric effect (particle properties).
- **Statement 3 is incorrect:** Light does not always move in straight lines; it bends or refracts when it passes from one medium to another with a different refractive index, such as from air to water or glass.

**Thus, the correct answer is (b) Only two.**

**59.** *(c)* Only three pairs

- **Reflection is correct:** Light bounces off surfaces, such as mirrors.
- **Refraction is correct:** Light changes speed and direction when moving between different media, like air to water.
- **Dispersion is correct:** Light spreads into its constituent colours, as seen in a prism.
- **Polarisation is incorrect:** Polarisation involves aligning the vibrations of light waves in a single direction, not increasing intensity.

**Thus, the correct answer is (c) only three pairs.**

**60.** *(c)* Only three

- **Statement 1 is correct:** LEDs are a photonic device, emitting light when an electric current passes through a semiconductor, making them widely used in displays and lighting.
- **Statement 2 is correct:** Lasers are one of the most important photonic devices, producing highly coherent light for applications in communications, medicine and industry.
- **Statement 3 is correct:** Fiber optic cables are a fundamental component of photonic technology, transmitting light signals over long distances for high-speed data communication.
- **Statement 4 is incorrect: Cathode Ray Tubes (CRTs) are not photonic devices;** they rely on electron beams and phosphorescent screens to display images and do not operate on the principles of photonics.

**Thus, the correct answer is (c) Only three.**

**61.** *(b)* The development and application of electronic devices that source, detect and control light.

- **Option (b) is correct:** Optoelectronics is a specialised field that combines principles from both optics and electronics to develop and apply devices that source, detect and control light. This field is crucial for various technologies, including:
  - **Light Emitting Diodes (LEDs):** Used in lighting and displays, LEDs convert electrical energy into visible light.

- Photovoltaic cells (solar cells): These devices convert sunlight into electrical energy, contributing to renewable energy solutions.
- Laser diodes: Critical in telecommunications, laser diodes facilitate high-speed data transmission through fibre optic networks.
- Photodetectors: Employed in sensors and communication systems, photodetectors capture light and convert it into electrical signals.

- **Option (a) is incorrect:** Optoelectronics involves the interaction of electronic systems with light, contrary to the description in option (a).
- **Option (c) is incorrect:** While optoelectronics includes fibre optics, it is not limited to this area alone. It encompasses a broader scope involving various light-managing electronic devices.
- **Option (d) is incorrect:** Optoelectronics is not restricted to solar panel technology; it covers a wide range of applications where light interacts with electronic systems.

**Thus, option (b) is the correct answer.**

**62.** *(b)* Only two

- **Statement 1 is correct:** OLED displays can turn off individual pixels to produce true blacks, giving them high contrast ratios.
- **Statement 2 is correct:** OLEDs consume less power than LCDs, especially when displaying dark images, as they don't require a backlight and can turn off pixels individually.
- **Statement 3 is incorrect:** OLED displays typically have a shorter lifespan compared to traditional LED displays, primarily due to organic materials that can degrade over time.

**Thus, the correct answer is (b) Only two.**

**63.** *(b)* Only two

- **Statement 1 is correct:** LEDs generally have a higher initial cost, though their energy savings over time help offset this.
- **Statement 2 is correct:** Extreme temperatures can impact the performance and lifespan of LEDs, particularly in very hot or cold environments.
- **Statement 3 is incorrect:** LEDs, especially those used in screens and displays, emit blue light, which can cause eye strain and potentially affect sleep if exposed to excessively.

**Thus, the correct answer is (b) Only two.**

**64.** *(c)* Only three pairs

- **Pair 1 is correct:** Li-Fi provides internet connectivity using visible light.
- **Pair 2 is correct:** Laser technology is used for precision cutting and other manufacturing applications.
- **Pair 3 is incorrect:** Photovoltaic cells are used for converting solar energy into electricity, not for data transmission.
- **Pair 4 is correct:** LED lighting is widely used for energy-efficient lighting in various settings.

**Thus, only three pairs are correctly matched.**

**65.** *(b)* 1 and 3 only

- **Statement 1 is correct:** LEDs are energy-efficient and have a longer operational life than traditional incandescent bulbs, which makes them ideal for various lighting applications.
- **Statement 2 is incorrect:** Unlike incandescent bulbs, LEDs do not work by heating a filament. Instead, they emit light through a process called electroluminescence, where electrons recombine with holes in the LED material, releasing photons.
- **Statement 3 is correct:** LEDs can produce a variety of colours without using colour filters due to semiconductor materials that emit light at specific wavelengths.

**Thus, the correct answer is (b) 1 and 3 only.**

**66.** *(d)* 1, 2 and 3

- **Statement 1 is correct:** Li-Fi technology transmits data through visible light, which is inherently confined to line-of-sight and short-range. This limited reach reduces the risk of external interception, making it more secure for transmitting sensitive data within closed environments.
- **Statement 2 is correct:** The absence of RF interference in Li-Fi allows it to operate in